W9-DES-385

by JOHN HENRIK CLARKE

Rebellion in Rhyme (Poetry). The Dicker Press, Prairie City, Ill., 1948.

The Lives of Great African Chiefs. Pittsburgh Courier Publishing Co., 1958.

edited by JOHN HENRIK CLARKE

Harlem, A Community in Transition. Citadel Press, New York, 1964 (enlarged edition 1970).

Harlem, U.S.A. Seven Seas Publishers, Berlin, 1965.

American Negro Short Stories (Anthology). Hill and Wang, Inc., New York City, 1966.

William Styron's Nat Turner: Ten Black Writers Respond. Beacon Press, Boston, 1968.

Malcolm X The Man and His Times. Macmillan Co., New York, 1969.

Slavery and the Slave Trade. Edited with Vincent Harding. Holt, Rinehart and Winston, Inc., New York, 1970.

Black Titan: W. E. B. Du Bois. Edited with the Editors of *Freedomways*. Beacon Press, Boston, 1971.

Harlem: Voices From the Soul of Black America. New American Library, New York, 1970.

Harlem, U.S.A. (Revised American Edition). Collier Books, New York, 1971.

World's Great Men of Color. Vols. 1 and 2, by J. A. Rogers (revised and updated edition, with commentary). Collier-Macmillan Co., New York, 1972.

Marcus Garvey and the Vision of Africa. Random House, New York, 1973.

MARCUS GARVEY AND THE VISION OF AFRICA

Marcus Garvey and the Vision of Africa

EDITED, WITH AN INTRODUCTION
AND COMMENTARIES, BY

John Henrik Clarke

WITH THE ASSISTANCE OF

Amy Jaques Garvey

VINTAGE BOOKS
A DIVISION OF RANDOM HOUSE
NEW YORK

FIRST VINTAGE BOOKS EDITION, January 1974
Copyright © 1974 by John Henrik Clarke and Amy Jacques Garvey

All rights reserved under International and Pan-American Copyright
Conventions. Published in the United States by Random House,
Inc., New York, and simultaneously in Canada by Random House of
Canada Limited, Toronto. Originally published by Random House,
Inc., in 1974.

Grateful acknowledgment is made to the following for permission to
reprint previously published material:

Harcourt Brace Jovanovich, Inc.: For excerpts from "The Flowering
of Black Nationalism: Henry McNeal Turner and Marcus Garvey,"
reprinted from *Key Issues in the Afro-American Experience*, Volume
II, by Nathan I. Huggins, Martin Kilson, Daniel M. Fox, copyright ©
1971 by Harcourt Brace Jovanovich, Inc.

The Institute of Race Relations: For "Marcus Garvey and African
Nationalism," by Jabez Ayodale Langley, *Race*, Volume XI, Number
2, October, 1969, published for the Institute of Race Relations,
London, by the Oxford University Press, copyright © 1969 by the
Institute of Race Relations; and for "Marcus Garvey, Pan-Negroist:
The View from Whitehall," by Robert G. Weisbord, *Race*, Volume
XI, Number 4, April, 1970, published for the Institute of Race
Relations, London, by the Oxford University Press, copyright ©
1970 by the Institute of Race Relations.

International Publishers Co., Inc.: For "The Garvey Movement: A
Marxists View," from The Negro People in American History, by
William Z. Foster. Copyright 1954 by International Publishers Co.,
Inc.; and for "Memoirs of a Captain of the Black Star Line," from A
Star To Steer By, by Captain Hugh Mulzac. Copyright © 1963 by
International Publishers Co., Inc.

Institute of Caribbean Studies (University of Puerto Rico): For
"Marcus Garvey, The Negro World and the British West Indies:
1919–1920," by W. F. Elkins, from *Black Power in the British West
Indies 1918–1920*, by W. F. Elkins.

Library of Congress Cataloging in Publication Data
Clarke, John Henrik, 1915–   comp.
Marcus Garvey and the vision of Africa.
Bibliography: p.
1. Garvey, Marcus, 1887–1940.   I.   Title.
[E185.97.G3C55   1974]   301.45'19'6024   [B]   73–4732
ISBN 0–394–71888–7 (pbk.)

Manufactured in the United States of America

68B975

DEDICATION

To Amy Jacques Garvey and all of the Garveyites throughout the world who held on to the dream of nationhood for African people until the dream was realized.

ACKNOWLEDGMENTS

This book was researched and compiled with the assistance of Amy Jacques Garvey, who placed at my disposal her extensive files of information about her late husband and the rise and transition of the Garvey Movement. The basic information for most of the commentary was obtained from two extensive taped interviews with Mrs. Garvey during the summers of 1969 and 1970, and a long article that she wrote for this book. Mrs. Garvey agreed in the main with my interpretation of the material, but I am responsible for whatever errors occur in the adaptation of the material, which does not necessarily coincide with the data Mrs. Garvey shared with me. Further, I wish to acknowledge the use of the research of the young Jamaican historian, Robert Hill, who has examined the government files and court records relating to the Garvey Movement.

Contents

THE DECLARATION OF RIGHTS OF THE NEGRO
　PEOPLES OF THE WORLD

Introduction

IT IS NO accident that Marcus Garvey had his greatest success in the United States among Black Americans. There is an historical logic to this occurrence that seemed to have escaped most of the interpreters of the life of Marcus Garvey and the mass movement that he built. He came to the United States and began to build this movement at a time of great disenchantment among Afro-Americans, who had pursued the "American Dream" until they had to concede that the dream was not dreamed for them. They had listened to the "American Promise" and also conceded that the promise was not made to them. These concessions only complicated their lives, because they could not disassociate themselves from the "American Dream" and the "American Promise." No other dream and no other promise was being held out to them.

Bishop Henry McNeal Turner (1835–1915), the most prominent and outspoken American advocate of Black emigration in the years between the Civil and the First World War, had died. His dream of African reclamation by the hands of Black Americans, seemed to have died with him. There was nothing new about this dream. Men and movements had evolved around it before. Marcus Garvey only reintroduced the longing for Africa and gave the dream a new vitality and an organization.

In his book *New World A-coming*,[1] Roi Ottley (1943) observed that "Garvey leaped into the ocean of Black unhappiness at a most timely moment for a savior. He had witnessed the Negro's disillusionment mount with the progress of the war. Negro soldiers had suffered all forms of Jim Crow, humiliation, discrimi-

Marcus Garvey and the Vision of Africa

nation, slander, and even violence at the hands of a white civilian population. After the war there was a resurgence of Ku Klux Klan influence; another decade of racial hatred and open lawlessness had set in, and Negroes again were prominent among the victims. Meantime, administration leaders were quite pointed in trying to persuade Negroes that in spite of their full participation in the war effort they could expect no changes in their traditional status in America."

This attitude had helped to create the atmosphere into which a Marcus Garvey could emerge. In many ways the scene was being prepared for Marcus Garvey for over one hundred years before he was born. There is no way to understand this fact without looking at the American antecedents of Marcus Garvey, i.e., the men, forces and movements that came before him.

The Africans who were brought to the United States as slaves started their attempts to reclaim their lost African heritage soon after they arrived in this country. They were searching for the identity that the slave system had destroyed. Concurrent with the Black man's search for an identity in America has been his search for an identity in the world, which means, in essence, his identity as a human being with a history, before and after slavery, that can command respect.

Some Afro-Americans gave up the search and accepted the distorted image of themselves that had been created by their oppressors. As early as 1881, Dr. Edward Wilmot Blyden, the great West Indian scholar and benefactor of West Africa, addressed himself to this situation when he said: "In all English-speaking countries the mind of the intelligent Negro child revolts against the descriptions of the Negro given in elementary school books, geographies, travels, histories . . . having embraced or at least assented to those falsehoods about himself, he concludes that his only hope of rising in the scale of respectable manhood is to strive for what is most unlike himself and most alien to his peculiar tastes."

Despite the alienation spoken of here by Dr. Blyden, the Afro-American's spiritual trek back to Africa continued.

Dr. W. E. B. Du Bois, the elder statesman among the Afro-Americans, addressed himself to the broader aspects of this situation on the occasion of the celebration of the Second

Anniversary of the Asian-African (Bandung) Conference and the rebirth of Ghana on April 30, 1957, when he said:

> From the fifteenth through the seventeenth centuries, the Africans imported to America regarded themselves as temporary settlers destined to return eventually to Africa. Their increasing revolts against the slave system, which culminated in the eighteenth century, showed a feeling of close kinship to the motherland and even well into the nineteenth century they called their organizations "African," as witness the "African Unions" of New York and Newport and the African churches of Philadelphia and New York. In the West Indies and South America there was even closer indication of feelings of kinship with Africa and the East.
>
> The planters' excuse for slavery was advertised as conversion of Africa to Christianity; but soon American slavery appeared based on the huge profits of the Sugar Empire and the Cotton Kingdom. As plans were laid for the expansion of the slave system, the slaves themselves sought freedom by increasing revolt which culminated in the eighteenth century. In Haiti they won autonomy; in the United States they fled from the slave states in the South to the free states in the North and to Canada.
>
> Here the Free Negroes helped form the Abolition Movement, and when that seemed to be failing, the Negroes began to plan for migration to Africa, Haiti and South America.
>
> Civil war and emancipation intervened and American Negroes looked forward to becoming free and equal here with no thought of return to Africa or of kinship with the world's darker peoples. However, the rise of the Negro was hindered by disfranchisement, lynching and caste legislation. There was some recurrence of the "Back to Africa" idea and increased sympathy for [other] darker folk who suffered the same sort of caste restrictions as American Negroes.

During the eighteenth century there was strong agitation among certain groups of Black people in America for a return to Africa. This agitation was found mainly among groups of "free Negroes" because of the uncertainty of their position as freed men in a slave-holding society. "One can see it late into the eighteenth century," Dr. Du Bois explains in his book *Dusk of Dawn*;[2]

". . . the Negro Union of Newport, Rhode Island, in 1788, proposed to the Free African Society of Philadelphia a general exodus to Africa on the part of at least free Negroes."

The Back-to-Africa idea has been a recurring theme in Afro-American life and thought for more than a hundred years. This thought was strong during the formative years of the Colonization Society and succeeded in convincing some of the most outstanding Black men of the eighteenth and nineteenth centuries, such as Lott Carey, the powerful Virginia preacher. Later the Society fell into severe disrepute after an argument with the Abolitionists.

Marcus Garvey was not the first West Indian to play a vital role in the Afro-American freedom struggle. West Indians have been coming to the United States for over a century. The part they have played in the progress of the Afro-American in his long march from slavery to freedom has always been an important factor. More important is the fact that the most outstanding of these Caribbean-Americans saw their plight and the plight of the Afro-American as being one and the same.

As early as 1827 a Jamaican, John B. Russwurm, one of the founders of Liberia, was the first Black man to be graduated from Bowdoin, an American college, and to publish a newspaper with Samuel E. Comish. Sixteen years later his fellow countryman, Peter Ogden, organized in New York City the first lodge of Odd Fellows for Negroes. Prior to the Civil War, the West Indian contribution to the progress of Afro-American life was one of the main factors in the fight for freedom and full citizenship in the northern part of the United States.

In his book *Souls of Black Folk*,[3] Dr. W. E. B. Du Bois says that the West Indians were mainly responsible for the manhood program presented by the race in the early decades of the last century. Indicative of their tendency to blaze new paths is the achievement of John W. A. Shaw of Antigua, who in the early 1890's passed the civil service tests and became deputy commissioner of taxes for the County of Queens in New York.

In eighteenth-century America two of the most outstanding figures for liberty and justice were the West Indians Prince Hall and John B. Russwurm. When Prince Hall came to the United

States the nation was in turmoil. The colonies were ablaze with indignation. Britain, with a series of revenue acts, had stoked the fires of colonial discontent. In Virginia, Patrick Henry was speaking of liberty or death. The cry "No Taxation Without Representation" played on the nerve strings of the nation. Prince Hall, then a delicate-looking teenager, often walked through the turbulent streets of Boston.

A few months before these hectic scenes he had arrived in the United States from his home in Barbados, where he had been born about 1748, the son of an Englishman and a free African woman. He was, in theory, a free man, but he knew that neither in Boston nor in Barbados were persons of African descent free in fact. At once he questioned the sincerity of the vocal white patriots of Boston. The colonists held in servitude more than a half million human beings, some of them white; yet they engaged in the contradiction of going to war to support the theory that all men were created equal.

When Prince Hall arrived in Boston that city was the center of the American slave trade. Most of the major leaders of the revolutionary movement were slave holders or investors in slave-supported businesses. Hall, like many other Americans, wondered what these men meant by freedom.

The condition of the free Black men, as Prince Hall found them, was not an enviable one. Emancipation brought neither freedom nor relief from the stigma of color. They were still included with slaves, indentured servants, and Indians in slave codes. Discriminatory laws severely circumscribed their freedom of movement.

By 1765, Prince Hall saw little change in the condition of the Blacks. He saw his people debased as though they were slaves still in bondage. So through diligence and frugality he became a property owner, thus establishing himself in the eyes of white people as well as the Blacks.

But the ownership of property was not enough. He still had to endure sneers and insults. He decided then to prepare himself for a role of leadership among his people. To this end he went to school at night and later became a Methodist preacher. His church became the forum for his people's grievances. Ten years after his arrival in Boston he was the accepted leader of the Black community.

In 1788 Hall petitioned the Massachusetts legislature protesting the kidnapping of free Negroes. This was a time when American patriots were engaged in a constitutional struggle for freedom. They had proclaimed the inherent rights of all mankind to life, liberty and the pursuit of happiness. Hall dared to remind them that the Black men in the United States were human beings, and as such were entitled to freedom and respect for their human personality.

Prejudice made Hall the father of African secret societies in the United States. He was the founder of what is now known as "Negro Masonry." Hall first sought initiation into the white Masonic Lodge in Boston, but was turned down because of his color. He then applied to the Army Lodge of an Irish Regiment. His petition was favorably received. On March 6, 1775, Hall and fourteen other Black Americans were initiated in Lodge No. 441. When, on March 17, the British were forced to evacuate Boston, the Army Lodge gave Prince Hall and his colleagues a license to meet and function as a lodge. Thus, on July 3, 1776, African Lodge No. 1 came into being. This was the first lodge in Massachusetts established in America for men of African descent.

The founding of the African Lodge was one of Prince Hall's greatest achievements. It afforded the Africans in the New England area of the United States a greater sense of security and contributed to a new spirit of unity among them. Hall's interest did not end with the Lodge. He was deeply concerned with improving the lot of his people in other ways. He sought to have schools established for the children of the free Africans in Massachusetts. Of prime importance is the fact that Prince Hall worked to secure respect for the personality of his people and also played a significant role in the downfall of the Massachusetts slave trade. He helped to prepare the ground work for the freedom fighters of the nineteenth and twentieth centuries, whose continuing efforts have brought the Black American closer to the goal of full citizenship.

Samuel E. Cornish, who is virtually unknown today, was born about 1795 in Delaware and raised in the relatively free environments of Philadelphia and New York. He organized the first Black Presbyterian Church in New York City.

Russwurm and Cornish made an excellent team despite the difference in their backgrounds. In the prospectus for the proposed paper they idealistically stated: "We shall ever regard the constitution of the United States as our polar star. Pledged to no party, we shall endeavor to urge our brethren to use their rights to the elective franchise as free citizens. It shall never be our objective to court controversy though we must at all times consider ourselves as champions in defense of oppressed humanity. Daily slandered, we think that there ought to be some channel of communication between us and the public, through which a single voice may be heard in defense of five hundred thousand free people of color . . ."

On Friday, March 26, 1827, the first issue of *Freedom's Journal*, the first "Negro newspaper" in the Western world, appeared on the streets of New York. In their ambitious first editorial, Russwurm and Cornish struck a high note of positiveness that still has something to say to the Afro-Americans in their present plight. It read, in part:

> We wish to plead our own cause. Too long have others spoken for us. Too long has the republic been deceived by misrepresentations, in things which concern us dearly, though in the estimation of some mere trifles; for though there are many in society who exercise toward us benevolent feelings, still (with sorrow we confess it) there are others who make it their business to enlarge upon the least trifle which tends to discredit any person of color and pronounce anathema and denounce our whole body for the misconduct of this guilty one . . . Our vices and our degradation are ever arrayed against us, but our virtues are passed unnoticed . . .
>
> It is our earnest wish to make our Journal a medium of intercourse between our brethren in different states of this great confederacy.

For its timeliness and the dynamics of its intellectual content this editorial, written over a hundred years ago, is far ahead of most editorials that appear in present-day Afro-American newspapers. During the later years of his life John B. Russwurm moved to a position that today would be called Black Nationalism. After receiving his master's degree from Bowdoin College in 1829, Russwurm went to Liberia in West Africa where he established another newspaper, *The Liberia Herald*, and served as superintendent of schools. After further distinguishing himself as the Governor of the Maryland Colony of Cape Palmas, this pioneer editor and freedom fighter died in Liberia in 1851.

The same year John B. Russwurm died, another West Indian, Edward W. Blyden, went to Africa and established himself in Liberia. He was destined to become the greatest Black intellectual of the nineteenth century. He concerned himself with the plight of African people the world over and eventually built a bridge of understanding between the people of African origin in the West Indies, the United States and Africa. More than anyone else in the nineteenth and during the early part of the twentieth century, Edward W. Blyden called upon the Black man to reclaim himself and his ancient African glory. The concept now being called Negritude started with Blyden.

Blyden was born on the (then Danish) island of St. Thomas in 1832, but reacted against the treatment of his people in the New World by emigrating to Liberia in 1851. He was convinced that the only way to bring respect and dignity to the people of African descent was by building progressive new "empires" in Africa whose contribution, while remaining basically African, would incorporate useful elements of Western culture.

It was the great Edward W. Blyden who, with the immortal Frederick Douglass, placed before the bar of public opinion in England and other countries in Europe the case of the Black man in America. These men were reacting to the fact that the whole of the nineteenth century was a time of struggle for African people everywhere.

Two freedom struggles emerged early in the nineteenth century—one African, one Afro-American. While the Africans were engaged in their wars against colonialism, the American Blacks were engaged in slave revolts.

Some slaves took the Christian version of the Bible seriously and believed that God meant all men to be free. Such a slave was Gabriel Prosser of Virginia, who felt that he was inspired by God to lead his people to freedom. Over 40,000 slaves were involved in his revolt of 1800 before it was betrayed. In 1822 in Charleston, South Carolina, a carpenter, Denmark Vesey, planned one of the most extensive revolts against slavery ever recorded. He, too, was betrayed and afterwards put to death along with thirty-six of his followers. In 1831, the greatest slave revolt of all occurred in Virginia led by Nat Turner, a plowman and a preacher, whose father had escaped to freedom.

In 1839, Joseph Cinque, the son of a Mendi king of Sierra Leone, West Africa, was sold into slavery and shipped to Cuba. Cinque and his fellow Africans revolted on board the ship and ordered the ship's owners to sail to Africa. The Spanish owners of the ship steered northward when they were not being watched and eventually landed off the coast of Long Island. The Africans were arrested and sent to New Haven, Connecticut, where they were put on trial.

When the trial began, there was great excitement in the country. People talked about the case and took sides. Southern politicians wanted to give the Africans back to the Spaniards who had bought them. The trial lasted all winter.

In court, Cinque made a wonderful speech in his own language, telling the story of how he and his men fought to be free. After that speech, the court ordered the Africans set free.

Cinque and his men were sent to school to be educated and were found to be intelligent and quick to learn.

Meanwhile, the two Spaniards and the Spanish Government appealed to the United States Supreme Court to have the Africans returned to them as slaves. The friends of Cinque and his men asked John Quincy Adams, the former President of the United States and a great lawyer, to speak for the Africans. On March 9, 1841, after Adams had spoken, Chief Justice Roger B. Taney of the Supreme Court ruled that Cinque and the others were to be freed.

After that, Cinque continued his schooling, and in 1842 he and his men returned to Africa.

All America had been stirred by this case. The slave owners feared that the news about the freedom and return of Cinque and his fellow Africans would cause their slaves to revolt and also demand to be returned to their homeland.

In the years before the Civil War plans for the migration of the "free" Negroes back to Africa were revived, and agents were sent to South America, Haiti and Africa. Paul Cuffe, a free Black ship owner from New Bedford, Massachusetts, had founded the Friendly Society for the Emigration of Free Negroes from America and had taken a large number back to Africa at his own expense.

In the middle of the nineteenth century, while the issue of slavery was being debated in most of the country, the feeling for Africa among American Blacks was growing stronger. Publications like *Freedom's Journal* and *Douglass Monthly*, edited by Frederick Douglass, called attention to the plight of the people of Africa as well as the Black Americans.

Martin R. Delany was proud of his African background and his Mandingo heritage. He was one of the leaders of the great debate following the passage of the Fugitive Slave Act in 1850. He was the spokesman for the Black people who felt that the bitter climate in America had made life unbearable. Delany was the strongest voice in several conventions of free Blacks to discuss plans for emigrating to Africa. In 1859, he led the first and only exploratory party of American-born Africans to the land of their forefathers. In the region of the Niger River, in the area that became Nigeria, Delany's party carried out scientific studies and made agreements with several African kings for the settlement of emigrants from America.

Martin Delany was accompanied on this expedition by Robert Campbell, a Jamaican, who had been Director of the Scientific Department of the Institute for Colored Youth in Philadelphia and a member of the International Statistical Congress in London. His account of the expedition can be found in his book *A Pilgrimage to My Motherland: An Account of a Journey Among the Egbas and Yarubas of Central Africa in 1859–60.*[4]

About his report, Robert Campbell said, "After what is written in the context, if I am still asked what I think of Africa for a colored man to live and do well in, I simply answer that with as good prospects in America as colored men generally, I have determined with my wife and children, to go to Africa to live, leaving the inquirer to interpret the reply for himself."

What needs to be remembered about this mid-nineteenth-century back-to-Africa movement is that to a moderate degree it was successful. There was, of course, no mass exodus to Africa. Individual families did go to Africa at regular intervals for the next fifty years.

In a recent book by Dorothy Sterling,[5] Martin Delany is referred to as "the father of Black Nationalism." Delany was a multitalented freedom fighter who seemed to have crammed a half dozen lifetimes into one. He was a dentist, a writer, an editor, a doctor, an explorer, a scientist, a soldier and a politician. He was a Renaissance man of his day.

Martin R. Delany was with Frederick Douglass co-editor of the newspaper *North Star*. In Delany's own time, he was a famous figure, widely known for his lectures and for his associations with John Brown and others. Before the Civil War, he advocated the establishment of a state by Black Americans in the Niger Valley (in present day Nigeria). This interest in Africa was continued under the leadership of men like the Reverend Alexander Crummell and Bishop Henry McNeal Turner.

The Africa consciousness started during the closing years of the eighteenth century, and was articulated by the first Afro-American writers, thinkers and abolitionists. Professor E. U. Essien-Udom (University of Ibadon, Nigeria) outlined the beginning of this consciousness and how it developed in the C.B.S. Black Heritage television series in the summer of 1969. Professor Essien-Udom said that Black Americans have been forced by a set of circumstances to walk down several roads simultaneously going to and from America. This seems like a contradiction and maybe it is. The greater contradiction is America itself, and its relationship to Black people. Early in the nineteenth century some "free" Blacks and escaped slaves began to have second thoughts about the future of African people in this country. These Blacks, in large numbers, responded to the program of the "African Colonization Movement." Superficially, the program was good, and it had begun to function before a number of Blacks, mainly, Frederick Douglass and some of the men around him, examined the program and began to have some serious questions about it. The stated intent of the American Colonization Society was to solve the problems of slavery by advocating the removal of freed slaves to colonies along the west coast of Africa. The founders of the society believed this course would atone for the evil of the African slave trade, help put an end to slavery, restore the "Africans" to their divinely ordained homes, and help "civilize" Africa. By "civilize" the white supporters of the movement really meant Christianize. Some of the most able Black men and women of the nineteenth century were attracted to this movement and its concept. It is generally believed, according to Professor Essien-Udom, that the Black New England sea captain, Paul Cuffe, set in motion the ideas that led to the founding of the American Colonization Society. Paul Cuffe was one of the most unusual men of his time. He was a rare exception among the Black sailors of New Bedford, Massachusetts: he was a ship owner. He made a small fortune hauling cargo to different parts of the world, including Asia. He was a free Black whose father had been a slave. One of his early acts was to change his family name from Slocum to Cuffe. In this way, he was seeking his African identity. (His name must have been "Koh-fee," which is a Ghanian name.)

The Black intelligentsia of that day were obsessed with a yearning for nationality. This obsession caused them to look two ways—at Africa and at the United States. In 1811, Paul Cuffe sailed one of his ships, the *Traveler*, to Sierra Leone on the west coast of Africa, where he founded "The Friendly Society from America." In 1812 he used his personal funds to take thirty-eight Black emigrants to Sierra Leone.

But the most active years of "The American Colonization" came after the death of Paul Cuffe in 1817. At the Emigration Convention of 1852, Martin Delany projected additional plans for the settlement of Black Americans in Africa. "Settle them in the land which is ours," he said, "and there lies with it inexhaustible resources. Let us go and possess it. We must establish a national position for ourselves and never may we expect to be respected as men and women until we have undertaken some fearless, bold and adventurous deeds of daring, contending against every consequence."

This movement was not without its opposition. Frederick Douglass and several of his supporters thought that the emigration-to-Africa efforts would divert attention from the more important task of freeing the slaves from the plantations.

General interest in Africa continued through the pre-Civil War emigration, but efforts to establish an autonomous nation for Black Americans in Africa did not succeed. The Civil War and the promises to Black Americans that followed lessened some of the interest in Africa. Pat Singleton started an internal resettlement scheme. His plan was to settle Blacks in the unused areas of America—mainly, at that time, the state of Kansas. He hoped to establish free separate Black communities.

The betrayal of the Reconstruction and the rise in lynching and other atrocities against Black Americans made a new generation of Black thinkers and freedom fighters turn to Africa again. New men and movements entered the area of struggle. The most notable of the new personalities was Bishop Henry McNeal Turner. In his book, *Black Exodus*,[6] Edwin S. Redkey said: "Bishop Henry McNeal Turner was, without a doubt, the most prominent and outspoken American advocate of Black emigration in the years between the Civil War and the First World War. By constant agitation he kept Afro-Americans aware of their African heritage and their disabilities in the United States."

Like most Afro-Americans who can be called Black Nationalists, his vision of Africa grew out of his heartbreaking discovery that his love for America was unrequited. Earlier in his life, he thought that the status of a "free" Black man should be no different than that of a white man. His awakening to reality was not long in coming. The new cause that he had found for himself and his energies during the Civil War, and the new hope that he had for the future of Black Americans, was consumed in the bitter disappointments that followed the end of that war.

During the latter part of the nineteenth century, Edward Wilmot Blyden called attention to the important role that Africa could play in emerging world affairs. He was convinced that the only way to bring respect and dignity to his people was by building progressive new "empires" in Africa. He was of the opinion that the "New World Negro" had a great future in Africa. He saw Liberia, in West Africa, as the ideal place where African-Americans could build a great new civilization by making use of the things that they had learned in the West and preserving the best of the African way of life. Because of his work and the work of many others, the African consciousness was translated into useful programs of service to Africa. Afro-American institutions of higher learning joined in this service through their training of the personnel of the churches as well as their support of Africans studying in their institutions.

The idea of uniting all Africa had its greatest development early in this century. In 1900 a West Indian lawyer, H. Sylvester Williams, called together the first Pan-African Conference in London. This meeting attracted attention and put the word "Pan-African" in the dictionaries for the first time. The thirty delegates to the conference came mainly from England, the West Indies and the United States. The small delegation from the United States was led by W. E. B. Du Bois.

From the beginning this was a movement that was brought into being by Africans in the Western world. Years would pass before it would have any deep roots in Africa itself. The first conference was greeted by the Lord Bishop of London, and a promise was obtained from Queen Victoria through Joseph Chamberlain not to "overlook the interests and welfare of the native races." [7] The British were long on politeness and short on commitment.

At this conference there was no demand for self-government for African nations, though the thought pattern was set in motion for later development. In the book *Africa and Unity: The Evolution of Pan-Africanism*,[8] the Nigerian writer Vincent Bakpetu Thompson said:

> As a forum of protest, the conference snowed that Africa had begun jointly, through some of her sons, to make her voice heard against the excesses of western European rule—a sentiment which has been re-echoed in the second half of the twentieth century.

The aims of the conference were limited. They were obviously worded in order to appeal without offending. They were:

1. To act as a forum of protest against the aggression of white colonizers.

2. To appeal to the "missionary and abolitionist traditions of the British people to protect Africans from the deprivation of Empire builders."

3. To bring people of African descent throughout the world into closer touch with each other and to establish more friendly relations between the Caucasian and African races.

4. To start a movement looking forward to the securing to all African races living in civilized countries, their full rights and to promote their business interests.

Mr. Thompson further observed that, "both protest and fellowship were to re-emerge in the 'African Redemption' movement, formed by the Afro-Jamaican, Marcus Garvey, to uplift his downtrodden brethren." Garvey said: "I know no national boundary where the Negro is concerned. The whole world is my province until Africa is free."

In his assessment of what the conference achieved, Mr. Thompson says: "First, it achieved the idea of oneness in experience and ideal." The spirit of fellowship reaffirmed at the 1900 conference was never lost. It has reasserted itself again and again. This was demonstrated when in the post-war period Afro-Americans and Afro-West Indians joined forces with those who clamored for the dismantling of colonialism in Africa. The spirit lives on, though today the Afro-American interest in the freedom of Africa and the success of Pan-Africanism has three main themes:

1. The continuance of the idea of fellowship which has existed since slavery first took Black men away from the shores of Africa.

2. Self-interest—a hope for the enhancement of the stature for the Afro-American in the United States. The success of Africa, it is believed, will hasten integration for the Afro-American in American society; whether this is so or not is another matter, but the belief was present in the "back to Africa" fervor of the mid-nineteenth and the twentieth centuries.

3. A genuine interest in the study of African history and culture with a view to taking a hand in rehabilitating what they genuinely believe through "scientific" research, to be the true picture of life in Africa in pre-imperialist days. This is seen in the formation of organizations such as "The American Society of African Culture."

In the preface to *Africa as Seen by American Negroes* Alioune Diop, president of the International Society of African Culture, states: "It is not without emotion that we welcome this evidence of solidarity between Negro intellectuals of America and Africa. What links us first of all is assuredly our common origin . . . So long as our African nations are not independent, SAC's duty is to avoid the influence of the massive power of both Washington and Moscow. This must be absolutely clear to anyone who would understand the meaning of our solidarity with Negro Americans.

"Furthermore, the struggle that African people are waging for their independence and entry upon the scene of international responsibility is followed with understandable sympathy by Negro Americans. The liberation, unification and development of African countries will be a real contribution to the success of the struggle of Black people in America for their rights as citizens."

In *The American Negro Writer and His Roots* (selected papers from the First Conference of Negro Writers), the historian, novelist and teacher Saunders Redding addressed himself to the role of the writer in the self-discovery and the restoration of a people's pride in themselves. "The human condition, the discovery of self, community identity—surely, this must be achieved before it can be seen that a particular identity has a relation to a common identity, commonly described as human."

What we have here is a continuation of the search for identity, definition and direction that started among Black Americans early in the nineteenth century. This search led to the founding of the first Black societies, publications and institutions in this country. In the years following the betrayal of the Reconstruction (1875–1900), these Black societies and institutions were in serious trouble. Most of the white defenders of the Blacks had either died or had given up the fight. Black leadership was in transition. The great Frederick Douglass was losing his effectiveness at the end of the nineteenth century. A world-wide imperialism, and the acceptance of the Kipling concept of "taking up the white man's burden," gave support to American racism. Like England, France, and some other European nations, the United States had now acquired overseas colonies.

A new "leader," approved by the whites, appeared among the Blacks. His name was Booker T. Washington. Washington took no action against the rising tide of Jim Crow, lynchings and the mass disenfranchisement of Black voters. He advised his people to put their energies into industry, improved farming and the craft trades. He said, "Agitation of questions of social equality is the extreme 'folly' because an opportunity to earn a dollar in a factory first, now is worth infinitely more than the opportunity to spend a dollar in an opera house."

White America, mostly editorial writers on white newspapers, responded favorably to the words of Booker T. Washington and made him the leader of Black America. These words, taken from his famous Atlanta Cotton Exposition Speech, were still re-echoing early in this century when an anti-Booker T. Washington school of thought was developed and led by W. E. B. Du Bois.

In what can still be referred to as "The Booker T. Washington Era" (1895–1915) new men and movements were emerging. The Niagara Movement, under the leadership of W. E. B. Du Bois and Monroe Trotter, was born in 1905. Some of the ideas of the Niagara Movement went into the making of the NAACP in 1909.

During the years leading to the eve of the First World War and those that immediately followed, the flight from the South continued. Over a half million Blacks migrated northward in search of better paying wartime jobs, better schools for their children and better housing. For a short while, they entertained the illusion that their lot had been improved and that they had escaped from the oppression of the South. The illusion was short lived. Race riots in wartime East St. Louis (1917) and in post-war Chicago (1919) awakened the new urban settlers to reality. In Washington, D. C., the President, Woodrow Wilson, and the Southern Democrats who had come to power with him, had introduced segregation in federal facilities that had long been integrated. Booker T. Washington had died in 1915. An investigation into his last years revealed he had privately battled against disenfranchisement and had secretly financed law suits against segregation, but publicly he maintained his submissive stance. With Washington gone and the influence of the "Tuskegee Machine" in decline, a new class of Black radicals came forward. For a few years, W. E. B. Du Bois was at the center stage of leadership. As founder-editor of the NAACP's *The Crisis*, Du Bois urged in 1918, "Let us, while this war lasts, forget our special grievances and close ranks shoulder to shoulder with our fellow citizens . . ." The continued discrimination against Black Americans, both soldiers and civilians, soon made W. E. B. Du Bois regret having made this statement. The end of the war brought no improvement to the lives of Black Americans. The then prevailing conditions made a large number of them ripe for the militant program of Marcus Garvey. This was the beginning of the heroic and troubled years of the Black urban ghetto.

JOHN HENRIK CLARKE
January 1973
New York, N. Y.

Part One

The Formative Years, 1912-1920

Commentary

BY JOHN HENRIK CLARKE

IN THE APPENDIX to the second edition of his book, *The Black Jacobins*, the Caribbean scholar C. L. R. James observes that two West Indians "using the ink of Negritude wrote their names imperishably on the front pages of the history of our times." [1] Professor James is referring to Aimé Cesaire and Marcus Garvey. He places Marcus Garvey at the forefront of the group of twentieth-century Black radicals whose ideas and programs still reverberate within present-day liberation movements. Marcus Garvey was a man who, in retrospect, was far ahead of his time. This is proved by the fact that his ideas have resurfaced and are being seriously reconsidered as a major factor in the liberation of African people the world over.

To call the movement he brought into being a "back-to-Africa movement" is to narrow its meaning. This was only one aspect of his movement. Marcus Garvey's plan was for total African redemption. The crucial legacy of slavery and colonialism helped to produce a Marcus Garvey. When he was born in 1887, in Jamaica, West Indies, the so-called "scramble for Africa" was over. All over Africa the warrior nationalists, who had opposed European colonialism throughout the nineteenth century, were being killed or sent into exile. The Europeans with territorial aspirations in Africa had sat at the Berlin Conference of 1884 and 1885 and decided how to split up the continent among them. In the United States, Black Americans were still suffering from the betrayal of the Reconstruction in 1876. The trouble within the world Black community that Marcus Garvey was later to grapple with had already begun when he was born. In the years when he was growing to early manhood, his people entered the twentieth century and a new phase of their struggle for freedom and national identity.

In 1907 Marcus Garvey was involved in the Printers' Union strike in Jamaica. After this unsuccessful strike ended in defeat for the printers, he went to work for the Government Printing Office and soon after edited his first publication, *The Watchman*.

In 1909 Garvey made his first trip outside of Jamaica to Costa Rica. In this poor and exploited country he observed the condition of Black workers and started an effort to improve their lot. His protest to the British consul was answered with bureaucratic indifference. He was learning his first lesson about the arrogant stubbornness of a European colonial power.

Garvey made several attempts to start a newspaper, hoping that it could expose the bad working conditions of the Blacks. These workers had no funds to support such a venture. He then went to Bocas-del-Toro, Panama, where he met a large number of Jamaicans who had originally come into the country to work on the Canal. With their help he was able to start a newspaper, *La Prensa*. The paper and Garvey's stay in Bocas-del-Toro lasted only a few months. He left Panama and went to Ecuador, Nicaragua, Honduras, Colombia and Venezuela. Again he observed that Black workers were being taken advantage of in the mines and in the tobacco fields; the Black man totally lacked power to improve his lot.

In 1912 Garvey was in London working, learning, growing, and seeing new dimensions of the Black man's struggle. The ideas that would go into the making of his life's work were being formulated. His close association with Duse Mohammed Ali, Egyptian scholar and nationalist of Sudanese descent, helped to sharpen his ideas about African redemption. He worked for a while on the monthly *The African Times and Orient Review*, edited by Ali, an association that was a continuation of Marcus Garvey's political education. It was not by accident that he came to London, the administrative headquarters of the British Empire, to continue his education, an education more practical than formal. He set out to acquaint himself with the realities of dealing with massive power and London was a storehouse of information about the colonial world.

A year before Marcus Garvey arrived in London the city had been host to a World Congress on Race (July 1911), more often referred to as the Races Congress. The Congress had been planned by Gustave Spiller working under the auspices of the English Ethical Culture Movement. Felix Adler was among the distinguished persons who took part.

The literature, the attitudes and the debates about the Congress were very influential when Marcus Garvey began his London years. Also important was the new anticolonial literature coming out of West Africa, such as the writings of the great Gold Coast (now Ghana) nationalist E. Casely Hayford and the Caribbean scholar Edward W. Blyden.

Dr. W. E. B. Du Bois,[2] a future adversary of Marcus Garvey, attended and gives this account of the Races Congress in his book *Dusk of Dawn*: "The Congress would have marked an epoch in the cultural history of the world if it had not been followed so quickly by the World War. As it was, it turned out to be a great and inspiring occasion, bringing together representatives of numerous ethnic and cultural groups, and new and frank conceptions of the scientific bases of racial and social relations of people." [3]

Dr. Du Bois further states that he not only had his regular assignment, but, due to the sudden illness of Sir Harry Johnson, represented him at one of the main sessions and made a speech on race and colonialism that was widely quoted in the London press. "Thus," he said, "I had a chance twice to address the Congress."

Dr. Du Bois wrote one of the poems that greeted the assembly. The interesting thing about the poem is that in tone and content it is similar to some of the poems that Marcus Garvey would later write:

> Save us, World Spirit, from our lesser selves,
> Grant us that war and hatred cease,
> Reveal our souls in every race and hue;
> Help us, O Human God, in this Thy truce,
> To make Humanity divine.

"Even while the Races Congress was meeting," Dr. Du Bois reported, "came the forewarning of coming doom: in a character-istic way a German war vessel sailed into an African port, notifying the world that Germany was determined to have larger ownership and control of cheap Black labor: a demand cam-ouflaged as a need of 'a place in the sun.' " And thus, the issue was joined.

Some of the questions about the future of colonial peoples had been put forward by the Races Congress. While trying to understand these questions, Garvey was seeing the British at close range and learning more about the difficult job still ahead of him. He obtained a copy of the book *Up from Slavery* [4] by Booker T. Washington. This book and its ideas had a strong influence on his concept of leadership and its responsibility and helped form the theoretical basis of what would later become Garveyism.

Black Americans had entered the twentieth century searching for new directions politically, culturally and institutionally: Booker T. Washington's Atlanta Cotton Exposition address (1895) had set in motion a great debate among Black people about their direction and their place in the developing American social order. New men and movements were emerging. Some, principally Bishop Henry McNeal Turner, the best known of the Back-to-Africa advocates before the emergence of Marcus Gar-vey, were questioning whether Black people had any future in America. Bishop Turner, now with failing health, continued to direct the last phase of his Back-to-Africa program which had been started in the closing years of the nineteenth century.[5] In an outlined history of his movement, *Bishop Henry McNeal Turner: A Political Biography*,[6] Anne Kelley made the following assess-ment of his career:

When considering the historical period between 1890 and 1915, when Bishop Turner's political thought was at its most mature level, two powerful black figures come to mind, namely Booker T. Washington and W. E. B. Du Bois. Most blacks are familiar with Washington's major theme of accommodation and Du Bois' major theme of integration; but, few are equally as aware of Turner's presence and nationalist theme with emphasis on emigration of blacks back-to-Africa. . . . During this particular period both

Washington and Du Bois advanced plans that were basically aimed at "liberation" of the black middle class. Washington's plan sought the creation of a class of black entrepreneurs; Du Bois sought to create a black intelligentsia. But Turner's back-to-Africa brand of black nationalism was rooted in a concern for the masses of black people, i.e., that most oppressed segment of black society represented by the southern rural population.

Other Black Americans answered the question of direction in a more affirmative way, by pouring massive energy into the building of new institutions, mainly schools. The institutional building aspects of the Booker T. Washington Program were an attraction for Marcus Garvey.

Marcus Garvey returned to Jamaica in 1914 and founded the Universal Negro Improvement and Conservation Association and African Communities League (UNIA and ACL). These organizations were not an instantaneous success. For nearly two years, he struggled to bring a semblance of unity to Jamaicans and to make some of the educated classes conscious of the needs of poor people.[7] He was up against the plutocracy—the land barons and the white shipping and fruit companies who made millions exploiting the cheap labor of the islands. The newspapers and all public media were against him. Also against him was an English institution, "prejudice based on class," that was compounded in Jamaica by color. He continued to struggle to bring a people's organization into being though at times it seemed like a stillborn child.

In the pamphlet "Marcus Garvey," Adolph Edwards gives the following capsule history of the early days of the Universal Negro Improvement Association: "Garvey landed in Jamaica on 15th July, 1914. The Caribbean isle had not changed. Kingston remained hot, depressing, inactive; above all, the social atmosphere was just as stultifying as before. Garvey's brain was afire and his existence was a world of thoughts. Within five days of his arrival he organized and founded the movement whose name was destined to be on the lips of millions—The Universal Negro Improvement Association. Briefly, the purpose of the Association was to unite 'all the Negro peoples of the world into one great body to establish a country and government absolutely their own.' The Association's motto was short and stirring: 'One God! One aim! One destiny!' " Garvey was designated President and Travelling Commissioner.

The UNIA not only had plans for the universal improvement of the Negro, but it also had plans for the immediate uplift of the Negro in Jamaica. The most important of these was the proposed establishment of educational and industrial colleges for Jamaican Negroes on the pattern of the Tuskegee Institute in Alabama, which had been founded by Booker T. Washington. This plan received the support of a few prominent citizens, including the Mayor of Kingston and the Roman Catholic bishop, but on the whole, it came in for sharp criticism within the more articulate circles. Garvey said about his persecutors and the decision he made: "Men and women as black as I and even more so, had believed themselves white under the West Indian order of society. I was simply an impossible man to use openly the term 'negro'; yet every one beneath his breath was calling the black man a 'nigger.' I had to decide whether to please my friends and be one of the 'black-whites' of Jamaica, and be reasonably prosperous, or come out openly, and help improve and protect the integrity of the black millions, and suffer. I decided to do the latter."

In *Philosophy and Opinions* Marcus Garvey would later ask himself: "Where is the black man's government? Where is his king and his kingdom? Where is his president, his country and his ambassador, his army, his navy, his men of big affairs?" He could not answer the question affirmatively, so he decided to make the black man's government, king and kingdom, president and men of big affairs. He taught his people to dream big again; he reminded them that they had once been kings and rulers of great nations and would be again. The cry "Up you mighty race, you can accomplish what you will" was a call to the black man to reclaim his best self and re-enter the mainstream of world history.

When Marcus Garvey came to the United States in 1916, Booker T. Washington was dead and World War I had already started. The migration of Black workers from the South to the new war industries in the northern and eastern parts of the United States was in full swing. Dissatisfaction, discontent and frustration among millions of Black Americans were accelerating this migration.

In the book *New World A-Coming* Roi Ottley[8] observed that Marcus Garvey leaped into the ocean of black unhappiness in the United States at a most timely moment for a savior. The Negro's disillusionment had mounted with the progress of the World War. Negro soldiers had suffered all forms of Jim Crow, humiliation, discrimination, slander, and even violence at the hands of the white civilian population. After the war, there was a resurgence of Ku Klux Klan influence; another decade of racial hatred and open lawlessness had set in, and Negroes again were prominent among the victims. Meantime, administration leaders quite pointedly tried to persuade Negroes that, in spite of their full participation in the war effort, they could expect no change in their status in America. Newton D. Baker was particularly vocal on this issue. The liberal white citizens were disturbed by events, but took little action beyond viewing with alarm.

Negroes were more than ready for a Moses, and only a Black man could express the depth of their feelings. Intellectuals of the race tried to rationalize the situation, but not so the broad masses; their acknowledged leader, Du Bois, had gone overboard on the war effort and now found himself estranged from his people. Negroes were faced with a choice between racialism and radicalism. Marcus Garvey settled the question for thousands by forming the United States branch of the Universal Negro Improvement Association (UNIA) and preaching with great zeal for a pilgrimage of Black men "back to Africa." He rallied men to the slogan, "Africa for Africans!"

The appearance of the Garvey Movement was perfectly timed. The broken promises of the post-war period had produced widespread cynicism in the Black population which had lost some of its belief in itself as a people. Adam Clayton Powell, Sr. wrote of Garvey: "He is the only man that made Negroes not feel ashamed of their color." In his book, *Marching Blacks*,[9] Adam Clayton Powell, Jr. wrote, "Marcus Garvey was one of the greatest mass leaders of all time. He was misunderstood and maligned, but he brought to the Negro people for the first time a sense of pride in being Black."

The Garvey Movement had a profound effect on the political development of the Harlem community. The migrations from the South during the First World War had, by the time Marcus Garvey arrived, made this an almost solidly Black community. In the freer atmosphere of the North, many Blacks who could not vote in local elections before were now demanding the right to run for public office. In these formative years of the Movement, Marcus Garvey had awakened in Black people a desire to be the masters of their own destiny.

One year after he entered the United States, he made a speaking tour (1917) of the principal cities, building up a national following. By 1919, a banner year for the growth of the UNIA, he had branches established all over the world. These branches were already preparing to send delegates and representatives of fraternal organizations to "The First International Convention of the Negro People of the World" that was planned for the following year.

Reaction to this growth and to the grievances of Black Americans in general came hard and fast. Race riots flared in nearly every part of the United States. Most of them occurred in the summer, and are collectively referred to as "the red summer of 1919."

These riots[10] convinced Marcus Garvey more than ever that the Black man had no secure place in America. His newspaper, the *Negro World*, became the most widely read weekly in America. The Black Star Line Steamship Company had been founded. The UNIA as an organization had been transformed from a wild dream to a reality that now commanded worldwide attention. Great masses of Black Americans began to relate to Garvey and his Movement. Harlem was his window on the world; from this ethnic ghetto he inspired millions of Black people to hope again and dream again.

Also, in 1919, under the leadership of Dr. W. E. B. Du Bois, then editor of the NAACP magazine *The Crisis*, another drama claiming African redemption as its objective was displayed in the capitals of Europe. It was the 1919 Pan-African Congress[11] called by W. E. B. Du Bois.

Dr. Du Bois had mapped out a scheme that he would attempt to present to President Woodrow Wilson and other heads of state, or their representatives, who were meeting at the Peace Conference at Versailles. Dr. Du Bois' dream was that the Peace Conference could form an internationalized Africa, its basis the former German colonies with their 1,000,000 square miles of territory and population of 12,500,000. "To this," his plan reads, "could be added by negotiation the 800,000 square miles and 9,000,000 inhabitants of Portuguese Africa. It is not impossible that Belgium could be persuaded to add to such a state the 900,000 square miles and 9,000,000 natives of the Congo, making an international Africa with over 2,500,000 square miles of land and over 20,000,000 people.

"This Africa for the Africans could be under the guidance of international organizations. The governing international Commission should represent not simply Governments, but modern culture, science, commerce, social reform, and religious philanthropy."

This was a plea by the Western-educated elite for a place in the African sun. True, they had the interest of what they called "the natives" at heart. But there was no question about who would rule if the plan materialized. The plan brought nothing but scorn from Marcus Garvey.

An excerpt from Dr. Du Bois' report on the Congress:

> Members of the American delegation and associated experts assured me that no congress on this matter could be held in Paris because France was still under martial law; but the ace that I had up my sleeve was Blaise Diagne, the black deputy from Senegal and Commissaire-General in charge of recruiting native African troops. I went to Diagne and sold him the idea of a Pan-African Congress. He consulted Clemenceau, and the matter was held up two wet, discouraging months. But finally we got permission to hold the Congress in Paris. "Don't advertise it," said Clemenceau, "but go ahead." Walter Lippmann wrote me in his crabbed hand, February 20th, 1919: "I am very much interested in your organization of the Pan-African Conference, and glad that Clemenceau has made it possible. Will you send me whatever reports you might have on the work?

The *Dispatch*, Pittsburgh, Pennsylvania, February 16, 1919, said:

> Officials here are puzzled by the news from Paris that plans are going forward there for a Pan-African Conference to be held

February 19th. Acting Secretary Polk said today the State Department had been officially advised by the French Government that no such Conference would be held. It was announced recently that no passports would be issued for American delegates desiring to attend the meeting. But at the very time that Polk was assuring American Negroes that no Congress would be held, the Congress actually assembled in Paris.

The international Garvey Movement continued its preparation for its great convention of 1920. This convention ended the formative years of the Garvey Movement and projected it into a new era of "Triumph and Tragedy." The following description of the convention was taken from the book, *Garvey and Garveyism*, by Amy Jacques Garvey:

> The first International Convention of the Negro Peoples of the World held its opening meeting at night at Madison Square Garden—the largest completely covered auditorium in New York. The first half of the program was musical, and the best talent in the race took part. The second half was devoted to speeches. White newspapers estimated the crowd inside and outside as between 20,000 to 25,000 persons; it was like an invasion of the white section. The thousands who could not get in the auditorium just stayed around the adjacent streets and discussed the day's happenings as something they never thought possible.
>
> The other sessions were held at Liberty Hall for thirty days, strenuous days for the Speaker-in-Convention. The first item on the agenda was reports from delegates on conditions in their localities and territories. For the first time in history all peoples of African descent sat together in brotherly understanding and sympathy to listen to accounts of the awful conditions and handicaps under which they were born, lived and worked. Even this privilege and the results were worth the enormous costs involved.
>
> Spanish and French interpreters helped those who could not speak English fluently. Africans were helped by others to write their speeches in basic English. Committees were appointed to deal with various matters; their terms of reference were investigatory, planning and advisory. This saved time, and the best informed and trained persons were given opportunities to serve in their particular line. The Committee on Africa had to hear certain delegates

privately. These had to register under assumed names, for their freedom and lives might be endangered if they openly exposed conditions in their home territories.

The culmination of this work was the Declaration of Rights of the Negro Peoples of the World, which commenced with a preamble, then twelve causes for grievous complaints of injustices, and fifty-four demands for future fair treatment of our people everywhere. The UNIA held sessions for members only, at which the association's business was discussed, constitutional amendments made, and officers elected.[12]

The Caribbean Antecedents of Marcus Garvey

BY JOHN HENRIK CLARKE

MARCUS GARVEY EMERGED from a historical setting that began to develop early in the fifteenth century. The European awakening that had started with the Crusades had by this time led to a movement to explore and exploit large areas of the world outside Europe. For the great states of West Africa it was a time of tragedy and decline. Europe's era of exploration and the internal strife in Africa were contributing factors to the start of the slave trade; the slave trade, in turn, was a contributing factor to the development of the philosophy of mercantilism that would dominate political and economic thought for the next 300 years.

The story of the African slave trade is essentially the story of the consequences of the second rise of Europe. In the years between the passing of the Roman Empire in the eighth century and the partial unification of Europe within the framework of the Catholic Church in the fifteenth century, Europeans were engaged mainly in internal matters. With the opening of the New World and the expulsion of the Moors from Spain during the latter part of the fifteenth century, the Europeans started to expand into the broader world. They were searching for new markets, new materials, new manpower, and new land to exploit.

The African slave trade was created to accommodate this expansion.

The rationale justifying the slave trade developed with Europeans attempting to justify the enslavement of other Europeans. This discord was a result of the religious wars that had existed in Europe for hundreds of years. In most European countries peace was unknown. Kings ruled like tyrants. The farmers were without land and had to work most of their lives on the farms of strong and rich landlords who had private armies to put down all unrest. During the religious wars many Roman Catholic kings would burn their Protestant subjects to death because they were not Catholic. Then Protestant kings would burn their Roman Catholic subjects for not being Protestant. These internal disputes were only partly settled when the Europeans began to explore Africa, Asia and the Americas.

By the time exploration began, the basis for the European industrial revolution had already been established. Europeans had created an embryo technology including the gun. In the years that followed, they also used other advantages, mainly a large fleet of ships and rabble soldiers and sailors who had no sentimental attachment to non-European people, to take over most of the world. In so doing, they destroyed a large number of nations and civilizations that were older than any in Europe.

The Europeans did not initially come to Africa to find slaves. For years they had heard stories about the great riches of Africa. At the Battle of Ceuta against the Moslems in 1415, Prince Henry of Portugal, later known as Prince Henry the Navigator, heard about the prosperity of Timbuktu and the wealth of the great states along the west coast of Africa. About the middle of the fifteenth century the Portuguese began trading with the people along the west coast of Africa, to which they gave the name "Guinea" after the Sudanic Empire of Ghana. Before the end of the century Portuguese sailors had come to know the general shape of the continent of Africa. They traded regularly with West African countries from 1471 on. Because of the large profits gained by the Portuguese in their trading in this country, they called it the Gold Coast.

At first the Portuguese traded mainly in gold, but before long they began to take slaves also.

During the latter half of the fifteenth century European nationalism was reflected in the expansion of trade in both slaves and manufactured goods. The marriage of Isabella and Ferdinand gave Europe the unity to drive the Moors out of Spain. Both Spain and Portugal were becoming powerful Mediterranean nations and began to vie for spheres of influence. As good Catholic nations, they went to the Pope to settle the dispute, and the Pope told them, in essence, you (Portugal) take the east and you (Spain) take the west.

In 1488 Bartholomew Diaz sailed around the southern tip of Africa. About ten years later, another Portuguese sailor, Vasco da Gama, sailed past the point reached by Diaz. With the help of an Arab pilot, Vasco da Gama reached India in 1498. For Europe, the door to the vast world of Asia was open.

When the Moors were expelled from Spain, they returned to Morocco, where the emperor El Mansur arranged with them to invade Equatorial Africa, the old empire of Songhai. This invasion broke up the structure of the last great empire in Western Africa, and the chaos that followed set up Africa for the future European slave trade.

Social and political unrest began to develop among the nations of West Africa at about the time Europe was regaining its strength and a degree of unity. The first Europeans to visit the west coast of Africa did not have to fight their way in; they came as guests and were treated as guests. Later, they decided to stay as conquerors and slave traders. In order to gain a position strong enough to attain these ambitions, they began to take sides in African family disputes, very often supplying the family or tribe they favored with arms and using the favorites as slave catchers. A number of African nations went into the slave trade in order to buy guns and other European manufactured items. Others were forced to capture slaves or to become slaves.

The main problem of the African in dealing with the European during this early period was the African's tragic naïveté. He had never dealt with this kind of people. He came out of a society where nature was kind; nature furnished him enough food, enough land, enough of the basic things he needed to live a pretty good life. Old African societies were governed by honor and obligation. Land could neither be bought nor sold; the land belonged to everyone.

The European, coming from a society where nature was rather stingy and where he had to compete with his brother for his breakfast, his land, and his woman, had acquired a competitive nature that the African could not deal with. In order to justify the destruction of African societies, a monster that still haunts our lives was created. This monster was racism. The slave trade and the colonial system that followed are the children of this catastrophe.

The slave trade prospered, and Africans continued to be poured into the world. Figures vary, but it has been established that during the years of the slave trade, Africa lost from sixty to a hundred million people. This wholesale export of human beings was the greatest single crime ever committed against a people in world history. It was also the most tragic act of protracted genocide.

The first Africans who came to the New World were not in bondage, contrary to popular belief. Africans participated in some of the early expeditions, mainly with Spanish explorers. The best known of these African explorers was Estevanico, sometimes known as Little Steven, who accompanied the de Vaca expedition during six years of wandering from Florida to Mexico. The remarkable thing about Estevanico, who came to America in 1527, is that he was a remarkable linguist. He learned the language of the Indians in a matter of weeks. Because of his knowledge of herbs and medicines, he was accepted as a deity by some Indian tribes.

In 1539, Estevanico set out from Mexico in a party with Fray Marcos de Niza in search of the fabulous Seven Cities of Cibola. When most of the expedition, including Fray Marcos, became ill, Estevanico went on alone and explored what is now known as New Mexico and Arizona.

The greatest destroyer of African culture, and the greatest exploiter of the African, was the plantation system of the New World. The African was transformed into something called a "Negro." He was demeaned. No other slave system in the world dehumanized the slave more than that started by the Europeans in the fifteenth century. Using religion as an excuse, the slavers began to set up myths that nearly always read the African out of human history, beginning with the classification of the African as a lesser being. The Catholic Church's justification for slavery was that the African was being brought under the guidance of Christendom and that he would eventually receive its blessings.

There were several competing slave systems in the New World. In order to understand the effects of these various systems on the personality of the Africans, we have to look at each one individually. In Cuba and Haiti, the Africans were often a majority population. This is also true of certain portions of Brazil. Therefore, the system operated differently in these areas, and although it was still slavery, the African had some cultural mobility.

In South America and in the West Indies, the slave masters did not outlaw the African drum, African ornamentations, African religion, or other things dear to the African remembered from his former way of life. In the Portuguese areas, in the West Indies and often in South America, plantation owners would buy a shipload or half a shipload of slaves. These slaves usually came from the same areas in Africa, and they naturally spoke the same language and had the same basic culture. Families, in the main, were kept together. If a slave on an island was sold to a plantation owner at the other end of the island, he could still walk to see his relatives. This freedom permitted a form of cultural continuity among the slaves in South America, the West Indies, Cuba, and Haiti that did not exist in the United States and that later made their revolts more successful than revolts in the United States.

It can be said that these revolts, and the personalities involved, were the Caribbean antecedents of Marcus Garvey. It is against this historical background that he can best be understood. In an article, "A Birth of Freedom," by the Guyanan writer Sidney King, this point is graphically made when he reminds us that, "The Caribbean tradition, taken as a whole, is a revolutionary tradition. It is the stage on which acted Cudgoe and Cuffe, Accabreh and Accra, Toussaint, Quamina and Damon, Adoe and Araby [all leaders of slave revolts]. Blows delivered against the European system in 1750 or in 1850 served to shake that system, sometimes to its foundations, and to cause it to make democratic concessions as a price of recovery. It was never the same again; and although financial exploitation became more intense and complicated, a constitutional superstructure was raised for dealing with human anger and for sidetracking revolution into peaceful awe-inspiring chambers." [13]

The revolts referred to here were epitomized by the Berbice Revolution of 1763. This revolt, Sidney King observes, "struck the first blow for Guyanese independence. It was a blow that the theoreticians of human subjugation will never forget. It was part and parcel of the Caribbean Movement begun by the Caribs against European penetration and domination."

The Berbice slave revolt began when the slaves in Guyana made their first massive attempt to throw off the yoke of their masters; they realized that they would have to kill a large number of white people in order to do so. These killings are spoken of as rebellions and scores of them are recorded. But the Berbice slave rebellion was more than an attempt to abolish slavery; it had the germ of a true revolution—it was also an attempt to establish a nation. The importance of this slave rebellion is in the fact that it went far beyond a revolt against then prevailing conditions.

The 1763 rebellion[14] came in spite of the Dutch penal code that was set up to prevent it and it came at the time Spanish slave traders were challenging the Dutch traders both in South America and in the Caribbean Islands. (Between 1624 and 1654 the Dutch had lost their vast slave empire in Brazil.) Other nations—France, Britain and Portugal—were also trying to secure their spheres of influence in the New World.

The Dutch had established themselves in Berbice in 1624. During the years 1624 to 1763 they were the cruelest of slave masters. The Dutch slave code was much harsher than the Spanish code (the savagery of the Dutch code is shown by one provision of calculated cruelty: the burning alive of mutinous slaves over a slow fire). The Dutch had no institution comparable to the Spanish *audiencia*, a tribunal which included four judges. The ruthlessness of the Dutch created the situation that came to a climax in the Berbice slave rebellion.

A number of minor uprisings had occurred in 1762, a year before the February Revolution. In his book *Revolution to*

Republic the Guyanan writer P. H. Daly states that these uprisings "were not exclusively Black against white. In the outbreak of 1762, the rebels had killed many Africans who were fighting on the side of the whites. The prelude to the February Revolution, as seen in the minor uprisings in 1762, had shown many of the nationalist characteristics of the February Revolution itself. Fundamentally, a war of Black against white, the February Revolution gradually escalated into a class conflict, still fundamentally against the whites, but internally between the house-gang slaves and the field-gang slaves in the revolutionary leadership." [15] In this conflict over leadership lay the dangerous seed that would grow and destroy the effectiveness of the Revolution.

Cuffe, the leader of the revolt, was a house servant who had been brought to the colony very young and because of his intelligence had been taught carpentering by his master. When the rebellion started in February 1763, at Plantation Magdelenenburg on the Canje in Berbice, Cuffe had some misgivings about the outcome and the methods being used. He had hoped to secure better conditions for the slaves without having to resort to war.

In his introduction to P. H. Daly's *Revolution to Republic*,[16] Martin Carter calls attention to the conditions that existed within the slave society in Guyana and Cuffe's dilemma as the rebellion got under way. He writes of the "certificates of submissiveness which were the psychological credentials required of an African slave who aspired to enter the white man's house" and of the situations in which pregnant field-slave women were kicked to death. He identifies Cuffe with the former position and Akkara (the field slave) with the latter, and contends that as a consequence of the two different kinds of psychological conditioning it was "inevitable" that "different" ideas about waging war "would follow."

Ironically, while the slaves were rebelling, the Governor of Berbice was putting a plea for them to the Directors of the Association. But when he heard news of the rising he did not hesitate to send what help he could to the planters on the Canje.

By the beginning of March the rebellion had spread to the Berbice River, where the first plantations to be attacked were those of certain private planters who had been extremely cruel to their slaves. Plantation after plantation was overrun and the whites captured and killed. More than 900 rebels had joined the fight.

In the meantime the whites had rushed for places of safety, and finally took refuge in a brick house at Peerbroom. They turned the house into a fortress; each window was defended and the approaches were strewn with broken glass. But this did not stop the Africans who bombarded the building with hobnails bound around with burning cotton. Soon, the roofs of some of the houses were afire. Casala, the leader of this particular attack, told the whites that the Africans were determined to take the estate. The whites held a hasty council. They knew that the Governor of Berbice had planned to send a recently arrived slave ship to cover their retreat to the river with guns, but the ship was nowhere in sight and provisions were running out. The manager of one of the estates spoke to the Africans. He asked why they were treating the Christians in that manner. Casala's reply was virtually a declaration of independence: he said that the Christians were too cruel, and that they had decided that they would not tolerate any more Christians or whites in their country. Further, he said that they intended to be masters of Berbice since all the plantations belonged to them.

Every estate on the Canje River was sacked; new battles were fought at Fort Nassau. The revolutionary forces pushed their way to Port St. Andries and to New Amsterdam. The slaves on most of the plantations joined the rebels; only a few remained faithful to their masters.

P. H. Daly tells us further that, "On May 3, 1763, two vessels from St. Eustatius brought food stuffs and fresh troops for the besieged. The battle for Dageraad proved the decisive engagement of the Revolution. It was a revolutionary army weakened by dissension that confronted the whites in the final assault on Dageraad, the cultural and spiritual stronghold of the white community. But the revolutionary forces fought bravely. With the warrior-statesman Cuffe at the head of his men, titanic hand-to-hand battles between Blacks and whites distinguished this final and attritive conflict. The day was May 13. The hand-to-hand fighting lasted for hours. The whites had strengthened their defences. The revolutionary forces attacked with guns, cutlasses, agricultural tools and with the iron chains which formerly shackled them—every conceivable weapon was pressed into battle. They sprayed the strong point with cannon fire, showing remarkable determination and ruthlessness." [17]

Though the struggle for Guyana between the Blacks and the whites would go on for years, and though there would be other slave uprisings, Dageraad was the beginning of the end of the Berbice slave rebellion. In his book *History of the Guyanas* James Rodway says: "Had it not been for the last arrivals, it would probably have been the final catastrophe" [18]—for the whites.

In the Prologue and Summary to his book Daly says: "The great drama of the Revolution of February 23, 1763 . . . is the most significant event in the history of Guyana. . . . While it lasted, the maelstrom of events it churned still challenges the ability of the scientific historian to interpret and assess them." [19]

The War of the Maroons of Jamaica predated the Berbice rebellion and is better known in history. The word Maroons (usually escaped slaves and their descendants, more rarely freed slaves) once spread terror along the skirts of the blue mountains of Jamaica. The Maroons, whose revolt started in 1655, were never completely conquered.

Modern Jamaican history, in brief, and the events that led to this famous slave rebellion started with the coming of the Spaniards in 1494.[20] Jamaica was a Spanish colony for 149 years. During this time the original inhabitants, the Arawak Indians, were literally destroyed and replaced by African slaves. The British took over the island in 1655. Two years later, the Maroons in the hills of Jamaica gave some assistance to Don Cristobal Arnaldo de Ysassi, the last appointed Spanish Governor of Jamaica, in his desperate attempt to hold on to the island for Spain. The Maroons were troublesome to British authorities in Jamaica for the next 50 years. Open warfare between the British and the Maroons, under the leadership of a man referred to as Captain Cudgoe who had united several settlements under his leadership, broke out in 1728 and lasted for ten years.

In the protracted wars that followed the Maroons distinguished themselves militarily, but accepted a settlement that was less than independence. The settlement, still being questioned by some Caribbean historians, gave the Maroons internal autonomy while making them "responsible directly to the Governor of Jamaica."

A British colonist, Guthrie by name, conceived the plan of making the Maroons "friends" of the Government.[21] According to "The Gleaner Geography and History of Jamaica," Guthrie's idea was accepted by the Governor of Jamaica and a treaty of peace and friendship was drawn up between the Maroons and the Government. The Maroons were given land in different parts of the country, free of taxes. They were allowed to govern themselves and were to be tried and punished by their own chiefs, but no chief could pass a sentence of death on any of them. They were to capture all runaway slaves and take them back to their owners, and they were also to assist in suppressing any rebellion among the slaves.

Some of the more radical Black historians are of the opinion that the terms of this agreement were tantamount to the reinslavement of the Maroons.[22] What is called "The Bush Negro Movement of Surinam" (or Dutch Guyana) has a closer relationship to the Maroon Movement than to the Berbice Movement of 1763. In their cause and in the way they executed their battle strategy by withdrawing from the European-dominated plantations, they related directly to the Maroons. In fact, they are referred to as the Maroons of Surinam. Both of these movements used some of the same tactics, though the Surinam Movement was not as effective. These movements were pre-nationalist in their aims and scope. In general, they were freedom movements that given time would have developed into autonomous Black states.

In Surinam some of the Africans who had been brought into the country earlier had escaped into the wooded hinterlands and had established independent communities. These communities became havens for other Africans who escaped from the plantations. This situation in part helped to set the Surinam revolt in motion. The first open outbreak occurred in 1726 when the slaves on the plantations on the Seramica River revolted. After the government found it impossible to subdue these rebels they tortured eleven captives to death, thinking that this would frighten the other rebels into submission. This act of cruelty only made the rebellion spread into other areas. It continued for almost another generation. One of the leaders of the rebellion, a man named Adoe, signed a peace treaty in 1749. In 1761, when the Surinam rebels were under the leadership of two Black generals referred to as Captain Araby and Captain Baston, another treaty was signed.

The plantation owners did not seem to have learned anything from their experiences. They did not honor any of the treaties they had made with the Blacks. In 1772, another leader, named Baron, led the Surinam Maroons in another uprising. Some of the planters liberated their slaves and used them against the rebels. This move was only partly successful; in increasing numbers the "liberated" slaves joined the rebels. These wars lasted until 1831.

These revolts, collectively, helped to create the conditions and attitudes that went into the making of the most successful slave revolt in history, the Haitian Revolution. This revolt was brought into being by three of the most arresting personalities in Caribbean history, Toussaint L'Overture, Jacques Dessalines and Henri Christophe. The distinguishing feature of this revolution is in the fact that it achieved what the others had not, the creation of a nation.

Revolts and resistance to slavery were widespread throughout the Caribbean in the years between the Maroon revolts and the Haitian Revolution. In 1760, a formidable uprising of slaves took place at St. Mary in Jamaica under a leader named Tacky. The slaves seized the town of Port Maria, armed themselves, murdered all the white people that fell into their hands, and were preparing for further acts of vengeance when they were met by troops sent against them. Their courage and desperation in the fight against these troops, who were equipped with the modern arms of that day, is a high-water mark in the eighteenth-century struggle of the Africans in Jamaica for human status and nationhood. In the end they were defeated; 400 were killed in battle; 600 were deported to British Honduras. The ringleaders, who could be found, were put to death.

In the article, "Tacky and the Great Slave Rebellion of 1760," C. Roy Reynolds says: "The leader of the revolt which was to involve the island in nearly eighteen months of internal warfare, which apparently threatened the loss of Jamaica to the British crown, was Tacky. He was a young slave who was brought from the west coast of Africa. Through great ingenuity and organizing prowess, this incredible man, described as handsome and well built, had been able to formulate an islandwide revolutionary organization entirely unknown to the planters and their agents." [23]

The agitation against the slave trade, and against slavery itself, had already started in England. Lord Mansfield and other enlightened judges of this day had already declared that the moment a slave set foot on English soil he was a free man. This ruling came about as a result of the work of Grandville Sharpe and other British abolitionists. [24]

Resistance continued in Jamaica while the storm of revolution was developing in Haiti. In 1791 the white planters in Haiti, who were opposed to the French Revolution and who objected to their slaves being set free, eventually appealed to the English in Jamaica for help. France, now a republican country, became involved in a war with England and other European states. Some of the French Royalists came over to Jamaica and requested assistance in their fight against the African slaves and former slaves who wanted to free the country from French rule. Some of the French Royalists wanted to put the colony under the protection of the British Crown.

A detachment of British and Black troops went from Jamaica to Haiti. These troops began to die of diseases soon after they arrived in Haiti. The English were eventually defeated and expelled by Toussaint L'Overture.

The dramatic beginning of the Haitian Revolution is told in the following statement, taken from the book *Great Negroes Past and Present*, by Russell L. Adams: [25]

> In 1630 the French came to the island and took control of the western side of Saint Domingue. With the sweat of the blacks they made their territory the richest European colonial possession, sending to France a steady stream of sugar, cotton, and indigo. By the end of the seventeenth century, some 20,000 Frenchmen, 50,000 mulattoes and 2,000,000 blacks lived there in an uneasy balance. Caste and class separated the three groups. Complicating these divisions was the presence of the Spanish rule on the eastern

half of the island. High, well-nigh impassable mountains sliced Saint Domingue in two parts.

While France itself was astir with talk of the rights of man and of freedom, equality, and fraternity, autocratic governors-general held absolute sway over thousands of slaves who produced the wealth of Saint Domingue and over dissatisfied mulattoes who could own land but had no political or social standing. When the Bastille fell in 1789, the island trembled as though in anticipation of some dreaded catastrophe. In this same year the mulattoes revolted. France then loosened its rule a bit and allowed the mulattoes to have seats in the new colonial assembly.

But the enslavement of the blacks continued, harsh and cruel as ever. As the revolution in France gained momentum, the far away island of Saint Domingue became increasingly restless. The blacks became fired with the desire for freedom and deep in the forest at night they gathered and plotted. The tom-tom language of the Africans told the blacks of the planned uprising. . . .

After conquering all of the French territory, Toussaint established himself as Governor-General of Saint Domingue. Jacques Dessalines, his comrade-in-arms, was made Governor of the Province. Henri Christophe was promoted to the rank of General and made Governor of Cap François. To the south of Cap François, there was a region that was predominantly inhabited by mulattoes. This region was ruled over by Alexander Sabes Petion. Before Toussaint had time to pull the country together, the mulatto problem, which had been somewhat latent during the Revolution, surfaced and added new problems to Toussaint L'Ouverture's nation-building efforts.

While Toussaint was turning his attention to the arts of peace and domestic politics, Emperor Napoleon was planning the reconquest of Haiti. He ordered eighty-six ships to be built to carry 22,000 fighting men. The commander of this navy was General LeClerc. This fleet arrived in the waters of Saint Domingue in February 1802. The main force of the fleet was directed at Cap François, then under the Governorship of Henri Christophe, who refused to receive LeClerc. This led to an attack by the French forces. Christophe put a torch to the city, including his fabulous palace, and fled to the hills. Belatedly, the peasants rushed to join Christophe.

General LeClerc had attempted to re-enslave the Blacks and return all plantations to their former owners. When this tactic failed, he reversed himself and declared all Blacks free forever. He offered Christophe and Dessalines generalships in the French army. He went through the motions of retiring the aged Toussaint with honor. This was part of an overall scheme to destroy the three main leaders of Haiti. Toussaint was captured and taken to France where he died in prison in 1803. An attempt was made to assassinate Dessalines. This act of deception by LeClerc started another revolution. Christophe and Dessalines joined forces and drove the French army into the sea. In this crisis the mulattoes put aside their loyalty to the French and fought with the Blacks. Dessalines came to power, and after his assassination in 1806, Christophe, literally, rebuilt Haiti and ruled it until his death on October 8, 1820.

On August 28, 1833, slavery was abolished throughout the British Empire. The abolition of slavery did not automatically mean the abolition of servitude, however. Most of the Blacks were still landless and poor. Near the end of the nineteenth century, a large number of Jamaican Blacks, many of them skilled craftsmen, began to agitate against their condition. Marcus Garvey was born at a time of great agitation for reform and for the ownership of land (1887). The "Back to Africa" concept was introduced into the social thought of Jamaica by J. Albert Thorne while Marcus Garvey was growing to manhood.

Thorne was born in Barbados in 1860. He became a public-school teacher after finding government work closed to him. His plans for African colonization were set forth in a pamphlet that he had dedicated to the memory of William Wilberforce, the noted abolitionist, and David Livingstone, the famous missionary and explorer. His plans, unlike others, called for settlement in the parts of Central and East Africa that were then controlled by the British.

J. Albert Thorne founded the African Colonial Enterprise as an instrument for the work that he intended to do and as a means of raising funds for that work. The plan did not work and could not work in the colonial climate of that day. The so-called "Scramble for Africa" had started ten years before at the Berlin Conference of 1884–1885. The European powers who had claims on Africa had sat down and decided how Africa would be divided. All over Africa during the closing years of the nineteenth century warrior nationalists were engaged in a physical struggle to rescue Africa from its colonial masters. The Europeans who had finally agreed on their respective territorial claims and spheres of influence were in no way amenable to the settlement of Afro-Americans and Afro-Caribbean people in any part of Africa. In spite of this, J. Albert Thorne continued his back-to-Africa scheme.

Thorne believed that the British had a moral obligation to assist him. The British, in their usual ambiguous way, did not give him a positive yes or a positive no. Several Englishmen gave Thorne the impression that they approved of his scheme without letting him know that they were not speaking officially for the British government. After seeking assistance from Captain (later Lord) Lugard, Thorne quotes him as making this observation: "If undertaken by thoroughly capable men and if the families consist of capable and industrious artisans, the scheme should have in it the promise of success." [26]

J. Albert Thorne helped to shape the tradition out of which a Marcus Garvey would emerge. Marcus Garvey, who was of proud Maroon descent, would use this tradition to build the largest Black mass movement of this century.

The Early Years
of Marcus Garvey

BY AMY JACQUES GARVEY

ON THE ISLAND of Jamaica—the Isle Springs—ninety miles from Cuba, on the seventeenth day of August in 1887, was born to Marcus Garvey and his wife Sarah a baby boy, the eleventh child of the couple. Ma Garvey wanted him named Moses, as she liked Biblical names for her children, and had a hunch that this child would become a leader like Moses of old. But Pa Garvey had ideas about this little boy, too. He said the boy should be named Marcus after him, and maybe he would become a Marcus Aurelius, believing in the worth of every human being because "the Universe has need of them." Pa Garvey believed in planetary influences; the child was born under the sign of Leo the Lion, when the sun was in its ascendancy, a most favorable omen. Eventually a compromise was reached and the child was baptized as Marcus Mosiah Garvey, although many people called him Mose.

Pa Garvey was a stocky man, muscular and strong. He was descended from the Maroons, the African slaves who defied the English administrator and soldiers, fled to the hills and fought a guerrilla war. Fever and the unfamiliar tropical terrain forced the English to call peace. A treaty was signed, and the Maroons were given certain tax-free land areas and the right to govern themselves. In the 1665 slave rebellion the Maroons decoyed the brave rebel leader Paul Bogle and captured him for the English authorities; perhaps that was why Pa Garvey brooded so much as he looked back on the history of his people.

He was a stonemason by trade, cutting and shaping pieces of white rock, then jointing and pointing them to build walls and great houses on plantations. At home he stayed mostly in a room of his own, away from the family, where he had a collection of books, magazines and newspapers. He was called "the village lawyer," because he was well informed and advised the townfolk. Everyone called him Mr. Garvey, even his wife.

On the other side Sarah was slim with fine features and large black eyes. She was gentle and always helpful to her neighbors and a regular churchgoer. Pa Garvey went to funerals or big rallies, but his Bible was well marked, as he studied it so as to argue about the Scriptures.

Young Marcus Garvey spent his childhood in St. Ann's Bay, St. Ann, called the Garden Parish, because of its lush vegetation and good rainfall. As a child he learned to swim in the sea; he dodged sharks, fished and basked in the sun on the beach. Roaring River Falls was near, a great place for picnics. Later in life he grew to appreciate the grandeur and power of the falls; the roar of its turbulent waters could be heard miles away on a quiet night. He used to sit by the wharf and watch the ships loading products such as pimiento and logwood for Germany and citrus, bulk sugar and rum for America. He talked with seamen and heard not only tall tales from the seadogs, but picturesque descriptions of ports and towns they visited during their voyages around the world. He was thrilled by their accounts of adventure and would have loved to run away on a ship and see foreign countries and mix with new people. But Pa Garvey was no man to play tricks with, so he comforted himself with the thought that one day he would be a man and could go wherever he pleased.

Ma Garvey had a brother named Benjie at Chalky Hill with whom she shared the family property. From the time Mose was nine years old Ma Garvey would send him to help his uncle reap the crops which were sold to the produce dealer. Ma got a portion of the proceeds, which she used to help support the family when Pa was out of work; the money was also used to buy Mose's clothes and provide him with an allowance. Ma Garvey also sold delicious cakes and pastries made from guavas, coconuts and ripe plantains.

Pa argued with his neighbors over line fences, hanging trees and surveyors' pegs. He lost two holdings, either by court decree or by using them in lieu of money to pay his lawyers, and was left with only the house plot. So Mose could not be sent to Kingston to secondary school. His mother paid the head teacher at the primary school to give him private lessons in secondary school subjects; she knew he was a bright boy.

Pa Garvey was hard and stern, and he never seemed to warm up to his son. Mose remembered that one day he was helping his father build a vault for a planter's son who had died of pneumonia in England; when it was lunchtime Pa proceeded up the ladder, and immediately pulled it up, leaving Mose in the unfinished vault. When Mose shouted: "Pa! Pa! I am down here," and got no answer, he decided that this was another test. He tried to stay awake, but his legs shook and he imagined he saw the dead man peeping down at him, so he prayed for sleep, which came as he was tired and hungry. When Pa woke Mose up later he told him in rough voice: "Boy, this is a lesson to teach you never to be afraid."

When Mose was nearly fourteen Ma gave him a suit—not just a shirt and pants but a real suit with jacket and pants, made by a tailor. He was to attend the biannual garden party on the church grounds. Ma had given him money to buy ice cream and balloons, to take chances in the raffle and a dip in the grab bag.

But just as Mose was about to take a bath Pa sent him to buy a half pint of white rum and two cigars. The feeling of stepping out and posing big made him go round by the banana patch and taste the rum, one sip, then another sip. He lit a cigar and puffed and puffed; the cool breeze fanned his face. When he got up to go he staggered; he had to sit down again, and soon he was bringing up all he had. He attempted to stand up and walk, but his head was swimming so he had to lay down, and sleep took charge of him.

Pa was annoyed when Mose did not show up with his rum and cigars. Ma was worried about Mose. Something must have happened to make him so late for the garden party. So she climbed the little rise behind the house, cupped her hands to her mouth and called, "Mose! Mo-ose! Mo-ose!" just as if she were using the Abeng-talking horn, which echoes over the hills. Then she suspected that since he could not hear her call, he must be asleep somewhere; and so he was. She had to get help to put him in bed and lock the door so that his father could not flog him. The next day Pa felt that Mose had been punished enough by not being able to "spree himself" at the garden party, but he warned him: "Rum and cigar is not for BOY, that is for MAN." Mose never drank strong liquor, even when he came to manhood, and he never smoked until the winter of 1921 when he contracted asthma going from Key West, Florida, to Cuba and had to smoke asthma cigarettes.

At fifteen young Marcus was sent to learn printing at his godfather Burrows' shop. There was a back room at the shop containing books, magazines, and old newspapers, where he could read and think deeply. Mr. Burrows' old cronies and friends stopped by to exchange news and reminisce about the old slave days, plantation stories and slave rebellions. He admired leaders such as Cudjoe, Tacky, Sharp, Quaco, and Paul Bogle, who came down from Stony-Gut warning his people: "Remember your color and cleave to the blacks."

Mose read from the Jamaica *Advocate*, published by Dr. Robert Love, a Black man from Nassau. Dr. Love was a landed proprietor who qualified for the "better class" category (those who ignored the Black masses) but he attended all sick people, even those who could not pay him, and published a newspaper that voiced the opinions of the submerged "lower class." The following is an excerpt from one of his editorials dated May 18, 1895:

> Some are whispering that we are dangerous. We don't care if we are. If to speak out thoughts freely and fearlessly—if to advocate the equal rights of all citizens—if to denounce oppression and wrong—if to teach the class to which we belong their rights and privileges, as well as their duties and responsibilities, if to do these is to be dangerous, then we wish to be [as] dangerous as we can be, and no power can arrest our action in this direction.

Powerful words, written in 1895, while under British rule. These were the men who inspired Garvey and made him realize that the economic thraldom of the masses was part of a system to keep Black people down; for the Colonial Office in London saw to it that the local government provided incentives for better working and living conditions for English men and women and their kith and kin.

Looking up at the moon or gazing at the star-studded sky he felt the awe of a Divinity and a sense of the mystery of all nature far beyond the comprehension of many knowledgeable men. The roaring falls, the river peacefully flowing by, the mountains and their lonely, lofty peaks; the colors of the rainbow, the colors of the sunsets that defy a painter's skill; the hurricanes in the summer; the droughts and flood rains, planting time and reaping time; all these touched him, and he displayed their influences. The Maroon blood was stirring in his veins, and he felt that it was time for him to carry on the struggle for which the patriots of old had sacrificed.

At eighteen Marcus Garvey went to Kingston, the capital, and got a job at Benjamin's printery. He became involved in a printers' strike, and although he was young he rallied the men. The strike failed because the union treasurer ran away with the money sent by American printers to aid the workers.

Garvey went to work at the government printery and sent for his mother. She did not like city life. She missed her kitchen garden, chickens, fresh eggs and cool air. She passed on after nearly two years with Mose. His father died about ten years later.

In 1910 Garvey joined the National Club; among the club's members were Sir William Morrison, S. A. G. Cox, Alexander Dixon, W. A. Domingo, S. M. DeLeon and J. Coleman Beecher. Garvey became secretary. The club published a fortnightly called *Our Own*. The members of this political club took part in an election to the Legislative Council; Dixon and Cox were elected, but Cox was unseated for not having a proper residential qualification in St. Thomas. The club provided Garvey with his first experience in newspaper publishing and campaigning for a political candidate.

I asked Beecher just before he died what impressed him most

about Garvey, and he said: "He was fiercely proud of being black. He carried a pocket dictionary with him and said he studied three or four words daily, and in his room he would write a paragraph or two using these words." DeLeon had this to say: "He had a mature mind from the time he came to Kingston in his teens. He was always busy, planning and doing something for the underprivileged youth. Uplift work we called it, and he had us in the shaft with him."

There was so much he wanted to do for his people, and not having the means, he went to an uncle in Costa Rica who got him a job as timekeeper on a fruit farm. From there he moved on to Guatemala, Panama, Nicaragua, Bocas-del-Toro, then down to South America—Ecuador, Chile and Peru. In all these Spanish-speaking republics were West Indian workers who had left their overpopulated islands because of unemployment and poverty to work on the fruit farms of Guatemala, Costa Rica and Bocas-del-Toro and in the mines of South America. They had built the Panama Canal, but in the Canal Zone they were classified as "silver employees" and given less pay than white men who were called "gold employees." These islanders risked their lives working in the swamps and blasting rocks to build "the big ditch" linking the Atlantic with the Pacific Ocean.

They cleared the forests and planted bananas for the fruit companies but were poorly paid and made to live under wretched conditions. The native highwaymen of these republics robbed the immigrants on payday (they had to travel miles to get groceries and other necessities). Being thrifty they put their savings in the banks, but these banks were not under government control; they were more like money agencies, so sometimes they closed their doors, and the migrants lost their savings without any redress.

In all these republics Garvey tried to organize the West Indian immigrants and called on the British Consul to protect them. Invariably he was told that the Consul was there to see after the interests of His Majesty's government and did not intend to disrupt friendly relations with these republics because of West Indian migrants.

Whenever he could Garvey published a little paper to voice

the migrants' feelings and views. In Costa Rica it was called *La Nacionale*, in Panama *La Prensa*. But the people did not realize the importance of maintaining a paper and an organization for their own protection and interest. He kept trying and working, but the authorities harassed him as an agitator. After two years he felt sick at heart and worn out with malaria and he returned to Jamaica. He related the sufferings of the West Indian workers, who had asked him to see what their home governments would do in their behalf. He headed a delegation that put the workers' problems before the governor of Jamaica; the governor said that the workers should return home if conditions were that bad and not create any incidents for His Majesty's government. When Garvey asked him what the workers could expect at home in the way of jobs, the governor had no suggestions to offer.

The upper and middle classes had the same callous, indifferent attitude about the problems faced by West Indians working in foreign lands. Yet these migrants sent money home to support their close relatives and to buy property. If statistics were available it would be proved that millions of dollars were sent back yearly. These people were an asset, yet they were allowed to be mistreated and exploited, even to the point of reducing their earning power. They formed the nucleus of the soon-to-be-organized Universal Negro Improvement Association.

Finally Garvey felt that if he went to England he might be able to get help for West Indians working in foreign lands. In England he would contact men in high places as well as working-class people, none of whom knew what went on in the far-flung colonies of the Empire.

Garvey's only surviving sister, Indiana, was in England working as a child's nurse, so he got her help to pay his passage. During his stay there she continued to help him. He worked around the docks of London, Cardiff and Liverpool and gained a wealth of information from African and West Indian seamen. As he told them, they told him, and all concluded that suffering was indeed the common lot of the race, no matter where they lived. The seamen told him where to find Duse Mohammed Ali, an Egyptian nationalist, who did not confine his nationalism to Egypt. His place was a center for Africans and Asians. He published *The African and Orient Review*. Indian and Chinese seamen and students also visited Ali, giving reports of ghastly happenings in their respective homelands under Colonial rule. Garvey realized why India was called "the brightest jewel in the British Crown." Thus he became fully involved in all that went on there and contributed his views to the magazine. He spent hours in the libraries, and attended lectures at Birbeck College. Indiana always had a package of sandwiches for him when he visited her.

Rumblings of war were in the air, and early in 1914 Garvey returned to Jamaica and set up an organization for members of the Black race. He called it the Universal Negro Improvement Association and African Communities League. Its motto—One God! One Aim! One Destiny! Africanus was the cable address, and the officers were: Marcus Garvey, President and Travelling Commissioner; T. A. McCormack, Secretary General; and J. W. Milburn, Treasurer.

The mixed-blood and "better-off" Blacks resented being called Negroes; the word African conjured up in their minds "cannibals and heathens." Regardless of this opposition, Garvey pushed on with the cultural program—promoting elocution contests and concerts so as to develop and bring out the hidden talents of the poor blacks. Garvey also lectured on the true conditions in Africa. The Roman Catholic bishop and the Presbyterian minister helped him. The latter allowed him to use the Collegiate Hall for his activities.

The people whom he served had no money to finance the programs as they expanded, so he decided to establish a trade school so that his followers could acquire skills in order to earn better wages. He wrote Booker T. Washington, who replied, encouraging him to come to America. By the time he was able to raise enough money for the trip, Dr. Washington had died.

Garvey landed in New York in March 1916. Harlem was a Black city, but most of the businesses were owned by Jews, Greeks, Italians. The churches were well attended, mostly by women, who used them for recreation as well as worship.

Garvey soon found that Negroes in the South were heading North, leaving behind Jim Crow, lynching, peonage farms, disenfranchisement, serfdom and misery; but how did they fare in the industrial cities and towns of the North? They earned better wages in the factories, which had to feed the war machines, but they had to live in rundown houses in proscribed areas and their children were provided with very poor school accommodations. When the thrifty ones bought houses through white agents and moved into white areas they lived in fear of being bombed out, of their families being threatened on the streets.

The preachers and ward politicians were designated as leaders for these new Northerners. There was no all-Negro organization; the National Association for the Advancement of Colored People was, and is, an interracial organization. At that time its officers were mainly whites and mulattoes, like Dr. Du Bois, and later Walter White, who looked white.

Garvey started his campaign in Harlem as a soapbox speaker on street corners. Later on he got the use of St. Mark's Hall for special meetings. He rallied the people around him because he was talking about a positive international program, not just an anti-lynching protest. He opposed integration of the races as racial suicide and an easy solution put forward by persons who did not have the courage and determination to keep on fighting for their rights to live and work as other racial groups did.

The First England Years
and After, 1912-1916

BY ROBERT A. HILL

I

We still cannot be entirely certain of the exact date of
Garvey's arrival in Britain. Garvey himself later spoke of 1911 as
the year in which his visit commenced. We do know, however,
that it had to be sometime after the end of February 1912 since
Garvey had been an eyewitness to the Kingston Streetcar Riot,
which occurred on February 26, 1912.[27] Garvey would then have
been twenty-five years old, able to appreciate and seize upon the significant
opportunities that a period of stay in the Imperial Center
offered an energetic-minded young colonial, as was Garvey.

Garvey's first encounter with English society was a genteel
one. He has left us a clear picture of the equanimity of contact of
those early years. In a brief editorial reminiscence published in
1932, Garvey portrayed his successive encounters with English
society in the following terms:

When we visited England in 1911 we found a different state of
affairs. We of ourselves, who are not coloured but black, found no
difficulty in securing lodgings. We secured lodgings not only in
London but the different cities we visited, as also in different places

in Scotland. We were even offered employment during the time spent there at College.

When we returned there the second time, we found it a little changed, but not to any extent to speak of, or to become disgusted over; however, when we made our third visit in 1928 we were astounded to be confronted with a pronounced prejudice that shocked our concept of things English.[28]

Thus, although Garvey landed alone and penniless in a city renowned for its coldness to strangers, he was not forced, in addition, to suffer the shock of racial rejection, which progressively became a part of "things English."

We gain a further sense of an almost Victorian decorousness surrounding Garvey's encounter with English society from his own explicitly affective regard for the educational institution through which he had gained partial access to academic learning while in London.

In an editorial aimed at mocking the ex-Chief Justice of Jamaica, Sir Fiennes Barret-Lennard, who had imposed on Garvey a famous three-month term of imprisonment for contempt in 1929, we are told:

As far as we are concerned, it seems that there is to be a kind of inseparable relationship between us and the ex-Chief. By goodness, he is to be connected to our Alma Mater. Little did we believe twenty years ago that Sir Fiennes would have become a member of the faculty of the College where we spent a little time.

We would feel very much embarrassed on a visit to England, during a Commencement, to find him as the guest of the evening. The tradition of Berbeck [sic] College is one that every student can be proud of. On our last attendance at a Commencement, we had the honour of listening to Lord Balfour of Burleigh, the Chancellor, but next time we may have to listen to Sir Fiennes.[29]

There seems to be nothing insincere in this declaration of attachment and esteem for the Birkbeck College experience as felt by Garvey. And when we add to this statement the above stated fact, that Garvey was "offered employment during the time spent there at College," there is strong reason to believe that Garvey was untroubled by any serious encounter with racism in Britain. The available evidence would seem to suggest a situation of mutual respectfulness.

Birkbeck College functioned at that time, not as a constituent part of the University of London, but as an independent educational center for mainly working-class people. Thus it did not adhere to any set of rigid educational requirements for admission, which would help to explain Garvey's attendance at the College.[30] The exact subjects of the curriculum which Garvey pursued cannot be ascertained, though a general sense of Garvey's academic interest can be gleaned from his later remarks. On his return to Jamaica in December 1927, after deportation from the United States, Garvey reprimanded his listeners for "(having) been so darned lazy that you have allowed the other fellow to run away with the whole world and now he is bluffing you and letting you know that the world belongs to him and that you have no share in it," and then went on to point out to them:

> . . . he will have a hard time bluffing this Marcus Garvey who has been through the same schools he has been through, who has shouldered with him in college and university, who has met him on the same campus, and imbibed every idea from the same textbooks out of which he has studied, from Socrates and Plato, to Lloyd George and Woodrow Wilson. I have followed the rest of them in Roman and British Constitutional Law and American Law and International Law; I have followed them all the way to protect myself . . . In the Liberal Arts, in what field can they make a fool of me? [31]

As an integral part of the process of Garvey's own self-education in England the academic disciplines of Law and Philosophy would seem to have been his principal interests at Birkbeck College. Further confirmation might be found in the fact that the initials, "D.C.L.," which Garvey later appended to his name, stood for "Doctor of Civil Law."

Insofar as the esteem of others was concerned, young Garvey had significantly advanced his stature by his educational efforts. Upon his return to Jamaica and shortly after the establishment of the Universal Negro Improvement Association, one influential newspaper editorialized:

> Mr. Marcus Garvey, a young Jamaican, who *has been to England for a course of study,* has started here the Negro Universal Society (sic) which has excellent aims and has made a promising beginning.[32]

In addition to the aura of formal educational attainment, which seemed to qualify him for a useful role in the colonial society of the island, Garvey was also possessed of an undoubted self-confident manner gained through his travel experiences. The well known educative process to be derived through exposure to peoples and places would have applied to Garvey with special force, given his extremely sensitive disposition, his zealousness for knowledge and the impressiveness of Imperial power flaunted as the badge of Imperial civilization.

In the statement quoted above regarding his successive periods of stay in England Garvey mentioned that his first visit embraced not only London but "the different cities we visited, as also [the] different places in Scotland." [33] Elsewhere Garvey has spoken of how his "doom—if I may so call it—of being a race leader dawned upon me in London after I had travelled through almost half of Europe." [34]

We can turn now to the relationship that emerged between the young Garvey and the central figure of Pan-African thought and expression of the pre-1914 period, Duse Mohammed Ali. Before the lapse of too many years, their relationship would become a matter of considerable dispute and remains so even today.

Duse Mohammed Ali was a Sudanese-Egyptian who had lived in England for many years.[35] He was both journalist and stage-actor. Real prominence first came his way in 1911 with the publication of his book, *In the Land of the Pharaohs,* reputedly the first history of Egypt written by an Egyptian and a work that was critically well received.[36] The acclaim received by the book brought with it the offer, ironically, to organize entertainment for the First Universal Races Congress, also held in 1911. Many significant Pan-African figures were in attendance at the Congress, among them W. E. B. Du Bois from America, Tengo

Jabavu from South Africa, Antenor Firmin and ex-President
Legitime from Haiti, Theophilus E. S. Scholes of Jamaica, and
Pastor Majola Agbebi of the Niger Mission representing the
venerable Dr. Edward Wilmot Blyden.[37]

It was in this context of heightened Pan-African consciousness
that Duse Mohammed emerged, and out of which was launched
the vehicle for Pan-African thought and opinion that would lay
the intellectual foundations for a whole new generation of
African struggle. The vehicle was the journal *African Times and
Orient Review*, which began publication in July 1912 and from its
inception adopted a radical Pan-Afro-Asian perspective. The
opening leader of its first issue declared:

> The recent Universal Race Congress . . . clearly demonstrated
> that there was ample need for a Pan-Oriental, Pan-African journal
> at the seat of the British Empire which would lay the aims, desires
> and intentions of the Black, Brown and Yellow Races—within and
> without the Empire—at the throne of Caesar.[38]

Among the list of its more notable contributors and local
distributors were to be found Kobina Sekyi, William Ferris, John
E. Bruce, Majola Agbebi, F. E. M. Hercules, the Rev. Attoh
Ahumah, F. Z. Peregrino, J. E. K. Aggrey, and as a contributor in
the October 1913 issue, Marcus Garvey, Jr. These individuals all
represented the early-twentieth-century generation of Afro-West
Indian, African, and Afro-American nationalists. Duse Mohammed Ali's journal provided an indispensable forum for the
articulation of their anticolonial protests, and was undoubtedly
the central source from which emanated most of the ideological
currents regarding politics, culture, and economics in Pan-African consciousness. The following minutes taken from the West
African files of the Colonial Office reveal:

> In the old days, the magazine (ATOR) was considered to be of
> doubtful loyalty, owing to Duse Mohammed's Pan-Ethiopian
> programme. "C.S. 23.10.17."

> Duse Mohammed, the editor of the *African Times and Orient
> Review*, is a rather doubtful character whose paper, before the
> War, was *suspect*, being inclined to the Ethiopian movement and

believed to be in touch with undesirable elements in India and Egypt. "Mr. Williams." [39]

"Ethiopian movement" was the principal term currently describing the Pan-African consciousness (in the period before 1914). The connection between this early pre-war phase of African Nationalism and the even more embryonic efforts that took shape in 1900 around the London Conference of the Pan-African Association should also be pointed out. Ian Duffield provides information which makes it clear that people at the time were aware of the connection:

> Dr. R. Adinwande Savage, the (Gold Coast) *Leader's* editor, not only expressed these hopes (that the *African Times and Orient Review* should be representative of and supported by all the coloured peoples of the Empire), but also saw the *ATOR* as picking up from Sylvester Williams' abortive efforts to found such a journal in London in 1900 as the organ of the Pan-African Association. Since Savage had been present at the 1900 meeting of the Pan-African Association, this was a real mark of hope and confidence. [40]

In addition to the early Pan-African ideas to which Garvey was exposed within ATOR's circle of contacts and political relations, it seems likely as well that Garvey was indebted to Duse Mohammed Ali for his understanding of the importance of ancient Egyptian civilization and the African basis of that cultural and historical achievement. Finally, it must be pointed out that Duse Mohammed Ali's deep and persistent attachment to Pan-African commercial potential and projects constantly highlighting the exploitative nature of European control over Africa's resources might have left a significant impression on Garvey, as his own later attempts in the field of independent African commercial enterprise attested. Among the General Objects listed by Garvey in the Manifesto of the UNIA in 1914 was "To conduct a world-wide commercial and industrial intercourse."

Duse Mohammed Ali's efforts to dissociate himself from any significant relationship with Garvey can be seen in the report contained in a British War Office memorandum:

DUSE MOHAMMED has since been questioned about various matters including Marcus GARVEY. He says that Marcus GARVEY first came to see him in 1913, saying he was from Jamaica. He was stranded in this country and DUSE MOHAMMED gave him a job as a messenger in his office but as his conduct was unsatisfactory he was discharged after about three months. After that he claimed to have gone to the continent of Europe . . .[41]

Still later in 1921, in the process of applying for an American visa, Duse Mohammed Ali repeated almost verbatim his description of his early contact with Garvey in London:

Consul General reports he has again interviewed Ali and that his commercial projects appear to have no relation to any political matters. Ali says Marcus Garvey was a West Indian employed by him in London in 1913 as a messenger. Owing to his laziness and generally worthless character he was discharged. Ali says he intends, if possible, to bring libel action against *World's Work* in connection with article written by Garvey and published therein reflecting on Ali.[42]

What is interesting to note, however, and somewhat inexplicable, was the fact that Duse Mohammed Ali would shortly thereafter commence once again his relationship with Garvey, though on this occasion with the latter as the undisputed leader of the Black movement. In April 1922 Duse was to be found writing on behalf of the parent body of the UNIA to Major Robert Moton, Principal of the Tuskegee Institute, requesting his participation in the Third Annual International Convention of the Negro Peoples of the World.[43] Moreover, Duse's name appeared as one of the twenty signatories to the UNIA *Petition to the League of Nations* in July 1922, where he is described as "Foreign Secretary" along with the names and positions of other Executive Officers of the UNIA.

The title of Garvey's 1913 article was "The British West Indies in the Mirror of Civilization—History Making by Colonial Negroes." [44] The article began on a confidently optimistic note:

In these days when democracy is spreading itself over the British Empire, and the peoples under the rule of the Union Jack are freeing themselves from hereditary lordship, and an *unjust bureaucracy*, it should not be amiss to recount the condition of affairs in the British West Indies, and particularly in the historic island of Jamaica, one of the oldest colonial possessions of the Crown. [Emphasis mine.] [Page 158.]

This initial expression of nationalist consciousness, looking toward the reform of colonial rule, had as its principal target the highly bureaucratized colonial order of Crown Colony rule in Jamaica (i.e., direct rule from London by English officials). This criticism of Crown Colony rule was made explicit in the following manner:

> The country has passed through many forms of legal government; at one time it was self-governing; then it became a Crown Colony. For the last twenty years, it has enjoyed a semi-representative government, with little power of control, the balance of power resting in the hands of the *red-tapists*, who pull the strings of colonial conservatism from Downing Street, with a reckless disregard of the interests and wishes of the people. [Emphasis mine.] [Page 159.][45]

The imposition of Crown Colony rule was effected in 1866 as a consequence of the Morant Bay Rebellion of the previous year. The violent eruption of a section of the once-slave community so terrified the white planters that they took headlong flight into the waiting arms of the Colonial bureaucracy, in the process surrendering their long-cherished legislative rights as the lesser of two evils. Garvey's recounting of this seminal event in Jamaica's colonial political past allowed him to raise the alternative claim of national freedom. He told of the leaders of the Rebellion, George William Gordon and Paul Bogle, and added:

> They sounded the call of unmolested liberty, but owing to the suppression of telegraphic communication, they were handicapped and suppressed, otherwise Jamaica would be as free to-day as Hayti, which threw off the French yoke under the leadership of the famous Negro General, Toussaint L'Ouverture. [Page 159.]

Garvey, however, returned to his critique of the "unjust bureaucracy" contained in his opening statement. He informed his readers:

> Since the abolition of slavery, the Negroes have improved them-
> selves wonderfully, and when the Government twenty or thirty
> years ago, threw open the doors of the Civil Service to competitive
> examination, the Negro youths swept the board and captured every
> available office, leaving their white competitors far behind. This
> system went on for a few years, but as the white youths were found
> to be intellectually inferior to the black, the whites persuaded the
> Government to abolish the competitive system, and fill vacancies
> by nomination, and by this means kept out the black youths. The
> service has long since been recruiting from an *inferior class of
> sychophantic weaklings whose brains are exhausted by dissipation
> and vice before they reach the age of thirty-five.* [Emphasis mine.]
> [Page. 159.]

Who should govern? Garvey, the young nationalist, was here
giving voice to the incipient confrontation, namely, the right to
greater native representation and participation in colonial government based on the proven abilities of the native educated
class.

Garvey, however, was then envisaging more than the mere
question of Island government. At the conclusion of his article,
Garvey boldly looked toward a future Caribbean confederation:

> There have been several movements to federate the British West
> Indian Islands, but owing to parochial feelings nothing definite has
> been achieved. Ere long this change is sure to come about because
> the people of these islands are all one. They live under the same
> conditions, are of the same race and mind, and have the same
> feelings and sentiments regarding the things of the world. [Page
> 159.]

From this anticipated union of the British West Indian Islands,
there issued the final prophetic statement, the one with which
the article has traditionally been associated, namely:

> As one who knows the people well, I make no apology for
> prophesying that there will soon be a turning point in the history of

the West Indies; and that the people who inhabit that portion of
the Western hemisphere will be the *instruments of uniting a
scattered race* who, before the close of many centuries, will found
an Empire on which the sun shall shine as ceaselessly as it shines on
the Empire of the North to-day. This may be regarded as a dream,
but I would point my critical friends to history and its lessons.
Would Caesar have believed that the country he was invading in
55 B.C. would be the seat of the greatest Empire of the World? Had
it been suggested to him would he not have laughed at it as a huge
joke? Yet it has come true. England is the seat of the greatest
Empire of the World, and its king is above the rest of monarchs in
power and dominion. Laugh then you may, as what I have been
bold enough to prophecy, but as surely as there is an evolution in
the natural growth of man and nations, so surely will there be a
change in the history of these subjected regions. [Emphasis mine.]
[Pages 159–160.]

Such, at that time, was Garvey's vision of the future—"unmolested liberty" for the British West Indies, the uniting of a
scattered and subjected race through a federal grouping of the
various Islands on the foundation of which would in time be
established a Black West Indian "Empire." The vision was in all
respects a West Indian vision. It would still have some considerable distance to travel before it transformed itself into a vision of a
free and sovereign "African Empire."

The storm clouds of World War I were already hovering over
Europe and prior to this first published statement Garvey had
already set about making plans to return to his native Jamaica.
For assistance with his passage he turned to the traditional
English watchdog on colonial abuses of native African rights, the
Anti-Slavery and Aborigines Protection Society. Although at this
stage our knowledge of the connection between Garvey and the
Society is very rudimentary, we have unearthed the development
of a rather sympathetic tie between them, based on the following
chronology of correspondence between the Society and the
Colonial Office:

July 8, 1913. M. Garvey—applies for assistance in circumstances
              stated.
May 28, 1914. Repatriation of M. Garvey—if it is possible to

> provide fund for repatriation, Society will be willing
> to assist by a contribution. He is bearer of this letter.

June 9, 1914. Case of M. Garvey—he is endeavouring to raise a
fund to meet passage money. If the Colonial Office
will contribute, the Society will give an equal
amount.

June 19, 1914. Case of M. Garvey—he did not think it necessary
to fill up a form. He left for Jamaica on 17 June,
necessary funds having been raised by private
charity.[46]

Garvey boarded ship at Southampton on June 17 and landed in
Jamaica on July 15, 1914, a voyage lasting almost a month.

It was during the passage from Southampton to Jamaica that
the idea of the Universal Negro Improvement Association,
according to Garvey, was transmitted to him. He has left us a
very vivid account of how the whole process unfolded before and
within him:

> Where did the name of the organization come from? It was while
> speaking to a West Indian Negro who was a passenger on the ship
> with me from Southampton, who was returning home to the West
> Indies from Basutoland with his Basuto wife, that I further learned
> of the horrors of native life in Africa. He related to me in
> conversation such horrible and pitiable tales that my heart bled
> within me. Retiring from the conversation to my cabin, all day and
> the following night I pondered over the subject matter of that
> conversation, and at midnight, lying flat on my back, the vision and
> thought came to me that I should name the organization the
> Universal Negro Improvement Association and African Communi-
> ties (Imperial) League. Such a name I thought would embrace the
> purpose of all black humanity.[47]

While allowing for the possibility of great spontaneous illumina-
tion looming before Garvey's agitated mind as he wrestled in his
cabin with the reality of Africa's oppressed humanity, we need to
enquire very much deeper below the surface of that inspired
moment in order to locate the real sources of the young Garvey's
enlightenment.

II

The organization which Garvey launched on August 1, 1914, was given the name "The Universal Negro Improvement and Conservation Association and African Communities League." Its motto was, "One God! One Aim! One Destiny!" and in addition to the motto, it also gave great prominence to the Biblical injunction, "He created of one blood all nations of man to dwell on the face of the earth" (Acts 17:26).

All historical accounts of the beginning struggles of the Garvey movement have tended to simply *assume* these details as part of the record. We are convinced, however, that a re-opening to critical examination of this previously assumed information as well as its framework will lead to a new and deeper understanding of the significance of Garvey's sojourn in England. In addition, it is our belief that by no longer taking these details for granted, we shall arrive at a much clearer vision of the developmental pattern through which the UNIA emerged on to the historical stage.

In this section I shall try to explain the specific sources to which the following points may be referred for a fuller understanding of their meanings:

   (a) African Communities' League
   (b) Concept of "conservation"
   (c) The organizational Motto
   (d) Concept of "Improvement"
   (e) Theme of universal brotherhood

The basic hypothesis, drawn from an examination of these questions, has led me to believe that Garvey's outlook on the racial issue as well as his model of organization by which he hoped to implement his ideas was gained through his experience in England during the period 1912–1914. At a deeper level the conceptual framework as well as the racial organizational principle of the UNIA were at bottom drawn largely from nineteenth-century African and European thinking on race. Finally, our hypothesis implies that Garvey, by leaning heavily on

African and European formulations on the racial question, would be impelled to work himself free at some point of the contradiction inherent in such an antagonistic relation of ideas. The concluding section of this paper will attempt to demonstrate how Garvey was able to achieve that liberation.

The British Consul General's *Annual Report of Panama* for 1923 informed us that "when in London, Garvey met a number of his own race from Africa and the West Indies, many of whom were engaged in commerce, travelling for pleasure, or studying for various professional examinations in England." The report added further that "during Garvey's stay in London, he heard from the lips of his countrymen and other coloured people about the sufferings of the darker races, and of their desire to unite for mutual understanding and protection." [48]

Who precisely were these "countrymen and other coloured people"? We are certain that Garvey was associated on something more than a purely menial level with Duse Mohammed Ali. Besides Duse, however, it is possible that Garvey might have found acquaintance through the journal's offices with certain prominent West African figures who played a crucial part in the development of the journal. Ian Duffield describes the individuals concerned and how their connection with the *African Times and Orient Review* came about:

> By the time of the ATOR's second issue in mid-August 1912 he (John Eldred Taylor) had been pushed out of its management and ownership by a syndicate of West Africans: Frans and Fred Dove, C. W. Betts, Dr. Sapara (who was of Creole origin), Casely Hayford (one of the most respected intellectuals on the coast because of his successful defence of traditional Fanti land rights), Dr. Quartey-Papafio, Gold Coast barrister E. J. P. Brown, and a Nigerian Yoruba barrister practising in the Gold Coast, Rotomi Alade. Brown, Quartey-Papafio and Casely Hayford, all members of that important proto-nationalist organization, the Gold Coast Aborigines Rights Protection Society, were in London to protest further against the highly unpopular Gold Coast Forests Bill of 1911. The whole group was a microcosm of the top strata of educated West Africa . . . [ATOR's] backers may be reasonably claimed to represent an earlier germination than has been supposed of that spirit which flowered in the National Congress of

British West Africa . . . Containing men from the three major British West African colonies, the ATOR take-over group was virtually an NCBWA in miniature.[49]

After August 1912, the young Garvey might well have gained access to this very significant grouping of West African intellectuals and politicians which had coalesced around rescuing the floundering *African Times and Orient Review.*

The most outstanding of this West African group was the Gold Coast lawyer, J. E. Casely Hayford, later to become known as the "uncrowned king" of British West Africa.[50] The year before young Garvey arrived in London had seen the publication of Casely Hayford's classic, *Ethiopia Unbound—Studies in Race Emancipation* (1911). That same year had also witnessed the publication of a second work, *Gold Coast Land Tenure and the Forest Bill,* and in 1913 another book was published, *Truth About West African Land Question.* All of these were influential works which would very likely have come to Garvey's attention.

Indeed, a careful examination of the most influential of the three books, *Ethiopia Unbound,* provides very strong evidence of having played a creative role in the direction and development of Garvey's outlook. Moreover, the very theme of the book itself, a fictionalized account of a young Fanti intellectual's education in England and his subsequent return to the Gold Coast to a career of political protest, seemed to fit the picture of young Garvey in London amazingly well, and would have certainly appealed to him.

Ethiopia Unbound might be described as an extended sermon/parable on the theme of African racial salvation. The essential viewpoint of the book was drawn from the ideas and teaching of Edward Wilmot Blyden, who in fact had been Casely Hayford's teacher in Sierra Leone at Fourah Bay College, Freetown.[51] For Hayford and others, who had come under his powerful influence, the old teacher was the prophet of Race Emancipation. At the point in the book where Blyden was explicitly introduced, his significance was described in unequivocal terms of divinity:

In the self-same era a god descended upon earth to teach the Ethiopians anew the *way* of *life*. He came not in thunder, or with great sound, but in the garb of a humble teacher, a John the Baptist among his brethren, preaching racial and national salvation. From land to land, and from shore to shore, his message was the self-same one, which, interpreted in the language of the Christ, was: *What shall it profit a race if it shall gain the whole world and lose its own soul?* [Page 160.]

The author then made explicit the teachings of Blyden in the form of a lecture delivered by Kwamankra, the book's principal character, at Hampton Institute in 1907. In the course of the lecture, the speaker drew for his audience the following important comparison:

The work of men like Booker T. Washington and W. E. Burghart Du Bois is *exclusive and provincial*. The work of Edward Wilmot Blyden is *universal, covering the entire race and the entire race problem*. [Emphasis mine.] [Page 163.]

The lecturer went on to describe him as "the greatest living exponent of the true spirit of African nationality and manhood" (Page 164), and urging upon his putative Afro-American audience the following injunction:

To leave no possible doubt as to my meaning, Afro-Americans must bring themselves into touch with some of the general traditions and institutions of their ancestors, and, though sojourning in a strange land, endeavour to *conserve* the characteristics of the race. [Emphasis mine.] [Page 165.]

This call for the African in America to "conserve the characteristics of the race" by preserving his cultural originality and nationality was focused through a program of "national *conservancy* and evolution." The author further proposed that a program of "national conservancy" should become embodied in the form of "Ethiopian *Leagues*," which, he stated, was "worthy of consideration by the Ethiopian in the United States, in Sierra Leone, in the West Indies, and in Liberia" (Pages 175–176).

This proposal of Casely Hayford's, for the preservation of nationality, I am strongly inclined to believe, was the real source of Garvey's idea of "Conservation" contained in the original title

of the latter's organization in 1914 as well as the inspiration for
the title of the second half of the organization, "African
Communities' League." [52]

It is probable as well that the source from which would later
spring the UNIA motto, "One God! One Aim! One Destiny!" was
Hayford's discussion of W. E. B. Du Bois' book, *The Souls of
Black Folk*. It is well to note that Hayford gave to the chapter
dealing with Du Bois the conclusive title "The Crux of The
Matter." For Hayford the central question raised by Du Bois'
book was his famous plaintive statement:

> . . . One ever feels his twoness—an American, a Negro; two souls,
> two thoughts, two unreconciled strivings; two warring ideals in one
> dark body, whose dogged strength alone keeps it from being torn
> asunder.

To Du Bois' pained refrain of warring duality, Hayford ex-
claimed:

> Poor Ethiopia! how sorely hath the iron of oppression entered into
> the very soul of thy erring children! [Page 180.]

The author then drew the following contrast with the enthralled
and split condition of the Afro-American ideals, and here we can
identify the source of the UNIA's motto of a single, unified Black
consciousness:

> Now, fancy Candace, Queen of Ethiopia, or Chephron, the Master
> of Egypt, being troubled with a double consciousness. Watch that
> symbolic, reposeful figure yonder, and you can but see *one soul,
> one ideal, one striving, one line* of a natural, rational progress.
> [Pages 181–182.]

Finally, *Ethiopia Unbound* might well have been the occasion
which provided Garvey's fertile imagination with the inspiration
for perceiving his future destiny as that of a race leader. The
book's stirring appeals for new African leadership along with
renewed dedication to the cause of race would have struck a
deep, responsive chord in the young Garvey.

. . . today Africa's sons in the East and in the West can do peculiar service unto one another in the common cause of uplifting Ethiopia and placing her upon her feet among the nations. [Page 171.]

. . . the unfortunate part of it is that the way out is as yet but dimly dawning even upon such as would otherwise be qualified to lead the masses. It becomes, therefore, the sacred duty of those who can see a little more clearly ahead to point the way. [Pages 183–184.]

. . . The voice of the ancient universal God goes forth once more, who will go for us, who will show us any good? May there be a full, free, and hearty response from the sons of Ethiopia in the four quarters of the globe. [Page 197.]

Paradoxically, it is important to note here the extraordinary reciprocating effect of roles that would later develop between the two men in the years 1918–1920. In the latter year, Casely Hayford would voice the profound influence on his own political outlook and the stimulation of political consciousness generally in what was then British West Africa, created by the apocalyptic eruption in America, especially, but elsewhere throughout the Black world, of Marcus Garvey's movement and program of African Emancipation. The new consciousness created in part by that influence was channeled into the establishment in 1920 of the National Congress of British West Africa, otherwise known as the British West African Conference Movement.[53]

If Garvey's later emergence as the outstanding Black nationalist figure of the post-World War I period was to play an undoubted role in the evolution of political consciousness in West Africa, it can also be claimed that during his sojourn in England the young Garvey was exposed to and drew heavily upon the ideas of James Africanus Beale Horton, an extraordinarily gifted pioneer of African nationalism in the second half of the nineteenth century. It has been said he was "the first to voice national aspirations in the Gold Coast." [54] Physician, British army officer, entrepreneur, Africanus Horton was also a man prolific with the pen, whose writings spanned scientific as well as political matters in the cause of Africa's self-government.[55]

Chief among Horton's writings, however, and the one which is considered to have been the source of much of Garvey's thought, was his book that quickly became a classic, *West African Countries and Peoples, British and Native . . . And a Vindication of the African Race*, published in 1868. In his Introduction to a new edition of the book, Professor George Shepperson affirmed as part of the value of republishing the work "the appreciation of the beginnings of modern political thought in Africa" which it gave.[56]

My awareness of the importance of Horton's ideas for a study of the formation of Garvey's early racial consciousness was first suggested by the fact that the UNIA letterhead stationery between 1915–1916 listed as the organization's cable address AFRICANUS, Jamaica. This fact by itself, though symbolically significant, would not be sufficient to establish any deeper, substantive influence.[57] A careful textual reading of Horton's *West African Countries and Peoples*, however, has pointed up a significant similarity, of meaning as well as mode of expression, between the concluding statement by Horton in Part I ("The Negro's Place in Nature"), and the concluding paragraph in Garvey's October 1913 article in the *African Times and Orient Review*. The dominant conception at work in both these statements was their powerful trust in the cyclical nature of historical evolution, which would, it was felt, in time bring the African out of subjection and to occupy once more a commanding position in the march of world history.

Beyond the shared meaning, however, of this cyclical historical viewpoint, there was additional similarity in Garvey's use of the example of the ancient Britons. Africanus Horton had made great play of this historical precedent with the objective of proving that "the natural tendency of the new civilized European was exactly the same as the natural tendency of the now uncivilized African" (Page 27). Horton explained the historical proof thus:

Now let us ask would it be consistent with reason, with common sense and justice, with humanity, for Tacitus, Caesar, or Pliny, to have condemned the British island and the British nation to an eternity of Boeotian darkness—"to be the officina of hereditary bondage and transmitted helplessness?" And yet if we read some of the testimonies in the late parliamentary Report (1865) and most of

the writings of members of the Anthropological Society, we find
that the negro race, from some supposed moral and intellectual
inferiority, are condemned by men who, in many respects, can be
regarded as generous and honourable, to live in perpetual ignorance, misery, and barbarity, forgetting that as the present
untutored negroes appear to them, *Just such (their) sires appeared
in Caesar's eyes.* [Emphasis mine.] [Page 29.]

This passage by Horton now takes us to the central significance
of his book for understanding its influence upon Garvey's
development. We are referring here to the source of the concept
of "improvement," which Garvey gave to the title of his
organization. The reference in the above quotation to "the
writings of members of the Anthropological Society" will explain
it. In his Preface Horton, on the very first page, informed the
reader:

Its object is to prove him (the African) *unimprovable*, therefore
unimproved since the beginning, and consequently, fitted only to
remain a hewer of wood and drawer of water for the members of
that select society. [Emphasis mine.] [Page v.]

Horton again in the concluding sentence to his Preface defined
his purpose in writing in the following manner:

. . . I hope the following pages, although, I fear, full of imperfec-
tions, will convince [my readers] that the Africans are not
incapable of *improvement*; but that by the *assistance of good and
able men* they are destined to figure in the course of time, and to
take a prominent part in the history of the civilized world.
[Emphasis mine.] [Pages ix–x.]

The fundamental question in dispute was the capacity of the
African race for "improvement." Could the African be improved? And if not, what explained his impossibility of improvement. If the answer to the question was yes, then the explanation
would have to be that all human groups possessed the capacity of
improvement, i.e., there was no "specific" or species difference
among men, so that mankind was physiologically and spiritually a
unity. And beyond that, for those who agreed on the improve-

ment potential of the African, the relevant questions centered on the most feasible lines of improvement and the agencies of bringing about such improvement.

The "anthropological" racists and their supporters flatly denied any basis of a unified mankind and hence any generalized capacity for improvement as applying to all races. The outstanding spokesman of the group, James Hunt, denounced as illusory all claims to a common humanity and quoted from a paper read by a friend at Cambridge University as an example of such thinking:

> For as God made of one blood all the nations of the earth, and endowed them all with the same animal, intellectual, moral, and religious nature: so has he bound them all together—in accordance with the high behest that they should increase and multiply and replenish the earth—in one common bond of universal brotherhood.[58]

Hunt, intending the final destruction of this moral-ethical argument for the unity of mankind, went through a lengthy recapitulation of the negrophobist literature regarding the physical and mental character of the African and advanced the following "deductions":

> 1. That there is as good reason for classifying the Negro as a distinct species from the European as there is for making the ass a distinct species from the zebra; and if, in classification, we take intelligence into consideration, there is a far greater difference between the Negro and European than between the gorilla and chimpanzee. 2. That the analogies are far more numerous between the Negro and the ape than between the European and the ape. 3. That the Negro is inferior intellectually to the European. 4. That the Negro becomes more humanized when in his natural subordination to the European than under any other circumstances. 5. That the Negro race can only be humanized and civilized by Europeans. 6. That European civilization is not suited to the Negro's requirements or character.[59]

Therefore, when in 1914 Garvey raised as the guiding precept of the UNIA the Biblical injunction, "He created of one blood all nations of man to dwell on the face of the earth," it should be clearly evident that this concept of "universal brotherhood" was inextricably bound up with the whole question of racial "improvement." They were but opposite sides of the same coin. Without the former, there was no basis in the outlook of that period for racial improvement.[60] Where Europe did not give its brotherhood people were denied the potential for improvement. They, in turn, as the condition of asserting their right to and capacity for improvement were compelled to offer their brotherhood, whether Europe desired it or not. Human brotherhood and progressive improvement were therefore the twin terms of antithesis to the dominant ideology of European imperialism and the exclusivity of European culture and civilization, which Hunt *et al.* merely made explicit for the age.

Here is Garvey's own declaration of this idea in his address to the first annual meeting in 1915 of the Universal Negro Improvement Association, one year after his return to Jamaica:

> Our people have had seventy-seven years of unfettered liberty in this country, a liberty given us by the liberty-loving and Christian British people, during which period of time we have tried our best to adapt ourselves to the environments of the country, and to live up to the teachings of our Christian brothers.
>
> We have nothing to regret in adopting and living up to the teachings of our more fortunate and cultured friends, for in obeying their teachings and living up to their principles we have only done the right thing to *bring us on par with the civilized habits and customs of the most cultured and civilized of mankind.* Thank God there is no racial friction in Jamaica, and I pray that the day may never dawn to see anything of racial friction or open racial prejudice in this country.
>
> Jamaica has a lesson to teach the world, and it is—that people of different races can live together within one country as brothers and friends, on the best of terms, without prejudice, upholding one Government, ready to die for one flag, enjoying the same liberty of constitution (Christian and otherwise) and looking to one common destiny.
>
> I say thank God for this state of affairs, and it shall be the principle of the Universal Negro Improvement Association to live up to and

spread *the doctrine of brotherhood* and love among all mankind all over the world. We stand on the *platform of humanity*, and whether the man be black, white or blue, it shall be our mission to clasp his hand in *fellowship*. Any man who despises another because of his race only is mean and is in everything a coward. God made us all to dwell on the face of the earth, so whether we are this, that, or the other, we are all children of one common father . . . As President of the Universal Negro Improvement Association I now declare that it is not my intention nor the intention of the society to belabor any race question in this country as some may be inclined to believe, and as some envious and evil minds would care to suggest. The race question must never affect us. We must uphold the equity of the land irrespective of race under our constitution . . . What concerns us here is the development of our people and country. *As a society we realize that the negro people of Jamaica need a great deal of improvement.* The bulk of our people are in darkness and are really unfit for good society. To the cultured mind the bulk of our people are contemptible—that is to say, they are entirely outside the pale of cultured appreciation. You know this to be true, so we need not get uneasy through prejudice. Go into the country parts of Jamaica and you see there villainy and vice of the worst kind, immorality, obeah and all kinds of dirty things are part of the avocation of a large percentage of our people, and we, the few of cultured tastes can in no way save the race from infamy in a balanced comparison with other people, for the standard of races or of anything else is not arrived at by the few who are always the exceptions, but by the majority.

. . . Well, this society has set itself the task to go among the people and help them up to a better state of appreciation among the cultured classes, and *raise them to the standard of civilized approval. To do this we must get the co-operation and sympathy of our white brothers.* . . . [Emphasis mine.] [61]

III

Garvey did not waste much time in contemplation upon his return to Jamaica, for he swiftly set about launching the organization that would eventually enter his name in the annals of Black struggle. "The Universal Negro Improvement and

Conservation Association and African Communities' League"
was constituted on August 1, 1914, looking toward, as it said,
"the propagation and achievement of the following objects":

GENERAL OBJECTS

To establish a Universal Confraternity among the race.

To promote the spirit of race pride and love.

To reclaim the fallen of the race.

To administer to and assist the needy.

To assist in civilizing the backward tribes of Africa.

To strengthen the Imperialism of independent African States.

To establish Commissionaries or Agencies in the principal
countries of the world for the protection of all Negroes,
irrespective of nationality.

To promote a conscientious Christian worship among the native
tribes of Africa.

To establish Universities, College and Secondary Schools for the
further education and culture of the boys and girls of the race.

To conduct a worldwide commercial and industrial intercourse.

LOCAL (JAMAICA) OBJECTS

To establish educational and industrial colleges for the further
education and culture of our boys and girls.

To reclaim the fallen and degraded (especially the criminal class)
and help them to a state of good citizenship.

To administer to and assist the needy.

To promote a better taste for commerce and industry.

To promote a universal confraternity and strengthen the bonds of
brotherhood and unity among the races.

To help generally in the development of the country.[62]

The major orientation of the beginning UNIA, as can be
observed from both the General and Local Objects, was toward
moral and social improvement. The lead Object in the General
category specifically called for the creation of a fraternal union,
which as some of the succeeding objects made clear, would be
directed toward largely *altruistic* purposes. This original program, however, which I will describe as one of "racial altruism,"

contained an early evidence of Garvey's preoccupation with *European statecraft*, which had impressed itself strongly upon his racial sensibility during his stay in England. It was here enunciated in the form of "the imperialism of independent African States" and High Commissions.

In spite of this latter interest in statecraft, however, it is difficult to see how the program of the founding UNIA can be regarded as radical. Moreover, insofar as the "Local (Jamaica) Objects" were concerned, the program could not be said to have raised any challenges regarding the ruling colonial system. On the other hand, it has been commonly asserted that the young Garvey returned from his experience in England generally radicalized by what he had seen and learned while there. In other words, we have to ask the question, was Garvey really radicalized in England?

Garvey, in the second to last Object in his program, promised that the UNIA in Jamaica would "promote a universal confraternity and strengthen the bonds of *brotherhood and unity among the races*" (my emphasis). This was the practical application of the "all of one blood" injunction which Garvey set as the guiding precept of the organization. However, the promise of promoting "unity among the races" had an even more substantive meaning and was inherently rooted, as shown, in the improvement concept, and which Garvey was seeking to effect organizationally in 1914. Africanus Horton concluded the Preface to his book:

> . . . Africans are not incapable of *improvement*; but that by *the assistance of good and able men* they are destined to figure in the course of time, and to take a prominent part in the history of the civilized world. [Page x.]

Thus, the whole idea of improvement carried with it the presumption of agency and instrumentality which would be necessary to guarantee the improvement process. That agency, working from the basic premise of racial (i.e., some races being ahead of others) advancement and the existence of a common humanity, would perforce have to be European. As Shepperson points out in his Introduction, "To him [Horton], civilization was the application to West Africa of European learning, technology and religion" (Page xiii). Whereas Horton looked toward the agency of improvement operating through what Shepperson calls the "transmission of civilization" from *without*, Garvey at the inception of his organization sought basically the same thing in the functioning of racial cooperation and unity from *within* the society.

We should acknowledge Garvey's success, though ironic in terms of his later evolution, in this pursuit of racial cooperation as the agency of improvement. In a later account of the assistance which this approach brought him, it was reported:

> Garvey made a point of it that when he was trying in Jamaica his own race "turned him down," and all the assistance and encouragement he received were from men of the white race, mentioning specifically the Rev. William Graham, Sir William Henry Manning (Governor), Brigadier-General Blackden, and Mr. Bourne, the late Colonial Secretary.[63]

In an extensively detailed memorandum prepared for the visiting dignitary from Tuskegee, Major Robert Moton, who in early 1916 visited Jamaica for a two-day stay, Garvey laid bare the justification of racial cooperation and assistance. He informed Moton:

> It (the race problem) is a paradox. I personally would like to solve the situation on the broadest *humanitarian* lines. I would like to solve it on the platform of Dr. Booker T. Washington, and I am working on those lines hence you will find that up to now *my one true friend* as far as you can rely on his friendship is the *white man*. [Emphasis mine.]
>
> I do not mean to bring any estrangement between black and white. I want to have Jamaica a country of "Black and White" all living in peace and harmony but with equal rights and opportunities.

And in the covering letter to his Memorandum, Garvey spelled out for Moton the full extent of European involvement in the fledgling UNIA:

> My Association is well appreciated by the cultured white people of the country, and in a small way they have come to my assistance to

help me along. From His Excellency the Governor down, among the whites, I have been helped by kindly encouragement and I can say that some of the most influential of them have paid us the honour of coming among us. His Excellency the Governor, the Colonial Secretary, Hon. H. Bryan, C.M.G., Sir John Pringle, Hon. Brigadier-General, L. S. Blackden, all members of the Privy Council, have been our patrons on several occasions and they are still friends of the Association. The Brigadier-General has lectured to us, also His Lordship Bishop J. J. Collins, S.J., His Worship the Mayor of Kingston, Hon. H. A. L. Simpson, M.L.C., Mr. R. W. Bryant, J.P., ex-Mayor of Kingston who has visited us more than a dozen times, and many other prominent dignitaries of the country. The Hon. Colonial Secretary has himself attended a function along with his wife to which he was specifically invited.[64]

Such extraordinary support by the Colonial Establishment for Garvey's initial attempts at organization would have been remarkable under any circumstances. However, the condition of their support had to have been assured by Garvey by something more than the mere assertion regarding strengthening "the bonds of brotherhood and unity among the races." The very highest level of white support which Garvey had achieved became possible by his avowal of loyalty and devotion to the King and Empire. It was not something accidental. Rather it was the condition of European patronage. In a letter dated September 1914, Garvey wrote to the Secretary of State for the Colonies:

I have the honour to forward you, through His Excellency the Governor, the following resolution, passed by our Association at a general meeting, held in the Collegiate Hall, Kingston, on Tuesday evening the 15th September, 1914, which I beg that you accept as the genuine feeling of our members. Our love for, and devotion to, His Majesty and the Empire, stands unrivalled and from the depths of our hearts we pray for the crowning victory of the British Soldiers now at war.

I, therefore, beg that you convey the feelings of this resolution to His Gracious Majesty and people:

"That we the members of the Universal Negro Improvement and Conservation Association and African Communities League, assembled in general meeting at Kingston, Jamaica, being mindful of the *great protecting and civilizing influence of the English nation and people*, of whom we are subjects, and their justice to all men, and especially to their Negro Subjects scattered all over the world, hereby beg to express our loyalty and devotion to His Majesty the King, and Empire and our sympathy with those of the people who are in any way grieved and in difficulty in this time of National trouble.

"We sincerely pray for the success of British arms on the battle fields of Europe and Africa, and at Sea, in crushing the 'Common Foe,' the enemy of peace and further civilization.

"We rejoice in British Victories and the suppression of foreign foes. Thrice we hail, 'God save the King! Long live the King and Empire.' " [65]

Even considering the patriotic Imperial fervor of the time, which the Great War galvanized throughout the Empire, such a statement coming from Garvey can only be understood if it is realized how important politically it was within the framework of Garvey's program.

Thus far, we observe a program of "racial altruism" activating in the colonial setting of Jamaica the agency of official European assistance, as had been postulated in the whole conceptual framework of racial improvement. All of this hardly added up to Garvey as a radicalized leader or an organization with a radical orientation. In this light, the commonly held idea interpreting Garvey's early efforts in Jamaica as a failure must be re-examined. For if Garvey, on one level, can be said to have failed to achieve some of his goals, on another and more significant level he can be said to have succeeded in realizing for the purposes of his own organization "the bonds of brotherhood and unity among the races." In other words, the measure of failure or success to be applied to the first period of the UNIA in Jamaica has to be a relative one, for this initial period has to be evaluated in terms of Garvey's own evolving position. Any attempt, therefore, to read back into this period, on the basis of static criteria, the accomplishments of a qualitatively different and later stage of development must inevitably distort our understanding of what Garvey had brought back with him from England and what in reality, on the basis of that experience, he had originally set out to achieve in Jamaica.

What then did Garvey's radicalism at this period of his development consist? Put another way, what was in fact the source of decisive radicalization for Garvey? His experiences in England and Europe, in spite of the awareness which he undoubtedly acquired there about issues of worldwide moment and even the significant personal contacts which he had formed, did not produce in him anything that could be described as truly radical. Had it done so, his efforts at organization upon his return to Jamaica would have been much less collaborative with the colonial system.

I believe Garvey's moment of authentic radicalization occurred in the context of his struggle to cope with and overcome the rejection of the *colored Jamaican middle-class.* It was the repressive exclusion of the Jamaican "browns," as they were sometimes described, to keep Garvey in his social place and thereby maintain their *monopoly of influence as spokesmen for the society to the Colonial Establishment;* this fact triggered in him the beginning of a genuine radicalization. There was cruel irony at work here. Garvey's rejection came at the hands of the very persons whose abilities had been refused by the Colonial Establishment as entitling them to a place in government, a refusal and rejection which he himself had strongly protested in his article in 1913 attacking the abuses of Crown Colony rule. In that article, it was the cause of the native educated middle-class which was being advanced by Garvey, and it was they who now effectively stigmatized and stymied his efforts. Moreover, to compound the irony, it would appear that it was into the ranks of that class that Garvey, outfitted with some semi-professional training acquired during his period of stay in England, seemed to be heading upon his return to Jamaica in 1914. Whether subjectively he desired to gain admission among their number, we cannot be certain, but that would have been the objective destination of a "young Jamaican, who [had] been to England for a course of study," as he was described by one local newspaper, and shortly after whose return "had made a promising beginning." (See reference to *Jamaica Times* article, October 17, 1914, quoted above.) At any rate, the native colored middle-class in 1915 adamantly rejected the validity of Garvey's attempts to develop organization along racial lines, no matter how innocuous in real substance; nor would they allow the pretensions of Garvey, young and able and as black in complexion as he was, which *vied with them for the privileged ear of the Colonial Establishment.* Garvey himself was not unaware of these questions, as can be attested by his later statement:

> I had to decide whether to please my friends and be one of the "black-whites" of Jamaica, and be reasonably prosperous, or come out openly and defend and help improve and protect the integrity of the black millions and suffer. I decided to do the latter, hence my offence against "colored-black-white" society in the colonies and America. I was openly hated and persecuted by some of these colored men of the island who did not want to be classified as Negroes, but as white. They hated me worse than poison. They opposed me at every step, but I had a large number of white friends, who encouraged and helped me . . . But they were afraid of *offending the "colored gentry" that were passed for white.* Hence my fight had to be made alone. [Emphasis mine.]

> . . . Furthermore, I was a black man and therefore had absolutely no right to lead; in the opinion of the "colored" element, leadership should have been in the hands of a yellow or very light man.[66]

In this enveloping class and intraracial struggle, which during the period 1914–1916 saw Garvey in collision with the "browns," who rejected him in the defense of their own vested interests, a decisive turning-point was made in the development of an original radical consciousness.

Evidence for this authentic radicalization on Garvey's part can be seen in his correspondence with Major Robert Moton in early 1916. In his covering letter to Major Moton, Garvey outlined the deepening crisis in his position:

> My Association was founded in Jamaica eighteen months ago immediately after my return from a long tour and duty of Europe. Personally I have spent nearly every cent I possess to found the Society, and keep it alive, and I can only say that the work has been most *harassing and heartrending* . . .

> Whilst we have been encouraged and helped by the cultured

whites to do something to help in lifting the masses, the so-called *representatives* of our own people have sought to down us and ever since they have been waging a secret campaign to that end, hence even on your coming here you will find such men parading themselves as "wolves in sheep's clothing" who are desirous of destroying the existence of a Negro Society. I am engaged in fighting a battle with foes of my own all around, but I am prepared to fight on with the strength given me by Almighty God.

I have many large schemes on my mind for the advancement of my people that I cannot expose at the present to the public, as in such a case, my hope of immediate success would be defeated, as *my enemies are so many*, and they are ever anxious to misrepresent me . . .

One of your experience will readily realize what enemies in a cause mean. They are the carriers of poison, so the "tongue" of the serpent sometimes stings without doing harm . . . [Emphasis mine.] [67]

The deep hurt and frustration experienced by Garvey at the hands of the socially oppressive apparatus of colored domination had shattered his innocent expectations regarding his role in society. Toward the close of his accompanying Memorandum to Major Moton on the general conditions existing for the black majority of society, Garvey revealed how dislocative this loss of illusion had been:

This is the grinding system that keeps the blackman down, hence I personally, have very little in common with the educated class of our people for they are the bitterest enemies of their own race. Our people have no respect for one another, and all the respect is shown to the white and colored people. The reception that will be given you will not be genuine from more than one reason which I may explain later on to you.

Black men here are never truly honoured. Don't you believe like colored Dr. Du Bois that the "race problem is at an end here," except you want to admit the utter insignificance of the blackman.

It was never started and has not yet begun . . . [68]

At this point Garvey let drop the cryptic and especially

ominous statement regarding the place of the Black man in West
Indian society. Only by hindsight can we today perceive the slow
stirring that was occurring under the surface of Garvey's
consciousness. The statement reads as follows:

> I would not advise you to give yourself too much away to the desire
> and wishes of the people who are around you for they are mostly
> hypocrites. They mean to deceive you on the conditions here
> because *we can never blend under the existing state of affairs—it
> would not be fair to the blackman.* To blend we must all in equal
> proportion "show our hands." [69]

It was an oblique announcement by Garvey of the beginning of
that search for options laying outside the West Indies to which he
had been driven by the colored middle-class refusal to meet with
him. He could no longer continue to believe in the possibility of
ever "blend(ing) under the existing state of affairs." In the long
run, it was that failure which made him accept the awesome
challenge of Africa.

As the earlier vision of the West Indies and its people
becoming "the instruments of uniting a scattered race" receded
under the merciless blows heaped upon it by the colored
middle-class, Garvey was reacting by simultaneously discovering
the dim rays of the new vision being born in him, the vision of
Africa. This latter was contained in the pamphlet which he wrote
just prior to his embarkation for America. It was entitled, *A Talk
with Afro-West Indians: The Negro Race and Its Problems*, and
emerged from his critically radicalizing encounter with the
colored elite. In it Garvey provided a balance sheet of the efforts
and ideas which had brought him to that turning point. The
address opened pleadingly for the reader to share with Garvey in
the new vision of Africa:

> Dear Friend and Brother:
>
> I am moved to address you through the great spirit of love and the
> kindred affection that I have for the race African; and I am asking
> you to be good, loyal and racial enough as to take this address in
> the spirit of goodwill, and lend yourself to the worldwide
> movement of doing something to promote the intellectual, social,

commercial, industrial and *national interest* of the downtrodden
race of which you are a member. [Emphasis mine.] [70]

Garvey was here making the significant advance from the earlier
stage of racial altruism toward the new stage of *racial patriotism*.
He described his own progression and the achievement of this
new consciousness in the succeeding paragraph:

> For the last ten years I have given my time to the study of the
> condition of the Negro, here, there, and everywhere, and I have
> come to realize that he is still the object of degradation and pity
> the world over, in the sense that he has no status socially,
> nationally, or commercially (with a modicum of exception in the
> United States of America) hence the entire world is prone to look
> down on him as an inferior and degraded being, although the
> people as a whole have done no worse than others to deserve the
> ignominious snub. The retrograde state of the Negro is character-
> ized as accidental and circumstantial; and *the onus of his condition
> is attributable to the callous indifference and insincerity of those
> Negroes who have failed to do their duty by the race in promoting a
> civilized imperialism that would meet with the approval of
> established ideals.*

Once having embarked, however, on the new program of racial
patriotism, the outcome of his struggle with the Jamaican colored
middle-class, Garvey would rapidly, as the circumstances
changed, apply this racial patriotism to his ultimate vision of
"Africa for the Africans, at home and abroad." That transformation was to be wrought by a synthesis of the myriad upheavals
brought on by the First World War and the simultaneously
violent conflagrations in which the Black masses in America were
to be engulfed. When that time came, Garvey was ready and
waiting to move.

As we leave Garvey at this stage still in Jamaica, however, let
him speak the last words:

> Sons and daughters of Africa, I say to you arise, take on the toga of
> race pride, and throw off the brand of ignominy which has kept
> you back for so many centuries. Dash asunder the petty prejudices
> within your own fold; set at defiance the scornful designation of

"nigger" uttered even by yourselves, and be a Negro in the light of the Pharaohs of Egypt, Simons of Cyrene, Hannibals of Carthage, L'Overtures and Dessalines of Hayti, Blydens, Barclays and Johnsons of Liberia, Lewises of Sierra Leone, and Douglass's and Du Bois's of America, who have made, and are making history for the race, though depreciated and in many cases unwritten. [Page 3.]

⠿ MARCUS GARVEY
IN HIS OWN WORDS

A Journey of Self-Discovery*

I WAS BORN in the Island of Jamaica, British West Indies, on August 17, 1887. My parents were black negroes. My father was a man of brilliant intellect and dashing courage. He was unafraid of consequences. He took human chances in the course of life, as most bold men do, and he failed at the close of his career. He once had a fortune; he died poor. My mother was a sober and conscientious Christian, too soft and good for the time in which she lived. She was the direct opposite of my father. He was severe, firm, determined, bold and strong, refusing to yield even to superior forces if he believed he was right. My mother, on the other hand, was always willing to return a smile for a blow, and ever ready to bestow charity upon her enemy. Of this strange combination I was born thirty-six years ago, and ushered into a world of sin, the flesh and the devil.

I grew up with other black and white boys. I was never whipped by any, but made them all respect the strength of my arms. I got my education from many sources—through private tutors, two public schools, two grammar or high schools and two colleges. My teachers were men and women of varied experiences and abilities; four of them were eminent preachers. They studied me and I studied them. With some I became friendly in after years, others and I drifted apart, because as a boy they

wanted to whip me, and I simply refused to be whipped. I was
not made to be whipped. It annoys me to be defeated; hence to
me, to be once defeated is to find cause for an everlasting
struggle to reach the top.

I became a printer's apprentice at an early age, while still
attending school. My apprentice master was a highly educated
and alert man. In the affairs of business and the world he had no
peer. He taught me many things before I reached twelve, and at
fourteen I had enough intelligence and experience to manage
men. I was strong and manly, and I made them respect me. I
developed a strong and forceful character, and have maintained
it still.

To me, at home in my early days, there was no difference
between white and black. One of my father's properties, the
place where I lived most of the time, was adjoining that of a
white man. He had three girls and two boys; the Wesleyan
minister, another white man whose church my parents attended,
also had property adjoining ours. He had three girls and one boy.
All of us were playmates. We romped and were happy children
playmates together. The little white girl whom I liked most knew
no better than I did myself. We were two innocent fools who
never dreamed of a race feeling and problem. As a child, I went
to school with white boys and girls, like all other negroes. We
were not called negroes then. I never heard the term negro used
once until I was about fourteen.

At fourteen my little white playmate and I parted. Her parents
thought the time had come to separate us and draw the color
line. They sent her and another sister to Edinburgh, Scotland,
and told her that she was never to write or try to get in touch
with me, for I was a "nigger." It was then that I found for the
first time that there was some difference in humanity, and that
there were different races, each having its own separate and
distinct social life. I did not care about the separation after I was
told about it, because I never thought all during our childhood
association that the girl and the rest of the children of her race
were better than I was; in fact, they used to look up to me. So I
simply had no regrets. I only thought them "fresh."

After my first lesson in race distinction, I never thought of
playing with white girls any more, even if they might be

next-door neighbors. At home my sister's company was good enough for me, and at school I made friends with the colored girls next to me. White boys and I used to frolic together. We played cricket and baseball, ran races and rode bicycles together, took each other to the river and to the sea beach to learn to swim, and made boyish efforts while out in deep water to drown each other, making a sprint for shore crying out "shark, shark, shark." In all our experiences, however, only one black boy was drowned. He went under on a Friday afternoon after school hours, and his parents found him afloat half eaten by sharks on the following Sunday afternoon. Since then we boys never went back to sea.

At maturity the black and white boys separated, and took different courses in life. I grew up then to see the difference between the races more and more. My schoolmates as young men did not know or remember me any more. Then I realized that I had to make a fight for a place in the world, that it was not so easy to pass on to office and position. Personally, however, I had not much difficulty in finding and holding a place for myself, for I was aggressive. At eighteen I had an excellent position as manager of a large printing establishment, having under my control several men old enough to be my grandfathers. But I got mixed up with public life. I started to take an interest in the politics of my country, and then I saw the injustice done to my race because it was black, and I became dissatisfied on that account. I went traveling to South and Central America and parts of the West Indies to find out if it was so elsewhere, and I found the same situation. I set sail for Europe to find out if it was different there, and again I found the same stumbling-block— "You are black." I read of the conditions in America. I read *Up From Slavery*, by Booker T. Washington, and then my doom—if I may so call it—of being a race leader dawned upon me in London after I had traveled through almost half of Europe.

I asked, "Where is the black man's Government?" "Where is his King and his kingdom?" "Where is his President, his country, and his ambassador, his army, his navy, his men of big affairs?" I could not find them, and then I declared, "I will help to make them."

Becoming naturally restless for the opportunity of doing

something for the advancement of my race, I was determined that the black man would not continue to be kicked about by all the other races and nations of the world, as I saw it in the West Indies, South and Central America and Europe, and as I read of it in America. My young and ambitious mind led me into flights of great imagination. I saw before me then, even as I do now, a new world of black men, not peons, serfs, dogs and slaves, but a nation of sturdy men making their impression upon civilization and causing a new light to dawn upon the human race. I could not remain in London any more. My brain was afire. There was a world of thought to conquer. I had to start ere it became too late and the work be not done. Immediately I boarded a ship at Southampton for Jamaica, where I arrived on July 15, 1914. The Universal Negro Improvement Association and African Communities (Imperial) League was founded and organized five days after my arrival, with the program of uniting all the negro peoples of the world into one great body to establish a country and Government absolutely their own.

Where did the name of the organization come from? It was while speaking to a West Indian negro who was a passenger on the ship with me from Southampton, who was returning home to the West Indies from Basutoland with his Basuto wife, that I further learned of the horrors of native life in Africa. He related to me in conversation such horrible and pitiable tales that my heart bled within me. Retiring from the conversation to my cabin, all day and the following night I pondered over the subject matter of that conversation, and at midnight, lying flat on my back, the vision and thought came to me that I should name the organization the Universal Negro Improvement Association and African Communities (Imperial) League. Such a name I thought would embrace the purpose of all black humanity. Thus to the world a name was born, a movement created, and a man became known.

I really never knew there was so much color prejudice in Jamaica, my own native home, until I started the work of the Universal Negro Improvement Association . . . I had just returned from a successful trip to Europe, which was an exceptional achievement for a black man. The daily papers wrote me up with big headlines and told of my movement. But nobody wanted to be a negro. "Garvey is crazy; he has lost his head," "Is that the use he is going to make of his experience and intelligence?" Such were the criticisms passed upon me. Men and women as black as I, and even more so, had believed themselves white under the West Indian order of society. I was simply an impossible man to use openly the term "negro"; yet every one beneath his breath was calling the black man a negro.

I had to decide whether to please my friends and be one of the "black-whites" of Jamaica, and be reasonably prosperous, or come out openly and defend and help improve and protect the integrity of the black millions and suffer. I decided to do the latter, hence my offence against "colored-black-white" society in the colonies and America. I was openly hated and persecuted by some of these colored men of the island who did not want to be classified as negroes, but as white. They hated me worse than poison. They opposed me at every step, but I had a large number of white friends, who encouraged and helped me. Notable among them were the then Governor of the Colony, the Colonial Secretary and several other prominent men. But they were afraid of offending the "colored gentry" that were passing for white. Hence my fight had to be made alone. I spent hundreds of pounds (sterling) helping the organization to gain a footing. I also gave up all my time to the promulgation of its ideals. I became a marked man, but I was determined that the work should be done.

The war helped a great deal in arousing the consciousness of the colored people to the reasonableness of our program, especially after the British at home had rejected a large number of West Indian colored men who wanted to be officers in the British army. When they were told that negroes could not be officers in the British army they started their own propaganda, which supplemented the program of the Universal Negro Improvement Association. With this and other contributing agencies a few of the stiff-necked colored people began to see the reasonableness of my program, but they were firm in refusing to be known as negroes. Furthermore, I was a black man and therefore had absolutely no right to lead; in the opinion of the "colored" element, leadership should have been in the hands of a yellow or a very light man. On such flimsy prejudices our race has been retarded. There is more bitterness among us negroes because of the caste of color than there is between any other peoples, not excluding the people of India.

I succeeded to a great extent in establishing the association in Jamaica with the assistance of a Catholic Bishop, the Governor, Sir John Pringle, the Rev. William Graham, a Scottish clergyman, and several other white friends. I got in touch with Booker Washington and told him what I wanted to do. He invited me to America and promised to speak with me in the Southern and other States to help my work. Although he died in the fall of 1915, I made my arrangements and arrived in the United States on March 23, 1916.

The British West Indies in the Mirror of Civilization*

History Making by American Negroes

In these days when democracy is spreading itself over the British Empire, and the peoples under the rule of the Union Jack are freeing themselves from hereditary lordship, and an unjust bureaucracy, it should not be amiss to recount the condition of affairs in the British West Indies, and particularly, in the historic island of Jamaica, one of the oldest colonial possessions of the Crown.

It is right that the peoples of the vast Empire to which these colonies belong should be correctly informed on things affecting the welfare of these islands, being a comparatively neglected, if not unknown, region of the Atlantic Archipelago.

The history of the British possession of these islands is very interesting, as it reveals the many conflicts between the various powers that have been struggling for occupancy and supremacy in the Caribbean waters for three hundred years.

These islands were discovered by Christopher Columbus in the latter part of the fifteenth century, and the major portion of them were handed over to the Spanish throne. England and France laid claim to certain of these colonies, and the former, with her justifiable (?) means of warfare, succeeded in driving the Spaniards from their tropical "gold mines" with much regret on the part of the ejected, who had extinguished the Aborigines, an action quite in keeping with the European custom of depopulating new lands of their aboriginal tribes. The British West Indian Colonies today comprise Jamaica, Trinidad and Tobago, Barbados, British Guiana, Grenada, St. Vincent, St. Lucia, Dominica, Antigua and Montserrat, St. Kitts, and Nevis, the Virgin Islands and one or two others, scattered over the groups known as the Greater and Lesser Antilles, with a population of over three million souls.

When the Spaniards took possession of these islands they introduced cotton and sugar growing. To supply the labor that was necessary to make these industries solid and profitable, they started the slave traffic with Africa, from which place they recruited thousands of Negro slaves whom they took from their congenial homes by force. The sugar industry developed wonderfully with Negro labor, and the great output of sugar, as exported to Europe, brought incomputable wealth to the landed proprietors, which they used in gambling and feasting; and for exploration and further development of the veritable "gold mines" of the Western Hemisphere.

Piratical and buccaneering parties used to frequent the waters of the Caribbean, where they held up on the high sea merchant vessels laden with their rich cargoes bound for Europe and the West Indies. Filibustering [irregular military free booting] was carried on in a daring fashion on land, where a buccaneering invader would hold up one of these islands and force the wealthy landlords to capitulate on conditions suitable to filibustering requirements.

During the sixteenth century England drove the Spaniards from the wealthiest of these islands and established herself in possession. To the Plantations, as they were called, a large proportion of her criminal class was deported, as also a few gentlemen. The new occupiers took over the paying sugar industry, and, with their superior knowledge of agriculture, gave a new impetus to it. These new owners found it necessary to replenish their laborers with new arrivals to foster the industry, hence an agreement was entered into with John Hawkins, of infamous memory, who clandestinely obtained a charter from his sovereign to convey Negroes from Africa to the West Indies, thereby giving new life to the merciless traffic in human souls.

Jamaica was the most flourishing of the British West Indian islands, and the ancient capital, Port Royal, which has been submerged by earthquake, was said to be the richest spot on the face of the globe. The chief products of this colony were sugar and rum, but its assets were largely added to be its being the headquarters of European pirates and buccaneers who took their treasures thither, where they gambled and feasted in great luxury. It is amusing to note that many of the pirates who traversed the West Indies had been deprived of their ears as the result of the unsuccessful . . . encounters. Some of the early Governors of these islands, such as Sir Henry Morgan, were known as subtle rogues, and were themselves at some time or another, pirates and buccaneers.

Among the many piratical and buccaneering heroes or rogues, whichever you wish to call them, may be mentioned Teach, otherwise known as Blackbeard, Morgan, Hawkins, Rogers, Drake, Raleigh, Preston, Shirley, Jackson and Somers. Such terror did these villains strike in the hearts of the people of these islands, that up to the present day their names are held as auguries of fear among the people. It is common to hear a black or colored mother, in trying to frighten her child, count, "One, two, three, four," and then shout, "Preston, ah, com!" at which intimidation the child runs in terror.

Owing to the limit of space I shall confine myself to a few facts relating to the island of Jamaica, but I may say that conditions in the various islands are the same, and what is true of one is true of the whole.

Jamaica became a colony of England in 1665, under Oliver Cromwell, and has since remained under her control. The country has passed through many forms of local government; at one time it was self-governing; then it became a Crown Colony. For the last twenty years, it has enjoyed a semi-representative government, with little power of control, the balance of power resting in the hands of the red-tapists, who pull the strings of colonial conservatism from Downing Street with a reckless disregard of the interests and wishes of the people.

When the English took possession of this island they exploited it agriculturally for all it was worth, which was a great lot. As I have already mentioned they imported Negro slaves from Africa who tilled the soil under the severest torture, and who are the real producers of the wealth that the country has contributed to the coffers of Europe and the pockets of English adventurers who, in the early days, were men of foul and inhuman characters.

The slaves were inhumanly treated, being beaten, tortured and scourged for the slightest offence. One of the primitive methods of chastisement was to "dance the treadmill," an instrument that clipped off the toes when not danced to proper motion. In self-defense . . . the [former] slaves revolted on several occasions, but with little or no success, as being without arms they were powerless in the face of the organized military forces of the ruling class. In 1851 the ex-slaves in one of the North Western parishes of the island revolted, but were subdued with the loss to the planting proprietors of over three-quarters of a million sterling. They again revolted in 1865 in the East, under the leadership of the Hon. George William Gordon, a member of the Legislative Council, and Paul Bogle. They sounded the call of unmolested liberty, but owing to the suppression of telegraphic communication, they were handicapped and suppressed, otherwise Jamaica would be as free today as Haiti, which threw off the French yoke under the leadership of the famous Negro General, Toussaint L'Ouverture. The Gordon party killed fifteen of the native despots and a savage plutocrat by the name of Baron von Ketelhodt who had great control over the governor, Edward John Eyre. The victorious party hanged Gordon, Paul Bogle and several hundred Negroes, for which crime Governor Eyre was recalled to England and indicted for murder, but escaped by the "skin of his teeth."

In 1834 a law was passed by the Imperial Parliament declaring all slaves within the British Empire free forever, with the promise that such slaves should undergo an apprenticeship for a few years. On August 1, 1838, the Negro slaves of the West Indies became free. Twenty millions sterling was paid to the planters by the Imperial Government for the emancipation of the people whom they had taken from their sunny homes in Africa. The slaves got nothing; they were liberated without money, proper clothing, food or shelter. But with the characteristic fortitude of the African, the Negroes shouldered their burdens and set themselves to work, receiving scanty remuneration for their services. By their industry and thrift they have been able to provide themselves with small holdings which they are improving, greatly to their credit.

Since the abolition of slavery, the Negroes have improved themselves wonderfully, and when the Government twenty or thirty years ago threw open the doors of the Civil Service to competitive examination, the Negro youths swept the board and captured every available office, leaving their white competitors far behind. This system went on for a few years, but as the white youths were found to be intellectually inferior to the black, the whites persuaded the Government to abolish the competitive system and fill vacancies by nomination, and by this means kept out the black youths. The service has long since been recruited from an inferior class of sychophantic weaklings whose brains are exhausted by dissipation and vice before they reach the age of thirty-five.

The population of Jamaica, according to the last census, was 831,383, and is divided as follows: White, 15,605; Black, 630,181; Colored, 168,201; East Indian, 17,380; Chinese, 2,111 and 2,905 whose color is not stated. Thus it can be seen that more than two-thirds of the population of Jamaica (as also of the other West Indian Islands), are descendants of "the old African Slaves." The question naturally arises, How comes this hybrid or colored element? This hybrid population is accounted for by the immoral advantage taken of the Negro women by the whites who have always been in power and who practice polygamy with black women as an unwritten right. The old slave owners raped their female slaves, married or unmarried, and compelled them into polygamy much against their will, thus producing the "colored" element. The latter-day whites, much to their regret, have not the opportunity of compelling black girls to become their mistresses, but they use other means of bewitching these unprotected women whom they keep as concubines, thus perpetuating the evil of which their fathers were guilty. The educated black gentleman, naturally, becomes disgusted with this state of affairs; and in seeking a wife he generally marries a white woman. These are the contributing causes to the negroid or hybrid population of the West Indies. Unlike the whites in the United States the Negroes do not lynch white men when they rape and take advantage of black girls; they leave them to the hand of retributive justice.

There have been several movements to federate the British West Indian Islands, but owing to parochial feelings nothing definite has been achieved. Ere long this change is sure to come about because the people of these islands are all one. They live under the same conditions, are of the same race and mind, and have the same feelings and sentiments regarding the things of the world.

As one who knows the people well, I make no apology for prophesying that there will soon be a turning point in the history of the West Indies; and that the people who inhabit that portion of the Western Hemisphere will be the instruments of uniting a scattered race who, before the close of many centuries, will found an Empire on which the sun shall shine as ceaselessly as it shines on the Empire of the North today. This may be regarded as a dream, but I would point my critical friends to history and its lessons. Would Caesar have believed that the country he was invading in 55 B.C. would be the seat of the greatest Empire in the World? Had it been suggested to him would he not have laughed at it as a huge joke? Yet it has come true. England is the seat of the greatest Empire of the World, and its king is above the rest of monarchs in power and dominion. Laugh then you may, at what I have been bold enough to prophesy, but as surely as there is an evolution in the natural growth of man and nations, so surely will there be a change in the history of these subjected regions.

A Talk with
Afro-West Indians*

The Negro Race and Its Problems

Dear Friend and Brother:

I am moved to address you through the great spirit of love and
the kindred affection that I have for the race Afric; and I am
asking you to be good, loyal and racial enough as to take this
address in the spirit of good will and lend yourself to the
worldwide movement of doing something to promote the intellectual, social, commercial, industrial, and national interest of the
downtrodden race of which you are a member.

For the last ten years I have given my time to the study of the
condition of the Negro, here, there, and everywhere, and I have
come to realize that he is still the object of degradation and pity
the world over, in the sense that he has no status socially,
nationally, or commercially (with a modicum of exception in the
United States of America). Hence the entire world is prone to
look down on him as an inferior and degraded being, although
the people as a whole have done no worse than others to deserve
the ignominious snub. The retrograde state of the Negro is
characterized as accidental and circumstantial; and the onus of
his condition is attributable to the callous indifference and

* Pamphlet on file at the Institute of Jamaica at Kingston, printed about January 1916.
Marcus Garvey landed in the United States in March 1916.

insincerity of those Negroes who have failed to do their duty by the race in promoting a civilized imperialism that would meet the approval of established ideals.

Representative and educated Negroes have made the mistake of drawing and keeping themselves away from the race, thinking that it is degrading and ignominious to identify themselves with the masses of the people who are still ignorant and backward; but who are crying out for true and conscientious leadership, so that they might advance into a higher state of enlightenment whence they could claim the appreciation and honest comradeship of the more advanced races who are today ignoring us simply because we are so lethargic and selfish.

The prejudices of the educated and positioned Negro towards his own people have done much to create a marked indifference to the race among those of other races who are true to themselves, and who do not believe that environment or position removes one from the tie of blood relationship in race.

In America, Europe, Africa, and Australia the Negro is identified by his color and his hair, so it is useless for any pompous man of color to think because his skin is a little paler than that of his brother that he is not also a Negro. Once the African blood courses through the veins you belong to "the company of Negroes," and there is no getting away from it.

God places us in the world as men, so whether we are of an identical species or not, as far as accidental details are concerned, does not matter. What matters is that we are all human, and according to the philosophy of human relationship, all of us have one destiny, hence there should be no estrangement between the people who form the groups of mortals scattered in the different parts of the world.

It is true, that by accident and unfavorable circumstances, the Negro lost hold of the glorious civilization that he once dispensed, and in process of time reverted into savagery, and subsequently became a slave, and even to those whom he once enslaved, yet it does not follow that the Negro must always remain backward. There is no chance for the Negro today in securing a comfortable place with the *progressives* of mankind, as far as racial exclusiveness protects the achievements of the particular race; but there is a great chance for the Negro to do something for himself on the same standard of established customs among the *advanced;* and the *advanced* are eagerly waiting to stretch out the hand of compliment to the Negro as soon as he shall have done the *thing* to merit recognition.

The Negro is ignored today simply because he has kept himself backward; but if he were to try to raise himself to a higher state in the civilized cosmos, all the other races would be glad to meet him on the plane of equality and comradeship. It is indeed unfair to demand equality when one of himself has done nothing to establish the right to equality.

But how can the Negro ever hope to rise when the very men who should have been our props and leaders draw themselves away and try to create an impossible and foolish atmosphere of their own, which is untenable and never recognized?

The appeal I now make is: "For God's sake, you men and women who have been keeping yourselves away from the people of your own African race, cease the ignorance; unite your hands and hearts with the people Afric, and let us reach out to the highest idealism that there is in living, thereby demonstrating to others, not of our race, that we are ambitious, virtuous, noble, and proud of the classification of race.

Sons and daughters of Africa, I say to you arise, take on the toga of race pride, and throw off the brand of ignominy which has kept you back for so many centuries. Dash asunder the petty prejudices within your own fold; set at defiance the scornful designation of "nigger" uttered even by yourselves, and be a Negro in the light of the Pharaohs of Egypt, Simons of Cyrene, Hannibals of Carthage, L'Ouvertures and Dessalines of Haiti, Blydens, Barclays and Johnsons of Liberia, Lewises of Sierra Leone, and Douglass's and Du Bois's of America, who have made, and are making history for the race, though depreciated and in many cases unwritten.

To study the history of the Negro is to go back into a primitive civilization that teems with the brightest and best in art and the sciences.

You who do not know anything of your ancestry will do well to read the works of Blyden, one of our historians and chroniclers, who has done so much to retrieve the lost prestige of the race, and to undo the selfishness of alien historians and their history which has said so little and painted us so unfairly. . . .

The glories of the past should tend to inspire us with courage to create a worthy future. The Negro today is handicapped by circumstances; but no one is keeping him back. He is keeping back himself, and because of this, the other races refuse to notice or raise him. Let the Negro start out seriously to help himself and ere the fall of many more decades you will see him a "new man," once more fit for the association of the "gods" and the true companionship of those whose respect he lost.

I am pleading, yea, I am begging, all men and women within the reach of the blood Afric to wake up to the responsibility of race pride and do something to help in promoting a higher state of appreciation within the race. Locally, we are suffering from a marked shade prejudice, among ourselves, which is foolish and destructible. The established truism reigns the world over—that all people with . . . African blood in their veins are Negroes. The colored man who refuses to acknowledge himself a Negro has only to step into the outer world of Europe, Australia, or America, and even South Africa, to find his level and "place" whence he will find it even more advantageous, from a moral point of view, to be a "black nigger." It is so disgusting to hear some foolish people talk sometimes about their superiority in shade of color. The Caucasian is privileged to talk about his color for there is a standard in his breeding, and all of us have to respect him for his prowess and his might and his mastery, over established ideals. The Negro can attain a like position by self-industry and cooperation, and there is no one more willing to help him to attain that position than the genuine *man of Europe*, the lord of our civilization, today.

The *man of Europe* is longing to see the Negro do something for himself, hence I am imploring one and all to join hands with those millions across the seas, and particularly those in the Fatherland Africa, America, Brazil, and the West Indies, and speed up the brighter destiny of race in the civilized idealism of the day.

Let us from henceforth recognize one and all of the race as brothers and sisters of one fold. Let us move together for the one common good, so that those who have been our friends and protectors in the past might see the good that there is in us.

N.B. Mr. Marcus Garvey, Jr., President and Traveling Commissioner of the Universal Negro Improvement and Conservation Association and African Communities League, will be pleased to communicate or speak with anyone desiring to help in the worldwide movement for the advancement of the Negro. Mr. Garvey will be leaving Jamaica shortly on a lecturing tour through the West Indies, North, South and Central America, in connection with the movement; but all communications received during his absence will be dealt with by the officers in charge of the local division, 121, Orange Street and 34, Charles Street, Kingston, Jamaica.

West Indies in the Mirror of Truth*

I HAVE BEEN in America eight months. My mission to this country is to lecture and raise funds to help my organization —the Universal Negro Improvement Association of Jamaica—to establish an industrial and educational institute to assist in educating the Negro youth of that island. I am also engaged in the study of Negro life in this country.

I must say, at the outset, that the American Negro ought to compliment himself, as well as the early prejudice of the South, for the racial progress made in fifty years, and for the discriminating attitude that had led the race up to the high mark of consciousness preserving it from extinction.

I feel that the Negro who has come in touch with western civilization is characteristically the same, and but for the environment, there would have been no marked difference between those of the scattered race in the western hemisphere. The honest prejudice of the South was sufficiently evident to give the Negro of America the real start—the start with a race consciousness, which I am convinced is responsible for the state of development already reached by the race.

A Fred Douglass or a Booker Washington never would have been heard of in American national life if it were not for the

* *Champion* Magazine, January 1917.

consciousness of the race in having its own leaders. In contrast, the West Indies has produced no Fred Douglass, or Booker Washington, after seventy-eight years of emancipation, simply because the Negro people of that section started out without a race consciousness.

I have traveled a good deal through many countries, and from my observations and study, I unhesitatingly and unreservably say that the American Negro is the peer of all Negroes, the most progressive and the foremost unit in the expansive chain of scattered Ethiopia. Industrially, financially, educationally and socially, the Negroes of both hemispheres have to defer to the American brother, the fellow who has revolutionized history in race development inasmuch as to be able within fifty years to produce men and women out of the immediate bond of slavery, the latchets of whose shoes many a "favored son and daughter" has been unable to loose.

As I travel through the various cities I have been observing with pleasure the active part played by Negro men and women in the commercial and industrial life of the nation. In the cities I have already visited, which include New York, Boston, Philadelphia, Pittsburgh, Baltimore, Washington and Chicago, I have seen commercial enterprises owned and managed by Negro people. I have seen Negro banks in Washington and Chicago, stores, cafés, restaurants, theaters and real estate agencies that fill my heart with joy to realize, in positive truth, and not by sentiment, that at one center of Negrodom, at least, the people of the race have sufficient pride to do things for themselves.

The acme of American Negro enterprise is not yet reached. You have still a far way to go. You want more stores, more banks, and bigger enterprises. I hope that your powerful Negro press and the conscientious element among your leaders will continue to inspire you to achieve; I have detected, during my short stay, that even among you there are leaders who are false, who are mere self-seekers, but on the other hand, I am pleased to find good men and, too, those whose fight for the uplift of the race is one of life and death. I have met some personalities who are not prominently in the limelight for whom I have a strong regard as towards their sincerity in the cause of race uplift, and I think more of their people as real disciples working for the good of our race than many of the men whose names have become nationally and internationally known. In New York, I met John E. Bruce, a man for whom I have the strongest regard inasmuch as I have seen in him a true Negro, a man who does not talk simply because he is in a position for which he must say or do something, but who feels honored to be a member. I can also place in this category Dr. R. R. Wright, Jr., Dr. Parks, vice-president of the Baptist Union, and Dr. Triley of the M.E. church of Philadelphia, the Rev. J. C. Anderson of Quinn Chapel and Mrs. Ida Wells Barnett of Chicago. With men and women of this type, who are conscientious workers and not mere life service dignitaries, I can quite understand that the time is at hand when the stranger, such as I am, will discover the American Negro firmly and strongly set on the pinnacle of fame.

The West Indian Negro who has had seventy-eight years of emancipation has nothing to compare with your progress. Educationally, he has, in the exception, made a step forward, but generally he is stagnant. I have discovered a lot of "vain bluff" as propagated by the irresponsible type of West Indian Negro who has become resident of this country—bluff to the effect that conditions are better in the West Indies than they are in America. Now let me assure you, honestly and truthfully, that they are nothing of the kind. The West Indies in reality could have been the ideal home of the Negro, but the sleeping West Indian has ignored his chance ever since his emancipation, and today he is at the tail end of all that is worth while in the West Indies. The educated men are immigrating to the United States, Canada and Europe; the laboring element are to be found by the thousands in Central and South America. These people are leaving their homes simply because they haven't pride and courage enough to stay at home and combat the forces that make them exiles. If we had the spirit of self-consciousness and reliance, such as you have in America, we would have been ahead of you, and today the standard of Negro development in the West would have been higher. We haven't the pluck in the West Indies to agitate for or demand a square deal and the blame can be attributed to no other source than idolence and lack of pride among themselves.

Let not the American Negro be misled; he occupies the best

position among all Negroes up to the present time, and my advice to him is to keep up his constitutional fight for equity and justice.

The Negroes of the West Indies have been sleeping for seventy-eight years and are still under the spell of Rip Van Winkle. These people want a terrific sensation to awaken them to their racial consciousness. We are throwing away good business opportunities in the beautiful islands of the West. We have no banks of our own, no big stores and commercial undertakings; we depend on others as dealers while we remain consumers. The file is there open and ready for anyone who has the training and ability to become a pioneer. If enterprising Negro Americans would get hold of some of the wealthy Negroes of the West Indies and teach them how to trade and to do things in the interest of their people, a great good would be accomplished for the advancement of the race.

The Negro masses in the West Indies want enterprises that will help them to dress as well as the Negroes in the North of the United States; to help them to live in good homes and to provide them with furniture on the installment plan; to insure them in sickness and health and to prevent a pauper's grave.

Part Two

The Years of Triumph and Tragedy, 1920-1925

Commentary

BY JOHN HENRIK CLARKE

AFTER THE HISTORIC first UNIA International Convention of the Negro Peoples of the World at Madison Square Garden in 1920, the cry "Africa for the Africans, those at home and those abroad" became part of the folklore of the Black Americans. The most important document that came out of this convention was the Declaration of the Rights of the Negro Peoples of the World. Marcus Garvey had started negotiations with the President of Liberia for colonization and development of Africa by Western-world Blacks. This was the beginning of the hope and heartbreak of Marcus Garvey's colonization scheme.

Between 1920 and 1925 the Garvey Movement rose to great heights and, in spite of its troubles, continued to grow. This is the period in which the Movement had its greatest success and was under the severest criticism. The Convention of 1920 was a monumental achievement in Black organizations. This convention came in the years after the First World War, when the promises to Black Americans had been broken, lynching rampant, and when Blacks were still recovering from "the red summer of 1919" in which there were race riots in most of the major cities and the white unemployed took out their grievances on the Blacks, who many times were competing with them for the few available jobs. During this time, Marcus Garvey brought the Black Star Line into being and into a multiplicity of troubles. He divorced his wife and married another and made his name and his organization household words in nearly every part of the world where Black people lived.

The trials and tribulations of the Black Star Line would read like the libretto of a comic opera, except that the events were both hectic and tragic, and there were more villains than heroes involved in this attempt to restore to Black people a sense of worth and nationness.

Marcus Garvey's trouble with the courts started soon after the formation of the Black Star Line. The charges and counter-charges relating to the Black Star Line were the basis of most of his troubles and the cause of his conviction and sentencing to Atlanta Prison. This was the beginning of the end of the greatest years of the Garvey Movement.

The years of triumph and tragedy were building years, searching years and years of magnificent dreaming. Marcus Garvey's vision of Africa had lifted the spirit of Black Americans out of the Depression that followed the First World War. The UNIA's African Legions and Black Cross Nurses became familiar sights on the streets of Harlem. The UNIA grew in membership and in support of all kinds. Garvey was the beating heart of the Movement. His persuasive voice and prolific writings and his effective use of pageantry struck a responsive chord throughout the Black communities of America and abroad. Branches of the Movement were established in Latin America, wherever there were large Caribbean communities. An African Orthodox Church was founded in America. Now the Black man was searching for a new God as well as a new land.

The Garvey Movement began to take effective roots in America when millions of Blacks had begun to feel that they would never know full citizenship with dignity in this country where their ancestors had been brought against their will, and where they had contributed to the wealth and development of the country in spite of conditions of previous servitude. Against this background of broken promises and fading hope, Marcus Garvey began to build a worldwide Black movement. This, the first Black mass protest crusade in the history of the United States, began to pose serious problems for white America. This movement also posed serious problems for the then existing Black leadership, especially for Dr. W. E. B. Du Bois.

In the article "Du Bois versus Garvey: Race Propagandists at War" [1] Elliott M. Rudnick outlines the origins of the conflict between these two Black giants who looked at the world from different vantage points. Both of them were Pan-Africanists and both of them had as their objectives the freedom and redemption of African people everywhere. Yet there was no meeting of minds on the methods of reaching these desirable goals.

The two men were not strangers to each other before Garvey came to the United States in 1916. Du Bois had heard of Garvey when he vacationed in Jamaica in 1915; he had been very well received by both white and colored people, and Garvey and his associates had joined in the welcome.

After this brief first meeting, Garvey and Du Bois went their separate ways, organizationally and ideologically. Garvey had been accused of "introducing" the Jamaican-Black-Mulatto schism to the United States, where Du Bois claimed it had no relevance and only bred disunity.[2] While the color situation in the United States differed appreciably from that in Jamaica, both situations were serious and tragic. In my opinion, both Du Bois and Garvey erred in the way they handled this matter and in the way they handled each other. Du Bois often addressed advice to Marcus Garvey as if the President of the UNIA were a misguided child, and Garvey spoke of Du Bois as if he were a fraud and a traitor to his people. At a critical period this kind of conduct was a negation of the cause that had been the life work of both men.

Garvey's reaction to the Pan-African Congress of 1919 had not been positive. He accused Du Bois of sabotaging his work abroad, especially in Liberia. Du Bois was pictured as a fallen old warrior who had already seen his best days. The editorial writers on Garvey's newspaper, *Negro World*, joined A. Philip Randolph's *Messenger* Magazine in saying that W. E. B. Du Bois was "controlled" by the white capitalists on the NAACP's Board of Directors. Besides, Garvey thought that Du Bois was being given too much credit as the founder of Pan-Africanism.

Criticism notwithstanding, Du Bois began the preparation for the second Pan-African Congress during the early part of 1921. He stated that his intention was to invite not only "Negro Governments," but "all Negro organizations interested in the people of African descent." Du Bois was careful in pointing out the difference between the Pan-African Congress and the Garvey Movement. The NAACP printed a letter from the President of Liberia to the effect that his country would not be used as a base from which the Garvey Movement could harass other governments in Africa.

Now the issue was joined and the lines were drawn. After this date peace between Marcus Garvey and W. E. B. Du Bois seems to have been an impossibility. The second Pan-African Congress was held while crosscurrents of accusations were still passing between Du Bois and Garvey. In the booklet *History of the Pan-African Congress*,[3] Du Bois describes how the Congress started:

> The idea of Pan-Africa having been . . . established, we attempted to build a real organization. We went to work first to assemble a more authentic Pan-African Congress and movement. We corresponded with Negroes in all parts of Africa and in other parts of the world, and finally arranged for a Congress to meet in London, Brussels, and Paris in August and September, 1921. Of the 113 delegates to this Congress, forty-one were from Africa, thirty-five from the United States, twenty-four represented Negroes living in Europe, and seven were from the West Indies. Thus the African element showed growth. They came for the most part, but not in all cases, as individuals, and more seldom as the representatives of organizations or of groups.

> The Pan-African movement thus began to represent a growth and development; but it immediately ran into difficulties. First of all, there was the natural reaction of war and the determination on the part of certain elements in England, Belgium, and elsewhere, to recoup their war losses by intensified exploitation of colonies. They were suspicious of native movements of any sort. Then, too, there came simultaneously another movement, stemming from the West Indies, which accounted for our small West Indian representation. This was in its way a people's movement rather than a movement of the intellectuals. It was led by Marcus Garvey, and it represented a poorly conceived but intensely earnest determination to unite the Negroes of the world, more especially in commercial enterprise. It used all the nationalist and racial paraphernalia of popular agitation, and its strength lay in its backing by the masses of West Indians and by increasing numbers

of American Negroes. Its weaknesses lay in its demogogic leadership, its intemperate propaganda, and the natural fear which it threw into the colonial powers.

Speaking even more bluntly, Du Bois says in his book, *Dusk of Dawn*: [4]

> . . . the Pan-African movement ran into two fatal difficulties: first of all, it was much too early to assume, as I had assumed, that in 1921 the war was over. In fact, the whole tremendous drama which followed the war, political and social revolution, economic upheaval and depression, national and racial hatred, all these things made a setting in which any such movement as I envisaged [probably] at the time impossible. I sensed this in the bitter and deep opposition which our resolutions invoked in Belgium. Both the Belgian and French governments were aroused and disturbed and the English opposition hovered in the background.
>
> There came, too, a second difficulty which had elements of comedy and curious social frustration, but nevertheless was real and in a sense tragic. Marcus Garvey walked into the scene.

In 1921 Marcus Garvey made a tour of Central America, Cuba and Jamaica. He was encouraged by the growth of the Garvey Movement and the acceptance of his teachings throughout the Caribbean islands. His main objective was to boost the sales of Black Star Line stock. He achieved this while trouble was developing with the ships of the Black Star Line and the crews.[5]

After his tour Marcus Garvey was prevented from re-entering the United States for a while.

In the face of other troubles brewing, in Jamaica in June 1921, Marcus Garvey sent a letter to the *Daily Gleaner* that antagonized the ruling elite on the island, Black and white. The letter read, in part:

> Jamaica as I see it is controlled by a few inexperienced "imported strangers" whose position in Jamaica as officials and heads of departments has come to them as "godsends." These fellows know well that they could find no place in the body politic of their own native lands because of their inferiority and their inability to perform technical work, yet through the system of any white man

being better than a native, these "imported gentlemen" are continuously being sent out to the colonies ("dumping grounds") to administer the affairs of our governments. It is time that a halt be called. If Jamaica is to be saved, if Jamaica is to take her place among the progressive nations of the world, then we must have a change of policy. Jamaica is void of that National spirit that should characterise every country. Everybody in Jamaica seems to be looking to the Mother Country for everything . . . I feel that Jamaica wants a political awakening and it should come from within and not from without . . . We feel that we are quite competent to handle the affairs of our country and now all that we ask is a chance . . . Jamaicans as I can see, worship too much that which comes from abroad and from anywhere. If a thing, a man or an animal is imported it is supposed to be better than the native product. How silly! As for individuals, I have seen some of the greatest idiots abroad . . . I would recommend that the poorer classes of Jamaica, the working classes, get together and form themselves into unions and organizations and elect their members for the Legislative Council. With few exceptions the men in the Council represent themselves and their class . . .

When Garvey was eventually given permission to return to the United States he began immediately to prepare for the second UNIA Convention in 1921. This second Convention was not as impressive as the first one held the previous year. Rumors about the mismanagement of the Black Star Line were rampant, and no one was putting these rumors to rest. It was discovered that some of the funds of the Black Star Line had been deposited in the personal bank accounts of some of the officials.

In January 1922, Garvey and three of the main officials of the Line were arrested and indicted for using the mails to defraud. They were released on bail as the investigation of the Black Star Line continued.

The third Convention of the UNIA was held in August of 1922 but was not as well attended as the previous ones. Some of Garvey's enemies organized anti-Garvey rallies, and literally started a "Garvey Must Go" movement.

There was some indication of the worldwide influence of the Garvey Movement while the third Convention was being held: For a number of years the British secret service had been keeping a record of Garvey's activities and making efforts to halt the spread of Garvey's ideas in the colonies. There is some indication that the French were engaged in similar surveillance.

Also in 1922 Marcus Garvey had a talk with the members of the Ku Klux Klan that was seriously misinterpreted. The Imperial Wizard had expressed a desire to see and talk to Marcus Garvey. He was head of the largest organization of whites then existing in the country. Marcus Garvey was his Black counterpart. The meeting did not result in an alliance and was probably ill-advised, mainly because of the misinterpretation that has been put upon it through the years.

In September 1923 the reported failure of the Black Star Line and allegations of financial fraud in the UNIA led Du Bois to write Marcus Garvey off as a failure. Exactly one year later, while Garvey was awaiting bail in The Tombs, the government of Liberia honored W. E. B. Du Bois by inviting him to the inauguration of President Charles D. King. In the meantime, Marcus Garvey and the officials of the Black Star Line were being brought to trial in New York City. The following account of the trial was prepared by Mrs. Amy Jacques Garvey:

> After the indictment of the officers of the Black Star Line, the Federal District Attorney sent two trucks up to the offices of the Black Star Line, the local branch [of the UNIA] and the *Negro World* which were housed in three different buildings and which functioned independently. They took away files, books, records, etc. Garvey tried to stop them, as only the Black Star Line books, etc., should have been taken in order to get evidence in the case, but he was told that he would be cited for contempt if he dared to prevent them from "getting everything connected with Garvey." This was intended to halt the work of the organization; but the members, and even outsiders, realized that Garvey was being persecuted, not prosecuted, so the membership increased.

> The Black Star Line was incorporated under the laws of the State of Delaware. The four indicted officers were Marcus Garvey, President, Orlando Thompson, Vice-President, George Tobias, Treasurer, and Elie Garcia, Secretary. They were released on bail of $2,500 each, until the day of trial, which started May 21, 1923, in Federal Court, New York City. Each defendant had an attorney. Judge Julian Mack presided with a white jury. At the start of the

trial, Garvey, through his attorney, made application that the trial judge declare himself disqualified to try the case on the ground that he was a member or contributor to the NAACP, an association whose officers were actively opposed to Garvey and his Movement. Judge Mack admitted his connection with the NAACP, but denied bias. The motion was denied, and the same judge proceeded to try the case.

At the end of the second day of the trial, Garvey's attorney came to our flat and said he was acting on advice and in Garvey's interest. As his lawyer he was advising him to plead guilty to the technical charge. He had reasons to believe that he would be fined and admonished of future activities. Garvey was surprised at his suggestion and told him that he did not seem to understand what was behind the prosecution. After a lengthy argument on the matter, which brought out other facts, Garvey felt that his attorney was being used innocently to trap him, and asked him to withdraw from his court defense. In leaving, the attorney warned him, "It will go hard with you." Garvey retorted, "I will prove to the jury that I am not guilty of any fraud."

Party politics plays an important part in the judiciary, as judges are elected on their selection by politicians. Garvey tried to get another attorney, whose politics were Republican, as the judge and District Attorney were Republicans, but failed, as some were warned not to handle the Garvey defense. The trial lasted about four weeks, during which time the District Attorney's henchmen circulated rumors that Garveyites were armed so as to justify the indignity of searching them daily. The climax came when it was alleged that an anonymous letter was received at the District Attorney's office, stating that one of Garvey's men was "going to get the judge." The letter was released to the press, with the consequent exaggerated headlines. Bomb-squad men and Secret Service Police cordoned off the courtroom.

The attitude of the Prosecutor is summed up in his final plea to the jury: "Gentlemen, will you let the Tiger loose?" It was clear he was not prosecuting the officers of the Black Star Line, only Garvey. So the other three officers were acquitted, and Garvey found guilty on one count, to wit "that on or about December 13, 1920, for the purpose of executing said scheme and artifice Garvey placed in a post office of the Southern District of New York a certain letter or circular enclosed in a postpaid envelope, addressed to Benny

Dancy, 34 West 131st Street, New York City." An empty envelope was put in evidence, and the Prosecutor assumed that either a letter or circular was enclosed in it inducing Dancy to buy shares. Any one could have rubber-stamped the return address of the Black Star Line on that envelope, and Garvey never took letters to the post office. Nor was there any evidence that this envelope came from the president's office.

W. A. Domingo sent a telegram to Prosecutor Mattocks: "Congratulations on bagging the Tiger." When Garvey read about it, he commented, "There are millions of cubs loose all over the world who are determined to fight their way out of any corral." The judge said he would not pass sentence for a few days. The Prosecutor immediately asked that Garvey be held in custody without bail. He made the startling statement that Garvey had arms and ammunitions in Liberty Hall and that he was a menace to society. Garvey, in protest said, "I am disappointed that your Honor has taken into consideration the remarks made by the Prosecutor, for whom I have nothing but contempt. His statements are utterly false, and this trial has been a conspiracy to ruin Marcus Garvey . . . I am satisfied to let the world judge me innocent or guilty. History will decide." Several bomb-squad men and policemen closed in on him, and he was pushed toward a freight elevator. He was conveyed in armored car to The Tombs. Government raids were made on Liberty Hall, also the offices of the organization, but they did not find even a pistol or a cartridge. But the press did not publish the results of the raids.

On June 21, 1923, Garvey was escorted to the courtroom heavily guarded, and Judge Mack pronounced sentence of five years' imprisonment, $1,000 fine, and the costs of the case. Garvey's attorney gave notice of appeal. Bail was denied, and Garvey was hustled back to prison. He was kept in The Tombs for three months, during which time his attorney made several applications for bail. Each time the trial judge and the District Attorney refused to recommend same. When the judge left for Europe on vacation we were successful, but the bond was set at $15,000.

The lawyer contacted the leading bonding companies, but all refused when they heard the name Garvey. Some said, "Sorry, just can't touch it." One said, "Frankly, if we carried this man's bond, we would be blacklisted." The officers of UNIA and I had to arrange speaking tours in all the states and borrowed the bond money from the members. When the cash bond was posted, he was released.

In 1924, Marcus Garvey had completed plans for a large settlement of American Blacks to Africa. He intended to make Liberia the African headquarters of the UNIA. The European powers who were occupying Africa brought pressure on Liberia to deny Garvey the right to start a settlement in that country. They feared that the spirit of nationalism would spread throughout Africa and put an end to colonial rule. The President of Liberia eventually reversed the decision to permit the settlement, and Garvey suffered another defeat.

The party of UNIA engineers assigned to construct housing was arrested and deported the moment their ship reached Monrovia, and the police seized $50,000 worth of construction material that was to be used by the Black settlers.

Marcus Garvey never cried over defeats or wasted any time between them. While waiting for a hearing on the request for appeal in his case, he started another maritime venture—Black Cross Navigation and Trading Company to replace the defunct Black Star Line.

Early in 1925, Garvey's appeal came for a hearing and was dismissed. He was sent to federal prison in Atlanta. What can be called "The Golden Age of the Garvey Movement" was over, but the Movement itself was not over.

Back to Africa*

BY W. E. B. DU BOIS

IT WAS UPON the tenth of August, in High Harlem of Manhattan Island, where a hundred thousand negroes live. There was a long, low, unfinished church basement, roofed over. A little, fat black man, ugly, but with intelligent eyes and big head, was seated on a plank platform beside a "throne," dressed in a military uniform of the gayest mid-Victorian type, heavy with gold lace, epaulets, plume, and sword. Beside him were "potentates," and before him knelt a succession of several colored gentlemen. These in the presence of a thousand or more applauding dark spectators were duly "knighted" and raised to the "peerage" as knight-commanders and dukes of Uganda and the Niger. Among the lucky recipients of titles was the former private secretary of Booker T. Washington!

What did it all mean? A casual observer might have mistaken it for the dress rehearsal of a new comic opera and looked instinctively for Bert Williams and Miller and Lyles. But it was not; it was a serious occasion, done on the whole soberly and solemnly. Another might have found it simply silly. All ceremonies are more or less silly. Some negroes would have said that this ceremony had something symbolic, like the coronation, because it was part of a great "back-to-Africa" movement and represented self-determination for the negro race and a relieving of

America of her most difficult race problem by a voluntary operation.

On the other hand, many American negroes and some others were scandalized by something which they could but regard as simply child's play. It seemed to them sinister, this enthroning of a demagogue, a blatant boaster, who with monkey shines was deluding the people and taking their hard-earned dollars; and in High Harlem there rose an insistent cry, "Garvey must go!"

Knowledge of all this seeped through to the greater world because it was sensational and made good copy for the reporters. The great world now and then becomes aware of certain currents within itself—tragedies and comedies, movements of mind, gossip, personalities—in some inner whirlpool of which it had been scarcely aware before. Usually these things are of little interest or influence for the main current of events; and yet is not this same main current made up of the impinging of these smaller swirlings of little groups? No matter how segregated and silent the smaller whirlpool is, if it is American, at some time it strikes and influences the American world. What, then, is the latest news from this area of negrodom spiritually so foreign to most of white America?

The sensation that Garvey created was due not so much to his program as to his processes of reasoning, his proposed methods of work, and the width of the stage upon which he essayed to play his part.

His reasoning was at first new and inexplicable to Americans because he brought to the United States a new negro problem. We think of our problem here as *the* negro problem, but we know more or less clearly that the problem of the American negro is very different from the problem of the South African negro or the problem of the Nigerian negro or the problem of the South American negro. We have not hitherto been so clear as to the way in which the problem of the negro in the United States differs from the problem of the negro in the West Indies. For a long time we have been told, and we have believed, that the race problem in the West Indies, and particularly in Jamaica, has virtually been settled.

Let us note the facts. Marcus Garvey was born on the northern coast of Jamaica in 1887. He was a poor black boy, his father dying later in the almshouse. He received a little training in the Church of England grammar school, and then learned the trade of printing, working for years as foreman of a printing plant. Then he went to Europe and wandered about England and France working and observing until he finally returned to Jamaica. He found himself facing a stone wall. He was poor, he was black, he had no chance for a university education, he had no likely chance for preferment in any line, but could work as an artisan at small wage for the rest of his life.

Moreover, he knew that the so-called settlement of the race problem in Jamaica was not complete; that as a matter of fact throughout the West Indies the development had been like this: most white masters had cohabited with negro women, and some had actually married them; their children were free by law in most cases, but were not the recognized equals of the whites either socially, politically, or economically. Because of the numbers of the free negroes as compared with the masters, and because of their continued growth in wealth and intelligence, they began to get political power, and they finally either expelled the whites by uniting with the blacks, as in Haiti, or forced the whites to receive the mulattoes, or at least the lighter-hued ones, as equals.

This is the West Indian solution of the negro problem. The mulattoes are virtually regarded and treated as whites, with the assumption that they will, by continued white intermarriage, bleach out their color as soon as possible. There survive, therefore, few white colonials, save newcomers, who are not of negro descent in some more or less remote ancestor. Mulattoes intermarry, then, largely with the whites, and the so-called disappearance of the color line is the disappearance of the line between the whites and mulattoes, and not between the whites and the blacks or even between the mulattoes and the blacks.

Thus the privileged and exploiting group in the West Indies is composed of whites and mulattoes, while the poorly paid and ignorant proletariat are the blacks, forming a peasantry vastly in the majority, but socially, politically, and economically helpless and nearly voiceless. This peasantry, moreover, has been systematically deprived of its natural leadership because the black boy who showed initiative or who accidentally gained wealth and education soon gained the recognition of the white-mulatto group and might be incorporated with them, particulary if he married one of them. Thus his interests and efforts were identified with the mulatto-white group.

There must naturally arise a more or less insistent demand among the black peasants for self-expression and for an exposition of their grievances by one of their own group. Such leaders have indeed arisen from time to time, and Marcus Garvey was one. His notoriety comes not from his ability and accomplishment, but from the Great War. Not that he was without ability. He was a facile speaker, able to express himself in grammatical and forceful English; he had spent enough time in world cities like London to get an idea of world movements, and he honestly believed that the backwardness of the blacks was simply the result of oppression and lack of opportunity.

On the other hand, Garvey had no thorough education and a very hazy idea of the technic of civilization. He fell easily into the common error of assuming that because oppression has retarded a group, the mere removal of the injustice will at a bound restore the group to full power. Then, too, he personally had his drawbacks: he was inordinately vain and egotistic, jealous of his power, impatient of details, a poor judge of human nature, and he had the common weakness of untrained devotees that no dependence could be put upon his statements of fact. Not that he was a conscious liar, but dream, fact, fancy, wish, were all so blurred in his thinking that neither he himself nor his hearers could clearly or easily extricate them.

Then came the new economic demand for negro peasant labor on the Panama Canal, and finally the Great War. Black West-Indians began to make something like decent wages, they began to travel, and they began to talk and think. Garvey talked and thought with them. In conjunction with white and colored sympathizers he planned a small Jamaican Tuskegee. This failed, and he conceived the idea of a purely negro organization to establish independent negro states and link them with commerce and industry. His "Universal Negro Improvement Association," launched August 1, 1914, in Jamaica, was soon in financial difficulties. The war was beginning to change the world, and as white American laborers began to be drawn into war work there was an opening in many lines not only for Southern American negroes as laborers and mechanics, but also for West-Indians as servants and laborers. They began to migrate in larger numbers. With this new migration came Marcus Garvey.

He established a little group of his own Jamaica countrymen in Harlem and launched his program. He took no account of the American negro problem; he knew nothing about it. What he was trying to do was to settle the Jamaican problem in the United States. On the other hand, American negroes knew nothing about the Jamaican problem, and they were excited and indignant at being brought face to face with a man who was full of wild talk about Africa and the West Indies and steamship lines and "race pride," but who said nothing and apparently knew nothing about the right to vote, the horrors of lynching and mob law, and the problem of racial equality.

Moreover, they were especially incensed at the new West-Indian conception of the color line. Color lines had naturally often appeared in colored America, but the development had early taken a far different direction from that in the West Indies. Migration by whites had numerically overwhelmed both masters and mulattoes and compelled most American masters to sell their own children into slavery. Freedom, therefore, rather than color, became the first line of social distinction in the American negro world despite the near-white aristocracies of cities like Charleston and New Orleans, and despite the fact that the proportion of mulattoes who were free and who gained some wealth and education was greater than that of blacks because of the favor of their white parents.

After emancipation, color caste tended to arise again, but the darker group was quickly welded into one despite color by caste legislation, which applied to a white man with one negro great-grandfather as well as to a full-blooded Bantu. There were still obvious advantages to the negro American of lighter hue in passing for white or posing as Spanish or Portuguese, but the pressing demand for ability and efficiency and honesty within this fighting, advancing group continually drove the color line back before reason and necessity, and it came to be generally regarded as the poorest possible taste for a negro even to refer to differences of color. Colored folk as white as the whitest came to describe themselves as negroes. Imagine, then, the surprise and disgust of these Americans when Garvey launched his Jamaican color scheme.

He did this, of course, ignorantly and with no idea of his mistake and no wit to read the signs. He meant well. He saw what seemed to him the same color lines which he hated in Jamaica, and he sought here as there to oppose white supremacy and the white ideal by a crude and equally brutal black supremacy and black idea. His mistake did not lie in the utter impossibility of this program—greater upheavals in ideal have shaken the world before—but rather in its spiritual bankruptcy and futility; for what shall this poor world gain if it exchange one race supremacy for another?

Garvey soon sensed that somewhere he was making a mistake, and he began to protest that he was not excluding mulattoes from his organization. Indeed, he has men of all colors and bloods in his organization, but his propaganda still remains "all-black," because this brings cash from the Jamaica peasants. Once he was actually haled to court and made to apologize for calling a disgruntled former colleague "white"! His tirades and twistings have landed him in strange contradictions. Thus with one voice he denounced Booker T. Washington and Frederick Douglass as bastards, and with the next named his boarding-house and first steamship after these same men!

Aside from his color lines, Garvey soon developed in America a definite and in many respects original and alluring program. He proposed to establish the "Black Star Line" of steamships, under negro ownership and with negro money, to trade between the United States, the West Indies, and Africa. He proposed to establish a corporation which was going to build factories and manufacture goods both for local consumption of negroes and for export. He was going eventually to take possession of Africa and establish independent negro governments there.

The statement of this program, with tremendous headlines, wild eloquence, and great insistence and repetition, caught the attention of all America, white and black. When Mr. Garvey brought his cohorts to Madison Square Garden, clad in fancy costumes and with new songs and ceremonies, and when, ducking his dark head at the audience, he yelled, "We are going to Africa to tell England, France, and Belgium to get out of there," America sat up, listened, laughed, and said here at least is something new.

Negroes, especially West-Indians, flocked to his movement and poured money into it. About three years ago he had some 80,000 members in his organization, and perhaps 20,000 or 30,000 were paying regularly thirty-five cents a month into his chest. These numbers grew in his imagination until he was claiming 4,500,000 followers, and speaking for "Four hundred million negroes"! He did not, however, stop with dreams and promises. If he had been simply a calculating scoundrel, he would carefully have skirted the narrow line between promise and performance and avoided as long as possible the inevitable catastrophe. But he believed in his program and he had a childish ignorance of the stern facts of the world into whose face he was flying. Being an islander, and born in a little realm where half a day's journey takes one from ocean to ocean, the world always seemed small to him, and it was perhaps excusable for this black peasant of Jamaica to think of Africa as a similar, but slightly larger, island which could easily be taken possession of.

His first practical step . . . was to establish the Black Star Line, and here he literally left his critics and opponents breathless by suddenly announcing in 1919 that the *Frederick Douglass*, a steamship, had been bought by his line, was on exhibition at a wharf in New York, and was about to sail to the West Indies with freight and passengers. The announcement was electrical even for those who did not believe in Garvey. With a splendid, audacious faith, this poor black leader, with his storming tongue, compelled a word of admiration from all. But the seeds of failure were in his very first efforts. This first boat, the *Yarmouth* (never renamed the *Frederick Douglass* probably because of financial difficulties), was built in the year Garvey was born and was an old sea-scarred hulk. He was cheated in buying it, and paid $140,000 for it—at least twice as much as the boat was worth. She made three trips to the West Indies in three years and then was docked for repairs, attached for debt, and finally, in December, 1921, sold at auction for $1,625!

The second boat that Garvey bought was a steam yacht originally built for a Standard Oil magnate. It, too, was old and of doubtful value, but Garvey paid $60,000 for it, and sent it down to do a small carrying trade between the West Indies Islands. The boat broke down, and it cost $70,000 or $80,000 more to repair it than Garvey paid for it. Finally it was wrecked or seized in Cuba, and the crew was transported to the United States at government expense.

The third boat was a Hudson River ferry-boat that Garvey bought for $35,000. With this he carried excursionists up and down the Hudson during one summer and used it as a vivid advertisement to collect more money. The boat, however, ran only that summer, and then had to be abandoned as beyond repair.

Finally, Garvey tried to buy from the United States Shipping Board the steamship *Orion* for $250,000. This boat was to be renamed the *Phyllis Wheatley*, and its sailings were advertised in Garvey's weekly paper for several months, and some passages were sold; but the boat never was delivered because sufficient payments were not made.

Thus the Black Star Line arose and disappeared, and with it went some $800,000 of the savings of West Indians and a few American negroes. With this enterprise the initial step and greatest test of Mr. Garvey's movement failed utterly. His factories corporation never really got started. In its place he has established a number of local grocery stores in Harlem and one or two shops, including a laundry and a printing press, which may or may not survive.

His African program was made impossible by his own pig-headedness. He proposed to make a start in Liberia with industrial enterprises. From this center he would penetrate all Africa and gradually subdue it. Instead of keeping this plan hidden and working cautiously and intelligently toward it, he yelled and shouted and telegraphed it all over the world. Without consulting the Liberians, he apparently was ready to assume partial charge of their state. He appointed officials with high-sounding titles, and announced that the headquarters of his organization was to be removed to Liberia in January, 1922. Such announcements, together with talk about conquest and "driving

Europe out," aroused European governments to inquire about Garvey and his backing. Diplomatic representations were made to Liberia, asking it how far it intended to coöperate in this program. Liberia was naturally compelled to repudiate Garveyism, root and branch. The officials told Garvey that he or any one else was welcome to migrate to Liberia and develop industry within legal lines, but that they could recognize only one authority in Liberia and that was the authority of the Liberian Government, and that Liberia could not be the seat of any intrigue against her peaceful neighbors. They made it impossible for Garvey to establish any headquarters in Africa unless it was done by the consent of the very nations whom he was threatening to drive out of Africa!

This ended his African program and reduced him to the curious alternative of sending a delegate to the third assembly of the League of Nations to ask them to hand over as a gift to his organization a German colony in order that he might begin his work.

Thus the bubble of Garveyism burst; but its significance, its meaning, remains. After all, one has to get within Garvey to know him, to understand him. He is not simply a liar and blatant fool. Something of both, to be sure, is there; but that is not all. He is the type of dark man whom the white world is making daily, molding, marring, tossing to the air. All his life whites have laughed and sneered at him and torn his soul. All his life he has hated the half-whites who, rejecting their darker blood, have gloried in their pale sham. He stormed and fought within, and then at last it all burst out. He had to guard himself before the powers and be careful of law and libel and hunger, but where he could be free, he snarled and cursed at the whites, insulted the mulattoes with unpardonable epithets, and bitterly reviled the blacks for their cowardice.

Suppose, now, for a moment that Garvey had been a man of first-rate ability, canny, shrewd, patient, dogged? He might have brought a world war of races a generation nearer, he might have deprived civilization of that precious generation of respite where we have yet time to sit and consider if difference of human color must necessarily mean blows and blood. As a matter of fact,

Garvey did not know how to approach his self-appointed task; he had not the genius to wait and laboriously learn, yet he pompously seized the pose; he kept extremely busy, rushed hither and thither. He collected and squandered thousands, almost millions. He would, he must, succeed. He appeared in the uniforms of his dream triumphs, in 1921 with an academic cap and gown, weird in colors; in 1922 with cocked hat, gold lace, and sword—the commander-in-chief of the African Legion! He did not quite dare call himself King Marcus I, but he sunned himself awhile in the address of "your Majesty." He held court and made knights, lords, and dukes; and yet, as he feverishly worked, he knew he had failed; he knew he had missed the key to some dark arcanum. He grew suspicious, morose, complaining, furious at the "fools" and "scoundrels" who were "plotting" his ruin and the overthrow of his cause. With all the provincial backwoods love of courts and judges he rushed into and reveled in litigation, figuring in at least fifty suits, suing for libel, breach of contract, slander, divorce, assault—everything and anything; while in turn his personal enemies sued him, rioted against him, and one shot him, so that today he dares not stir without a sturdy body guard.

Beaten and overwhelmed with loss and disappointment, he will not yet surrender, and seeks by surrounding himself with new officials and by announcing new enterprises—a daily paper, a new line of steamships, and the like—to re-form his lines. So he sits today. He is a world figure in minute microcosm. On a larger field, with fairer opportunity, he might have been great, certainly notorious. He is today a little puppet, serio-comic, funny, yet swept with a great veil of tragedy; meaning in himself little more than a passing agitation, moving darkly and uncertainly from a little island of the sea to the panting, half-submerged millions of the first world state. And yet he means something to the world. He is type of a mighty coming thing. He voices a vague, formless, but growing, integrating, human mind which some day will arrest the world.

Just what it has cost the negro race in money to support Garvey it is hard to say, but certainly not less than a million dollars. And yet with all this there are certain peculiar satisfactions. Here has come a test to the American negro which he has not had before. A demagogue has appeared, not the worst kind of demagogue, but, on the contrary, a man who had much which was attractive and understandable in his personality and his program; nevertheless a man whose program anybody with common sense knew was impossible. With all the arts of the demagogue, Garvey appealed to crowds of people with persuasive eloquence, with the ringing of all possible charges of race loyalty and the bastardy of the mulatto and the persons ashamed of their race, and the implacable enmity of the whites. It was the sort of appeal that easily throws ignorant and inexperienced people into orgies of response and generosity. Yet with all this, coming at a critical time, when the negro was hurt at his war experience and his post-war treatment, when lynching was still a national institution and mob law a ready resort; when the rank and file of ignorant West-Indian negroes were going wild over Garvey, the American negroes sat cool and calm, and were neither betrayed into wild and unjust attacks upon Garvey nor into uncritical acceptance.

His following has ebbed and flowed. Its main and moving nucleus has been a knot of black Jamaica peasants resident in America as laborers and servants, mostly unlettered, poor, and ignorant, who worship Garvey as their ideal incarnate. Garvey is bold. Garvey lashes the white folk. Garvey downs the mulattoes. Garvey forever! no matter what he does. Does he steal? Better let him steal than let white folk. Does he squander? It's our money; let him waste. Does he fail? Others have failed.

It is this blind and dangerous nucleus that explains Garvey's success in holding his power. Around these are a mass of West Indians, resident in the islands and in the United States, who have honestly supported Garvey in the hope that this new leader would direct them out of the West-Indian *impasse* of low wages, little educational opportunity, no industrial openings, and caste. Especially they seized upon the Black Star Line, as isolated islanders would, as a plan of real practical hope. This group reached sixty or seventy thousand in number during Garvey's heyday, but with the failure of his enterprises it is rapidly falling away.

With these groups have always been a number of American negroes: the ignorant, drawn by eloquence and sound; the grafters who saw a chance of sharing spoils; and with these some honest, thinking folk who paused and inquired, "Who is Garvey, and what is his program?" This American following, though always small, grew here and there, and in centers like Norfolk, Chicago, and Pittsburgh reached for a time into the thousands. But, on the whole, American negroes stood the test well.

Garvey's proposal of such a new, autonomous, and hostile black world in league with the brown and yellow peoples brought from American negroes a simple Missouri "Show us." They asked: "What are you doing, and how? What are your concrete and practical proposals?" They did not follow the more impatient counsels of "Garvey must go." They did not slander or silence or ignore him. The two hundred negro weeklies treated him fairly, and audiences listened to his words and read his literature. And right here lay his undoing, for the more his flamboyant promises were carefully compared with his results, the sooner the utter futility of his program was revealed.

Here is a world that for a thousand years, from the First Crusade to the Great War, had been breaking down the barriers between nations and races in order to build a worldwide economic unity and cultural solidarity. The process has involved slavery, peonage, rape, theft, and extermination, but it is slowly uniting humanity. It is now proposed to turn back and cut out of this world its black eighth or its colored two-thirds. Not only is this virtually impossible, but its attempt today would certainly involve the white and colored worlds in a death struggle whose issue none can surely foretell. The power of the yellow, black, and brown worlds today is the economic dependence of the white world on them, and the power of the white world is its economic technic and organization. The super-diplomacy of race politics tomorrow is to transmute this interdependence into cultural sympathy, spiritual tolerance, and human freedom. Not in segregation, but in closer, larger unity lies interracial peace.

Not with entire clearness and yet with a certain fundamental and tremendously significant clarity the American negro realizes this, and as yet no demagoguery or pipe dreams have been able to divorce him from the facts. The present generation of negroes has survived two grave temptations, the greater one, fathered by Booker T. Washington, which said, "Let politics alone, keep in your place, work hard, and do not complain," and which meant perpetual color caste for colored folk by their own coöperation and consent, and the consequent inevitable debauchery of the white world; and the lesser, fathered by Marcus Garvey, which said: "Give up! Surrender! The struggle is useless; back to Africa and fight the white world."

It is no ordinary tribute to American negro poise and common sense, and ability to choose and reject leadership, that neither of these programs has been able to hold them. One of the most singular proofs of this is that the latest support of Garveyism is from the notorious Ku Klux Klan. When Garvey saw his Black Star Line disappear, his West-Indian membership fall off, and his American listeners grow increasingly critical, he flew South to consult the Grand Cyclops of the Invisible Empire. Whether the initiative came from him or from the Klan is not known, but probably the Klan invited him. They were indeed birds of a feather, believing in titles, flummery, and mumbo-jumbo, and handling much gullible money.

Garvey's motives were clear. The triumph of the Klan would drive negroes to his program in despair, while the Klan's sympathy would enable him to enter the South, where he has not dared to work, and exploit the ignorant black millions. The Klan's object was to encourage anything that would induce negroes to believe that their fight for freedom in America was vain. Garvey's secretary said that the Klan would probably finance the Black Star Line, and Garvey invited the Grand Cyclops to speak at his convention. But Garvey reckoned without his host. A storm of criticism rose among negroes and kept Garvey explaining, contradicting, and repudiating the unholy alliance, and finally drove it under cover, although Garvey openly advertised the Klan's program as showing the impossibility of the negro's remaining in America, and the Klan sent out circulars defending Garvey and declaring that the opposition to him was from the Catholic Church!

Again it is High Harlem, with its music and laughter, its conversations shouted aloft, its teeming, bantering, pushing crowds, its brown and black and creamlike faces, its crisp and curling hair. As the setting sun sends its last crimson light from the heights that hold the Hudson from the Harlem, it floods 138th

Street and lights three blocks. One is a block of homes built by
the Equitable Life Insurance Society, but now sold to negroes,
some crowded, some carelessly kept, but most of them beautiful,
even luxurious, perhaps as handsome a block as middle-class
America, white or black, affords. Next the sun softens the
newness of a brick block on Seventh Avenue, stretching low and
beautiful from the YWCA, with a moving-picture house of the
better class and a colored five-and-ten cent store built and owned
by black folk. Down beyond, on 138th Street, the sun burns the
raising spire of Abyssinian Church, a vast and striking structure
built by negroes who for a hundred years have supported one
organization and are now moving to their newest and luxurious
home of soft carpets, strained windows, and swelling organ.
Finally, the dying rays hit a low, rambling basement of brick and
rough stone. It was designed as the beginning of a church long
ago, but abandoned. Marcus Garvey roofed it over, and out of
this squat and dirty old "Liberty Hall" he screams his propaganda. As compared with the homes, the business, the church,
Garvey's basement represents nothing in accomplishment and
only waste in attempt.

Yet it has a right to be. It represents something spiritual,
however poor and futile today. Deep in the black man's heart he
knows that he needs more than homes and stores and churches.
He needs manhood—liberty, brotherhood, equality. The call of
the spirit urges him restlessly to and fro with all men of the
despised and forgotten, seeking, seeking. Misled they often are,
and again and again they play in microcosm the same tragic
drama that other worlds and other groups have played. Here is
Garvey yelling to life, from the black side, a race consciousness
which leaps to meet Madison Grant and Lothrop Stoddard and
other worshipers of the great white race. It is symptomatic and
portentous. If with a greater and more gifted and efficient Garvey
it sometime blazes to real flame, it means world war and eternal
hate and blood. It means the setting of the world clock back a
thousand years. And yet the world's Garveys are not solely to
blame, but rather every worshiper of race superiority and human
inequality. On the other hand, back of all this lurks the quieter,
more successful, more insistent, and hopeful fact. Races are living
together. They are buying and selling, marrying and rearing

children, laughing and crying. They are fighting mobs and lynchers and those that enslave and despise, and they have not yet failed in that fight. Their faith in their ultimate and complete triumph are these homes, this business block, this church, duplicated a hundred thousand times in a nation of twelve million. Here, then, are the two future paths, outlined with a certain sullen dimness in the world's blood-crimson twilight, and yet to be descried easily by those with the seeing hearts. Which path will America choose?

Garvey and Garveyism—
An Estimate*

BY A. F. ELMES

A CLOSE-UP VIEW of a picture frequently exaggerates elements out of all proportion to their true importance. This principle should also be borne in mind in estimating all human movements. History cannot be written fairly and dispassionately nor a just interpretation given to events in the midst of the ferment of such events, nor yet at a time, nor by a person, that stands too near the stage of such events.

The British Parliament has recently decided to give publicity to all the documents relating to the recent war. The world will look with more than ordinary interest and expectancy to such publications, and now seven years after the Armistice, judgment as to where full responsibility for the war should be placed, what were the causes primary and secondary—in a word, the interpretation of the facts in full fairness would do well to wait on these documents.

No one will refuse to admit this principle—the principle that human movements cannot be viewed in their true perspective at close range. History must have time to justify itself.

Lest there be any prejudice as to the identity of the writer, he wishes to say of himself at the outset, that he is not, nor ever was,

* *Opportunity*, May 1925.

a Garveyite, nor has he at any time shown a disposition to become an orthodox disciple of Garvey. He has no stock in the defunct Black Star Line, nor in any of the enterprises fostered by the movement. He claims no particular fitness to declare himself on the subject except that of an outsider, a student of human movements, a sympathetic observer of Garvey and the workings of the colossal and unwieldy program he inaugurated.

In Harlem and in other parts of the country the writer has had the experience of personal encounters, unaccompanied however by any physical violence, with ardent disciples of Garvey and he numbers among these some of his friends who themselves have been puzzled as to his (the writer's) inability, perhaps more frankly his mental obtuseness, in not being able to recognize this savior of his race.

His contacts have been wide and he has watched and studied the movement, read with avidity the *Negro World* and he has before him as he pens this article "The Constitution and Book of Laws, made for the Government of the Universal Negro Improvement Association, Inc., and African Communities' League, Inc., of the World. Revised and Amended August 1920."

Newspaper and magazine articles have appeared on both sides and the language of some of these have been poignantly sarcastic and many of them have descended to the plane of abuse and personal vilification of the man Garvey. And they have all had a wide circulation.

Now that the "tumult and the shouting" is about to subside in both pro- and anti-Garvey camps, now that Garvey himself has passed into the shadows of the federal prison and open opposition to him has necessarily been rendered futile, it were well for some sympathetic outsider whose state of mind thus characterized would fit him eminently to present the case, frankly and openly to do so.

Let it be observed that no man could stand in one of those teeming Liberty Hall audiences, see one of Garvey's ostentatious parades, hear Garvey's magnetic voice, read his *Negro World*, watch the sweep of his ideas and then say there was nothing to it. Let him do this and he would cast a serious doubt on his mental integrity. This is apart entirely from the goodness or the badness

of Garveyism. There is something to it; all reasonable men will
readily admit.

And how does this come to be? It is the personality of Garvey
himself. Call him what you will: a visionary, impossible idealist,
fanatical reformer, unprincipled opportunist; behind these epithets lie the unconquerable fact of Garvey, the personality of the
man who has dramatically attracted the attention of the world.

Contrary to much of what has hitherto been published, I
believe the man was not fundamentally insincere. What he saw,
he saw and there was no make believe in his own mind. True,
many of his followers have been disappointed, they were duped,
bewildered, bewitched and surrendered reason as well as ready
money. The thing has not worked out as they expected; but in
Garvey's own mind there was a close fit between what he gave
forth and what he held in his mind. I think he was substantially
and in the main sincere.

If I understand his program correctly he was sound in his basic
contention for his people. Above I gave a passing characterization to his program as being unwieldy. The objects of the UNIA
as given in its Constitution and Book of Laws make me smile as I
read them over. They go from reclaiming the fallen and assisting
the needy to the establishing of a Negro nation in Africa, from
helping backward tribes in Africa to the founding of universities,
colleges, academies and a worldwide commercial enterprise . . .
Comprehensive, colossal, topheavy and impossible! No one man
is wise nor powerful enough to sit astride so many horses at one
and the same time.

Interpreting these manifold objects synthetically and as Garvey sought to have them carried out in practice, what do we find?
He is contending for the principle of a self-sustaining, self-propa-
gating group life, that as a race the Negro will not rise into the
fullness of racial selfhood until his group becomes fully competent and adequate in resources for the demands of his economic,
political, moral and spiritual life. What is there against this? All
Negro organizations vote its full adoption with both hands up. In
principle; yes, we do.

No man who is content to remain poor, who for his normal
needs seeks dependence on others, merits much respect. No race
comes into the place of dignified selfhood that stays poor. Marcus

Garvey argues when the colored man needs a suit of clothes, there should be a colored tailor competent to fit him, a colored wholesale store from which the goods can be procured, colored factory for the preparation of the raw material, colored producers for this raw material and ships manned and owned by men of his race to transport the goods. He would close up the whole economic circle with agents and agencies of his own people. Thus he carried the doctrine in the other aspects of Negro life. Is not this principle valid for a program of uplift and advance for any people?

Marcus Garvey while fundamentally sincere, unhappily failed to realize his limitations, and the tremendous sweep of his mind was not balanced by adequate penetrating power. While he dreamed the emotional content of those dreams, the showy fabric of his visions bore him away in method from the immediate or remotely practicable. In short, for the carrying out of such universal aims there seemed wanting in the leader many of the intellectual prerequisites.

No estimate of Garveyism as a social movement can ignore the fact that his personality plus the mere size of the things he attempted to do gave him a a good measure of the power of his appeal. He thought in terms large and universal and would in one organization compass the Alpha to Omega of his people's progress. Such a mind is usually "short" in analytic power and penetrative capacity. Garvey's was eminently so. His very inability for clear-cut, analytical reasoning made him intolerant of interference and made him assume at times the investiture of divine rightness and supernatural inspiration for his scheme.

Garvey was a prophet. He was possessed of a great and noble passion. The fervor with which he believed in himself and his message, the full measure of his devotion to what he held to be right, cannot be successfully gainsaid. He missed the mark in method and procedure. Like other reformers that went before him, this passion for redemption of his people led him beyond the bounds of discretion and his inability to sense his limitations was really a dire element in his psychology. Garveyism came to be regarded by a number of well-thinking Negroes as a gospel of hate for white people and all that appertains to this group. This was worse than unfortunate. No program of permanent uplift for the Negro can successfully proceed on such an issue. Breathing out threatenings and slaughter against the dominant element among whom we live and move and have our being was common among the disciples of Marcus Garvey. Foolish and worse. Teach Negroes to hate white people and it will soon be impossible to teach them to love and think well of their own. Garveyism lost much of the intelligent sympathy, if not open avowal, it might have gained by the fiery ebulitions of its ardent ambassadors. Nevertheless, our judgment of Garvey and his movement, I will say, should not be given on this count only. It is meet to observe that reformers and seers are prone to deliver themselves in such manner. It is also true that the excesses to which a movement goes should not necessarily bias judgment in this direction. Reformers, prophets and human movements that would rectify an existing order have this habit.

"Liberty, equality, fraternity" are the accepted bulwarks of democracy. Turn to the story of the French Revolution and see the extravagance out of which these ideas were salvaged. They would tear down everything; yea, and religion also. On the corner of a street in Paris a red republican was heard to declare how they were going to destroy churches, crucifixes and shrines, all that stood for the perpetuation of religion. Yet history points proudly to that event as marking the birthday of the modern democratic movement.

Garvey's was a great idea. It had in it a remarkable power of appeal and contagion. When a great idea deeply lays hold of the minds of a group with other suggestive elements in its mental and social atmosphere cooperating, it is liable to cause commotion and as a result throw up to attention much frothy and extraneous matter.

The phenomenal spread of Garveyism, further, must be attributed to the leader's knowledge of the psychology of his people joined to the fact—and this is most significant—of the time and circumstances in which the movement was inaugurated. Mark the elements in Negro psychology which he took cognizance of and marshalled to his service. Garvey proves a conviction of my own that only the Negro can properly interpret the Negro. The love of symbols, the craving for power, titles, etc., plumed knights in showy parades—all these Garvey took and exploited for the UNIA. All the gorgeous periphery in dress, court display, fantastic titles were very relevant to his aim—the capture of the heart (if not the head) and the imagination of the masses of his people, and it worked. He captured moreover, some of the intellectuals. This was a splendid achievement. If only the leader had had the good sense to bind this latter class to himself for counsel, executive direction and business management in the special lines of his manifold enterprises the crash might have been postponed and made much less dramatic. I am not convinced that some crash would have been altogether avoided, for Garvey flattered by success grew dogged and impatient of the counsel of others. . . .

And now, Marcus Garvey is behind the bars convicted of using the mails to defraud and the most pertinent question is what of the UNIA? Orthodox disciples of his give the answer to the satisfaction of those within the fold. It could well be put: "Garvey's body lies . . . But his soul goes marching on." But for the masses of Negroes outside of the fold who do but ill to rejoice in the downfall of Garvey, it were well to discover if there is anything in this wreck of hopes and enterprise that may well be salvaged.

Here is one thing. Set this down to the eternal credit of Marcus Garvey that before him there has not been a man who stirred into expression the consciousness of the Negro peoples to the extent that he succeeded in doing—extent both in degree and geographical area over which his ideas swept. Negroes all over the world have come to think of themselves as a Race—one in hope and destiny, as never before. Now this I count to be a thing of high value. This consciousness of race has been perhaps more vocal in America than anywhere else among Negroes, and was there before Garvey, you will say; but Garvey gave to it larger proportions and doubtless a height to which it had never risen. Under the spell of his propaganda it was amplified to an extent that gives justification to the name of his organization, Universal Negro Improvement Association. Thus the present state into which Garveyism has fallen offers a new challenge; that new challenge is for some new leader of equal breadth of sympathy, more practical intellect and of sober counsel to give himself to the task of the conservation of this race consciousness for the future good of this people. Much as this great spiritual product has come to be regarded as a thing greatly needed, it would be a pity to see it lost under the crash of Garvey's fall. Perhaps this leader can be found in the ranks of the UNIA. . . .

Finally, it does not do to treat Garveyism with detached indifference; it does not do to blame, decry nor vilify in any sweeping, indiscriminate manner, nor yet "without sneering, others teach to sneer." Many an outsider like myself may be brought sooner or later to admit: after all there was something to it!

Memoirs of a Captain
of the Black Star Line*

BY CAPTAIN HUGH MULZAC

THE EVENTS WHICH drew me to the Garvey move-
ment in 1920 were also attracting millions of other colored men
and women. Chief among them was the outrageous discrimination to which they had been subjected during the war, both in
the Army and in civilian jobs. Though Afro-Americans constituted only 10 percent of the United States population, they
contributed 13 percent of the soldiers. President Wilson had
promised that "with thousands of your young sons in the camps
and in France, out of this conflict you must expect nothing less
than the enjoyment of full citizenship rights—the same as are
enjoyed by any other citizens." However, he lifted not a finger to
halt the vicious murders and pogroms which raged through the
South when the troops returned home. The spectacle of black
bodies dangling from southern trees or burned on the stake was
commonplace—their bones and the chains that bound them
often distributed to the mob as souvenirs. Afraid that U.S.
colored troops would learn too much from French democracy,
the Army issued its notorious Order No. 40, forbidding colored
troops to associate with white women, and Wilson sent Dr.
Robert Russa Moton, Booker T. Washington's successor at

* From A Star to Steer By, by Captain Hugh Mulzac, International Publishers, New
York, 1963.

Tuskegee Institute, to France to warn the Negro GI's not to expect freedom and equality when they return home.

In the flight from lynch terror and in search of opportunity, colored men and women had begun moving North as early as the second decade of the century. Individuals, families, whole communities gathered their meager belongings and set out for Hartford, New York, Philadelphia, Pittsburgh, Cleveland and Youngstown, Chicago, St. Louis, and Kansas City. Between 1915 and 1920 more than a million colored people found their way to the segregated tenements of the North.

If they were looking for a Promised Land they were doomed to disappointment. In the North factory doors were usually closed to them and most unions rigidly enforced the color bar. They met social abuse, debasement, the thwarting of ambition, caricature, and the disparagement of their culture. The government in Washington did not hide its disdain for its colored citizens, and the administrations of Wilson, and Harding's after him, viewed America's racial crisis with deep-seated unconcern.

With the founding of the National Association for the Advancement of Colored People in 1909, and the National Urban League in 1911, many leading colored intellectuals and professional men and women joined with sympathetic whites to launch an attack upon the political, social and economic proscriptions under which the Negro labored. But against the solid wall of American race prejudice, North and South, progress was painfully slow. The Negro intellectuals enjoyed very limited support among the colored masses. Racial pride had not yet developed to today's political level. Too few colored citizens could go to school. Too few voted, too few were able to free themselves from the daily hardship of earning a living. The honest, dedicated leaders, with few victories to show, could neither attract a militant following nor convince their hosts, however brilliantly their pleas for full citizenship were set forth, that their appeals needed to be answered.

It was in this setting of bitter disillusionment following the War to Make the World Safe for Democracy that Marcus Garvey for a brief time occupied the center of the stage in the unfolding drama of the black man's struggle. Garvey had been a teacher in his native Jamaica, and in 1914, at the age of 47 had founded the

Universal Negro Improvement Association. In 1916 the Association's headquarters moved to New York, and aided by the heavy Negro immigration from Puerto Rico, Haiti, Cuba, and the British West Indies, by 1921 had 418 chapters with a membership alleged to total more than two million in the United States alone.

The objective of the UNIA was to redeem the continent of Africa for Africans "at home and abroad." That mighty "dark" land had been the chief prize of the Western Powers following World War I, and if its vast natural and human resources were enough to set white men at each other's throats, Garvey reasoned, why could it not also move black men to action?

Garvey envisioned a sort of supergovernment which would unite the peoples of African descent in Africa, the United States, Latin and South America, and other parts of the world and direct their destinies—a Black Zion. He sought to bring these millions of disenfranchised black folk under one discipline "just as the Pope and the Catholic Church control millions in every land."

Garvey encouraged colored business and manufacturing enterprises, which were stimulated and guided by African Factories Corporation. He sought to win followers and bind them together through a militant organ, the *Negro World*. He advocated increased trade between the United States, the West Indies, and Africa, under black men's control. The Black Star Steamship Corporation was to be the means to this end.

Garvey was an inspired organizer with a flair for promotion; and he launched his enterprises with the most powerful appeals to black African nationalism. "Help float more ships," read one brochure, "and write the name of the race across the commercial history of the world." "White men have invested in their own propositions and today make millions while crushing the souls of the black men. What white men have done colored men can do," read another. The appeal to race patriotism, the promise of an African renaissance under their own control, and the attraction of rapidly multiplying dollars drew colored folk to the Garvey movement as they had not been drawn by any other since the Civil War and Reconstruction.

When I emerged at the subway exit on 135th Street and Lenox Avenue many a curious passer-by on the crowded street stopped to stare at my master's uniform, for I had dressed for the occasion. But as I made my way toward the UNIA headquarters —or to within a block of it—I discovered a line more than 100 yards long waiting to enter 56 West 135 Street. There were jobseekers and supplicants, stock-owners-to-be and a few hero worshippers who simply wanted to tell Mr. Garvey how proud they were of him for what he was doing for the race. Since I had an appointment, I walked past and up the stairway leading from the first floor to the second, and the second to the third. There in the topmost office was a counter stacked high with bundles of bills of small denomination—the savings of thousands of earnest, hard-working folk who had come to buy five-dollar shares of stock in the Black Star Line.

Off this room was Mr. Garvey's office. As I entered he rose from his desk and gave my hand a fierce shake.

"Glad to see you, Mulzac," he said, giving me a piercing look from his deep black eyes set in a fleshy but well-formed face. "Sit down, sit down," he ordered and started to unfold his dream before I had even obeyed his command.

Garvey was a short, stocky man of pure African descent. As he expounded, taking off every few moments in a flight of oratory, his black eyes flashed and his quick fingers drove home each point. At one moment he was wildly castigating white men for their cruelty and hypocrisy, and the next extolling the greatness of ancient African civilizations and recounting the unlimited wealth of the "mother continent."

Throughout our half-hour meeting, during which he outlined the greatest "Back To Africa" movement the world has ever seen, I sat transfixed with awe.

"I am going to make you chief officer of the *Yarmouth*," he said, "but this is only the beginning. You are going to help man a vast fleet of speedy ships engaged in the African trade. Afro-Americans shall come into their own."

"Yes, yes," I assented, entranced by the enthusiasm of this man who was obsessed with what he considered to be the great idea. Before I left I had purchased five shares of stock in the Black Star Line and cherished a clear vision of being commander of a great fleet.

Firsthand contact with one of Mr. Garvey's enterprises a few days later began to undermine my more grandiose illusions. Although a great deal of publicity had attended the "launching" of the first ship in the proposed Black Star fleet, the *Yarmouth* was not a vessel to set a sailor's heart aflame. She had been built in Scotland 34 years earlier, and was undoubtedly a fine vessel at the time of her christening, a year before my birth. But she had been used as a coal boat during the war and by the time Garvey acquired her she was something less than seaworthy. Her boiler crowns were in need of repair, and her hull was practically worn out. She could not have been worth a penny over $25,000 when the Black Star Line acquired her for $165,000. To add insult to injury, though she was always referred to as the S.S. *Frederick Douglass* in Black Star publicity, the *Yarmouth* she was and the *Yarmouth* she was to remain till the day she was sold for scrap.

Her career under Black Star operation had not been one to inspire confidence, either. On her second voyage she had been chartered to take a cargo of whiskey to Cuba, just a few days before Prohibition took effect. Mr. Garvey and Smith Green, vice-president, had drawn up a contract without consulting the ship's master, Captain Charles Cockburn, and though the cargo was worth in excess of a million dollars they had chartered her for $11,000—a sum insufficient even to get her to her destination, let alone return a dividend for the poor stockholders.

Unfortunately the vessel had been loaded in such haste that in heavy weather off Cape May the cargo had shifted, giving her a heavy starboard list. Part of the cargo had to be jettisoned, and the *Yarmouth* limped back to New York under a Coast Guard escort.

It was at this point, while she laid at anchor off the Statue of Liberty, that I went aboard, January 23, 1920. Captain Cockburn, a tall colored man who had sailed the African coast for years and had a British master's license, quickly brought me up to date on the *Yarmouth*'s misadventures and his differences with Mr. Garvey.

Still under the influence of Garvey's rhetoric, however, I declined to take sides. My immediate task was clear—to make the *Yarmouth* as shipshape as possible so we could resume our voyage. Not only was she carrying a heavy list, but the ashes from her furnaces had been dumped under the lifeboats, the cargo was topsy-turvy, dunnage was all over the vessel, much of the gear was not in operating condition and her plates were covered with rust.

I called for a gang of stevedores and made the crew snap to. Several days later Mr. Garvey came aboard and was so pleased with the appearance of the vessel that he hinted broadly that he intended to discharge Captain Cockburn and make me master of the vessel. I was anxious not to be put into such an ambiguous position, first because while Mr. Garvey was the boss ashore, Cockburn was the master at sea, but more to the point, since the *Yarmouth* was under British registry, my American license would not qualify me to take command. Also, I was imbued with the spirit of the Garvey movement and had no selfish ambitions. But I was soon to learn it was naive to suppose one could remain neutral in any undertaking involving Marcus Garvey. Wherever he went, whatever he undertook, excitement and controversy followed in his wake.

On February 27 we raised anchor and with the ship in as good shape as she had been in years, we sailed in clear weather and arrived in Havana March 3.

The *Yarmouth*'s arrival had been heralded by Cuban agents of the UNIA and sympathizers flocked from all parts of the island toward the docks to greet the first ship they had ever seen entirely owned and operated by colored men. They came out in boats when we arrived, showering us with flowers and fruit, but we couldn't let them aboard. We lay at anchor for five days waiting for a berth, and I worked the crew overtime cleaning and painting the ship so we would make a good impression. Finally, however, we moved to dock and were overrun with visitors from dawn until sunset.

Since the charter party's overriding interest had been in getting the cargo of whiskey out of the United States waters no arrangements had been made for a Cuban consignee. Normally the owners of a vessel are protected against delays by a demurrage clause in the contract. But because there was no formal consignee and the operators had failed to insist upon the protection of a demurrage clause in their contract with the owners of the liquor, every delay meant that the vessel lost more money. To the five-day wait at anchorage was added a two-week delay when we tied up because of a longshore strike. Thus, instead of collecting the value of its cargo space for each day's delay, including Sundays, which would have amounted to several thousand dollars daily, we not only lost our expenses and possible profits, but had to pay the maintenance of the 35 passengers bound for Jamaica and other Caribbean ports.

Though Captain Cockburn and I were almost constantly occupied with such dispiriting details we found time to enjoy the welcome of the Cuban people, from President Menocal on down. There was a party nearly every night. President Menocal honored us with a banquet at the Presidential Palace and expressed his great pride in seeing colored men make their own opportunities in the field of commerce. Before the evening was over he promised the support of the Cuban government for the ventures of the Black Star Line.

Many other Cuban businessmen and landowners also pledged their cooperation. One particularly influential Senator, who owned several thousand acres of sugar cane, said that he had been shipping all of his sugar by United Fruit Company vessels but would readily switch to Black Star if we would promise him seaworthy vessels and good service. In scores of formal and informal gatherings the officers and men of the *Yarmouth* were feted, and at every one some Cuban businessman promised us his trade. Many bought stock in the Black Star Line.

Finally, after thirty-two days in port, we discharged our cargo in bond and with only passengers aboard left for Jamaica. Again hundreds greeted us at the dock. With no cargo to load or discharge we remained only long enough to repair the boilers and take on bunkers and stores. Then we left for Colon, the Panama Canal Zone, and the biggest reception of all. Literally thousands of Panamanians swarmed over the docks with baskets of fruit, vegetables, and other gifts. I was amazed that the *Yarmouth* had become such a symbol for the colored citizens of every land.

Back in the 1880's and '90's, when two French companies had begun construction of the canal, several thousand West Indians had emigrated to the Canal Zone and had remained when the United States took over the project in 1904. When Americans succeeded the French as builders, however, they brought with them not only great resources of capital and technological skill, but also that characteristic hallmark of the United States civilization—flagrant racial discrimination.

The "colored" and "white" signs which designate public facilities throughout the South had been placed in Panama by "gold" and "silver" signs. The West Indians resented having to buy provisions from the "silver" commissary while their white colleagues purchased from the "gold" store, an indignity that applied even in the post office! An even more grievous affront, however, was that the "gold" pay envelopes invariably contained more money than the "silver" ones, even when the workers performed the same duties, side by side.

From 1904 on the West Indians had fought this treatment bitterly, defeating an effort to institute segregation on street cars and in theaters. Resentment was at a fever pitch when we tied up in 1920, and thousands were anxious to leave the Canal Zone. We finally agreed to take 500 to Cuba, which was then importing workers for the sugar and banana plantations. The accommodations I hastily constructed in the holds were terribly inadequate, and before we were to discharge our passengers at Santiago de Cuba we encountered many difficulties, including shortages of fuel, food, and equipment, but the migrants preferred risking these hazards to remaining a moment longer in a country where they were not free.

En route to Cuba, again at the insistence of Mr. Garvey, we put in at Bocas del Toro, Almirante, and Puerto Limon, Costa Rica. In all three we were accorded the welcome of conquering heroes. At Bocas del Toro thousands of peasants came down from the hills on horses, donkeys, and in makeshift carts, and by a special train provided by the United Fruit Company, which, since it was going to lose its employees for the day anyway, declared a legal holiday. The crowd on the dock was so thick that when we threw our heaving lines ashore the peasants seized the hawsers as they came out of the water and literally breasted us alongside the dock. In the tumult that followed dancing broke out on the deck, great piles of fruit and flowers mounted on the hatch covers, and UNIA agents signed up hundreds of new members.

Yet it was clear to me that we had no reason at all to be in these ports. There was no cargo to be loaded or discharged. We

had 500 passengers aboard to be fed and cared for. The
Yarmouth was simply being used as a propaganda device for
recruiting new members to the Universal Negro Improvement
Association. It was a helluva way to run a steamship.

When our passengers were finally discharged at Santiago de
Cuba the *Yarmouth* sailed for Kingston, Jamaica, for a cargo of
coconuts—and to have the boiler crowns repaired again, by this
time a routine job. Just before leaving Kingston we received fresh
orders from Mr. Garvey: coconuts or no coconuts, we were to
depart at once for Boston!

The British government still maintained wartime restrictions
on food exports from Jamaica, and it was impossible to secure
sufficient provisions for the trip home. Captain Cockburn therefore found it expedient to stop at Nassau and then Norfolk for
stores and fuel, and in the latter port new orders awaited us: a
UNIA celebration was being held in Philadelphia, and we should
put in there for a few days en route to Boston! Orders are orders,
even when 700 tons of coconuts for New York are rotting in the
hold. We dutifully steamed for Philadelphia.

The UNIA celebrations in both ports were spectacular affairs,
with thousands joining the parades. Garvey made impassioned
speeches, whipping the people into frenzied support of the
association. Luckily he had also scheduled a celebration in New
York, so the *Yarmouth* could finally deliver its cargo. The crew of
the *Yarmouth* joined the parade, which at its peak started at
116th Street and Lenox Avenue, and stretched down to 100th
Street, over to Seventh Avenue, and back up to 145th Street! As
far as I am aware it was the greatest demonstration of colored
solidarity in American history, before or since.

The coconuts, of course, were rotten. The incensed owners
promptly filed a damage suit against the Black Star Line, bringing
into bold relief another instance of the company's inefficiency:
the contract did not contain any limit upon company responsibility. Further, no one in the office had any idea how to check
damage claims submitted by the owners of the cargo, placing the
company completely at the mercy of the shipper and forced to
depend upon *his* estimate of the value of the cargo instead of its
own.

While in New York Captain Cockburn's differences with Mr.

Garvey reached the boiling point, and the first break in the solid black phalanx occurred: a Captain Dixon, a white Canadian with English papers, was hired as master. For propaganda purposes Mr. Garvey announced that I had been appointed master of the *Phyllis Wheatley*, a ship that didn't even exist.

The second voyage of the *Yarmouth*, but for one unusual incident, was virtually a repetition of the first. We were chartered to load fertilizer for Cuba, and after discharging there sailed for Port-au-Prince, Haiti, and another admiring throng. From Port-au-Prince we headed for Kingston and a final commercial debacle.

A Japanese vessel, the *Kyo Maru*, had gone aground on the Serrana Banks, 500 miles south of Jamaica, and for two weeks had been waiting for a rescue vessel to relieve her of part of her cargo so she could float or be pulled off. No ship, however, had been willing to risk this operation. Captain Dixon and I both assured Mr. Wilson, agent for Black Star in Kingston, that we could do the job and advised him to charter us for $45,000. The owners of the cargo, and Lloyds of London, would willingly have paid this sum, for this was salvage cargo with a freight value from three to five times the value of ordinary cargo.

Mr. Wilson, however, was a building contractor who understood even less of the shipping business than Mr. Garvey. For reasons understood only to himself, he drew up a contract for $12,000, barely enough to cover our expenses to the Banks and back again. On the strength of this contract we sailed for the Serrana Banks with an empty hold and 32 passengers. We got alongside the *Kyo Maru* with little trouble and with the assistance of the Japanese crew loaded 2,000 tons of her cargo in two days. She was pulled off the rocks without incident, and we sailed for New York with but one stop—in Charleston, South Carolina, to refuel and repair the ever-defective boilers.

After two such profitless trips, I found myself losing confidence in Mr. Garvey and his business acumen. I decided to make a firm effort to put the line's operations, at least, on a sound commercial basis, and drew up a cargo plan containing detailed proposals for accepting and handling freight by weight and cubic measure, and many other provisions which would assure a profitable cargo-handling operation. I submitted this plan to Mr. O. M. Thompson, general manager of the company. He could not have been less interested. With UNIA membership booming he could not be bothered with such irksome details.

As it turned out, I was too late anyway—the *Yarmouth* had made her last voyage. Her boilers were beyond repair and in most other respects she was no longer a seaworthy vessel. For a number of years she was laid up at Staten Island, and the transaction which separated her from Black Star ownership was of a piece with all the other dealings which marked her brief career under Garvey's auspices. She was finally sold for scrap for $6,000 to cover her wharfage fees.

The Black Star Line operated two other ships, the *Kanawha* and the *Shadyside*, an excursion boat, and their careers as harbingers of the colored people's commercial resurgence were equally short. Although Garvey boasted that all three vessels were to be placed under American registry and rechristened the *Booker T. Washington*, the *Frederick Douglass* and the *Phyllis Wheatley* after colored American heroes—and these names were widely used in UNIA publicity—this was never done.

In April of 1922 the Black Star Line collapsed, and with it many of Garvey's other far-flung commercial enterprises. In the court proceedings which followed it turned out that the line had lost nearly $700,000 in the few brief years of its existence, nearly half of it on the *Yarmouth*. It was also revealed that Garvey had kept no books, issued no financial reports. He was found guilty and sentenced to serve a five-year term at Atlanta in 1925. He was pardoned in 1927, deported to Jamaica, and died in England in 1940, a broken and embittered man.

Throughout the United States, and indeed the world, the impact of the failure of the UNIA and the Black Star Line was tremendous. Everyone wanted to know *why*, and in a series of articles published in the Cleveland *Public Journal and Gazette*, in October of 1923, I tried to give the answers.

First, I wrote, the management was incompetent. Not one of the company's officers had the most rudimentary understanding of the shipping business. Mr. Garvey was a great organizer but a poor businessman. Mr. Jeremiah Certain, the second vice-president, was a cigar maker. The executive positions in the company were staffed by opportunists and relatives from all walks of life except the shipping industry. Ocean commerce, especially in the '20's, was one of the most highly rationalized industries in the world. Not only was there a surplus of war-built vessels, and many large and efficiently-run companies engaged in cargo trade, but then as now there was a vast fleet of highly competitive tramp steamers sailing under British, Greek, and other registries fighting for the diminishing cargoes of the postwar world. To compete with such companies effectively meant having good ships, sound capital backing, an extensive network of good agents, and above all, efficient management.

More important, however, the use to which the worthless Black Star ships were put represented the triumph of propaganda over business. The *Yarmouth* lost hundreds of thousands of dollars putting into ports where no cargo awaited, and in being chartered below her worth.

Thus the great and bold dream of colored resurgence ended in catastrophe. For their hard-won dollars scores of thousands of humble black men and women received in dividends only a transitory inflation of their racial pride.

Nor was there anything wrong in that; in fact, it was to be encouraged among a folk so long depreciated. But when the bubble burst as it had to, upon the jagged rocks of incompetence and venality, the people were left with their dreams of a bright future blighted. They had no steamship line, no newspaper, no successful challenge to white domination, but had instead only monetary losses and, more serious; a deep loss of faith in their own capacities.

What had begun as a great adventure for me and hundreds of thousands of others ended in tragedy and disillusionment. It was difficult to compute the suffering that resulted from this idealism. Thousands had mortgaged their homes to buy Black Star stock, others had sold their furniture and possessions to buy passage to Africa on ships that would never leave port. One man in Cuba sold his profitable lumber business and came to New York to book passage. Dollars evaporated with the dreams, personal ambitions with the hopes and aspirations of a whole people. For a few brief years Marcus Garvey fired the torch that lighted the Negro night, bringing dreams of glory and equality. Just as quickly the torch flickered and was out, leaving us in darkness as before; poorer, sadder, and perhaps wiser . . . who knows?

Why the Black
Star Line Failed*

The Black Star Line Steamship Corporation that I organized in 1919, under the charter from the State of Delaware, was the great attraction that brought to the Universal Negro Improvement Association millions of supporters. . . .

Having traveled extensively throughout the world and seriously studying the economical, commercial and industrial needs of our people, I found out the quickest and easiest way to reach them was by steamship communication. So immediately after I succeeded in forming the Universal Negro Improvement Association in America, I launched the idea of floating ships under the direction of Negroes. . . . I thought if we could launch our ships and have our own Black captains and officers, our race, too, would be respected in the mercantile and commercial world, thereby adding appreciative dignity to our downtrodden people.

With this aim in view, I circulated the whole world for support of the Black Star Line. My appeal was heard and responded to immediately in such places as Cuba, Panama and Costa Rica and other Central American republics. Most of the people who responded were West Indians who could appreciate the value of steamship communication. The call to distant Africa was answered also. In the space of two or three months the corporation

---

* From a weekly series published in the Pittsburgh *Courier*, February 22, 1930, to May 31, 1931.

of the Black Star Line was able to purchase its first ship, the S.S. *Yarmouth*, which was rechristened the S.S. *Frederick Douglass*. . . . It was not until after the first ship was launched in New York that the American Negroes got to know what it was all about and subscribed speedily their quota to help purchase other ships. . . .

My great difficulties in leading the Universal Negro Improvement Association and directing the affairs of the Black Star Line came really through the invisible influences that were operating against me all over the world, caused through the secret propaganda of other Negroes against me in impressing prominent members of the white race and their government that I was a bad man. . . .

First my enemies in New York, namely, Samuel Duncan, Richard Warner, Edgar Gray, and Adolphus Domingo, did everything to influence the district attorney's office of New York to prevent me carrying out the idea of launching ships for the Negro race. Mr. Edwin P. Kilroe was then assistant district attorney. He on several occasions threatened me with imprisonment if I continued in the idea. . . .

When the organization of the Universal Negro Improvement Association was started in New York I had altercations with Samuel Duncan, whom I had to depose from the position of president of the first New York organization. This man's revenge ran so far that he wrote confidential letters to all the British colonial and imperial governments, warning them that . . . "Marcus Garvey, a dangerous Negro agitator," who desired to stir up hatred between the colored and white people, had now made a serious attempt to get in touch with the colored people of the world through the launching of steamships, and that it would be wise for all good governments to undertake to prevent the entry of the ships of the Black Star Line into the ports of their countries.

. . . Associated with Duncan in this was Adolphus Domingo, already referred to. Domingo was first associated with me as editor of the *Negro World*. We were friends from boyhood, but because of my success he became jealous of me and became a Communist. While editing my paper he attempted to impress his Communistic views upon the readers and myself, even though he knew we had no inclinations toward Communism; we disagreed on policy and he left the paper. . . . He linked up with other Communists like Cyril Briggs, who was running a magazine called *The Crusader* and Chandler Owen, another red Socialist. They kept up a continuous tirade against me; in fact Domingo and others did everything to sabotage the Black Star Line. They were never satisfied until the venture went under.

. . . As a retort to Kilroe, and all those who were endeavoring to intimidate me, I stated that "we would launch our ships even if we had to do so in an ocean of blood." This statement somewhat scared those who were trying to intimidate us. . . .

On a day in October 1919, we launched in the New York harbor the first boat of the line. That was a day never to be forgotten. It was a Sunday. Hundreds of thousands of people gathered at the foot of the 125th Street pier at the North River to see the boat sail under the Black captain. People also gathered in thousands on Riverside Drive to witness the wonderful spectacle. . . .

The fact that Negroes had launched a ship in New York became a world sensation and the news was flashed from one center of our civilization to the next. Thousands of letters of inquiry came from all parts of the world. The result of [all this] tended to create more branches of the Universal Negro Improvement Association.

There is no doubt that the Negro is his own greatest enemy. He is jealous of himself, envious and covetous. This accounts for most of our failure in business and in other things. This I know was responsible for the collapse of the Black Star Line, in addition to the dishonesty of the race to itself.

In calling our people dishonest to ourselves I do not mean to infer that the white or other races are not dishonest; but they are dishonest with a method or a system. The Negro has no method or system in his dishonesty. . . . The Negro should, like the Jews, adopt a method of dealing with himself. If he is to steal, he should, like the Jews, steal from others but not from himself.

. . . For one year I unreservedly gave over my entire self to talking for the Black Star Line, so as to influence the people in buying stock—a penny's worth of which I never sold myself, and a dollar of which money I never handled. . . . All the money for the Black Star Line went through the New York office, from which office I was generally absent nine months out of the year. The handling of the money took place generally when I was 2,000 or 3,000 miles away. I had, therefore, to rely on the honesty of the other officers, such as the secretary, the treasurer, and the vice-president. They betrayed me and destroyed the hopes I had in view, as made manifest by the fact that with such a splendid start—[we had accumulated] nearly $750,000 in ten months—the Black Star Line is nowhere today.

. . . Unfortunately, with the Negro growing up with the disposition for playing dishonest with himself, hence, the great difficulty to promote successful Negro enterprises on a large scale.

When I started the Black Star Line I had the greatest confidence in every Negro first. I believed every Negro felt like I did [and was] a great enthusiast to see the race go forward in success. . . . Therefore, in selecting directors and officers of the Black Star Line, I did so with an open mind to everybody. I had Americans, West Indians, South Americans: I gave everybody a chance, and the story is that very nearly every one that I placed in responsible position fleeced the Black Star Line.

The fellow that I made secretary . . . (a clever, well-trained accountant from British Guiana, who could not be eclipsed for competency anywhere), after three months was unable to account for 50,000 shares of the stock of the Black Star Line. He was one of the original members of the New York division of the Universal Negro Improvement Association. It was during the war period, and he could earn much more money at Trenton, New Jersey, working in ammunition factories than he could in New York. He left New York and went to Trenton. When the Black Star Line was formed and I was looking for men of ability, I thought of him. I offered him a position. . . . He accepted the offer, but stated to me that he had not enough money to pay the railroad fare to New York. I sent him the money. The fellow, through his poor financial condition, would be rated just as an ordinary working man with about three or four suits of clothes. He came to New York. . . . [and] was inducted into office as secretary of the corporation.

We started to sell stock and the people bought it with a tremendous go. Thus, this man, earning $50 a week, started to handle thousands of dollars daily. He was the man who received all the cash. Sometimes $15,000 would pass through the mails . . . and sometimes he would take over the counter at the office in New York and at Liberty Hall $10,000 a day. . . . About one month after he was with us I noticed a great change in his personality; he had become a fashionable sport. He used to change his suits almost twice a day. At the end of the second month he came to me and said, "Mr. Garvey, aren't you going to buy an automobile?" I replied: "Buy an automobile? For what, and with what?" I was then getting $50 a week also. I said: "I can't afford to buy an automobile." He said: "Chief, I would like to buy a knockabout, but I was watching you." I became suspicious of the man, and after three months when an inventory was made, we found that 50,000 shares could not be accounted for.

There is another fellow whom I may bring out pointedly, whom I gave the position of passage and traffic superintendent. This man, although possessing very fine qualifications like the secretary, couldn't do better than work in a factory. It was out of a factory that I took him. He was in ordinary circumstances when he came to us, his clothes were not of the best, but after two months this Negro was the best-dressed man in Harlem, a fashion plate. He had all the women around and to my surprise after a while, he also had under his influence my first wife.

. . . The interested or inquiring person may ask: "How is it your secretary was not able to account for 50,000 shares and your treasurer and other officials were able to do so many things to the failure of the Black Star Line; did you not keep proper books?" The answer is: "Yes." In the history of the Black Star Line I had two of the best firms of chartered accountants in New York to open and start the sets of books to be used by the corporation and to audit them. I had competent men to keep the books in keeping with the instructions and advice of the accountants. But . . . they would not make the regular and proper entries . . . [and] by the end of the month they had forgotten a dozen times. Whenever I called in an outside party to give me expert information the rest of the fellows in the inside would organize themselves against the person getting the kind of information [he needed]. It was always a case of Mr. So and So has been using it and it can't be found, or some such excuse. Whenever anyone suspected that an investigation was going to be made by me that person would find an excuse to leave the position, another one would take charge and then whatever the wrong it was shifted to some other person or persons not to be identified.

If Jesus was the accountant or president of the Black Star Line he could not have done better than I or the accountant did, because the men had the disposition to steal and hide. They did everything to embarrass an honest investigation, and because I was president of such a corporation I had to bear the blunt.

. . . In the early part of January [of 1920] I was in Canada on my honeymoon, having been married on December 25, 1919. Whilst [I was away] several scheming white business sharpers from Wall Street, who had, during my presence in New York, tried to involve me and the Black Star Line in shady transactions . . . took advantage of my absence in striking up some arrangement with the secretary and the treasurer of the company—who like most Negroes felt that they had as much right as their superior officers to negotiate and handle vital business matters. . . . The result was that our first ship, the S.S. *Frederick Douglass*, was chartered to a company of irresponsible brokers for the removal of . . . a cargo of whiskey and other spiritous liquors, under prohibition by the 17th of the month. According to the new prohibition law that was to come into effect all spiritous liquor had to be disposed of in a limited time in the United States or be confiscated.

. . . I knew nothing about the contract when it was negotiated, no one mentioned anything to me about it, not until it was discovered that the company was to receive $7,000 for removing the cargo that was valued at $5,000,000, at the tremendous risk of being responsible for the cargo to its full value and with the possibility of losing our ship if the ship did not sail an hour before prohibition law went into effect. . . . On my arrival in New York . . . there was only one thing for me to do, that was to see that the contract was immediately executed so as to avoid other liabilities. I called upon the captain, therefore, to make preparations for the ship to sail with the cargo. . . . It turned out that under the direction of the captain $11,000 had to be spent for repairs. I was therefore called upon to spend $11,000 for repairs in order to have the ship sail with the cargo valued at $5,000,000 on which the company was collecting only $7,000 as freight, all because of the disobedience of two officers of the company, who took advantage of my absence in dealing with men I had already turned down.

After this my suspicions in all things were aroused and I made certain investigations, and found out that the Black Star Line and I as its president had often been called upon to pay repair bills for the ships running into the thousands, on which certain officers of the ships collected from 20 to 30 percent, from the engineers, on repairs that were called upon to be done that were not necessary, unless to supply the officers with their percentages. This kind of a fraud was also practiced in buying supplies for the ships, when ship chandlers were given orders running into thousands of dollars, out of which they had to pay the officers of the company on the ships responsible between 15 to 35 percent commission. . . . I determined to bring the employment of the captain and secretary to an end. . . . But in the separation of the captain and the secretary from the Black Star Line a loss was left behind of hundreds of thousands of dollars.

After having gotten rid of one group, I thought I would have been safe in the hands of another. This Barbadian, whom I made first vice-president and general manager of the Black Star Line came to me with a sad story . . . that he wanted me to give him a chance, which I was glad to do. There was no doubt about this man's qualifications; if he were a white man and honest he could have made his fortune for his company and himself in Wall Street. . . . After the management was passed over to this man, who had so much business experience, I had to take my circuit on the road in helping to improve my organizations as usual. This man . . . went about and made connections in the shipping and commercial areas which turned out to be connections with the very white men who were desirous of destroying the Black Star Line. At this time we had under repairs at the Morse dock in Brooklyn the S.S. *Antonio Maceo*, a yacht that we had bought from the interests of H. H. Rogers, which we were reconditioning for passenger service between Central America and the West

Indies. I was to have sailed on this boat on the trip contemplated to Central America and the West Indies. It happened, however, that whilst I made an arrangement with Morse to repair the boat for $15,000 and left for a trip to California and the West, Morse found out that his profit would not have been enough at $15,000, so during my absence he entered into an agreement with the vice-president . . . which gave Morse the option to violate the first agreement I made not only concerning the boat, but the specified time and for $15,000, which he changed to an indefinite time and unlimited amount for the repairs.

My indictment for using the United States mails to defraud occurred as follows: First I was the only person indicted, in that I was the only person wanted. I was arrested around 4 o'clock in the afternoon, and between my being taken from my home to the U.S. Commissioner's office for bail, the secretary handed over the books [to the district attorney's office] . . . without my instructions or any information to me. This made me feel that there was a conspiracy to "get me alone." When the matter was thoroughly gone into, it probably was discovered that the attempt to "get me alone" was too glaring, in that I was only president of the corporation and there were others who took as prominent part, if not more, than myself, in the daily routine of the corporation's business. So several months after there was another indictment which included the vice-president, the secretary, the treasurer, with myself. Through private information I knew, however, that the other men were only brought in to take off the suspicion of wanting to "get me singularly."

During the time of indictment, I had occasion also to have the secretary of the Black Star Line [who was the auditor-general of the UNIA] arrested for forgery and embezzlement. . . . The Chancellor of the Universal Negro Improvement Association one day made up his lodgement of the Association's funds for the bank. He had the money—checks and American greenbacks resting on the sideboard of his desk. The auditor-general . . . came down from his office to the chancellor's office and engaged him in a conversation [then] . . . slipped in among the lodgement money a forged check for $50, made out in the name of . . . [James Moore] who resided in Kansas and was formerly an official of the Kansas division of the Universal Negro Improvement Association, and a barber well known to me. The auditor-general took out $50 of American greenbacks. . . .

Immediately after this . . . I entered the chancellor's office just by curiosity to find out what the amount of lodgement for that day was. . . . The chancellor immediately turned to the amount he had for lodgement and started to check over. I watched carefully and I saw a peculiar looking check. I asked him where he got it from. He said he could not remember seeing it before. I [saw that] . . . the signature on the check was that of James Moore, but the writing was that of the secretary of the Black Star Line. . . . I took the check from the chancellor; [half an hour later] I called down the stenographer from the secretary's office to inquire where the secretary was. The young lady said he was out for about a half hour. I immediately ordered his office closed and . . . nailed up the door.

It was evident that the news of my discovery got to him, because he kept away all day. I remained in my office up to 6 o'clock that afternoon. . . . As I was about to leave, he came into the building . . . and confessed. . . . He beseeched me to give him another hearing before I took steps to prosecute. I promised him I would. . . . The next morning . . . he offered to give up the securities he had in the organization and immediately vacate his position. I told him I could not accept that because it was a bad example. I therefore summoned him before the magistrate at the Highgate court, where he was examined and held for the grand jury. He was indicted and tried in the Petty Session Court and found guilty and was to be sentenced at a later hearing. . . . Later . . . the combination of my enemies became his protectors, and at the second hearing he was acquitted. . . .

This man . . . had under his control all the books of the corporation for two years. He had been carrying on that kind of practice as explained above with no one to check him. . . .

What the secretary did in his way is an indication of what the vice-president did in his way. So when I stood indicted along with these men I found myself in the company of enemies who were working with my outside enemies to defeat me and send me to prison, because I stood in their way to making easy fortunes.

At the trial I was represented by an array of counsel, but after the first day's hearing I discovered that there was an arrangement whereby I was to be found guilty and disposed of as the court felt, after my attorney made the plea for mercy to further humiliate me. I detected that I would have been sent to prison on the twenty-six counts on which I was to be tried, each of which carried five years imprisonment and a fine of $1,000. . . . I found out that the counsel had arranged with the district attorney to give him two weeks for the prosecution and to take one week for me in my defense, so as to allow the judges and others to go on their vacations. I immediately lost faith in my counsel and urged him to retire from the case which I tried myself. . . .

The trial took five and one-half weeks, and every day of it was a terrible fight between myself and the district attorney, one Mr. Maxwell Mattock. As I went through the trial I saw where it was almost an impossibility for me to escape the traps that were laid for me in which the press, rival organizations, personal enemies, big business; foreign and other governments were interested to the point of seeing me convicted. . . . No one, not even the ablest attorney could have fought for me as I fought for myself . . . because he would be risking the friendship and good will of the powerful influences that were aligned against me. . . .

The evidence on which I was convicted is told as follows: Benny Dancy, who worked at the Pennsylvania Railroad in the postal department, testified that he received a letter from the Black Star Line. He could not tell what was contained in the letter nor could he identify the letter, [only] the empty envelope with his name typed on it which bore the rubber stamp to the Black Star Line. He testified having received the envelope through the mail. . . . It isn't necessary to go into the merits of the evidence here, but . . . it could have been easy for my enemies to have the rubber stamp of the Black Star Line affixed to the envelope and posted to the man.

The principle witness to state that fact that letters were mailed from the office of the Black Star Line to different places and parties was a boy who I never saw . . . who could not even remember the persons employed by the Black Star Line during the time he was supposed to be employed there. . . . He was unable to tell where the general post office of Harlem was . . . He could not even tell who used to pay him during the time he was supposed to be working with the Black Star Line. Nevertheless, with all that was said and done, I was convicted on one count [out of the original twenty-six], the penalty a sentence of five years or a fine of $1,000 or both, the passing of sentence resting with the discretion of the judge. . . . The judge, however, sentenced me to five years, with a fine of $1,000 and cost of the trial. He also denied me the right to bail, pending appeal to the District Court of Appeals. I was therefore confined in the Tombs Prison for several months, awaiting the decision of the Appellate Court. It was only through the good office of President Harding that I was allowed out on bail; when the question of bail came up the trial judge . . . insisted on a bond of $50,000, but President Harding prevailed with the district attorney, Colonel Haywood, and I was released on a bond of $1,500.

It was rumored during my conviction and pending appeal before the District Court of Appeal that if I would keep quiet the appeal would not be heard, or would be decided in my favor . . . There was no doubt that several governments of Europe were feeling the effects of the new spirit of racial consciousness that had come over the Negro people of the world. Big commercial houses in America were afraid of the result of my encouraging Negroes to develop their own business enterprises and trading among themselves. . . . The big shipping companies were also determined to keep the Negro off the high seas. When I was told of what would happen if I kept quiet, I became more determined to prosecute the idea that was uppermost in my mind, so I launched out immediately to organize a new line of steamships—the Black Cross Navigation and Trading Company.

The forces fighting me heard about it and launched more propaganda against me. But not two months after my release from the Tombs, the people rallied around me and we purchased our then biggest ship, the S.S. *General Goethals*—afterwards rechristened the S.S. *Booker T. Washington*—from the Panama Railroad Company in A-1 condition. When the boat was acquired the sentiment of my enemies was stirred to force the decision of the District Court of Appeal, and so the . . . very day that the S.S. *General Goethals* was to sail from Norfolk, Virginia, to the West Indies to engage in the banana business and the conveyance of general freight, the decision was given against me in the appeal. Two days after I had to surrender for imprisonment.

Speech before Incarceration in The Tombs Prison, June 17, 1923

Now, UNDERSTAND ME well, Marcus Garvey has entered the fight for the emancipation of race; Marcus Garvey has entered the fight for the redemption of a country. From the graves of millions of my forebears at this hour I hear the cry, and I am going to answer it even though hell is cut loose before Marcus Garvey. From the silent graves of millions who went down to make me what I am, I shall make for their memory, this fight that shall leave a glaring page in the history of man.

I did not bring myself here; they brought me from my silent repose in Africa 300 years ago, and this is only the first Marcus Garvey. They have thought that they could for 300 years brutalize a race. They have thought that they could for 300 years steep the soul of a race in blood and darkness and let it go at that. They make a terrible mistake. Marcus Garvey shall revenge the blood of his sires. So don't be afraid of Marcus Garvey. When Marcus Garvey goes to jail the world of Negroes will know. They have come at the wrong time.

I repeat that if they think they can stamp out the souls of 400,000,000 black men, they make a tremendous and terrible mistake. We are no longer dogs; we are no longer peons; we are no longer serfs—we are men. Tell us about fear; we were not born with fear. Intimidation does not drive fear into the soul of

Marcus Garvey. There is no fear, but the fear of God. Man cannot drive fear into the heart of man, because man is but the equal of man. The world is crazy and foolish if they think that they can destroy the principles, the ideals of the Universal Negro Improvement Association.

Letter to Guy M. Walker

March 10, 1924

My dear Mr. Walker:

I am charged with the duty and responsibility of writing to you on a subject which I feel that you are interested in, because of your high and elevated position in the nation, and because of your humanitarianism which is felt to be beyond question. The subject is that of the Negro problem as it confronts us, not only in America, but in the world.

There is a deep and earnest desire on the part of some of the world's most forward looking statesmen and humanitarians, to make an immediate effort for the settlement of the perplexing and grievous question of race. We in America should not delay the settlement of this great question, because it cannot settle itself.

The Universal Negro Improvement Association, an organization of six million scattered members of which I am President-General, is working for a solution of the problem through the founding and establishing in Africa of a nation for Negroes, where the race will be given the fullest opportunity to develop itself, such as we may not expect in countries where we form but a minority in a majority Government of other races.

There is no doubt that the twentieth-century Negro in America is different from the Negro of the last century. Today he is forward looking and ambitious. He is the product of our best schools, colleges and universities. With his training, he is not prepared to be satisfied as a secondary consideration in the social, economic and political life of the nation. By his ambition, he is aspiring to the highest in political office and industrial and social positions. This, under the Constitution, cannot be reasonably denied him, but in the midst of a majority race that is not inclined to allow the minority to enjoy the benefits of the best that the nation affords, we have the great problem that must be solved.

It is not the humanitarians like you, of the white race, that the Negro fears, nor those who are broad-minded enough to consider the rights of man regardless of color, but it is the great mass that does not think in the higher terms of humanity, but who are guided purely and simply by their economic, social and political relationship to others.

We of the Universal Negro Improvement Association, after having taken into consideration the impossibility of the liberal and humanitarian few to curb successfully the passion of the great mass, are endeavoring to so create sentiment among the fifteen million Negroes of America and other parts of the world as to lead them to see that the only and best solution for the race problem, is for us to have a nation of our own in Africa, whereby we would not be regarded in countries like America as competitors of the white race for the common positions in politics, industry and society, but that we would be regarded as a people striving in our own country to present to the world a civilization and culture of our own. Knowing that you must have some feeling on a question like this led the Universal Negro Improvement Association to direct me to write you, asking for a frank and open opinion of our program. The opinion that you give will be kept private if you so desire. Your wishes on this matter shall be respected in every particular.

The following symposium is therefore submitted to you most respectfully, and we are asking that you be good enough to answer each question in conjunction with this communication, so that we may be able to judge how much sympathy there is among the leaders of the white race in this country, as touching the effort we are making for the solution of the vexed problem of race in America, which is very annoying.

SYMPOSIUM:

1. Do you believe the Negro to be a human being?

2. Do you believe the Negro entitled to all the rights of humanity?

3. Do you believe that the Negro should be taught not to aspire to be the best imitation of the white man, but the best product of himself?

4. Do you believe that the Negro should be encouraged to develop a society of his own, that is for social intercourse and marrying within his own race?

5. Do you believe that the Negro should be taught not to aspire to the highest political positions in Governments of the white race, but to such positions among his own race in a Government of his own?

6. Do you believe that the Negro should have a Government of his own in Africa?

7. Would you help morally or otherwise to bring about such a possibility?

8. Do you believe that the Negro should be encouraged to aspire to the highest industrial and commercial positions in the countries of the white man in competition with him and to his exclusion?

9. Do you believe that the Negro should be encouraged to create positions of his own in industry and commerce in a country of his own with the privilege of trading with the other races of the world?

10. Do you believe that the Negro should be encouraged to regard and respect the rights of all other races in the same manner as other races would respect the rights of the Negro?

11. Should five or six million or any large number of Negroes in the United States of America desire a repatriation to Africa for the peaceful building up of a country of their own, or for the

settlement of such countries as are established among Negroes without any serious handicap to the industries of America, would you assist in this direction?

It is felt that you will give deep consideration to this communication and receive it in the spirit in which it is written—that of a desire to settle amicably a vexed question.

I am forwarding you along with this letter three pamphlets which we ask that you read without prejudice, but with a feeling of broad-mindedness, and a desire to help settle a troublesome problem that confronts your race.

Knowing your broadness of vision, and your liberality of soul leads me to feel that you will judge the subject matter of the pamphlets with fairness to my race that has suffered in slavery for two hundred and fifty years, and still confronted with obstacles to be sympathetically overcome.

With very best wishes for your health and success, and hoping for an immediate reply,

I have the honor to be

Your humble and obedient servant,
MARCUS GARVEY

African Fundamentalism*

**A RACIAL HIERARCHY AND EMPIRE FOR NEGROES
NEGRO'S FAITH MUST BE CONFIDENCE IN SELF
HIS CREED: ONE GOD, ONE AIM, ONE DESTINY**

The time has come for the Negro to forget and cast behind
him his hero worship and adoration of other races, and to start
out immediately to create and emulate heroes of his own. We
must canonize our own saints, create our own martyrs, and
elevate to positions of fame and honor black men and women
who have made their distinct contributions to our racial history.
Sojourner Truth is worthy of the place of sainthood alongside of
Joan of Arc: Crispus Attucks and George William Gordon are
entitled to the halo of martyrdom with no less glory than that of
the martyrs of any other race. Toussaint L'Ouverture's brilliancy
as a soldier and statesman outshone that of a Cromwell,
Napoleon and Washington; hence, he is entitled to the highest
place as a hero among men. Africa has produced countless
numbers of men and women, in war and in peace, whose luster
and bravery outshine that of any other people. Then why not see
good and perfection in ourselves? We must inspire a literature
and promulgate a doctrine of our own without any apologies to

* Published by UNIA, copyright 1925.

the powers that be. The right is ours and God's. Let contrary sentiment and cross opinions go to the winds. Opposition to race independence is the weapon of the enemy to defeat the hopes of an unfortunate people. We are entitled to our own opinions and not obligated to or bound by the opinions of others.

A PEEP AT THE PAST

If others laugh at you, return the laughter to them; if they mimic you, return the compliment with equal force. They have no more right to dishonor, disrespect and disregard your feeling and manhood than you have in dealing with them. Honor them when they honor you, disrespect and disregard them when they vilely treat you. Their arrogance is but skin deep and an assumption that has no foundation in morals or in law. They have sprung from the same family tree of obscurity as we have; their history is as rude in its primitiveness as ours; their ancestors ran wild and naked, lived in caves and in branches of trees, like monkeys, as ours; they made human sacrifices, ate the flesh of their own dead and the raw meat of the wild beast for centuries even as they accuse us of doing; their cannibalism was more prolonged than ours; when we were embracing the arts and sciences on the banks of the Nile their ancestors were still drinking human blood and eating out of the skulls of their conquered dead; when our civilization had reached the noonday of progress they were still running naked and sleeping in holes and caves with rats, bats and other insects and animals. After we had already fathomed the mystery of the stars and reduced the heavenly constellations to minute and regular calculus they were still backwoodsmen, living in ignorance and blatant darkness.

WHY BE DISCOURAGED?

The world today is indebted to us for the benefits of civilization. They stole our arts and sciences from Africa. Then why should we be ashamed of ourselves? Their *modern improvements* are but *duplicates* of a grander civilization that we reflected thousands of years ago, without the advantage of what is buried and still hidden, to be resurrected and reintroduced by the intelligence of our generation and our posterity. Why should we be discouraged because somebody laughs at us today? Who can tell what tomorrow will bring forth? Did they not laugh at Moses, Christ and Mohammed? Was there not a Carthage, Greece and Rome? We see and have changes every day, so pray, work, be steadfast and be not dismayed.

NOTHING MUST KILL THE EMPIRE URGE

As the Jew is held together by his *religion*, the white races by the assumption and the unwritten law of superiority, and the Mongolian by the precious tie of blood, so likewise the Negro must be united in one *grand racial hierarchy*. Our union must know no *clime*, *boundary* or *nationality*. Like the great Church of Rome, Negroes the world over must practice one faith, that of Confidence in themselves, with One God! One Aim! One Destiny! Let no religious scruples, no political machination divide us, but let us hold together under all climes and in every country, making among ourselves a Racial Empire upon which "the sun shall never set."

ALLEGIANCE TO SELF FIRST

Let no voice but your own speak to you from the depths. Let no influence but your own rouse you in time of peace and time of war; hear all, but attend only to that which concerns you. Your allegiance shall be to your God, then to your family, race and country. Remember always that the Jew in his political and economic urge is always first a Jew; the white man is first a white man under all circumstances, and you can do no less than being first and always a Negro, and then all else will take care of itself. Let no one innoculate you with evil doctrines to suit their own conveniences. There is no humanity before that which starts with yourself. "Charity begins at home." First, to thyself be true, and "thou canst not then be false to any man."

WE ARE ARBITERS OF OUR OWN DESTINY

God and Nature first made us what we are, and then out of our own created genius we make ourselves what we want to be. Follow always that great law. Let the sky and God be our limit and Eternity our measurement. There is no height to which we cannot climb by using the active intelligence of our own minds. Mind creates, and as much as we desire in Nature we can have through the creation of our own minds. Being at present the scientifically weaker race, you shall treat others only as they treat you; but in your homes and everywhere possible you must teach the higher development of science to your children; and be sure to develop a race of scientists par excellence, for in science and religion lies our only hope to withstand the evil designs of modern materialism. Never forget your God. Remember, we live, work and pray for the establishing of a great and binding racial hierarchy, the founding of a racial empire whose only natural, spiritual and political limits shall be God and "Africa, at home and abroad."

Part Three

The Movement in Transition, 1925-1927

Commentary

BY JOHN HENRIK CLARKE

THE CONVICTION OF Marcus Garvey and the fragmenting of his great movement during his imprisonment at Atlanta, Georgia, were events of great sadness in Black America. It was the end of a brief era in which Marcus Garvey, would instill in a people the gift of dreaming that would make them visualize again being a whole people ruling nations. Many critics of Marcus Garvey, including W. E. B. Du Bois, began to have second and somewhat more reasonable thoughts about him after he was behind prison bars. They began to deplore the internal strife that was pulling apart what so recently had been the largest Black movement in America. Factions within the UNIA began to bid for power, and this power struggle destroyed the effectiveness of this orgnization. The greatest losers were the ordinary Black people who had found a home within the movement, who had been a part of something that had hope and possibly a future for them, and for their children.

Garvey's impact was still felt from behind prison bars. The period referred to as the Harlem Renaissance was midway in its ten-year existence. Garvey had brought about a political awareness that was influencing this literary awareness. His imprisonment and deportation did not break his spirit; he proceeded to Jamaica, through Panama, where he was hailed as a hero who had not failed his people but who had been betrayed by the people he trusted. Garvey's conduct on this occasion was characteristic. He rarely ever had a defeatist attitude. In Jamaica he attempted to pick up the pieces of his organization and continue his work.

There is serious doubt about whether Dr. W. E. B. Du Bois had enough influence alone to persuade the Liberian Government to reverse its decision on permitting the members of the UNIA to establish a settlement. The important point here is that the settlement dream and the steamship line were being lost before Marcus Garvey was sent to jail. While in jail, his enemies made every effort to wreck the rest of these plans. It should be remembered that in spite of the charge that can be made against Dr. Du Bois for not understanding the objective of the UNIA and its leader, Marcus Garvey, there were other adversaries probably more dangerous. These were the people who pretended to believe in Marcus Garvey, and who functioned within the framework of the UNIA. During the time Marcus Garvey was in jail and in the years immediately following his release, this motley crew of self-seeking pretenders destroyed the national and international structure of the UNIA.

In Garvey's absence, Mrs. Amy Jacques Garvey and a few loyal followers of the Movement held the organization together. At a UNIA Convention that was held in 1927, a petition was sent to President Calvin Coolidge requesting clemency for Marcus Garvey. He was released later that year but was not permitted to return to the UNIA headquarters in Harlem. He was put on a ship at New Orleans and deported to his home country—Jamaica.

After Garvey—What?*

BY ROBERT MINOR

AT CARTERET, NEW JERSEY, a few days ago, a body of armed men drove the entire Negro population from the town, burned a Negro church and generally conducted an organized reign of terror of the sort which America calls a race riot and which the old Russia of the now-dead czar called a pogrom.

In the state of Kentucky there has been during the past few weeks a series of lynchings of new character—lynchings in which the state government participated, no longer as a "silent partner" merely permitting unofficial murder, but this time as an open, active leader in official murder without trial: In Kentucky courts of law Negroes accused of crime are being given "eighteen minute trials"—and the latest was a "ten-minute trial"—with a mob outside the courtroom, twelve actual members of the mob in the jury box, a virtual member of the mob as judge, usually a "confession" extorted by torture in a back room before the "trial," no defense whatever for the Negro victim (with the lack of defense concealed behind the presence of so-called attorneys for the victim), and a verdict of hanging delivered to the cheering mob from ten to eighteen minutes after the ceremony began. A body of state troops, acting in fact as uniformed lynchers, is in these cases stationed between the rest of the mob and the victim

* *Workers Monthly*, June 1926.

until the farce can be completed, and a few days later the sheriff acts as the mob's master of ceremonies in placing the noose and pulling the trap of the gallows. Then the ruling class of Kentucky leers into the faces of the Negro population and says: "The nigger got a trial didn't he?"

The 12,000,000 Americans known to be wholly or partly of African descent occupy a position which cannot much longer be tolerated by them. Enslaved as landless peasants or serfs in the agricultural southern states, working at odd jobs in extremest poverty in cities north and south, and just now breaking into big industrial plants as the workers at the heaviest labor, excluded from more attractive forms of labor, working for a wage much below that of other workers, often excluded from trade unions, living in miserable segregated slums, systematically degraded as a low caste by a rigid social code—the Negro masses have a score of issues which are worth life and death to them.

For a half-century these or similar issues have existed, but the forces which could deal with them did not emerge. At last the Negro has touched the transforming chemical—by entering into large industrial labor. By becoming a part of the modern industrial proletariat—a process through which many thousands of Negro former peasants are now going—the Negro masses are reaching the epoch in which their liberation is placed on the agenda of history. The flood of black population into the cities of the north has generated a culture which takes the form of a fever for organization. This culture has already gone through the stage of the exclusive devotion to the exaltation of favored individuals of the race. It has reached the stage where a serious mass movement for organization and mass emancipation has come into being.

The most modern of these movements—one which promises a mass character—is expressed in the American Negro Labor Congress. Simultaneously several particular movements, such as the successful organization of the Pullman porters, and the pressure upon the American Federation of Labor for the organization of other and more basic groups, show the trend of development.

At this time all promises and realizations of mass organization among Negroes are more or less recognized as being objectively movements against capitalism. In a formal "theoretical" way—in thought divorced from the concrete realities—it might be reasoned that the special burdens borne by the Negro are essentially relics of feudalism having no necessary place in capitalist society, and that therefore these burdens can be removed within capitalist society. It might be thought that the maintenance of a system of racial inequality within the borders of a highly developed capitalist country is not necessary to capitalist society, and that therefore when the forward pressure of an unfavored racial group begins to express a serious contradiction, capitalist society can accomplish the removal of the racial discrimination. But in concrete reality in a concrete world, it is not so. There is not and never was a purely capitalist society; by the term "capitalist society" is meant a society in which capitalist forms predominate. In all capitalist societies there are some remainders of feudal society which become interwoven with and interdependent with the capitalist economic and state systems. In no case has the complete removal of the feudal impurities taken place, and each proletarian revolution that we have experienced has overtaken a capitalist society still retaining much of the forms of feudalism. The mere existence of a peasant class is itself a relic of feudalism, and out of this comes the "alliance of the proletariat and peasantry" against capitalism.

In the case of America today, the existence of the "Negro question" is the existence in capitalist society of a remainder of a previous social system, and at the same time it is an integral part which cannot be separated from the capitalist system as it exists here and now. For the race question is interwoven with the class question; the special disabilities put upon the Negro toilers (real proletarians and peasants), are a built-in part of the concrete system of class exploitation. To any empty words about the ability of the capitalist society to abolish the special inferiority of the position of the Negro, we may answer that the capitalist system does not abolish this condition and that the struggle of the Negro as a racial group against the inferior racial caste status shows signs of beginning to merge with the proletarian movement against capitalism.

When the American Negro Labor Congress was founded in Chicago at the end of last year, the thing which caused a flurry

among high capitalist and government circles was not the fact
that some Communists were among its leaders, but the fact that
the Congress represented the merging of cause of Negro equality
with the cause of the labor movement. Some Communists had
been among those who called together the Negro Sanhedrin
Conference the year before; but the government did not send
any of its agents to harass the Sanhedrin; it was the combination
of "Negro" and "Labor" that caused fear. This is borne out
further by the fact that when the Pullman porters (not a basically
important element in the railroad industry, but an influential
element in the Negro city populations) started to organize their
trade union, the government supplied an assistant of the Attorney
General of the United States to act as an organizer of strike-
breaking. There were other anxious counter-movements such as
Coolidge's recent appointment of a commission of several
prominent Negroes of the job-seeking type, charged with the
duty of finding "solutions" for questions of race friction—a
commission which, of course, it is understood, must not meddle
in such matters as segregation or murder or disfranchisement of
Negroes.

It is seen that there are new developments among the masses
of Negroes, developments which lead forward, and which are
causing a shifting of landmarks.

But we are concerned here chiefly with a movement which is
not so new—with the first of the organized mass movements of
Negroes, and which appears still to be the largest now in
existence, the Universal Negro Improvement Association.

The Universal Negro Improvement Association, which seems
at one time to have had about a half-million adherents, has been
in a state of constant crisis during the past four years, and now
appears to be in a process of rapid disintegration. When this
movement first appeared about eight years ago, with something
of a working-class character and even some traces of a working-
class program mingled with utopian theories somewhat resembling that of Jewish Zionism adapted to Africa and the Negro, the
United States government assumed that its effect would be
anti-capitalist and began an uninterrupted course of persecution.
Under the leadership of Marcus Garvey the Association has

retreated before every attack into a more and more fantastic opportunism.

The decay of this first great experience of the Negro in mass organization is one of the tragedies of the struggle for emancipation—and it is a tragedy of the most disgracefully treacherous leadership ever known, a leadership which has never hesitated to desert its followers and which today has degenerated into the gutter of scramble for direct material gain for individuals.

Take up a copy of the *Negro World*, organ of the Universal Negro Improvement Association, and try to get from it a reflection of this great world-full of struggle of the Negro people—or of the beginning crystallization of the forces of the Negro masses for the struggle. What do you find about these tremendous affairs in the organ of what still claims to be the mass organization of the exploited black people?

You find nothing whatever except a seething stew of controversy about the financial affairs—not precisely the financial affairs of the organization itself, but the financial affairs of various officers or ex-officers of the organization who have been or are now struggling for position for themselves in the effort to obtain financial gain for themselves out of the organization. For instance, the current number of the *Negro World* (May 8) shows that the sole present activities of the organization are devoted to a violent controversy over control of the remaining property of the organization in New York, the controversy over mortgages, etc., and, second, the effort to raise more money for—what?

For the organization and struggle against lynching of the Negro in the old or new form? No. For the struggle against segregation? No. For the struggle for the political rights of the Negro? No. For the struggle of the Negro working masses for equality in the labor movement, for equality of pay and equal access to all kinds of jobs for organized Negro workers with organized workers in general? No. For the struggle against the Ku Klux Klan? No. For any effort of any sort whatever to put the Negro upon a plane of equality? No. Is there even a consistent, aggressive flight for the release of the imprisoned president, Marcus Garvey himself, whom the United States government framed . . . and jailed on the mistaken idea that Garvey in some way represented an effort of liberation of the exploited Negro masses? No, not even that; Garvey's political bankruptcy is nowhere better exemplified than by the fact he understands nothing of the possibilities of his case for mass organization in his defense; his only policy is to crawl and beg and bargain for his release. There is nothing in this organ in any way even suggesting a claim that the Negro has any rights whatever in this country. . . .

Two events of the last convention of the Universal Negro Improvement Association correctly foreshadowed the present situation:

The first in importance relates to program. Since Mr. Marcus Garvey appeals in big type for the support of "the great program," let us look again at the program that was adopted at the last convention in Detroit. The substance is:

The Nature of Race Problems Produced by the Contact of Races

Race problems move on to solution and they cannot be solved except by separation or amalgamation.

Thomas Jefferson proclaimed the nature of race problems and proposed separation.

Bushrod Washington, James Madison, John Marshall, James Monroe, Henry Clay, John Randolph of Roanoke, Abraham Lincoln, and Ulysses S. Grant are among the eminent men and women who took part in the African colonization movement of the blacks.

The Virginia General Assembly and others through resolutions and acts, supported the colonization of Liberia.

The present resolution has high historical precedent, and, in effect, memorialized the Congress to assist an important group of Negroes who wish to continue the colonization of Liberia as an independent Negro nation.

The essence of this "program" is simply the deportation of the masses of American Negroes to the African colony of the Firestone Company. Of course it is idiotic. The only reality it has is as a means of raising money.

The only other important incident of the convention aside

from the fight for control was one which had to do with the method of employing officers of the organization. It had been a custom for several years, begun at the high point of prosperity of the organization, to fix handsome salaries for officers and the custom of the officers, acting as representatives of the organization, to make contracts with each individual officer for these large salaries which ranged up to many thousands of dollars a year. This was supposed to be necessary to the "dignity" of the fancy-titled men who obligingly took the position of leadership. The result was that during the past few years the UNIA has found that with every internal dispute there came an ousting of some officer and a consequent law suit of the officer for the enormous salaries stipulated in the contract of employment. Of course, the treasury was drained with constant court judgments in favor of the ousted officers. It can be said that with very few exceptions the treasury was looted and gutted with every ousting of an officer—and these ousters were many. It was inevitable that after several years of this, at the last convention a naive delegate offered a motion to the effect that no more contracts be made of a sort that would enable discharged officers to sue the organization for salaries for unexpired terms. The proposal was a challenge to the sincerity of every newly elected officer present.

The test was effective, in a certain way. Immediately the proposal was made, the newly elected acting president, Fred A. Toote, jumped to his feet excitedly to declare that if the motion was not withdrawn he would resign. Toote explained that "You can't obtain the services of competent men unless you give them some security of a means to support their families." What he meant was, of course, that the officers of the organization placed a value upon the power to milk the treasury and upon their independence of control by the organization. The motion was withdrawn, not one delegate having the courage to speak plainly of the character of officers who would serve the Negro organization—the "great program"—only on condition of a strangle hold on the often-looted treasury.

The Universal Negro Improvement Association became at its last convention, so far as its officers were concerned, an organization of private plunder for "leaders" and nothing else, excepting its character as a promoter in the ranks of the Negroes themselves, of the program of the Ku Klux Klan for the submission of the Negroes to hopeless servitude.

The inevitable result is found in the present situation in which a war of money-grabbing leaders is accompanied by the rapid break up and disintegration of what once was a magnificently promising mass organization.

A peculiar feature of the policy of Marcus Garvey is that it results in the destruction even of the machine itself. The organization for several years fixed its center of gravity in a scheme for a steamship line in connection with a utopian venture of "trade with Africa." Now the salary-takers have lost the "steamship line" in the sheriff's sale of the steamship *General Goethals* (re-named the *Booker T. Washington*). Almost nothing of value is left to the contract-holding officers except a piece of property on 138th Street in New York City, the headquarters of the organization, for the possession of which two sets of officers are fighting in the courts. The New York division of the organization has split away from the parent body and controls the mortgaged property, and the faction of Garvey is fighting for its recovery.

What will be the fate of the Universal Negro Improvement Association? That an organization of masses of exploited Negroes should throw off the disintegrating influences, discard its Garvey-imposed opportunism, take on a clear program of struggle, and find new health and strength, must be the wish of any one who desires the emancipation of the Negro. Whether the saving of the Universal Negro Improvement Association is possible or not cannot be said now. Every effort should be made to save it from destruction and perversion. The tendency of most observers is to regard the organization as inseparable from Garvey and Garveyism, and to consider that the two will disappear from the scene together.

But this is not a sound conclusion. The broken fragments of the UNIA contain some of the best rank-and-file material to be found—material which has not been corrupted by false leadership, as its resistance proves. If the organization cannot be saved, at least out of the best of the fragments something will grow that is more in line with the new tendencies.

But Garveyism has been the dominant note in Negro mass activity in America for nearly a decade.

When Garveyism evaporates what will remain?

An article by Abram L. Harris in the April number of *The Crisis* contains the following interesting observation:

> The social unrest among the Negro race over which we waxed philosophical a few years back was not completely exhausted by the Garvey movement fiasco. Much of the ferment remains. Two years ago a friend of mine wrote this about the Garvey movement: "It is just another name for the psychology of the American Negro peasantry—for the surge of race consciousness felt by Negroes throughout the world, the intelligent as well as the ignorant. Though visionary and perhaps impossible of accomplishment, it afforded a mental relaxation for the long submerged Negro peasantry. Balked desire, repressed longings, must have an outlet." My friend then queried, "After Garvey—What?" Had I known what I think I know today I would have answered, "Communism."

If what the writer means is the merging of the mass unrest of the Negro population with the advanced section of the labor movement, I believe the quoted prediction is correct.

The Decline of
the Garvey Movement*

BY CYRIL BRIGGS

GARVEYISM, or Negro Zionism, rose on the crest of the wave of discontent and revolutionary ferment which swept the capitalist world as a result of the post-war crisis.

Increased national oppression of the Negroes, arising out of the post-war crisis, together with the democratic slogans thrown out by the liberal-imperialist demagogues during the World War (right of self-determination for all nations, etc.) served to bring to the surface the latent national aspirations of the Negro masses. These aspirations were considerably strengthened with the return of the Negro workers and poor farmers who had been conscripted to "save the world for democracy." These returned with a wider horizon, new perspectives of human rights and a new confidence in themselves as a result of their experiences and disillusionment in the war. Their return strengthened the morale of the Negro masses and stiffened their resistance. So-called race riots took the place of lynching bees and massacres. The Negro masses were fighting back. In addition, many of the more politically advanced of the Negro workers were looking to the example of the victorious Russian proletariat as the way out of their oppression. The conviction was growing that the proletarian

* *The Communist*, June 1931.

revolution in Russia was the beginning of a world-wide *united* movement of downtrodden classes and oppressed peoples. Even larger numbers of the Negro masses were becoming more favorable toward the revolutionary labor movement.

This growing national revolutionary sentiment was seized upon by the Negro petty bourgeoisie under the leadership of the demagogue, Marcus Garvey, and diverted into utopian, reactionary, "Back to Africa" channels. There were various other reformist attempts to formulate the demands of the Negro masses and to create a program of action which would appeal to all elements of the dissatisfied Negro people. None of these met with even the partial and temporary success which greeted the Garvey movement.

The leadership of the Garvey movement consisted of the poorest stratum of the Negro intellectuals—declassed elements, struggling businessmen and preachers, lawyers without a brief, etc.—who stood more or less close to the Negro masses and felt sharply the effects of the crisis. The movement represented a split away from the official Negro bourgeois leadership of the National Association for the Advancement of Colored People which even then was linked up with the imperialists.

The main social base of the movement was the Negro agricultural workers and the farming masses groaning under the terrific oppression of peonage and sharecropper slavery, and the backward sections of the Negro industrial workers, for the most part recent migrants from the plantations into the industrial centers of the North and South. These saw in the movement an escape from national oppression, a struggle for Negro rights throughout the world, including freedom from the oppression of the Southern landlords, and for ownership of the land. To the small advanced industrial Negro proletariat, who were experienced in the class struggle, the Garvey movement had little appeal.

While the movement never had the millions organizationally enrolled that its leaders claimed, it did have in 1921, at the time of its second Congress, nearly 100,000 members on its books, as revealed in an analysis made by W. A. Domingo[1] of the deliberately confused financial statement given by the leadership to the delegates at the second Congress. Moreover, the movement exercised a tremendous ideological influence over millions of Negroes outside its ranks.

The movement began as a radical petty bourgeois national movement, reflecting to a great extent in its early stages the militancy of the toiling masses and in its demands expressing their readiness for struggle against oppression in the United States. From the very beginning there were two sides inherent to the movement: a democratic side and a reactionary side. In the early stage the democratic side dominated. To get the masses into the movement, the national reformist leaders were forced to resort to demagogy. The pressure of the militant masses in the movement further forced them to adopt progressive slogans. The program of the first Congress was full of militant demands expressing the readiness for struggle in the United States.

A Negro mass movement with such perspectives was correctly construed by the imperialists as a direct threat to imperialism, and pressure began to be put on the leadership. A threat of the imperialists, inspired and backed by the leadership of the NAACP, to exclude Garvey from the country on his return from a tour of the West Indies brought about the complete and abject capitulation of the national reformist leaders. Crawling on his knees before the imperialists, Garvey enunciated the infamous doctrine that "the Negro must be loyal to all flags under which he lives." This was a complete negation of the Negro liberation struggle. It was followed by an agreement with the Ku Klux Klan, in which the reformists catered for the support of the Southern senators in an attempt to secure the "repatriation" of the Negro masses by deportation to Liberia.

The objective difficulties and subjective weakness of the movement, arising out of reformist leadership and its attempt to harmonize the demands of all the dissatisfied elements among the Negro people, inevitably led to the betrayal of the toiling masses.

While never actually waging a real struggle for national liberation the movement did make some militant demands in the beginning. However, these demands were soon thrown overboard as the reactionary side of the movement gained dominance. There followed a complete and shameful abandonment and betrayal of the struggles of the Negro masses of the United States and the West Indies. The right of the Negro majorities in the

West Indies and in the Black Belt of the United States to determine and control their own government was as completely negated by the Garvey national reformists as by the imperialists. The Garvey movement became a tool of the imperialists. Even its struggle slogans for the liberation of the African peoples, which had always been given main stress, were abandoned and the movement began to peddle the illusion of a *peaceful return to Africa*.

At first giving expression to the disgust which the Negro masses felt for the religious illusions of liberation through "divine" intervention, etc., the Garvey movement became one of the main social carriers of these illusions among the masses, with Marcus Garvey taking on the role of High Priest after the resignation and defection of the Chaplain-General, Bishop McGuire. Feudal orders, high sounding titles and various commercial adventures were substituted for the struggle [demanded in the earlier stages].

How completely the reactionary side came to dominate the movement is shown in (1) its acceptance of the Ku Klux Klan viewpoint that the United States is a white man's country and that the Negro masses living here are rightfully denied all democratic rights; (2) the rejection by the leaders at the 1929 convention in Jamaica, B. W. I., of a resolution condemning imperialism.

In both cases the betrayals just noted were carried to their logical conclusion, in Garvey's bid for an alliance with the Ku Klux Klan, and in an article he wrote in the *Blackman* (Jamaica organ of the movement) shortly after the 1929 convention in which he attacked the Jamaica workers for organizing into unions of the TUUL to better their conditions. In this article he attacked Communism as a menace to the imperialists and warned the Negro masses of Jamaica that they "would not dare accept and foster something tabooed by the mother country." So complete was the counterrevolutionary degeneration of the national reformists that the oppressing imperialism was openly accepted by them as their "mother country"! The imperialist oppressors were presented to the masses as "friends who have treated him (the Negro) if not fairly, with some kind of consideration!"

The decline of the movement synchronized with the subsiding of the post-war crisis. As a result both of the lessening of the

economic pressure on the masses and the awakening of the most
militant sections of the membership to the betrayals being
carried out by the national reformist behind the gesture of
struggle phrases and demagogy, the masses began to drop away
from the movement. Relieved of the pressure of the militant
masses the movement began to assert more and more its
reactionary and antidemocratic side.

Already at the second Congress it was evident that the national
reformists were losing their grip on the masses. As a result of the
widespread exposures carried on by the Negro radicals[2] against
the dishonest business schemes and consistent betrayals of the
national Negro liberation movement by the Garvey reformists,
the sympathetic masses outside of the organization were becoming more and more critical of the national reformists. Within the
organization itself there was such widespread dissatisfaction that
the top leadership was forced to make sacrifical goats of several
rubber-stamp lieutenants. Within a few months of the closing of
the second Congress, the first big mass defections occurred
(California, Philadelphia). These revolts, however, were led by
reformists and were significant only from the point of view of the
growing disintegration of the movement. From 1921, the movement has undergone a continuous process of deterioration and
break-up, as the masses increasingly came to realize the treacherous character of the national reformist leaders.

The recent decision of Garvey to sell the Jamaica properties of
the organization (pocketing the proceeds) and take up his
residence in Europe (far from the masses he has plundered and
betrayed), denotes a high stage in the collapse of this reactionary
movement, whose dangerous ideology, as pointed out by the C. I.
[Communist International], bears not a single democratic trait.

Historically however the movement has certain progressive
achievements. It undoubtedly helped to crystallize the national
aspirations of the Negro masses. Moreover, the Negro masses
achieved a certain political ripening as a result of their experience and disillusionment with this movement.

The betrayal of these aspirations and the national liberation
struggle by the Garvey national reformists was facilitated by (1)
the immaturity of the Negro working class; (2) the weakness both

in theoretical and in organizational strength of the revolutionary labor movement in the United States at that time.

Today as the result of large-scale migrations into the industrial centers of large numbers of Negroes from the plantations, a strong Negro proletariat has come into being, developing in the class struggle and freeing themselves of petty bourgeois influences and reformist illusions. Further, as the result of the present crisis and the correct application by the Communist Party of the U.S.A. of the C.I. line on the Negro question, the Negro liberation movement again goes forward, this time under the sign of proletarian hegemony, and wages a relentless fight against imperialism and for unconditional Negro equality, including the right of self-determination of the Negro majorities in the Black Belt of the South, in the West Indies and the Negro peoples of Africa.

Before concluding, it is necessary to emphasize here that the Garvey movement, while in decline and on the verge of collapse, still represents a most dangerous reactionary force, exercising considerable ideological influence over large masses of Negroes. It will not do to ignore this movement which is most dangerous in its disintegration because of the desperate attempts being made by the national reformist leaders to maintain their influences over the Negro masses, either by saving the movement as it is or by luring the dissatisfied masses into other organizations under the control of the national reformists.

The situation affords considerable opportunity for the winning of the Negro masses away from the influence of the reformists and in another article I will deal with the tasks of the Party in relation to the disintegration and decline of the Garvey Movement.

The Impact of Marcus Garvey on the Harlem Renaissance

BY JOHN HENRIK CLARKE

THE PERIOD OF the Harlem Renaissance is nearly always written about with major emphasis on writers, artists and other cultural figures. Though these dimensions are important, there are other aspects of this period that deserve attention and analysis. In some ways, the 1920's were a time similar to that time. Black Americans were discarding some old illusions and were taking on new ones. It was a period of self-discovery and we were calling ourselves "New Negroes" with the same vigor that some present day Afro-Americans are using to say that they are "Black and Beautiful."

In the years following the end of the First World War, when America's promises to us had been betrayed, again, we looked once more toward Africa and dreamed of a time and place where our essential manhood was not questioned.

A leader emerged and tried to make this dream into a reality. His name was Marcus Garvey. The personality and the movement founded by Marcus Garvey, together with the writers and artists of the Renaissance period, helped to put the community of Harlem on the map. While the literary aspect of the Renaissance was unfolding, Marcus Garvey and his Universal Negro Improvement Association, using Harlem as his base of operation, built the largest mass movement among Black people that this country has ever seen. This movement had international importance and was considered to be a threat to the colonial powers of Europe who were entrenched in Africa.

For about twelve years Harlem was Marcus Garvey's window on the world. From this vantage point, he became a figure of international importance. This magnetic and compelling personality succeeded in building a mass movement after other men had failed. His success may have been due to the fact that he was born and reared in an age of conflict that affected the world of African people everywhere.

When he was born in 1887, in Jamaica, the West Indies, the so-called "scramble for Africa" was over. All over Africa the warrior nationalists who had opposed European colonialism throughout the nineteenth century were either being killed or sent into exile. The Europeans with territorial aspirations in Africa had sat at the Berlin Conference of 1884 and 1885 and decided how to split up the continent among them. In the United States, the Black Americans were still suffering from the betrayal of the Reconstruction in 1876. The trouble within the world Black community that Marcus Garvey would later grapple with had already been started when he was born. In the years when he was growing to early manhood, his people entered the twentieth century and a new phase of their struggle for freedom and national identity.

The Black Americans at this time were still involved in a great migration movement that had started during the latter part of the nineteenth century and was increased during the First World War. At the turn of the century, large numbers of Blacks began to leave the farms and the cities of the South to search for employment opportunities and a better way of life in the cities of the North and along the eastern seaboard of the United States. They moved mainly into the urban areas between 1910 and 1920—New York and Chicago. Harlem was transformed from a white neighborhood into a Black metropolis and subsequently into the culture capital of the Black world.

The migration and the First World War had reoriented the Black man's thinking. Black soldiers had fought in large numbers to make the world safe for democracy. They now wondered, out loud, about why the world was not safe for them. In Harlem this wondering helped to develop a political Renaissance that had started much earlier. This was Harlem's first use of its political strength to gain control of the institutions that effected power in the community. The movement would later create the political atmosphere that prevailed in Harlem during the Literary Renaissance.

Harlem had become a Black community early in this century. From the beginning, politics was a form of community activity. After 1900, public recognition was made of this fact. Requests that Harlem politicians had made for offices and appointments in the 1890's were now being reconsidered. Spokesmen arose on all levels of municipal politics and demanded greater recognition of the community. Before this time, Black Americans' almost religious devotion to the Republican party had hampered their effectiveness in the politics of this city: the Republican party was sure of the Black vote and did not feel compelled to cater to it. The Democratic party was not sure of this vote and had not decided to make a serious attempt to bring Harlem voters into the Democratic camp. The activity of Harlem's first major politicians changed this situation and started both parties to catering to the city's Black voters.

Early in the twentieth century the first Black politician of great significance in the history of the city arose in the Republican party. His name was Charles W. Anderson. Anderson was a self-educated and self-made man. Born in Oxford, Ohio, a year after the Civil War ended, he came to New York at the age of twenty. He immediately became active in local Republican politics. In 1890 he was elected president of the Young Men's Colored Republican Club of New York County. As a reward for political work, he was appointed to the position of Gauger [exciseman] in a district office of the Internal Revenue Service. From this not too important position, Charles W. Anderson became "the recognized colored Republican leader of New York." He quickly rose from Gauger to private secretary of New York State's Treasury (1895–1898), to Supervisor of Accounts for the New York Racing Commission (1898–1905). In 1905 he was appointed to what was undoubtedly the most responsible and important federal office held by any Black politician in the early twentieth century: Collector of Internal Revenue for the Second New York District—the Wall Street District. Charles W. Anderson was a friend of both W. E. B. Du Bois and Booker T. Washington in spite of the conflict between these two men. More important, he was an astute and effective community politician. He had the welfare of the entire Harlem community at heart. To Charles W. Anderson, improving the race most often meant using his influence to find more and better-paying jobs for New York's Black community. He was responsible for the political pressure that got Samuel J. Battle appointed the first Black policeman on the New York City force.

More than any other politician before him, Charles W. Anderson made sure that the people of Harlem got their share of what the politicians call "the little plums"—the political appointee jobs. Anderson was the first leader in New York City history to push open the doors of political opportunity for Blacks. The rise of Charlie Anderson in many ways typified the political awakening of the Black people of New York City. He was the most able politician to emerge from Harlem during its formative years.

In 1898, Edward E. Lee (called "Chief") helped to establish the United Colored Democracy as a Black subdivision of the Democratic party. The Harlem community, still mainly Republican, denounced Lee and his followers. The Democratic party saw fit to reward Lee and his small group by giving them a measure of political patronage. James D. Carr, a Harlem lawyer who had graduated from Columbia University Law School in 1885, was appointed Assistant District Attorney. Edward E. Lee was made Sheriff. More and better appointments followed.

The United Colored Democracy continued its existence as a special "Negro" organization within the city's Democratic party. Its leader after 1915 was Harvard-educated Ferdinand Q. Morton, Chairman of the Municipal Civil Service Commission.

During this period Harlem was still a developing community. Several forces were in motion, helping that development. Politically, the Republican forces led by Charles W. Anderson were growing stronger. The competing Democratic force was gaining influence and demanding more patronage for the community. Marcus Garvey and his "back-to-Africa" movement was preaching a kind of Black nationalism that had never before been heard in this country. These competing forces started the campaign for Black district leadership in Harlem. When this campaign was won, they raised their sights and once more aimed at making Harlem a Congressional District. The early participants in this campaign were: Fred R. Moore, editor and publisher of *The New York Age;* T. Thomas Fortune, former editor of *The Age;* then editor of the Garvey publications; Charles W. Anderson, the leading Harlem Republican; Ferdinand Q. Morton, leading Harlem Democrat; Edward A. Johnson, Harlem's first Assemblyman; and the militant Black socialist, Black nationalist and Garveyite, Hubert H. Harrison.

The Black cultural explosion referred to as "The Negro Renaissance" or "The Harlem Literary Renaissance," was born around 1920 and developed during the artificial prosperity and gaiety that followed the First World War. In 1921, an all-Black variety show called *Shuffle Along* opened at the 63rd Street Theater in New York. This show that played to packed houses night after night brought to public attention a large number of Black performing artists for the first time and opened doors for other Black performers in other areas of the theater, including drama. Throughout the twenties, as Langston Hughes has said, "The Negro was in vogue." White interest in Black people, especially Black artists, writers and performers, became a national pastime.

Harlem became the new entertainment arena, literally a magnet drawing thousands of white people to its night clubs. They came uptown to Harlem to engage in a kind of pseudo-social equality with Black people. The white night club owners, who did not welcome "Negro patronage," misread the signs of the times and lost some white patronage because of their Jim Crow policies.

Entertainment by Black performers soared to new heights. The best known names were Roland Hayes, Paul Robeson, Florence Mills, Bessie Smith, Ethel Waters and Louis Armstrong.

In the theater, Black actors were, mainly, appearing in plays written by white writers. Charles Gilpin became one of the first

Black romantic stars when he appeared playing the leading role in "The Emperor Jones" by Eugene O'Neill in 1920. In 1923, another O'Neill play, "All of God's Chillun Got Wings," starred Paul Robeson. Other plays presented during this period were: "In Abraham's Bosom," by Paul Green; "Porgy" by Dubose Heyward; "Scarlet Sister Mary" by Julia Peterkin and "Green Pastures." Two of these plays won Pulitzer prizes.

The new interest in the theater and the success of a growing number of Black stars affected the Harlem community in many ways. Local theater groups were established. They performed plays by Black playwrights, but, more often preferred popular plays by white writers that had already been successfully staged on Broadway.

The visual arts were going through a period of transition. The Black artists lost their doubts about painting Black subjects though some of them were more interested in success than in artistic integrity. The painters Thomas Benton, Winold Reiss and others led the way. The Harmon Foundation that awarded annual prizes for the best paintings by "Negro artists" made a major contribution toward making Black subjects popular with Black artists.

The creative beating heart of the Harlem Renaissance was its writers, and their interpreter, Alain Locke. The personality of Alain Locke stood astride this period in such a way that no competent history of the period can be written without a reference to him. His ability extended far beyond the appraisal of writers and their works; he was a major intellect. No other person saw the Harlem Literary Renaissance with greater insight into its dimensions and the potential that it held for the future.

In 1925 Alain Locke expanded the special Harlem issue of the magazine *Survey Graphic,* which he edited, into the anthology *The New Negro.*[3] This book, recently reissued in paperback, is a milestone and a guide to Afro-American thought, literature and art in the middle 1920's. The announced objective of the volume, "to register the transformation of the inner and outer life of the Negro in America that had so significantly taken place in the last few preceding years," was achieved, and the book went far beyond this achievement. The poet and teacher Robert Hayden writing in the introduction of the new edition of this work says it "was the definitive presentation of the artistic and social goals of the New Negro movement. Perhaps," he continues, "it is no exaggeration to say that this book helped to create the movement. Certainly it had the effect of a manifesto when it appeared, and it remains an invaluable document of the cultural aspects of the Negro struggle as they were revealed by the work of artists and writers in Harlem during the 1920's."

Dr. Locke observed that his generation of Black writers and artists had opened new doors and asked new questions that could not be ignored. He saw the Harlem Literary Renaissance as a significant sign of racial awakening on a national and perhaps even a world scale.

Within the pages of *The New Negro* he brought together the essence of the creative writing talent of the 1920's. Many of these writers were being introduced to a large general audience for the first time. His choices had long range significance. Most of the writers whose work is included in the book went on to fulfill the promise that was evident in their early offerings.

The Harlem Literary Renaissance was now full grown. Several publications were competing for the attention of the new Black thinkers, the most notable of which were *The Crisis* (NAACP), edited by W. E. B. Du Bois, *Opportunity* (National Urban League), edited by Charles S. Johnson, *The Messenger*, edited by A. Philip Randolph and Chandler Owen, and Marcus Garvey's *Negro World*.

The three main poetic spokesmen for the "New Negro" period were Countee Cullen, Claude McKay, and Langston Hughes. They wrote with a considerable awareness of race consciousness. They were saying, more than forty-five years ago, that "Black is beautiful." They were also saying, in a poetic way, the same thing as Marcus Garvey: "Up you mighty race! You can accomplish what you will!"

This literary movement and its participants were soon "discovered" by an assortment of white celebrities, pseudoliterary figures with good publishing connections and some moderately wealthy liberal whites who were lost from their social moorings. They sponsored some Black writers and opened doors for others. Most of these well-wishers were somewhat paternalistic and possessive about the particular writer or writers they favored.

Some of them became overnight "authorities" on the new literature and its creators and these "authorities" were as wrong then as they are now.

The literary outpouring continued. Some of the main books and writers receiving wide circulation were: Walter White, *Fire in the Flint*; Jessie Fauset, *There is Confusion*; *Home to Harlem* by Claude McKay; *Quicksand* by Nella Larsen; *The Walls of Jericho* by Rudolph Fisher; and *The Blacker the Berry* by Wallace Thurman.

There was a "little renaissance" unfolding in the area of Boston, Massachusetts, under the leadership of a competent short-story writer and essayist named Eugene Gordon who was supported by Dorothy West, Gertrude West and others.

White writers could not resist the temptation to write about "Negro life" as they saw it. The novel that caused the greatest amount of heated debate among Black people was *Nigger Heaven*, by Carl Van Vechten, published in 1926. This novel created a demand for the so-called exotic novel and started some whites to searching for the "exotic Negro" or "the noble savage." Carl Van Vechten's greatest contribution to this period was the use of his influence to open to Negro writers doors of publishing houses that had not been open before.

Near the end of the decade, the Harlem Literary Renaissance had run its course and was fading away. The stronger writers and artists who came out of this period continued to produce high-caliber work, but the Great Depression helped to end the Negro Renaissance. Artists and writers could not make a living writing books and painting pictures. Claude McKay had a harsh and bitter explanation of the decline of the Negro Renaissance. His explanation should be read, but not without some reservations. He said, in *A Long Way from Home*, "The Harlem Renaissance movement of the artistic '20's was really inspired and kept alive by the interest and presence of white bohemians. It faded out when they became tired of the new plaything."

Let us now return to one of the sadly neglected aspects of this movement, the rise and decline of Marcus Garvey and what seemed to have been his impossible dreams of African reclamation and the redemption of Black people the world over.

Marcus Garvey's glorious, romantic and riotous movement

exhorted the Black race and fixed their eyes on the bright star of a future in which they would reclaim and rebuild their African homeland and heritage.

The self-proclaimed Provisional President of Africa never set foot on African soil. He spoke no African language. But Garvey managed to convey to members of the Black race everywhere (and to the rest of the world) his passionate belief that Africa was the home of a civilization which had once been great and would be great again. When one takes into consideration the slenderness of Garvey's resources and the vast material forces, social conceptions and imperial interests which automatically sought to destroy him, his achievement remains one of the great propaganda miracles of this century.

Garvey's voice reverberated inside Africa itself. The King of Swaziland later told Mrs. Marcus Garvey that he knew the names of only two Black men in the Western world: Jack Johnson, the boxer who defeated the white man Jim Jeffries, and Marcus Garvey. From his narrow vantage point in Harlem, Marcus Garvey became a world figure.

The Garvey movement began to fragment and decline concurrently with the end of the Harlem Renaissance. This period had a meaning that is generally missed by most people who write about it. This movement had indigenous roots and it could have existed without the concern and interest of white people. This concern, often overstated, gave the movement a broader and more colorful base, and may have extended its life span. The movement was the natural and logical result of years of neglect, suppression and degradation. Black Americans were projecting themselves as human beings, and demanding that their profound humaneness be accepted. It was the first time a large number of Black writers, artists and intellectuals took a unified walk into the sun.

๛ MARCUS GARVEY
IN HIS OWN WORDS

First Message to the Negroes of the World from Atlanta Prison*

February 10, 1925.

MY WORK IS just begun, and when the history of my suffering is complete, then future generations of Negroes will have in their hands the guide by which they shall know the "sins" of the twentieth century. I, and I know you, too, believe in time, and we shall wait patiently for two hundred years, if need be, to face our enemies through our posterity.

After my enemies are satisfied, in life or death I shall come back to you to serve even as I have served before. In life I shall be the same: in death I shall be a terror to the foes of Negro liberty. If death has power, then count on me in death to be the real Marcus Garvey I would like to be. If I may come in an earthquake, or a cyclone, or plague, or pestilence, or as God would have me, then be assured that I shall never desert you and make your enemies triumph over you. Would I not go to hell a million times for you?

If I die in Atlanta my work shall then only begin, but I shall live, in the physical or spiritual [sense] to see the day of Africa's

* From *The Philosophy and Opinions of Marcus Garvey*, Amy Jacques Garvey, ed., Atheneum, New York, 1969.

glory. When I am dead wrap the mantle of the Red, Black and Green around me, for in the new life I shall rise with God's grace and blessing to lead the millions up the heights of triumph with the colors that you well know. Look for me in the whirlwind or the storm, look for me all around you, for, with God's grace, I shall come and bring with me countless millions of black slaves who have died in America and the West Indies and the millions in Africa to aid you in the fight for Liberty, Freedom and Life.

The civilization of today is gone drunk and crazy with its power and by such it seeks through injustice, fraud and lies to crush the unfortunate. But if I am apparently crushed by the system of influence and misdirected power, my cause shall rise again to plague the conscience of the corrupt. For this I am satisfied, and for you, I repeat, I am glad to suffer and even die. Again, I say, cheer up, for better days are ahead. I shall write the history that will inspire the millions that are coming and leave the posterity of our enemies to reckon with the hosts for the deeds of their fathers.

With God's dearest blessings, I leave you for a while.

In Prison in Atlanta*

. . . TWO MONTHS AFTER I was confined at Atlanta,
they [my enemies] succeeded in taking away the new ship from
the unfaithful men who represented me. The same group of men
in Wall Street who . . . had used the old officers to destroy the
Black Star Line maneuvered to get the officers of the Black Cross
Navigation and Trading Company to sign up with them to accept
a cargo to Miami through a Negro broker. This Negro broker
influenced the men to allow him to accept the freight. . . . The
result was, in working out the scheme to get the ship, they got
one or two shippers to place aboard the boat a small tonnage of
cargo and then they went around to prospective shippers and
influenced them not to ship any freight on the boat to Miami.
The ship could not sail with the small amount of cargo; these
men in turn libeled the boat for non-performance of contract
with a demand to the extent of $25,000 . . . so the boat that was
purchased and equipped for $200,000 was taken away while I
was in prison for $25,000. Efforts were also made to get the
$22,250 lodged with the Shipping Board for the Black Star Line.

When I was sent to Atlanta my enemies made sure that would
have been the last of me. From what I could gather it seemed
that they had reached even the Deputy Warden of the prison
with their influence, with the suggestion of making it hard for me
whilst there. The Deputy Warden of the institution made every
effort to carry out the wishes of my enemies. When I was drafted

* Excerpt from Pittsburgh *Courier*, May 3, 1930.

for work he gave me the hardest and dirtiest tasks in the prison, thinking that would have ruffled my spirits to cause further punishment. But I philosophically accepted the duties and executed them to the best of my ability. After being so engaged for a short while, the Warden (a high-typed man of character and consideration), Mr. J. W. Snooks, called me into his office and had me transferred to the best position that a colored man could have in prison; this I also executed to the best of my ability during the entire time that I remained there. I have absolutely no complaint to make during the time I spent at Atlanta under Warden Snooks.

Whilst I was confined efforts were made to secure for me a pardon or communication [commutation?]. I was informed that President Coolidge would have acted immediately upon the application for pardon a few months after I was in Atlanta but [for] the pressure brought to bear upon him by my enemies. Instead of signing the papers for my release he returned them with a statement of "Premature." It was not until two years after he finally granted me communication.

I had hoped that on my release from Atlanta I would have had the opportunity of returning to New York to straighten out the affairs of the Universal Negro Improvement Association, the Black Star Line and the Black Cross Navigation and Trading Company, but my enemies made sure of their game in not allowing me to return to New York. They had already swallowed up all the assets of the companies, which could be removed only by my presence in New York. So they skillfully influenced the Department of Labor and the Department of State to deport me to Jamaica. On the order of President Coolidge I was shunted to New Orleans, and from there to my homeland—Jamaica.

Part Four

Marcus Garvey and His Critics

Commentary

BY JOHN HENRIK CLARKE

MARCUS GARVEY'S MANNER of dealing with those who had disagreed with him seemed to have been designed to create adversaries, of which there were many. While the best known of these adversaries were W. E. B. Du Bois and W. A. Domingo, he had several lesser known opponents. The main article in this section was written by Richard B. Moore, who lived through the rise and fall of the Garvey era. Mr. Moore, formerly a member of the Communist Party, was in opposition to Marcus Garvey because at that time a lot of the Black radicals were either Communists or Socialist-inclined, and they thought of Marcus Garvey's Movement as a negation of this ideology. Some of Marcus Garvey's critics had formerly been his supporters.

In the United States Marcus Garvey moved into an atmosphere that in some ways was being prepared for him before he was born. He managed to strike the right chords in the temperament of Black Americans and achieved what other leaders had not achieved; he managed to build a Black mass movement where others had failed. Some of his critics were those who had failed. In the rapid rise of the Garvey Movement some of the observers acted as though they were witnessing the impossible and had to deny it.

It is generally assumed that the greatest opposition to Marcus Garvey came from the NAACP and Dr. W. E. B. Du Bois.[1] This is not true. Opposition to his program and his teachings came from many quarters, including the Caribbean community in the United States and abroad. Opposition to Marcus Garvey by the Black working class was practically nonexistent. Now that we know what class of people opposed Marcus Garvey, the next question is, why?

Dr. Du Bois and the NAACP did not at first oppose Marcus Garvey. *The Crisis* published fine articles on Marcus Garvey. The first two appeared in March 1920 and January 1921 and ended with: "To sum up: Garvey is a sincere, hardworking idealist; he is also a stubborn, domineering leader of the mass; he has worthy industrial and commercial schemes but he is an inexperienced businessman. . . ."

The third and fourth articles dealt with the Black Star Line and the Universal Negro Improvement Association and were based on published documents with little comment. It was not until September 1922 that *The Crisis* had a sharp word of criticism. This was based on Garvey's threats against his critics, his connection with the Ku Klux Klan and his distribution of pamphlet propaganda against American Negroes. Quoted, among other things, was: "The white race can best help the Negro by telling him the truth, and not by flattering him into believing that he is as good as any white man."

The Crisis commented:

> Not even Tom Dixon or Ben Tillman or the hatefullest enemies of the Negro have ever stooped to a more vicious campaign than Marcus Garvey, sane or insane, is carrying on. He is not attacking white prejudice, he is grovelling before it and applauding it; his only attack is on men of his own race who are striving for freedom; his only contempt is for Negroes; his only threats are for black blood.

On the other hand Garvey's attacks on the NAACP in the pages of the *Negro World* were continuous, and according to the NAACP, preposterous. Some of the charges he made against them were:
1. That they kept his representative from activity in Paris in 1919.
2. That Moorfield Storey came from Boston to secure his conviction in 1924.

3. That the collapse of the Black Star Line came about "because men were paid to make this trouble by certain organizations calling themselves Negro Advancement Associations. They paid men to dismantle our machinery and otherwise damage it so as to bring about the downfall of the movement."

4. That the NAACP was responsible for his incarcerations and deportation.

The NAACP denied all of the charges.

All Black intellectuals did not oppose Marcus Garvey;[2] some of the most able in America supported him, to name a few: William H. Farris, author of *The African Abroad*; T. Thomas Fortune, Editor of the *Negro World* from 1923 until his death in 1927; and Hubert Harrison, one of the foremost Afro-American intellects of his time. Some Black intellectuals were sufficiently interested in the Garvey Movement to ally themselves with it at one time or another. Emmett J. Scott, for example, became "Duke of the Nile" in Garvey's visualized African Empire.

Another cause for opposition was Garvey's repatriation schemes.[3] Black Americans have been divided on this issue since the early days of the nineteenth century. This was the period when the African Colonization Movement began.

In his article "The Negro Intellectuals' Criticism of Garveyism"[4] Charles Willis Simmons describes Garvey's early days in Harlem and the introduction of his program:

> Garvey brought his program of Negro Zionism to New York on March 23, 1916. There among the transplanted, poorly educated, superstitious and disillusioned southern Negroes, he found fanatical supporters for his schemes. He made use of each opportunity to present his beliefs. On one occasion he was invited to speak for the organization of a Liberty League at Bethel A.M.E. Church. His speech when it came was not for such a league, but for the Universal Negro Improvement Association and its programs.

On this occasion Marcus Garvey was introduced by Hubert Harrison, founder of the Liberty League. This Black Socialist, who was also a nationalist, had a profound influence on the thinking of Marcus Garvey during the formative years of his movement in America.

George S. Schuyler, then a young man, but later a severe journalistic critic of the foibles of the American Negro, in a letter to the editor of *The Messenger*, wrote of Garvey:

> An ass was created to be ridden. Keep on riding Garvey by all means. Remember the much quoted maxim of Mr. P. T. Barnum and don't let up brother Marcus as long as he continues his mess, lest more foolish Negroes be taking in by this sable Ponzi.

When William Pickens, field organizer for the NAACP, was offered a position in the UNIA, he refused, saying, "I cannot feel myself quite bad enough to accept any honor or alliance with such organizations as the Ku Klux Klan or the Black Hand Society . . . You compare the aim of the KKK in America with your aim in Africa—and if that be true, no civilized man can endorse either of you."

Later Pickens gave additional expression to his contempt of the alliance between Garveyism and the Ku Klux Klan. [Here Pickens is distorting the facts. There was never any alliance between Marcus Garvey and the Ku Klux Klan.]:

> Dr. Du Bois in later years described the movement as a "grandiose and bombastic scheme, utterly impractical as a whole . . ." but Du Bois considered the movement sincere and said of Garvey that he "proved not only an astonishingly popular leader but a master of propaganda." Displaying even greater admiration for the leader of the UNIA and seemingly refusing to acknowledge that the profound impact of that organization had fallen upon United States Negroes, Du Bois wrote that Garvey had "made vocal the great and long suffering grievances and spirit of protest among the West Indian peasantry." He describes the UNIA as "one of the most interesting spiritual movements of the modern world."

Other Black intellectuals, who at first had been overtly critical of Marcus Garvey, began to look at him with more respect.[5]

E. Franklin Frazier, in 1926, commenting upon Garvey and his movement, wrote: "As a leader of a mass movement among Negroes, Garvey has no equal." Later, in 1949, Frazier described Garvey as being the "leader of the most important, though ephemeral, nationalistic movement among Negroes."

Alain Locke, in *The New Negro*, saw in Garveyism "the sense of a mission of rehabilitating the race in world esteem from the loss of prestige for which the fate and conditions of slavery have so largely been responsible. Garveyism may be a transient, if spectacular, phenomenon, but the possible role of the American Negro in the future development of Africa is one of the most constructive and universally helpful missions that any modern people can lay claim to."

A. Philip Randolph, one of Garvey's persistent opponents, pointed out that the UNIA "had stirred Negroes to the realization of a need for organization and had demonstrated the ability of Negroes to organize under Negro leadership." Randolph credited Garvey and his organization with having aided in the destruction of the "slave psychology which throttles and strangles Negro initiative."

One Negro intellectual, observing the impression which Garvey was making upon the American Negro said that "whatever may happen to his grandiose schemes of finance and politics, he is the best point at which to study what is going on inside the hearts of ten million colored people of the United States."

James Weldon Johnson believed that if Garvey had possessed a more tactful personality and had used more moderation he would have been successful in his back-to-Africa Movement. "He had," wrote Johnson, "energy and daring and the Napoleonic personality, the personality that draws masses of followers . . . he had great power and possibilities within his grasp, but his deficiencies as a leader outweighed his abilities. To this man came an opportunity such as comes to few men, and he clutched greedily at the glitter and let the substance slip from his fingers."

The reappraisal of Marcus Garvey went on for years—until some of his original critics and opponents became defenders of his movement.

Marcus Garvey*

BY W. E. B. DU BOIS

MARCUS GARVEY WAS born at St. Ann's Bay, Jamaica, about 1885. He was educated at the public school and then for a short time attended the Church of England Grammar School, although he was a Roman Catholic by religion. On leaving school he learned the printing trade and followed it for many years. In Costa Rica he was associated with Marclam Taylor in publishing the *Bluefield's Messenger*. Later he was on the staff of *La Nacion*. He then returned to Jamaica and worked as a printer, being foreman of the printing department of P. Benjamin's Manufacturing Company of Kingston. Later he visited Europe and spent some time in England and France and while abroad conceived his scheme of organizing the Negro Improvement Society. This society was launched August 1, 1914, in Jamaica, with these general objects among others:

> To establish a Universal Confraternity among the race; to promote the spirit of race pride and love; to administer to and assist the needy; to strengthen the imperialism of independent African States; to conduct a worldwide commercial and industrial intercourse.

His first practical object was to be the establishment of a farm

* *The Crisis*, December 1920, pages 58–60; January 1921, pages 112–115.

school. Meetings were held and the Roman Catholic Bishop, the Mayor of Kingston, and many others addressed them. Nevertheless the project did not succeed and Mr. Garvey was soon in financial difficulties. He therefore practically abandoned the Jamaica field and came to the United States. In the United States his movement for many years languished until at last with the increased migration from the West Indies during the war he succeeded in establishing a strong nucleus in the Harlem district of New York City.

His program now enlarged and changed somewhat in emphasis. He began especially to emphasize the commercial development of the Negroes and as an islander familiar with the necessities of ship traffic he planned the "Black Star Line." The public for a long time regarded this as simply a scheme of exploitation when they were startled by hearing that Garvey had bought a ship. This boat was a former coasting vessel, thirty-two years old, but it was put into commission with a black crew and a black captain and was announced as the first of a fleet of vessels which would trade between the colored peoples of America, the West Indies and Africa. With this beginning, the popularity and reputation of Mr. Garvey and his association increased quickly.

In addition to the *Yarmouth* he is said to have purchased two small boats, the *Shadyside*, a small excursion steamer which made daily excursions up the Hudson, and a yacht which was designed to cruise among the West Indies and collect cargo in some central spot for the *Yarmouth*. He had first announced the Black Star Line as a $5,000,000-corporation, but in February, 1920, he announced that it was going to be a $10,000,000-corporation with shares selling at $5. To this he added in a few months the Negro Factories Corporation capitalized at $1,000,000 with 200,000 $1 shares, and finally he announced the subscription of $5,000,000 to free Liberia and Haiti from debt.

Early in 1920 he called a convention of Negroes to meet in New York City from the 1st to the 31st of August, "to outline a constructive plan and program for the uplifting of the Negroes and the redemption of Africa." He also took title to three apartment houses to be used as offices and purchased the foundation of an unfinished Baptist church which he covered over and used for meetings, calling it "Liberty Hall." In August,

1920, his convention met with representatives from various parts
of the United States, several of the West India Islands and the
Canal Zone and a few from Africa. The convention carried out its
plan of a month's meetings and culminated with a mass meeting
which filled Madison Square Garden. Finally the convention
adopted a "Declaration of Independence" with sixty-six articles,
a universal anthem and colors—red, black and green—and
elected Mr. Garvey as "His Excellency, the Provisional President
of Africa," together with a number of various other leaders from
the various parts of the Negro world. This in brief is the history of
the Garvey movement.

The question comes (1) Is it an honest, sincere movement? (2)
Are its industrial and commercial projects businesslike and
effective? (3) Are its general objects plausible and capable of
being carried out?

The central and dynamic force of the movement is Garvey. He
has with singular success capitalized and made vocal the great
and long-suffering grievances and spirit of protest among the
West Indian peasantry. Hitherto the black peasantry of the West
Indies has been almost leaderless. Its natural leaders, both
mulatto and black, have crossed the color line and practically
obliterated social distinction, and to some extent economic
distinction, between them and the white English world on the
Islands. This has left a peasantry with only the rudiments of
education and with almost no economic chances, grovelling at
the bottom. Their distress and needs gave Garvey his vision.

It is a little difficult to characterize the man Garvey. He has
been charged with dishonesty and graft, but he seems to me
essentially an honest and sincere man with a tremendous vision,
great dynamic force, stubborn determination and unselfish desire
to serve; but also he has very serious defects of temperament and
training: he is dictatorial, domineering, inordinately vain and
very suspicious. He cannot get on with his fellow workers.[6] His
entourage has continually changed. He has had endless law suits
and some cases of fisticuffs with his subordinates and has even
divorced the young wife whom he married with great fanfare of
trumpets about a year ago. All these things militate against him
and his reputation. Nevertheless I have not found the slightest
proof that his objects were not sincere or that he was consciously

diverting money to his own uses. The great difficulty with him is that he has absolutely no business sense, no *flair* for real organization and his general objects are so shot through with bombast and exaggeration that it is difficult to pin them down for careful examination.

On the other hand, Garvey is an extraordinary leader of men. Thousands of people believe in him. He is able to stir them with singular eloquence and the general run of his thought is of a high plane. He has become to thousands of people a sort of religion. He allows and encourages all sorts of personal adulation, even printing in his paper the addresses of some of the delegates who hailed him as "His Majesty." He dons on state occasions a costume consisting of an academic cap and gown flounced in red and green!

Of Garvey's curious credulity and suspicions one example will suffice: In March, 1919, he held a large mass meeting at Palace Casino which was presided over by Chandler Owen and addressed by himself and Philip Randolph. Here he collected $204 in contributions on the plea that while in France, W. E. B. Du Bois had interfered with the work of his "High Commissioner" by "defeating" his articles in the French press and "repudiating" his statements as to lynching and injustice in America! The truth was that Mr. Du Bois never saw or heard of his "High Commissioner," never denied his nor anyone's statements of the wretched American conditions, did everything possible to arouse rather than quiet the French press and would have been delighted to welcome and cooperate with any colored fellow-worker.

When it comes to Mr. Garvey's industrial and commercial enterprises there is more ground for doubt and misgiving than in the matter of his character. First of all, his enterprises are incorporated in Delaware, where the corporation laws are loose and where no financial statements are required.[7] So far as I can find, and I have searched with care, Mr. Garvey has never published a complete statement of the income and expenditures of the Negro Improvement Association or of the Black Star Line or of any of his enterprises, which really revealed his financial situation. A courteous letter of inquiry sent to him July 22, 1920, asking for such financial data as he was willing for the public to know, remains to this day unacknowledged and unanswered.

Now a refusal to publish a financial statement is no proof of dishonesty, but it *is* proof that either Garvey is ill-advised and unnecessarily courting suspicion, or that his industrial enterprises are not on a sound business basis; otherwise he is too good an advertiser not to use a promising balance sheet for all it is worth.

There has been one balance sheet, published July 26, 1920, purporting to give the financial condition of the Black Star Line after one year of operation; neither profit or loss is shown, there is no way to tell the actual cash receipts or the true condition of the business. Nevertheless it does make some interesting revelations.

The total amount of stock subscribed for is $590,860. Of this $118,153.28 is not yet paid for, leaving the actual amount of paid-in capital charged against the corporation, $472,706.72. Against this stands only $355,214.59 of assets (viz.: $21,985.21 in cash deposits and loans receivable; $12,975.01 in furniture and equipment, $288,515.37 which is the alleged value of his boats, $26,000 in real estate and $5,739 of insurance paid in advance). To offset the assets he has $152,264.14 of other liabilities (accrued salaries, $1,539.30; notes and accounts payable, $129,224.84; mortgages due, $21,500). In other words, his capital stock of $472,706.72 is after a year's business impaired to such extent that he has only $202,950.45 to show for it.

Even this does not reveal the precariousness of his actual business condition. Banks before the war in lending their credit refused to recognize any business as safe unless for every dollar of current liabilities there were *two* dollars of current assets. Today, since the war, they require *three* dollars of current assets to every *one* of current liabilities. The Black Star Line had July 26, $16,485.21 in current assets and $130,764.14 in current liabilities, when recognition by any reputable bank called for $390,000 in current assets.

Moreover, another sinister admission appears in this statement: the cost of floating the Black Star Line to date has been $289,066.27. In other words, it has cost nearly $300,000 to collect a capital of less than half a million. Garvey has, in other words, spent more for advertisement than he has for his boats!

This is a serious situation, and even this does not tell the whole story: the real estate, furniture, etc., listed above, are probably valued correctly. But how about the boats? The *Yarmouth* is a wooden steamer of 1,452 gross tons, built in 1887. It is old and unseaworthy; it came near sinking a year ago and it has cost a great deal for repairs. It is said that it is now laid up for repairs with a large bill due. Without doubt the inexperienced purchasers of this vessel paid far more than it is worth, and it will soon be utterly worthless unless rebuilt at a very high cost.

The cases of the *Kanawha* (or *Antonio Maceo*) and the *Shadyside* are puzzling. Neither of these boats is registered as belonging to the Black Star Line at all. The former is recorded as belonging to C. L. Dimon and the latter to the North and East River Steamboat Company. Does the Black Star Line really own these boats, or is it buying them by installments, or only leasing them? We do not know the facts and have been unable to find out. Under the circumstances they look like dubious "assets."

The majority of the Black Star stock is apparently owned by the Universal Negro Improvement Association. There is no reason why this association, if it will and can, should not continue to pour money into its corporation. Let us therefore consider then Mr. Garvey's other resources.

Mr. Garvey's income consists of (a) dues from members of the UNIA; (b) shares in the Black Star Line and other enterprises, and (c) gifts and "loans" for specific objects. If the UNIA has "3,000,000 members" then the income from that source alone would be certainly over a million dollars a year. If, as is more likely, it has under 300,000 paying members, he may collect $150,000 annually from this source. Stock in the Black Star Line is still being sold. Garvey himself tells of one woman who had saved about $400 in gold: "She brought out all the gold and bought shares in the Black Star Line." Another man writes this touching letter from the Canal Zone: "I have sent twice to buy shares amounting to $125 (numbers of certificates 3752 and 9617). Now I am sending $35 for seven more shares. You might think I have money, but the truth, as I stated before, is that I have no money now. But if I'm to die of hunger it will be all right because I'm determined to do all that's in my power to better the conditions of my race."

In addition to this he has asked for special contributions. In the spring of 1920 he demanded for his coming convention in August, "a fund of two million dollars ($2,000,000) to capitalize this, the greatest of all conventions." In October he acknowledged a total of something over $16,000 in small contributions. Immediately he announced "a constructive loan" of $2,000,000, which he is presumably still seeking to raise.

From these sources of income Mr. Garvey has financed his enterprises and carried on a wide and determined propaganda, maintained a large staff of salaried officials, clerks and agents, and published a weekly newspaper. Notwithstanding this considerable income, there is no doubt that Garvey's expenditures are pressing hard on his income, and that his financial methods are so essentially unsound that unless he speedily revises them the investors will certainly get no dividends and worse may happen. He is apparently using the familiar method of "Kiting"—*i.e.*, the money which comes in as investment in stock is being used in current expenses, especially in heavy overhead costs, for clerk hire, interest and display. Even his boats are being used for advertisement more than for business—lying in harbors as exhibits, taking excursion parties, etc. These methods have necessitated mortgages on property and continually new and more grandiose schemes to collect larger and larger amounts of ready cash. Meantime, lacking businessmen of experience, his actual business ventures have brought in few returns, involved heavy expense and threatened him continually with disaster or legal complication.

On the other hand, full credit must be given Garvey for a bold effort and some success. He has at least put vessels manned and owned by black men on the seas and they have carried passengers and cargoes. The difficulty is that he does not know the shipping business, he does not understand the investment of capital, and he has few trained and staunch assistants.

The present financial plight of an inexperienced and headstrong promoter may therefore decide the fate of the whole movement. This would be a calamity. Garvey is the beloved leader of tens of thousands of poor and bewildered people who have been cheated all their lives. His failure would mean a blow to their faith, and a loss of their little savings, which it would take generations to undo.

Moreover, shorn of its bombast and exaggeration, the main lines of the Garvey plan are perfectly feasible. What he is trying to say and do is this: American Negroes can, by accumulating and ministering their own capital, organize industry, join the black centers of the south Atlantic by commercial enterprise and in this way ultimately redeem Africa as a fit and free home for black men. This is true. It is *feasible*. It is, in a sense, practical; but it will take for its accomplishment long years of painstaking, self-sacrificing effort. It will call for every ounce of ability, knowledge, experience and devotion in the whole Negro race. It is not a task for one man or one organization, but for co-ordinate effort on the part of millions. The plan is not original with Garvey but he has popularized it, made it a living, vocal ideal and swept thousands with him with intense belief in the possible accomplishment of the ideal.

This is a great, human service; but when Garvey forges ahead and almost singlehanded attempts to realize his dream in a few years, with large words and wild gestures, he grievously minimizes his task and endangers his cause.

To instance one illustrative fact: there is no doubt but what Garvey has sought to import to America and capitalize the antagonism between blacks and mulattoes in the West Indies. This has been the cause of the West Indian failures to gain headway against the whites. Yet Garvey imports it into a land where it has never had any substantial footing and where today, of all days, it is absolutely repudiated by every thinking Negro; Garvey capitalizes it, has sought to get the cooperation of men like R. R. Moton on this basis, and has aroused more bitter color enmity inside the race than has ever before existed. The whites are delighted at the prospect of a division of our solidifying phalanx, but their hopes are vain. American Negroes recognize no color line in or out of the race, and they will in the end punish the man who attempts to establish it.

Then, too, Garvey increases his difficulties in other directions. He is a British subject. He wants to trade in British territory. Why then does he needlessly antagonize and even insult Britain? He wants to unite all Negroes. Why then does he sneer at the work of the powerful group of his race in the United States where he finds asylum and sympathy? Particularly, why does he decry the excellent and rising business enterprises of Harlem—intimating that his schemes alone are honest and sound when the facts flatly contradict him? He proposes to settle his headquarters in Liberia—but has he asked permission of the Liberian government? Does he presume to usurp authority in a land which has successfully withstood England, France and the United States—but is expected tamely to submit to Marcus Garvey? How long does Mr. Garvey think that President King would permit his anti-English propaganda on Liberian soil, when the government is straining every nerve to escape the Lion's Paw?

And, finally, without arms, money, effective organization or base of operations, Mr. Garvey openly and wildly talks of "Conquest" and of telling white Europeans in Africa to "get out!" and of becoming himself a black Napoleon! [8]

Suppose Mr. Garvey should drop from the clouds and concentrate on his industrial schemes as a practical first step toward his dreams: the first duty of a great commercial enterprise is to carry on effective commerce. A man who sees in industry the key to a situation must establish sufficient businesslike industries. Here Mr. Garvey has failed lamentably.

The *Yarmouth*, for instance, has not been a commercial success. Stories have been published alleging its dirty condition and the inexcusable conduct of its captain and crew. To this Mr. Garvey may reply that it was no easy matter to get efficient persons to run his boats and to keep a schedule. This is certainly true, but if it is difficult to secure one black boat crew, how much more difficult is it going to be to "build and operate factories in the big industrial centers of the United States, Central America, the West Indies and Africa to manufacture every marketable commodity" and also "to purchase and build ships of larger tonnage for the African and South American trade" and also to raise "$5,000,000 to free Liberia" where "new buildings are to be erected, administrative buildings are to be built, colleges and universities are to be constructed" and finally to accomplish what Mr. Garvey calls the "Conquest of Africa"?

To sum up: Garvey is a sincere, hardworking idealist; he is also a stubborn, domineering leader of the mass; he has worthy industrial and commercial schemes but he is an inexperienced businessman. His dreams of Negro industry, commerce and the ultimate freedom of Africa are feasible; but his methods are bombastic, wasteful, illogical and ineffective and almost illegal. If he learns by experience, attracts strong and capable friends and helpers instead of making needless enemies; if he gives up secrecy and suspicion and substitutes open and frank reports as to his income and expenses, and above all if he is willing to be a co-worker and not a czar, he may yet in time succeed in at least starting some of his schemes toward accomplishment. But unless he does these things and does them quickly he cannot escape failure.

Let the followers of Mr. Garvey insist that he get down to bedrock business and make income and expense balance; let them gag Garvey's wilder words, and still preserve his wide power and influence. American Negro leaders are not jealous of Garvey—they are not envious of his success; they are simply afraid of his failure, for his failure would be theirs. He can have all the power and money that he can efficiently and honestly use, and if in addition he wants to prance down Broadway in a green shirt, let him—but do not let him foolishly overwhelm with bankruptcy and disaster one of the most interesting spiritual movements of the modern Negro world.

The Critics and Opponents of Marcus Garvey

BY RICHARD B. MOORE

WHAT OF THE opposition to Marcus Garvey and to the specific leadership which he projected in the U.S.A. in the affairs of people of African descent? That such an opposition was considerable and varied was reflected by Garvey himself in his writings, as collected and edited by his second wife, Amy Jacques Garvey, in *Philosophy and Opinions of Marcus Garvey*.[9] Even a cursory look through these writings will provide ample proof of this many-sided and well-nigh continuous opposition.

But hardly known at all is the cardinal fact that at the very beginning Marcus Garvey found himself in opposition to the principal leaders of the Afro-American people in the United States. In a comparatively early article, written in answer to his critics, Garvey stated that shortly after his arrival from Jamaica in the United States: "I immediately visited some of the so-called Negro leaders, only to discover that they had no programs, but were mere opportunists . . ."[10]

Due consideration must be given to such opposition in any historical study of the man and the movement which he led, if such a study is to be adequate and comprehensive. An account of this opposition seems particularly relevant and required when it is realized that such opposition may have played an important part in hastening the decline of this mass movement and its rapid reduction to a number of ineffective splinter groups.

However, in the opinion of some of the more emotional adherents of the Garvey movement, no consideration whatever should be given to any opposition to their leader. Indeed, to these followers it appears to be *lèse majesté* or intolerable disrespect of their revered leader to give countenance to such an opposition. To these uncritical partisans, any opposition to the leader's thought and will is not worthy of examination, but ought to be thrust aside peremptorily with severe condemnation and disdain.

Yet history shows that the greatest leaders of mankind are often seen to have committed grave errors in judgment and policy. Such mistakes, moreover, have caused serious setbacks and even great harm to the causes which these leaders have advocated. In the assessment of historical leaders, therefore, it is necessary to consider errors as well as correct responses, failures as well as achievements, and the position of opponents as well as the platform projected by the movement under consideration.

A widely known Afro-American historian, John Hope Franklin, has lamented in his foreword to the first (then the only full-length) biography of Marcus Garvey, written by Edmund Davis Cronon: "Yet Garvey remains an enigma—stolid, almost sphinxlike in his defiance of analysis and understanding. . . . We do not know how to assess the relative influence of the opposition and of Garvey's own mistakes, unwitting and otherwise, in bringing about his own downfall." It seems high time, then, that an endeavor be made toward such a desired and necessary assessment.

It is apparent from the record . . . that Marcus Garvey began his public career in the United States in opposition to the Afro-American leadership which then existed. His sweeping statement [that they had no programs but were mere opportunists] . . . calls for examination and more specific knowledge of the principal Afro-American organizations and leaders functioning during the years 1916–1927.

Prominent among these organizations was the National Association for the Advancement of Colored People. Founded in 1909

after the horrible massacre of Afro-Americans by a lynch mob
which had raged for two days through Springfield, Illinois, the
NAACP projected the following program:

> To promote equality of rights and eradicate caste or race prejudice
> among the citizens of the United States; to advance the interests of
> colored citizens; to secure for them impartial suffrage; and to
> increase their opportunities for securing justice in the courts,
> education for their children, employment according to their ability,
> and complete equality before the law.

This program launched by Afro-American militants together
with Euro-American liberals, was clearly a direct challenge to
"white supremacy." Dr. W. E. B. Du Bois, director of publicity
and research of the NAACP launched its organ *The Crisis* as "A
Record of the Darker Races." This magazine was developed into
a scholarly and powerful force against the injustice imposed upon
the Afro-American people. Court actions against segregation and
discrimination, pressure for federal legislation and action against
lynching, as well as protest actions, were constantly carried
forward.

The silent Protest Parade led by the NAACP in New York on
July 28, 1917, against increasing lynch murders, particularly
against slaying of over forty Afro-Americans in East St. Louis,
marshaled some 10,000 people who marched down Fifth Avenue
with placards and banners. Marcus Garvey, then living in New
York City, must have seen or read reports of this significant
demonstration. Garvey should have known too of the Pan-African Conference Movement launched by H. Sylvester Williams of
Trinidad in London during 1900. If not of the foregoing, then
certainly Garvey must have known of the Pan-African Congress
organized by Dr. W. E. B. Du Bois during 1919 in Paris and
during 1921 in London.

Similar in program and likewise stressing human rights and
equal status was the National Equal Rights League led by
William Monroe Trotter. Based specifically upon an Afro-American membership, this league and its publication *The Guardian*
strove uncompromisingly for complete and immediate equality in
every phase of American life. The National Association of

Colored Women, led by Mary Church Terrell, also championed full equality and civil rights, emphasizing rights for women as well. The National Negro Business League promoted business activity among Afro-Americans. The National Urban League, with its organ *Opportunity* sought to secure employment and better housing for the Afro-American people in urban centers.

The Liberty League of Afro-Americans, which was the last organized, with Hubert H. Harrison at its head and its newspaper *The Voice*, fostered a program of liberation of all peoples of African descent while stressing the demand for full human rights in the U.S.A. Several active and rising groups of younger radicals, the African Blood Brotherhood with Cyril V. Briggs as leader and the *Crusader* as organ, advocated human rights, an end to colonialism, and basic changes in society. The Socialists of Harlem, with *The Messenger* magazine and *The Emancipator* newspaper, took their stand against colonialist subjection, against all forms of racist discrimination and oppression, and for the fundamental reconstruction of society.

It does not appear to one conversant with the Afro-American scene during the years 1916 to 1927 how these widely publicized programs and [the] continuous activities of these organizations could be considered as constituting "no program." Nor can it be understood how Garvey, with his several prior attempts at organization and leadership in Jamaica and in Central America, could possibly fail to realize that a frontal attack upon these organizations and their leaders would call forth inevitable counterattacks. Besides, how could all the leaders of these various organizations be totally adjudged and dismissed as "mere opportunists"?

It is important now to recall the aims and objects or program projected during 1917 by Garvey in the UNIA. This should be borne in mind as a basis for comparison with the stated programs of the chief contemporary Afro-American organizations. This is necessary, besides, to understand the emphasis and thrust of the UNIA as later developed by its leader. The UNIA Manifesto of 1917 set forth the objectives as follows:

> To establish a Universal Confraternity among the race; to promote the spirit of race pride and love; to reclaim the fallen of the race; to

administer to and assist the needy; to assist in civilizing the
backward tribes of Africa; to strengthen the imperialism of
independent African states; to establish Commissioners or Agencies in the principal countries of the world for the protection of all
Negroes, irrespective of nationality; to promote a conscientious
Christian worship among the native tribes of Africa; to establish
Universities, Colleges, Academies and Schools for the racial
education of the boys and girls of the race; to conduct a worldwide
commercial and industrial intercourse.

Moreover, the Declaration of Rights of the Negro peoples of
the world, signed by 122 delegates, was duly adopted by the first
UNIA Convention on August 13, 1920. This broad Declaration
included specific demands for the basic human and civil rights for
which the NAACP, the Equal Rights League, and several other
Afro-American organizations were already fighting.

For example, Articles 4, 5, and 6 of this UNIA Declaration
demanded the right of "Negroes . . . to elect their own
representatives," "to even-handed justice before all courts of law
and equity," and "to representation on the jury." Articles 7, 9,
and 17 inveighed against "taxation without representation,"
against any law specifically aimed at the Negro . . ." because of
his race or color, and severely condemned lynching as "a
barbarous practice." Article 20 particularly protested "against
segregated districts, separate public conveyances, industrial discrimination, lynchings and limitations of political privileges of
any Negro citizen in any part of the world on account of race,
color, or creed." Article 22 protested "against the system of
education in any country where Negroes are denied the same
privileges and advantages as other races." Article 23 declared it
"inhuman and unfair to boycott Negroes from industries and
labor in any part of the world."

Obviously the foregoing rights, as affirmed in the UNIA
Declaration, as well as the stated aims of that body, were in no
sense basically opposed to the objectives set forth by the
Afro-American organizations then functioning in the U.S.A. Nor
opposed was the significant objective which was added in the
revised UNIA Manifesto of 1920: "To establish a central nation
for the race."

This last objective of the UNIA was by no means new in substance. It had been spelled out before, and even more fully, as the main object of the African Civilization Society, founded by Henry Highland Garnet in 1858, thus "to establish a grand center of Negro nationality from which shall flow the streams of commercial, intellectual and political power which shall make colored people respected everywhere."

Such a nation had been envisaged many times before by several leaders and organized bodies in the U.S.A. from Paul Cuffe during 1788 to 1818, on down to Chief Alfred C. Sam in 1897–1914, two years before Garvey came to the United States. This roster included two of Garvey's Jamaican fellow countrymen, John B. Russwurm and Robert Campbell, who had emerged on the scene long before. These pioneers of modern African nationality actually went to Africa, which Garvey never accomplished, and took steps toward the realization of such a nation.

John B. Russwurm migrated from the U.S.A. to Liberia and played an important role from 1830 until his death in 1851 as a journalist, educator, and administrator in the development of the Liberian nation. Robert Campbell, associated with Martin R. Delany in the expedition to the Niger Valley, concluded a treaty during 1859 with the rulers of Aboekuta, in what is now Nigeria in West Africa, for the right to settle and develop a nation there. An account was left by Robert Campbell in the book *A Pilgrimage to My Motherland*.[11] Yet these pioneers, Russwurm and Campbell, are almost wholly forgotten and are hardly ever mentioned in Jamaica, where they deserve to be honored for their achievements toward African nationhood and liberation alongside Marcus Garvey, who has been proclaimed as a national hero of Jamaica.

The attitude taken by Robert Campbell toward the indigenous African rulers appears to be quite important to an understanding here. It must be duly considered whether the conflict with officials of the Liberian nation would not have been avoided by Marcus Garvey had he adopted the attitude felt and expressed by Robert Campbell, especially so, when it is seen that this conflict contributed directly to the failure of the UNIA to achieve any more concrete results and thus hastened its decline.

A penetrating student of Pan-African nationalism, Hollis R.

Lynch, has noted the significant attitude of Robert Campbell thus: "But his goal was that of a 'national government' which would require the cooperation and support of native Africans. He therefore advised prospective emigrants to 'remember that the existing rulers must be respected, for they alone are the *bona fide* rulers of the place. The effort should be to fit them up to the proper standard, and not to supersede or crush them.'"

African nationhood had likewise been projected and publicized through the Pan-African Congress called by Dr. W. E. B. Du Bois in 1919 at Paris, and in the representation made and agitation conducted by William Monroe Trotter and the National Equal Rights League in connection with the Paris Peace Conference of 1918–1919.

While stress, therefore, was generally put by people of African origin in the U.S.A. upon the struggle for human rights, consciousness of their African origin and connection had never been wholly lost. The persistence of African consciousness had prepared the way and the conditions during and after the First World War contributed to the heightening of such African consciousness.

In order to achieve a fairly comprehensive and balanced understanding of the leadership conflict which contributed largely to the eclipse of Garvey's leadership and to the decline of the UNIA, it is necessary now to review more in detail Garvey's attitude and relationships to other leaders and bodies from the start of his public career in the United States.

It is noteworthy that the response of Dr. Du Bois to Garvey and his movement was at first favorable and quite constructive. In *The Crisis* of January 1921, Du Bois adjudged the "main lines" of Garvey's plan to be "perfectly feasible." Garvey was presented by Du Bois as declaring "American Negroes can, by accumulating and administering their own capital, organize industry, join the black centers of the South Atlantic by commercial enterprise, and in this way ultimately redeem Africa."

Subsequently, however, Marcus Garvey more and more emphasized differences rather than agreements, and soon came to regard himself as *the sole* protagonist of nationhood and empire for "the 400,000,000 Negroes of the world." Garvey now saw himself as thus advocating "the only solution" to the various ills,

economic, political, and social which people of African ancestry
generally suffered in diverse but basically kindred forms throughout the entire world.

"The difference between the Universal Negro Improvement
Association and other movements of this country," Marcus
Garvey declared, "is that the Universal Negro Improvement
Association seeks independence of government while the other
organizations seek to make the Negro a secondary part of existing
governments." The latter can hardly be considered as a fair
statement, since most of the leaders so characterized by Garvey
were in fact fighting *against secondary status and for primary
equal rights and parity for their people in every phase of
American life.*

The first considerable and fairly typical relationship of Marcus
Garvey to the leaders of existing organizations in the U.S.A. is to
be seen in his connection with the Liberty League of Afro-Americans and its leader, Hubert H. Harrison. The newcomer Garvey
was welcomed by Harrison and given a favorable introduction at
a mass meeting of Afro-Americans held by the Liberty League in
Bethel A.M.E. Church in Harlem on June 12, 1917. This
introduction gave Garvey his first significant contact with people
of African descent in the United States.

The attempt made by Marcus Garvey earlier to organize a
mass meeting in the parish hall of St. Mark's Roman Catholic
Church had been a failure. Only a few persons had attended, and
in his striving to make an impression, Garvey had stepped too far
forward and fallen off the platform. Nor were the first efforts to
reach the people through street-corner speeches in Harlem
notably successful.

Despite the welcome and favorable introduction accorded to
him by Harrison, Garvey was not slow to take advantage of the
schism which developed in the Liberty League. This dissension
arose over the ownership of *The Voice*, which Harrison insisted
was his own while several members held that this newspaper,
which was supported by the League, should belong to the
organization. In the split which ensued, Garvey influenced a
number of dissenters to join with him to launch in New York the
Universal Negro Improvement Association and African Communities League. Garvey's prior attempt, made some three years

before, to build such an organization in Jamaica had been largely unsuccessful.

Within this first small New York group of the Universal Negro Improvement Association there soon developed considerable conflict. In the course of a petty struggle involving personalities and power, one of Garvey's opponents read a letter from a former employer of Marcus Garvey, Duse Mohammed, which was said to have made damaging charges against Garvey's character.

Duse Mohammed was a Sudanese-Egyptian nationalist who had brought forward the slogan "Africa for the Africans," and who had published *The African Times and Orient Review* in London. It appears that Garvey had learned much from Duse Mohammed, but had decided to strike out himself for leadership. This conflict, heightened by Duse Mohammed's letter, caused the reduction of the membership to some fifty members.

Another conflict has been recorded by Garvey as due to "political designs" on the part of those who opposed him. Prominent among these opponents were Isaac B. Allen, the lawyer Louis A. Lavelle, and Samuel Augustus Duncan.

Against this opposition Garvey leveled the charge of "political designs" and attempts to use the organization in support of candidates for political office. This charge, however, could hardly have been based upon the principle of nonpolitical activity. For Garvey himself later gave endorsement and support through the Universal Political Union to the Republican candidate for President, Calvin Coolidge. Marcus Garvey, in utter disregard of his advocacy of "race first" even supported the Euro-American candidate Royal Weller for election in the 21st Congressional District of New York City in direct opposition to the Afro-American candidate, Dr. Charles H. Roberts.

It does appear, then, that the charge of "political designs" was insufficient to warrant Garvey's severe condemnation of this early opposition to his leadership, certainly so in the cases of Allen and Levelle. But the opposition of Duncan was shown to have been unprincipled, though on different grounds. For Samuel Augustus Duncan later, as head of the renamed West Indian Protective Society of America, addressed a letter to the British governor of the colony of St. Lucia which shamefully betrayed the oppressed

Caribbean people. In the despicable role of informer, Duncan branded the UNIA as "anti-white" and "anti-British," and as calculated "to create disturbance between white and colored people in the British possessions." Duncan further proposed that the *Negro World* be banned and called upon this British governor to ferret out among those seeking to enter the colony all persons in any way connected with the UNIA, the Black Star Line, or the *Negro World*, and then "to exercise your official discretion as to their admission into the colony."

During the summer of 1919 Marcus Garvey was repeatedly summoned for questioning by Assistant District Attorney Kilroe concerning the receipt of moneys for the projected Black Star Line. Kilroe is said to have warned Garvey several times against taking money or selling stock in business ventures unless in full accord with legal business procedure. Angered by what he deemed to be unwarranted harassment, Garvey publicly charged that "certain sinister forces" were working through Assistant District Attorney Kilroe to "scatter the sheep by striking the shepherd."

Indicted for libel as a result of this accusation against Kilroe, Garvey was forced to publish a retraction of this charge in order to avoid prosecution. It is important to note that Garvey is quoted as saying that Kilroe required him to "close down the Black Star Line" and warned him "to watch his step in the future." Mrs. Amy Jacques Garvey in *Garvey and Garveyism*[12] considered that Kilroe's action was "the result" of intervention of "two former associates" of Marcus Garvey. This view, however, overlooks the very likely probability that the effective motivation of Kilroe's attempt to stop Garvey from promoting the Black Star Line went far beyond the "two former associates" to the much more highly placed, hostile and powerful colonialist and "white supremacist" forces.

As the year 1919 wore on, the opposition to Marcus Garvey assumed a more dangerous and deadly character. A former employee, George Tyler, demanded to see Garvey at his office at 56 West 135th Street in New York City. As it was reported, when Garvey appeared Tyler accused the leader of swindling him out of a $25 debt, pulled a gun and opened fire; one bullet grazed Garvey's forehead and the next wounded him in the leg. It was further reported that Amy Ashwood, then secretary to Marcus Garvey and soon to be his first wife, rushed in front of Garvey and grappled with the assistant.

In jail after his arrest, Tyler is said to have declared that he had been sent to get Garvey. Later it was reported that Tyler jumped to his death from a window while being taken through a corridor by prison guards. But here, disturbing questions arise in the thinking mind. Were not the circumstances surrounding Tyler's attack upon Garvey and the subsequent "suicide" very strange and decidedly suspicious? Was George Tyler actually "sent to get Garvey?" If so, what forces sought to dispose of Garvey and stop the campaign to achieve the projected goal of free nationhood and the building of a powerful empire in Africa?

These questions raise the still more basic one which must be answered in order to arrive at a clear understanding and an adequate criterion or standard of judgment, and, therefore, to assess correctly the opposition to Marcus Garvey. Who was or what forces were "The Negro's Greatest Enemy"? Was the chief hostile and dangerous enemy the leaders of African descent, or the still higher and more powerful forces which controlled Western societies and upheld "white supremacy"? Reflection should make it clear that the ultimate compelling force would not be the leaders of African descent but the European colonizers and Euro-American controllers of vast wealth and great political power.

At the outset of his leadership career in the U.S.A., Marcus Garvey proclaimed "Africa for the Africans at home and abroad." In the UNIA organ, the *Negro World* of October 16, 1918, Garvey declared the African colonies, then ruled by European powers, to be the property of blacks and challenged "by God we are going to have them now or some time later, even if all the world is to waste itself in blood." Similarly, Garvey had affirmed in the *Negro World*: "Africa must be redeemed, and all of us pledge our manhood, our wealth and our blood to this sacred cause."

During the first Convention of the Universal Negro Improvement Association at the mammoth mass meeting held at Carnegie Hall in August 1920, Marcus Garvey thundered: "We say to the white man who now dominates Africa that it is to his interest to clear out of Africa now, because we are coming . . . 400,000,000 strong, and we mean to retake every square inch of the 12,000,000 square miles of African territory belonging to us by right Divine."

Unquestionably, this proclamation of intended reconquest of the entire continent of Africa caused the Garvey movement to be considered dangerous by the European colonialist powers which dominated almost all of Africa. This colonial system of European empire-builders showed itself directly and indirectly in onerous oppression and a whole vicious syndrome of thought, feeling, and action known generally as "white supremacy."

The counterpart of such colonialist domination in Africa manifested itself in somewhat different form in the United States of America, where the majority of the population was of European origin. In the U.S.A., there had existed for centuries chattel slavery imposed upon people of African descent. This slavery was followed after the Civil War and Emancipation of 1861–1865 by the less rigorous, but still onerous, oppressive and terrorist regime of peonage, debt slavery, forced labor, discrimination, disfranchisement, segregation, lynch murder, and the denial of almost all human and civil rights.

The Afro-American people were thus ruthlessly kept down at the bottom of the social order, even as the African and other colonial peoples were held down at the base of the structure of empire. Unfortunately, the basic connection and similar results of colonialism in Africa and of its counterpart in America were too often ignored by Marcus Garvey, as well as by several leaders of the Afro-American people in the United States. Thus the primary and most dangerous opposition of the "white supremacist" forces in Africa and the European centers of control, as well as in America, was tragically glossed over, underestimated, and sometimes even wholly forgotten.

This paramount "white supremacist" opposition operated covertly, and at times openly, to curb and to repress both the Garvey movement and the movement for civil rights and human status in the United States. But despite such racist repression which he only infrequently recognized, Marcus Garvey more and more came to see Afro-American leaders not only as his rivals but as his chief opposition, and "The Negro's Greatest Enemy." In turn these leaders frequently came to look upon Garvey as a challenging intruder who opposed the vital struggle of Afro-Americans for full human rights in the land of their birth or adoption.

The die was soon irrevocably cast; the relations between Garvey and other Afro-American leaders rapidly worsened and hardened. All prospect disappeared of essential unity, of fruitful cooperation, or even of symbiosis of tolerable coexistence. Meanwhile, the primary opposition, that of colonialist oppressors and all upholders of racist white supremacy, was woefully ignored. Marcus Garvey and many of the principal Afro-American leaders allowed themselves to fall into the most bitter opposition to each other and to engage in fratricidal and destructive conflict. Due recognition of this basic and fatal error now appears in retrospect to be the chief lesson of the rise and decline of the UNIA and the leadership of Marcus Garvey.

To these questions comment will later be made, since they involve an important aspect of this entire matter. Reference should now be made to the opposition to Richard E. Warner and Edgar M. Gray, two executive officers of the Black Star Line, who were discharged by Marcus Garvey and charged by him with misappropriation of the company's funds. These two officers retaliated by bringing libel suits against Garvey. It has been charged, although not proved, that Warner and Gray collaborated with Assistant District Attorney Kilroe against the leader Garvey.

The case of these officers of the Black Star Line has assumed importance because they were typical of many others who subsequently did not receive all their salaries and who came to feel themselves imposed upon by Marcus Garvey. This [situation] became frequent rather than exceptional in the organizations and business enterprises which Garvey launched and controlled. Garvey promised salaries on the mere hope of future income. When this income proved insufficient, Garvey expected the employees to endure this lack of pay stoically. To their demand for payment, Marcus Garvey frequently countered with accusations, from inefficiency and delinquency to outright misappropriation of funds.

A few more examples of the development of opposition and

leadership conflict should now be considered. Quite similar were the stated programs of the UNIA and those of the African Blood Brotherhood led by Cyril V. Briggs and fostered by its organ *The Crusader*. A very early issue of *The Crusader* projected a "Race Catechism" which extolled the present virtues and past achievements of "the Negro race" and stressed "duty to his race" in the following statement:

> To love one's race above one's self and to further the common interests of all above the private interest of one. To cheerfully sacrifice wealth, ease, luxuries, necessities and, if need be, life itself to attain for the race that greatness in arms, in commerce, in art, the three combined without which there is neither respect, honor, nor security.

The program of the ABB specifically called for a Federation of "all Negro organizations" within which a protective self-defense body would be ready to act at a moment's notice. In the African colonies, ABB representatives were to rally "Africans in the hinterland" into a "great Pan-African army." Accordingly, the ABB sought to cooperate with the UNIA. When in the April 1920 issue of *The Crusader* Briggs made certain criticisms of the Garvey movement, he was at pains to make it clear that he offered such criticisms as "friendly and constructive."

Yet Garvey soon attacked Briggs as a "white man," taking advantage of the latter's light complexion. Briggs answered by entering a libel suit in court against Garvey. A verdict in favor of Briggs was found by the court, but the jury rendered hardly any damages. Followers of Garvey took up the racist hue and cry against Briggs as "that white man passing as a black." On one occasion Cyril V. Briggs courageously went into Liberty Hall, the chief center of Garvey adherents, and amid a group of threatening Garveyites made a long and powerful speech. Remarkably, Briggs thus temporarily overcame his impediment of speech in order to defend himself and his position.

The breach between Garvey and Briggs became permanent during the UNIA Convention of 1922. No reply having been received in response to this written request for an alliance of the two organizations, Briggs had printed programs of the ABB distributed at this Convention. Because Briggs had hailed the Russian Revolution, particularly due to Lenin's Declaration of the Rights of Oppressed Nations to Self-Determination, Garvey now condemned Briggs as a "dangerous Bolshevik."

The program of the African Blood Brotherhood was never officially brought before the UNIA Convention, though the call for this Convention had urged attendance of delegates from "Negro organizations." Briggs afterwards declared that Garvey "felt it necessary to prevent them from officially presenting for the consideration of the delegates the program formulated by the ABB . . . because he saw that program gaining favor in the eyes of most of the delegates who had given cheerful consideration to the printed forms distributed by the ABB."

Not wholly to be endorsed, but appropriate for consideration here, is the conclusion reached by Theodore G. Vincent in the book just published, *Black Power and the Garvey Movement*:[13]

> The Garveyites broke with the ABB, then, because of the Brotherhood's extremism, not because of white Communist Party influence . . . Yet Garvey also lost as the ABB would have provided a most useful wedge in the UNIA's fight with its black American opposition. With a militant left-wing organization, the UNIA could have exposed the conservatism of Randolph, Du Bois and others. But the Brotherhood left Garvey no choice; it wanted revolution now.

It is certain, however, that the most formidable and withering opposition to Garvey proceeding from Afro-American leaders in the United States, was that which centered around the NAACP led by W. E. B. Du Bois, William Pickens, Robert W. Bengall, etc. Let it not be overlooked, however, that the really crippling opposition to Garvey came from the colonialist and white supremacist forces. What thinking person can doubt that these forces were behind the prosecution, conviction, and deportation of Marcus Garvey?

The opposition centered in the NAACP coalesced in time with that of A. Philip Randolph and Chandler Owen of *The Messenger* magazine. Starting out with a decidedly militant and radical stance, and thus encountering arrest by the U.S. government,

Randolph elected to remain and to go along with the Socialist Party, which failed to develop any consistent or effective struggle on behalf of the doubly oppressed Afro-American people. Randolph and Owen joined in the "Garvey Must Go" campaign though it was patently inconsistent with their professed socialist principles to aid the government of a capitalist state to deport or otherwise to abridge the civil rights of any of the working and oppressed people or any of their leaders.

The ire of Du Bois and other Afro-American leaders was fully aroused when Garvey shifted from condemnation of white supremacist attitudes and practices to questionable accommodation, then to virulent racism. When in a speech at Birmingham, Alabama, in 1921, President Warren G. Harding made a pronouncement to the effect that there are fundamental, inescapable, and eternal differences between the races which would forever forbid them from living together on the basis of equality, Marcus Garvey hastened to dispatch a telegram, and to publicize this widely, congratulating President Harding on this statement.

The People's Educational Forum, led by militant Afro-American Socialists of Harlem, adopted a resolution condemning President Harding for this harmful racist utterance and criticizing Marcus Garvey for his endorsement of the same. This was done in the spirit of principled opposition and constructive criticism. But Garvey was never known publicly to accept, or even seriously to consider, any criticism, however, restrained in tone or constructive in aim.

In this racist position, Garvey, therefore, persisted. What caused Afro-American leaders to heighten their opposition to the nth degree was Garvey's visit to the Ku Klux Klan headquarters in June 1922. This fateful visit has been judged by Theodore G. Vincent in *Black Power and the Garvey Movement* as "the one event which did more than any other to strengthen this opposition. . . . Garvey had committed his most grievous error." [14]

Not only the NAACP, but also many organizations and their leaders, deemed Garvey's visit to these most ruthless and murderous enemies of the Afro-American people to be treacherous truckling to vicious and deadly white supremacists. This situation was worsened by Garvey's publicly agreeing with the

Imperial Wizard of the Ku Klux Klan that "this is a white man's country."

Anger flared again when Garvey, by some specious and inverted mode of rationalization, declared to a crowd in North Carolina that white Southerners should be thanked for having "lynched race pride into the Negro." Fuel was added to the fire when Garvey asserted that "the black people should not be encouraged to remain in white people's countries and expect to be Presidents, Governors, Mayors, Senators, Congressmen, Judges and social and industrial leaders."

Infuriated by these statements boldly and unilaterally made by Marcus Garvey, which they saw as yielding precious rights and basic claims of the Afro-American people in the land of their birth and adoption, the chief Afro-American leaders roundly repudiated Garvey's position and disavowed his leadership. For in their eyes Garvey had bartered away three and a half centuries of toil and sweat and tears and blood of people of African descent.

In *The Crisis* of May 1924, Du Bois struck back. "Marcus Garvey is, without doubt, the most dangerous enemy of the Negro race in America and the world . . . either a lunatic or a traitor." Admittedly, the provocation was great, but it is all too clear that Du Bois had now fallen into the same error which Garvey had made when he branded certain Afro-American leaders as "the Negro's Greatest Enemy," as publicized in September 1923.

Du Bois had also descended into personalities and name-calling which had long become the common resort of Garvey. In an editorial of *The Crisis*, Du Bois characterized Garvey as a "little, fat, black man, ugly, but with intelligent eyes and a big head." When in this description Du Bois characterized Garvey as "black" and also as "ugly," Du Bois there used an expression connected with the contemptuous racist stereotype of people of African ancestry, which was generally employed by prejudiced white racists.

This statement, which used "black" along with "ugly" appeared in the eyes of many to give substance to Garvey's attack upon "mulattoes" as being thoroughly biased and hostile to "blacks." The term "mulatto" should be recognized for what it is, a derogatory term which equates people so branded with mules, which are the unnatural offspring of two different species, the horse and the donkey, and as such are sterile and unable to reproduce their kind. The racist characterization "mulatto" was devised by the Euro-American slave holder to stigmatize his own offspring by African women or by those of both African and European descent. "Mulattoes," "octoroons," "miscegenationists," such were the brands hurled by Garvey at his light-skinned opponents.

Garvey's animus against light-skinned Afro-Americans was doubtless the result of his experiences in Jamaica where the ruling Euro-Americans, being a small minority of some two percent of the total population, sought to maintain people of both European and African ancestry as a middle and buffer class. This brown middle class syndrome was developed more highly in Jamaica than in any of the other Caribbean areas, except perhaps Haiti. The "brown man" or "colored man" was encouraged by the ruling "white man" to look down upon the "black man" who was thus kept down, being the most exploited of toilers on the plantations and workers in the towns.

The true nature and specific source of this race prejudice, which utilized shades of color, is clearly to be seen in the secret instructions which Napoleon sent to Le Clerc in Haiti. . . . These revealing instructions have been quoted in *The Black Consul* [15] by Anatolil Vinogradov.

> You should give particular attention to the castes of colored people. Put them in a position to develop their national prejudices on a wide scale and give them the opportunity to rule over the blacks, and by these means you will secure the submission of both.

> Place full confidence, at any rate upon the surface, in mulattoes, Creoles, and colored people. Treat them, at any rate on the surface, the same as the whites; encourage marriages between colored people and white or mulatto women, but organize an absolutely contrary system in your relations with the black leaders.

Heedless of such admonitory facts, Garvey persisted in easy but faulty and facile generalizations about skin color. These generalizations he applied in the United States where shade prejudice did not prevail to such a degree, since Euro-Americans were here a majority of the population. The leader of the UNIA had become thoroughly dominated by the European colonialist concept of "race." To Garvey "race" was now the primary and all-important thing, the dominant force in every phase of life, even involving minute shades of color or other aspects linked with "race" rather than class position and the related modes of thought and feeling.

Garvey himself had emphasized the opposition of the group called the Friends of Negro Freedom, particularly the eight prominent Afro-Americans who signed a petition to the United States Attorney General, Harry M. Daugherty, urging that he "use his full influence completely to disband and extirpate this vicious movement and speedily push the government's case against Marcus Garvey for using the mails to defraud." The noted signatories were Harry H. Pace, John E. Nail, and Julia P. Coleman who were business people; the publishers Robert S. Abbott of the *Chicago Defender,* Chandler Owen of *The Messenger* and George W. Harris of the *New York News*; and William Pickens and Robert W. Bagnall, officers of the NAACP. It is noteworthy here that Dr. W. E. B. Du Bois never signed this petition.

These so-called Friends of Negro Freedom . . . were damaging the cause of freedom whether they were fully conscious [of it] or not. Such collaboration upheld the denial of basic civil and human rights and also helped to establish a precedent for further repressive acts against organizations and leaders of the oppressed Afro-American people.

That these Friends of Negro People were of African descent did not cause them to think correctly or to act upon principles of freedom. One of the biggest possible mistakes, therefore, is to assume that everybody who has a lot of pigment under the skin is by that token a genuine "soul brother" or "soul sister." For example, Moishe Tshombe who collaborated with Belgian and other European oppressors to remove the President of the Congo Republic, Patrice Lumumba, from the scene, can in no wise be considered to be a "soul brother." Judgment must be duly made, not upon the color and shade of skin or so-called "racial" classification, but upon what position is or is not taken to assure freedom and to enhance basic human status. This appears to be the proper basis for judgment rather than color and "race" which came to aggravate the conflict between Marcus Garvey and most of his opposition.

Significant among those whose opposition shook the confidence of many people in the leadership of Marcus Garvey was a former friend and associate, W. A. Domingo. A Jamaican of African descent, as was Garvey, Domingo edited the *Negro World* for a considerable period. But like so many others who worked with Marcus Garvey, Domingo also reached the point where human dignity made it impossible for him to tolerate Garvey's overbearing manner any longer. Domingo then became one of Garvey's most active, knowledgeable, and powerful opponents.

In *The Emancipator* newspaper Domingo keenly analyzed Garvey's failed or failing business projects, and tellingly exposed the inconsistencies of Garvey's racial position and actions. *The Emancipator*, which had secured most of its funds from militant labor unions, did not have enough money to continue publishing beyond ten issues. The effect of those ten issues, however, certainly operated to portray and to expose Garvey as "a giant with feet in clay."

Editorials of *The Emancipator*, like that captioned "Bubbles," marshaled facts not generally known which showed Garvey's enterprises had failed or were failing principally because of mismanagement. One such editorial commented upon the inconsistency of the man who preached "race first" to the "Negro," but who had his clothes made by a Jewish tailor. This fact had been carefully established by Domingo, who caused the advertising manager to secure and to insert an advertisement from that tailor which boldly proclaimed "Tailor to Marcus Garvey."

Since there were scores of fine tailors who were members of the UNIA, not to speak of hundreds of capable tailors throughout Harlem, it was difficult if not impossible for Garvey to explain away this undeniable contradiction between preachment and practice. Though apparently a small matter, this exposure had a far-reaching effect in questioning the trustworthiness of the leader of the "race" movement. Regrettably, no file of *The Emancipator* has been available for some time now, but it is to be hoped that such a file will be found, since this should throw great light on Garvey's leadership, the opposition, and on the subsequent decline of the UNIA mass movement.

It must be said that Domingo also allowed himself to fall into an unprincipled position. When Garvey was convicted of using the mails to defraud in connection with the promotion and operation of the Black Star Line, Domingo sent a telegram to a government prosecutor congratulating him upon having "caged the Tiger." This action was taken by Domingo without consulting any of his associates in the publication of *The Emancipator*.

On the other hand, it is to be observed that W. A. Domingo had been stabbed in the back with a penknife by a Garveyite, but escaped with a skin wound because of a heavy overcoat. The Rev. E. Ethelred Brown, an Afro-Jamaican Unitarian Minister, was slashed in his pulpit by an adherent of the Garvey movement because of his attempt constructively to criticize some of the weakness of the leadership of Marcus Garvey. The contributor of this chapter was seriously endangered when fanatical followers of Garvey rushed the ladder from which he was speaking at the corner of Seventh Avenue and West 138th Street. The timely action of a listener, who brandished a weapon against the attackers, saved the speaker from being thrown to the ground with who knows what evil or fatal consequences.

Typical of such all too numerous attacks was that made upon the Basuto "Prince" Mokete Manoedi, author of a pamphlet challenging Garvey's claims to represent Africans. Manoedi declared that Africans were "not favorably impressed with [the] unmitigated presumption of this man Garvey in electing himself Provisional President of Africa." Police had to protect Manoedi from the menacing crowd of Garveyites.

Another intellectual leader who was finally driven into opposition to Marcus Garvey was Bishop George Alexander McGuire who had come from Antigua. Aiding Garvey in the projection of a black God and a black Christ to counter the white Christ imposed upon people of African descent, Bishop McGuire wrote a catechism for the UNIA and developed the African Orthodox Church. Standing with Garvey in numerous conflicts with associates and opponents McGuire now found himself under attack.

At a meeting held at Rush Memorial Church in Harlem, when Bishop McGuire attempted to state his case in relation to Garvey, followers of the latter crowded into the church and made such a commotion that Bishop McGuire could not be heard. These followers of Garvey became so menacing that the organizers of the meeting found it necessary to surround McGuire and take him out through a back door in order to escape those who were threatening to kill him.

The opposition of the Reverend J. W. Eason to the chief leader of the UNIA was to end in his death in New Orleans. As the leader designated by the UNIA movement for the United States, Eason had become quite popular with the crowds who thronged Liberty Hall in Harlem, but he had found it necessary to oppose certain positions taken by Garvey, especially in respect to the Ku Klux Klan. Before the Rev. Eason died of the wounds inflicted upon him, he stated that he recognized his assailants as belonging to the Garvey "police" forces. In his biographical sketch of Marcus Garvey in *The World's Great Men of Color,* J. A. Rogers wrote that Eason had been killed by a fanatical Garveyite, it was charged at Garvey's instigation.[16]

Such a charge, of course, was difficult to prove, but was not considered improbable in view of the frequent attacks upon the critics of Garvey. Indeed, a clause in the UNIA constitution, which, if not written, was certainly endorsed by Marcus Garvey, could be and was interpreted as giving support to such criminal assaults. This clause declared: "No one shall be received by the Potentate and his consort who has been convicted of felony, except such crime or felony was committed in the interest of the Universal Negro Improvement Association."

Progressive and positive nationalism, expressing the right of the African, as of all other peoples, to self-determination, self-government, and self-realization, now gave way in Garvey's consciousness more and more to unrestrained and reactionary nationalism. It should be noted that progressive nationalism is marked by due regard for the rights and liberties of other nations and peoples while cherishing, promoting, and defending the best interests of one's own nation. On the contrary, reactionary nationalism is evident in the selfish and ruthless disdain for the freedom and welfare of other nations and their people, and in the elevation of the supposed interests of a particular nation above those of all others.

The essence of progressive nationalism is, therefore, *love for one's nation within the framework of regard for and observance of the liberties and well-being of all others*. The absence of such consideration or feeling indicated a reversion to the most antisocial, repressive, inhuman, and destructive attitudes and policies. "Nationality is sacred to me," wrote Mazzini, advocate of the unity and freedom of Italy, "because I see in it the instrument of labor for the well-being and progress of all men."

Examples of these two differing and opposite types of nationalism and nationalist attitudes may be seen in the experience of many peoples. An excellent contrast of these two attitudes is evident in the comparison of Napoleon and Washington with Toussaint L'Ouverture made by Wendell Phillips in his oration on the outstanding leader of the Haitian Revolution. He declared: "I would call him Napoleon, but Napoleon made his way to empire over broken oaths and through a sea of blood. This man never broke his word . . . I would call him Washington, but the great Virginian held slaves. This man risked his empire rather than permit the slave trade in the humblest village of his dominions." Similarly, the progressive nationalism of President Alexander Petion of Haiti was noted by the Haitian scholar Dantes Bellegrade in *La Nation Haitienne*. "Petion showed that he did not wish liberty and independence only for Haiti but for all the people weighed down by the insupportable yoke of foreign domination . . . President Petion gave him (Simon Bolivar), in order to allow him to resume the war against the Spanish, money, arms, ammunitions, some provisions, and a small printing press. Some Haitians enrolled under the colors of Bolivar." [17]

By contrast repressive nationalism is evident in Mussolini's fascist Italian nationalism projected in the horrendous slaughter of Ethiopian people including deluging noncombatants, men, women, and children, with poison gas from airplanes. In the same way Nazi nationalism, as propounded and practiced by Hitler, his armies, and storm troopers, rode roughshod with frightful massacre over millions of other nations and minority groups.

Marcus Garvey "worshipped Napoleon," as J. A. Rogers had
noted. This has prime significance because of the final reactionary political role and ruthless sacrifice of human rights and
lives by the man who transformed the revolutionary French
nation into an Empire woefully oppressing other nations and
peoples. The fact that Napoleon, with a vast and murderous
force, had striven to re-enslave the liberated Haitian people did
not affect Garvey's adulation of this white supremacist. That
Napoleon had caused the peerless leader of the Haitian Revolution, Toussaint L'Ouverture to be seized, imprisoned, and
hastened to his death, did not deter Marcus Garvey from
continued worship and emulation of this reactionary and deadly
enemy of people of African descent.

The Napoleonic tendencies and ambitions of Marcus Garvey
were recognized by certain UNIA aides, particularly by Ulysses
S. Poston who had been "minister of industries" of the UNIA but
had been defeated for re-election through Garvey's determination to secure absolute power over all offices and every aspect or
ramification of the UNIA. Poston admonished Garvey: "In your
mad rush to serve your race, in your mad rush to serve humanity,
pause long enough to study yourself introspectively . . . Remember Napoleon was ambitious to serve his people." But this
effort at counsel and restraint went altogether unheeded.

Garvey could, therefore, readily seek alliance with such
terrorist and racist prototypes of fascist organizations as the Ku
Klux Klan and later the Anglo-Saxon Clubs of America. As
Rogers recalled: "He had John Powell, head of these clubs, speak
from his platform on October 28, 1925, where Powell praised and
sold 'White America,' by Ernest Sevier Cox, a pseudohistory
intended to prove that Negroes were an inferior race from the
dawn of time." The Anglo-Saxon Clubs were notorious for their
vicious campaign of racist hatred and incitement to deadly
violence against Afro-Americans and against Jews, Catholics, and
Southern European immigrants.

The following characterization of the position which Marcus
Garvey had then reached has been given by J. A. Rogers in
World's Great Men of Color.

It was in short, racial fascism. He seemed to believe honestly that
the best way to right the wrong of his people was to retort by

adopting the *modus operandi* of the racial imperialists he was fighting. . . . He, himself, declared that his movement was fascistic. He said, "We were the first fascists . . . Mussolini copied fascism from me . . ." [18]

Corroborating the foregoing pronouncements, which Rogers declared were made while they both were in London, is the further bold pronouncement and prescription which Garvey published in his monthly magazine, the *Blackman*: "What the Negro needs is a Hitler."

It seems requisite now to summarize briefly conclusions from this review of the historical development of and around Marcus Garvey, his leadership, and the movement he founded.

1. The tendency on the part of Marcus Garvey to underestimate, and often to disregard, the *primary* opposition of European and Euro-American racists to all significant endeavors to improve the condition of people of African descent.

2. The attitude of Garvey which increasingly regarded other Afro-American leaders as his rivals in an inevitable struggle for power and thus as constituting "The Negro's Greatest Enemy."

3. The acceptance of the European colonialist concept of "race" as valid, natural, fundamental, and requiring the separation of so-called "races" in order to maintain "race purity." This view led directly to opportunist disregard of the necessary and vital struggle for basic human rights, and even to accommodation to the most hostile Euro-American racist forces like the Ku Klux Klan.

4. The adoption of the European imperialist assumption of rule over Africans as demonstrated in the title, "Provisional President of Africa."

5. The observable trend in the views and policies of Garvey away from progressive and healthy nationalism toward self-centered and reactionary nationalism.

6. The unresolved inner contradictions between progressive and reactionary aims, drives, and policies, with the reactionary tendencies gaining increasing force and dominance.

7. The resulting egocentric and aggressive personality which could brook no other leaders and intellectual figures standing beside himself nor tolerate anything short of total dominance.

8. The leanings of Marcus Garvey toward fascist aims and methods as evidenced in the Napoleonic complex he displayed and in his favorable judgments of Hitler and Mussolini.

Still relevant apparently is the estimate made of Marcus Garvey in "Africa-Conscious Harlem" published in *Freedomways* magazine in 1963. From this estimate the following statements may now be quoted, in conclusion of this chapter.

It appears that the founder and leader of the UNIA demonstrated two powerful drives which were basically opposed to each other. One was clearly the progressive tendency which projected "the redemption of Africa" and the "Declaration of Rights of the Negro Peoples of the World." The other was obviously reactionary in its Napoleonic urge for personal power and empire, with the inevitable accompaniment of racial exclusiveness and hostility. This latter tendency was evident when Garvey declared, on taking the title of Provisional President of Africa in 1920: "The signal honor of being Provisional President of Africa is mine . . . It is like asking Napoleon to take the world."

Unfortunately, Marcus Garvey veered evermore toward the more extreme forms of empire building, unlimited individual control, and unrestrained racism. At length these destructive forces were allowed to overshadow and outweigh the constructive pristine ideas of African nationalism, liberation, and independence . . . Besides, the constant attacks which Marcus Garvey made upon people of both African and European ancestry, whom he derisively called "the hybrids of the Negro race," did not conduce to the unifying of all people of African descent, who, regardless of varying shades of color and other physical characteristics, were compelled to suffer similar oppression whether as colonial subjects or as oppressed minority groups . . .

Finally, the open condemnation of Liberian officials by Garvey, his several reprisals against several of his chief associates, his poor choice of certain officers, and the inept conduct of the business enterprises which he controlled, left the movement wide open to the disastrous blows of those who began to fear its growing power . . . Nevertheless, the Garvey movement did heighten and spread the consciousness of African origin and identity among the various peoples of African descent on a wider scale than ever before. This was its definite and positive contribution.

Garvey: A Mass Leader*

BY E. FRANKLIN FRAZIER

THE GARVEY MOVEMENT is a crowd movement essentially different from any other social phenomenon among Negroes. For the most part American Negroes have sought self-magnification in fraternal orders and the church. But these organizations have failed to give that support to the Negro's ego-consciousness which the white masses find in membership in a political community, or on a smaller scale in Kiwanis clubs and the Ku Klux Klan. In a certain sense Garvey's followers form the black Klan of America.

The reason for Garvey's success in welding the Negroes into a crowd movement becomes apparent when we compare his methods and aims with those of other leaders. Take, for example, the leadership of Booker Washington. Washington could not be considered a leader of the masses of Negroes, for his program commended itself chiefly to white people and those Negroes who prided themselves on their opportunism. There was nothing popularly heroic or inspiring in his program to captivate the imagination of the average Negro. In fact the Negro was admonished to play an inglorious role. Certain other outstanding efforts among Negroes have failed to attract the masses because they have lacked the characteristics which have distinguished the Garvey movement. It is only necessary to mention such an

* *Nation*, CXXIII, August 18, 1926, pages 147–148.

organization as the National Urban League and its leadership to realize that so reasoned a program of social adjustment is lacking in everything that appeals to the crowd. The leadership of Dr. Du Bois has been too intellectual to satisfy the mob. Even his glorification of the Negro has been in terms which escape the black masses. The Pan-African Congress which he has promoted, while supporting to some extent the boasted aims of Garvey, has failed to stir any considerable number of American Negroes. The National Association for the Advancement of Colored People, which has fought uncompromisingly for equality for the Negro, has never secured, except locally and occasionally, the support of the masses. It has lacked the dramatic element.

The status of Negroes in American life makes it easy for a crowd movement to be initiated among them. In America the Negro is repressed and an outcast. Some people are inclined to feel that this repression is only felt by cultured Negroes. As a matter of fact many of them can find satisfaction in the intellectual and spiritual things of life and do not need the support to their personalities that the average man requires. The average Negro, like other mediocre people, must be fed upon empty and silly fictions in order that life may be bearable. In the South the most insignificant white man is made of supreme worth simply by the fact of his color, not to mention the added support he receives from the Kiwanis or the Klan.

Garvey came to America at a time when all groups were asserting themselves. Many American Negroes have belittled his influence on the ground that he is a West Indian. It has been said that Garvey was only able to attract the support of his fellow countrymen. The truth is that Garvey aroused the Negroes of Georgia as much as those of New York, except where the black preacher discouraged anything that threatened his income, or where white domination smothered every earthly hope. Moreover, this prejudice against the West Indian Negro loses sight of the contribution of the West Indian to the American Negro. The West Indian, who has been ruled by a small minority instead of being oppressed by the majority, is more worldly in his outlook. He has been successful in business. He does not need the lodge, with its promise of an imposing funeral, or the church, with its hope of a heavenly abode as an escape from a sense of inferiority.

By his example he has given the American Negro an earthly goal.

Garvey went even further. He not only promised the despised Negro a paradise on earth, but he made the Negro an important person in his immediate environment. He invented honors and social distinctions and converted every social invention to his use in his effort to make his followers feel important. While everyone was not a "Knight" or "Sir" all his followers were "Fellow-men of the Negro Race." Even more concrete distinctions were open to all. The women were organized into Black Cross Nurses, and the men became uniformed members of the vanguard of the Great African Army. A uniformed member of a Negro lodge paled in significance beside a soldier of the Army of Africa. A Negro might be a porter during the day, taking his orders from white men, but he was an officer in the black army when it assembled at night in Liberty Hall. Many a Negro went about his work singing in his heart that he was a member of the great army marching to "heights of achievements." And even in basing his program upon fantastic claims of empire, Garvey always impressed his followers that his promise was more realistic than that of those who were constantly arguing for the theoretical rights of the Negro. In the *Negro World* for October 18, 1924, he warned his followers that

> Those who try to ridicule the idea that America is a white man's country are going to find themselves sadly disappointed one of these days, homeless, shelterless, and unprovided for. Some of us do harp on our constitutional rights, which sounds reasonable in the righteous interpretation thereof, but we are forgetting that righteousness is alien to the world and that sin and materialism now triumph, and for material glory and honor and selfishness man will slay his brother. And in the knowledge of this, is the Negro still so foolish as to believe that the majority of other races are going to be so unfair and unjust to themselves as to yield to weaker peoples that which they themselves desire?

And after all this is essentially what most Negroes believe in spite of the celebrated faith of the Negro in America.

A closer examination of the ideals and symbols which Garvey always held up before his followers shows his mastery of the technique of creating and holding crowds. The Negro group becomes idealized. Therefore he declares he is as strongly against race-intermixture as a Ku Kluxer. He believes in a "pure black race just as all self-respecting whites believe in a pure white race." According to Garvey, civilization is about to fall and the Negro is called upon "to evolve a national ideal based upon freedom, human liberty, and true democracy." The "redemption of Africa" is the regaining of a lost paradise. It is always almost at hand.

This belief has served the same purpose as does the myth of the general strike in the syndicalist movement. Garvey, who is dealing with people imbued with religious feeling, endows the redemption of Africa with the mystery of the regeneration of mankind. He said on one occasion: "No one knows when the hour of Africa's redemption cometh. It is in the wind. It is coming one day like a storm. It will be here. When that day comes, all Africa will stand together."

Garvey gave the crowd that followed him victims to vent their hatred upon, just as the evangelist turns the hatred of his followers upon the Devil. Every rabble must find someone to blame for its woes. The Negro who is poor, ignorant, and weak naturally wants to place the blame on anything except his own incapacity. Therefore Garvey was always attributing the misfortunes of the Negro group to traitors and enemies. Although the identity of these "traitors" and "enemies" was often obscure, as a rule they turned out to be Negro intellectuals. The cause for such animosity against this class of Negroes is apparent when we remember that Garvey himself lacks formal education.

Garvey, who was well acquainted with the tremendous influence of religion in the life of the Negro, proved himself matchless in assimilating his own program to the religious experience of the Negro. Christmas, with its association of the lowly birth of Jesus, became symbolic of the Negro's birth among the nations of the world. Easter became the symbol of the resurrection of an oppressed and crucified race. Such naive symbolism easily kindled enthusiasm among his followers. At other times Garvey made his own situation appear similar to that of Jesus. Just as the Jews incited the Roman authorities against

Jesus, other Negro leaders were making the United States authorities persecute him.

Most discussions of the Garvey movement have been concerned with the feasibility of his schemes and the legal aspects of the charge which brought him finally to the Atlanta federal prison. It is idle to attempt to apply to the schemes that attract crowds the test of reasonableness. Even experience fails to teach a crowd anything, for the crowd satisfies its vanity and longing in the beliefs it holds. Nor is it surprising to find Garvey's followers regarding his imprisonment at present as martyrdom for the cause he represents, although the technical charge on which he was convicted is only indirectly related to his program. But Garvey has not failed to exploit his imprisonment. He knows that the average man is impressed if anyone suffers. Upon his arrest he gave out the following statement: "There has never been a movement where the Leader has not suffered for the Cause, and not received the ingratitude of the people. I, like the rest, am prepared for the consequence." As he entered the prison in Atlanta he sent a message to his followers which appeared in his paper, the *Negro World,* for February 14, 1925. He paints himself as a sufferer for his group and blames his lot on a group of plotters. In commending his wife to the care of his followers he says: "All I have, I have given to you. I have sacrificed my home and my loving wife for you. I intrust her to your charge, to protect and defend in my absence. She is the bravest little woman I know." Such pathos he knew the mob could not resist, and the final word he sent to his supporters under the caption, "If I Die in Atlanta," with its apocalyptic message, raises him above mortals. He bade them "Look for me in the whirlwind or the storm, look for me all around you, for, with God's grace, I shall come and bring with me the countless millions of black slaves who have died in America and the West Indies and the millions in Africa to aid you in the fight for liberty, freedom, and life."

Since his imprisonment Garvey has continued to send his weekly message on the front of his paper to his followers warning them against their enemies and exhorting them to remain faithful to him in his suffering. It is uncritical to regard Garvey as a common swindler who has sought simply to enrich himself when the evidence seems to place him among those so-called cranks who refuse to deal realistically with life. He has the distinction of initiating the first real mass movement among American Negroes.

After Marcus Garvey—
What of the Negro?*

BY KELLY MILLER

GARVEY ARRIVED IN New York at the psychological moment. The European nations were engaged in titanic conflict. America had, so far, stood aside in benevolent aloofness and apologetic neutrality. The Negro caught the sound of such expressions as "the rights of the minority" and "a war for self-determination," and was thrilled by their reverberations. . . . The Negro, along with the rest, was conscripted to fight for the freedom of white men in Europe, himself being denied full participation in the benefits of freedom at home.

Harlem was just becoming the great Negro metropolis. The necessities of the war were bringing tens of thousands of Negroes to New York from all parts of the country. Thousands were also attracted from the West Indian Islands. . . . The West Indians were radical beyond the rest and seemed to be better adepts in mob psychology. The West Indian Negro in America is a political conundrum. Conservative at home, he becomes radical abroad. About this time the Negroes in New York, native and West Indian, were asserting the rights and recounting the wrongs of the race in such severe terms of denunciation as to cause the government much uneasiness. The espionage department kept the more assertive ones under surveillance, suppressed the most

* *Contemporary Review*, CXXXI, April 1927, Pages 492–500.

outspoken publications and threatened the orators, editors, and authors with serious punishment.

In those days Marcus Garvey arrived in Harlem. . . . He built "Liberty Hut"—a crude tabernacle, with a seating capacity of six thousand, where on every Sunday evening he addressed overflowing crowds who hung breathless upon his words. The magnetic power of his charm and spell seemed never to wane.

At this stage Mr. Garvey appeared to be a crass pragmatist, relying wholly upon the instrumentality of material agencies to accomplish his remote spiritual objective. He hoped to develop race consciousness through race patronage and cooperative enterprise. Grocery stores, laundries, restaurants, hotels, and printing plants were organized under the auspices of the Universal Negro Improvement Association. These all failed as fast as they were founded. But the fanatic is never daunted by failure. How Mr. Garvey could hope that the operation of a few shops in Harlem could seriously affect the fate of the continent of Africa surpasses normal human understanding. But no whit abashed by the failure of his business ventures, the undaunted dreamer forthwith proceeded to launch the "Black Star Line" of steamships to trade with the West Indies and with the continent of Africa, a stupendous act of folly. The combined genius and wealth of America has not been able to operate competitive ocean-carrying trade. But the fanaticism and faith of Marcus Garvey performed miracles in inspiring his followers with confidence and zeal for the impossible. As fast as one steamship failed they were ready to provide for another. . . .

It was in 1921, in the presence of six thousand of his followers and admirers in "Liberty Hut," that he proceeded to the formal inauguration of the Empire of Africa. Garvey himself was crowned President-General of the United Negro Improvement Association and Provisional President of Africa, who with one Potentate and one Supreme Deputy Potentate constituted the royalty of the Empire of Africa. Knights of the Nile, Knights of the Distinguished Service Order of Ethiopia, and Dukes of the Niger and of Uganda, constituted the nobility. But pride goeth before a fall. The inevitable end was near. Dissension broke out within the ranks. The question of who shall sit on the right hand

and on the left hand in the kingdom always precipitates
unfriendly rivalry among the disciples. Internal dissensions,
however, were easily settled by the last word of the President-
General. Mr. Garvey's personal authority so far transcended that
of his following that no other name than his figures conspicuously
in the movement. . . .

He preaches that the Negro must build on his own basis apart
from the white man's foundation, if he ever hopes to be a master
builder. He therefore urges the race to look to the land of their
mothers across the sea for future growth and expansion. In the
United States the African sojourners will never be permitted to
rise above the level of hewers of wood and drawers of water. It is
said that he sought conference with the rulers of the Ku Klux
Klan and found himself in accord with the hooded order on this
basic proposition of racial relations, though each side reached the
same conclusion by different processes of reason. This doctrine of
inevitable subordination, naturally enough, aroused the bitterest
antagonism of the Afro-American leaders who have staked all
their hopes on the opposite proposition.

Again, Mr. Garvey believes, with frenzied fanaticism, in the
continent of Africa as the destined end and way of all the
scattered fragments of the black race who are now sojourning
among the whiter nations of the earth. The educated Afro-American has little interest and no enthusiasm for his motherland.
Frederick Douglass epitomized this sentiment in the sententious
saying: "I have none of the banana in me." Dr. Du Bois has been
trying for a number of years to promote a Pan-African Congress
for the discussion of the race question on a worldwide scale.
There are probably not half a dozen educated Negroes in
America who have evinced any genuine enthusiasm or passionate
interest for Garvey's proposition. . . .

At the climax of antagonism, Mr. Garvey took up the
apotheosis of blackness as offset to the existing deification of
whiteness. He would have God painted black. This caused a
violent revulsion of feeling on the part even of black men who
had become habituated to bow down and worship at the shrine
of a color alien to their own. . . . They simply held up their
hands in frantic disgust at such a revolting blasphemy.

With this wide difference the battle between the antagonists became war to the death. Negro newspapers and magazines were filled with criticisms and denunciations of this new and dangerous doctrine. The Garvey Movement became the Garvey menace. This interloper was denounced as a trouble maker, dangerous to whites and blacks alike. His motives and his honesty were impugned. It was strongly urged that he should be deported as a foreigner stirring up strife among native-born Americans. . . . No personal wrongdoing was attributed to him by way of improper personal profit. In the eyes of those who believe in him, he is as much a martyr to his cause as Gandhi of India. Both have sinned against the technicalities of the law and must suffer under the law. This is the price which the reformer must reckon to pay when his propaganda is at vital variance with established public policy. . . .

If we consider, as it now seems reasonable to do, that the Garvey Movement is a spent force, it might be profitable to consider the present and future effect of this hectic movement upon the Negro race and upon the permanent relations of the black and white races. The chief achievement of Marcus Garvey consists in his quickening the sense of race consciousness and self-dignity on the part of the common people among black folks all over the world. The effect of all the movements which have been launched by the intelligentsia among Negroés is that they have never been able to penetrate below a certain level of social grade. They do not reach the common people or stir their imagination. The National Association for the Advancement of Colored People, with its capable and consecrated leadership, so far has been able to make no great impression on the heart and imagination of the proletariat. But Garvey arouses the zeal of millions of the lowliest to the frenzy of a crusade. . . .

Various missionary societies for centuries have been operating in Africa but have made little headway in lighting up the dark continent. Now comes Marcus Garvey, if not with a new principle, at least with a new program. . . . He believes that philanthropy paralyzes the energies of the black peoples of the world and pauperizes their spirit. He has an unfathomable faith in the possibilities of his people. No greater vision has ever haunted the human mind. The accomplishment of the dream is worth a thousand years of the united endeavor of mankind. It is impossible to conceive of any task which will inure to greater advantage to the human race.

⚇ MARCUS GARVEY
IN HIS OWN WORDS

An Answer to His Many Critics

IMMEDIATE RELEASE

THE FOLLOWING LETTER is released at the American Head-Quarters of The Universal Negro Improvement Association, 52–54–56 West 135th Street, New York City, To the White Press of the World by Marcus Garvey as an Explanation of the Aims and Objects of the Universal Negro Improvement Association of Which He Is President-General.

THE EDITOR
Sir:

You have, for quite some time, been publishing news, letters and other articles in your paper purporting to be information about the activities of the Universal Negro Improvement Association, the "Back to Africa Movement," so named by critics, the Black Star Line Steamship Corporation and myself, but you have never been fair enough to give to the public and your readers the other side of the story of the picture painted by you.

It has been my policy not to pay any attention to prejudiced and unfair criticism, in that I always believed that truth of any kind cannot be permanently crushed; but whilst I personally still feel this way, a large number of my friends and wellwishers have far more than a thousand times endeavored to have me place the

Association I represent in a proper light before the public so that the general misrepresentations of the Movement can be clarified. I still would not have yielded but for the increasing demands made upon me by those whose interest I serve and because this misrepresentation has been conveyed to a large number of your readers who seem to regard me as some "hideous" person who hates all white people.

I am not blaming you for the stand you have taken against me and against the Movement I represent because I know that you have arrived at your conclusions through the misrepresentations made to you directly or indirectly by my enemies within my own Race who, being jealous of my success in assembling together more members of my Race throughout this country and the world than any other person has done, have been and are endeavoring to so misrepresent me as to cause an opposition sentiment to develop that would eventually handicap and thwart the objects of the organization I am leading.

The real function of the Press is public service without prejudice or partiality; to convey the truth as it is seen and understood without favoritism or bias.

You have already by your many reports published one side of my activities. I feel that you will be honest enough to now publish at least a part [of the other side].

First of all, let me say that all that has been published about the Universal Negro Improvement Association and about me tending to show that there is any hatred of other people, any scheme for personal gain, any desire to stir up race antagonism, and that my organization tends to promote race friction, are all false. . . .

The oft repeated statement that the Movement is sponsored and supported by the ignorant and gullible is so frivolous as to need no comment. Our Movement reflects the highest intelligence of the race, and as proof of this we have challenged and still challenge anyone within the race to debate our differences. No one has been manly enough out of the critics to accept the challenge.

Among our bitterest critics and opponents are W. E. B. Du Bois, James Weldon Johnson and their National Association for the Advancement of Colored People. Yet, these persons have not the manhood to match the intelligence of their Association with that of the Universal Negro Improvement Association by accepting the challenge.

Our organization stands for the highest in racial ideals, yielding to all races the right to ascend to the loftiest peak of human progress and demanding for ourselves a similar privilege.

Starting our organization in New York four and one half years ago with thirteen members, we have now grown into an approximate membership of five million people scattered all over the world, but principally . . . in the United States of America, Canada, South and Central America, the West Indies and Africa. It is because of the rapid growth and success of this organization that other Negroes have sought to defeat me by hostile propaganda in their own newspapers and with the misrepresentations they supply to the white press . . .

Every effort among Negroes has been made and exhausted by my enemies to defeat me and yet they have failed, hence they resort to the government and the white press for the accomplishment of this purpose. To repeat, it is not because I fear defeat or the sting of unfriendly or unfair criticism that I write to you, because I owe my success in organization to no one. . . . I am not personally disturbed, but I would like the public to be correctly informed about the Movement I represent. . . .

The Negro problem in America and elsewhere must be solved. We cannot do this by postponing the issue or by sidetracking it. We might as well face it now.

Some Negroes, such as the faction of the mulatto W. E. B. Du Bois, believe that the problem will be solved by assimilation and miscegenation. At least they believe that the black race will become, through social contact and intercourse, so mixed up with the white race as to produce a new type, probably like Du Bois himself, which will in time be the real American. It is for such a contingency that he and his associates are consciously or unconsciously working.

We of the Universal Negro Improvement Association believe in a pure black race, just as now all self-respecting whites believe in a pure white race as far as that can be.

We are conscious of the fact that slavery brought upon us the curse of many colors within one race, but that is no reason why we of ourselves should perpetuate the evil, hence, instead of encouraging a wholesale bastardy in the race, we feel that we should now set out to create a race type and standard of our own which could not, in the future, be stigmatized by bastardy but could be recognized and respected as the true race type anteceding even our own time.

We believe that the Negro has at least a social, cultural, and political destiny of his own and any attempt to make a white man of him is bound to fail in the end. In like manner, we believe that you cannot successfully make a Negro out of a white man in that he too has at least a social, cutural and political destiny of his own. Therefore, the fullest opportunity should be given to both races to develop independently a civilization of their own, meaning not to infer thereby that either race would not, in a limited degree, become a part of the civilization of each without losing their respective racial, cultural, social and political identities.

If this can be done, then we feel that the Negro too should have a government of his own and not remain in the countries of whites to aspire for and to positions that they will never get under the rule of the majority group upon their merely asking for or demanding such positions by an accidental Constitutional right. . . .

How far the two races will travel together socially, industrially and politically in America before a serious civil clash ensues is the speculation of all earnest thoughtful people. It is because I personally want to prevent such a clash that I am advocating the cause of the Universal Negro Improvement Association.

My interest in the Negro peoples of America and of the world is purely racial, because I feel proud of my race; I have the highest regard for the Motherhood of the race and I see absolutely no reason why all Negroes should not be as proud of themselves as other races are.

Now let us look at the race problem reasonably.

We are educating the Negro, the slave of the last century. He is so advanced educationally that he claims scholastic recognition everywhere. Place him in any school, college or university and he comes out with honors. In science, music, art and literature he is holding a place of equality with other races everywhere. His ability fits him no longer for the farm cotton field or plantation as a race. He seeks broader opportunities in every field. He is a citizen. He pays taxes. He observes the law. He supports the government. He applies for and seeks the position that attracts him.

"Why shouldn't I be President?" he asks himself. "I have the education and the ability."

"Why shouldn't I be Governor of the State; Mayor of the City; a judge of the Supreme Court, Police Commissioner or President of the Board of Aldermen?"

"Why shouldn't I be Chief Clerk in Gimbel Brothers, Macy's or Wanamaker's?"

"Why shouldn't I be a conductor on the railroad, on the Pullman car or tramp car service?"

"Why shouldn't I be employed in all the useful and productive industries of the nation?"

All these are positions and jobs sought by the majority group of whites in America and elsewhere. As the Negro becomes more insistent on these demands for Constitutional rights and privileges and threatens the more to compete with the white man for the job that the latter seeks and believes worthwhile having, then the inevitable conflict will come, and the group that is not strong enough to hold its own will go down, irrespective of the law and of the government because the law and the government are but executive expressions of the sober will of the people; when the people, through prejudice or any mass opinion, become dissatisfied, the law and the government are no longer able to control them in their action.

In this respect I would refer you to the industrial riots of East St. Louis and Chicago; the political riot of Washington and the commercial riot of Tulsa, Oklahoma. The things that the white majority want in their own countries they will not yield to the Negro or to any other race and that is natural. . . .

Those Negroes who are too lazy to work and lay the foundation for such a government are among those who criticize us.

Pilgrim Fathers we had in America before we enjoyed the delights of New York, Chicago or Boston. Pilgrim Fathers we must have if Africa is to rise from her slumber and darkness.

We of the Universal Negro Improvement Association are satisfied to be called ignorant and gullible in working toward this end.

A Barefaced Colored Leader*

W. E. B. DU BOIS is the most brazen fellow that one knows in Negro leadership. Because of the unfortunate mental condition of the masses of Negroes, this man, who secured many free scholarships to obtain his education, has consistently used his "white" education to mislead and humbug the millions of his race in the United States.

The Negroes in America, since Emancipation, have ever been looking for honest and upright leaders to point them to the way of political, economic, social and general development. Du Bois offered himself immediately after he left Harvard and the people were glad to receive him, but jealous as he was of every other Negro leader, his first effort was to attack the honest, upright and useful leader—Booker T. Washington. By so doing he divided American Negro opinion, and the confusion springing therefrom has continued up to the present, but Du Bois took pride and pleasure not only in attacking Booker Washington but he has attacked and tried to discredit every other Negro leader of importance who has sprung up in America. . . .

The very fact that the man up to now has no program shows that he never intended any, and his profession of being a leader . . . was only to deceive the American Negro and at the same time satisfy his white patrons who had the scheme to suppress an

* The *Blackman* Magazine, July 1935.

independent development of his race. It is good to make Du Bois speak for himself, and so it is good to quote him from an article he has written for the June [1935] number of *Current History*. Under the caption of "A Negro Nation within the Nation," Du Bois has the following confession to make: *"No more critical situation ever faced the Negroes of America than that of today—not in 1830 nor in 1861, nor in 1867. More than ever the appeal of the Negro for elementary justice falls on deaf ears."* Now, here is a man who fought the program of the Universal Negro Improvement Association, tried to discredit its leaders, assisted to have him imprisoned and deported after that organization and its leader stood boldly out in the United States for a program, which, if it were supported by men like Du Bois as it was supported by a large number of the masses of the Negroes, would have today placed the American Negro in a position not to be pitied but to be admired, confessing the helplessness of the race. Can anyone believe in his sincerity? It is evident that his plan of action originally was to keep the Negro in a condition that would always necessitate the propaganda of complaint of which Du Bois seems to be master. His National Association for the Advancement of Colored People, when he was active in it, stood for nothing else but complaint. It had no constructive program. It could only find usefulness in protesting against lynchings and discriminations, and in such an agitation Du Bois occupied himself for more than a quarter of a century. Now the conditions have grown worse, so his job is still there for him to complain. . . .

Whilst there may be a few good white men in America, there is no white man in America honest enough, sympathetic enough, humane enough, liberal enough to really take up the Negro's cause and fight it to a successful conclusion for the race's benefit, because in so doing it would be creating displeasure to the masses of white men and women who have always claimed superiority over the Negro and felt that his place should be limited in the body politic.

Those who can remember the activities of the Universal Negro Improvement Association in the United States and its great program of nationalism, coupled with genuine industrial and economic activities, will readily realize the difference between that Association and the National Association for the Advancement of Colored People. When that Association fought for wider opportunities for the Negro in America, it was with the view of warding off the terrible economic reactions that would come after the war. That was why ships were placed on the seas, factories were to be erected and great industries to be promoted. The leaders foresaw the unfortunate position of the Negro in these years, but Du Bois did not care and so he sabotaged the movement and would have hanged the leader if the white man was not even a little merciful. Now, let us listen to him again in *Current History*. He says: "Long before the depression Negroes in the South were losing 'Negro' jobs." Didn't we tell Du Bois that in 1917, '18, '20, up to 1925? Those who doubt that we told him and the American Negroes that, let them go to the volume known as *The Philosophy and Opinions of Marcus Garvey*[20] . . . and all the things that Du Bois is now confessing will be found in that volume as a warning to the Negroes of the United States. He goes on further in his article. He says: "Since 1929 Negro workers, like white workers, have lost their jobs, have had mortgages foreclosed on their farms and homes, have used up their small savings, but in the case of the Negro worker everything has been worse in larger or smaller degree; the loss has been greater and more permanent." . . .

When Du Bois dies he will go down in his grave to be remembered as the man who sabotaged the Liberian colonization scheme of the Negro, the man who opposed the American Negro launching steamships on the seas, the man who did everything to handicap the industrial and commercial propositions of the American Negro, the man who tried to wreck the industrial, educational system of Tuskegee, the man who never had a good word to say for any other Negro leader, but who tried to down every one of them.

Part Five

The Rebuilding of the Movement, 1927-1934

Commentary

BY JOHN HENRIK CLARKE

AFTER MARCUS GARVEY returned to Jamaica he attempted to rebuild the UNIA. He was now dealing with an organization, once massive, that had been divided against itself. Many of the units in the United States did not cooperate with the main unit, now in Jamaica under Garvey's leadership. In addition to attempting to rebuild the movement, he began an active political career, being elected to public office in Jamaica and serving out one term before the opposition to him had destroyed his effectiveness as a public official. He immediately began to organize conventions in Jamaica and subsequently, would bring to that island Blacks from large areas of the world who still held on to the dream of African redemption.

Back in Jamaica, as in the United States, maybe Marcus Garvey tried to build too many things and could not have possibly done justice to all of them. Many times, on tours of Jamaica, he would speak as often as five times a day. In addition to building the UNIA, he attempted to build business enterprises reflecting his more successful years in the United States. By 1932, his efforts in Jamaica had begun to fail and the movement was once more divided against itself. This would lead to the calling of the last massive UNIA convention in 1934 before Marcus Garvey went to London to set up new headquarters.

The last Jamaican years started as his eleven years in the United States ended. He did not leave the country a broken man, though he had every reason to be. Mrs. Garvey gives this account of his deportation:

> On November 18, 1927, President Coolidge signed a pardon for Garvey. When the order reached Atlanta, the deportation order was served simultaneously. Secrecy prevailed, but we were able to rush Attorney Armin Kohn to New Orleans, as this was the nearest seaport to Atlanta. He tried to get a stay of the deportation order, but his application was denied. On his return to New York City, he gave the following statement to reporters: "In my twenty-three years of practice at the New York Bar, I have never handled a case in which the Defendant has been treated with such manifest unfairness and with such a palpable attempt at persecution as this one."
>
> Under heavy guard Garvey was put on board the S. S. *Saramacca*. He spoke from the deck of the ship to hundreds of Garveyites who had rushed to the docks to see him off. He thanked the millions who had helped and supported the cause, and for their confidence in him despite the machinations of his enemies. His desire to serve was greater than ever, as the work had to be completed. Said he, "The UNIA is not something I have joined, it is something I have founded. I have set everything aside to do this work. It is a part of me, I dream about it, I sacrifice and suffer for it, I live for it, and I would gladly die for it. Go forward come what may. We must win by God's help and guidance."
>
> [When] the ship docked at Cristobal, Panama, he was not allowed ashore, but Garveyites secured permission to send a delegation on board. They presented him with a purse and discussed the future of the organization. He was transferred to the S. S. *Santa Marta*. He got a hero's welcome in Jamaica. The people pushed his car from the wharf to Liberty Hall.

Marcus Garvey arrived back in Kingston with Mrs. Garvey on December 10, 1927, and was indeed given a welcome befitting a popular head of state. The humble Jamaicans who came to see him were welcoming home a man who, in spite of setbacks, had given them status in the eyes of the world. They were not thinking about the loss of the ships and those who opposed him both in America and Jamaica; they were reacting to the hope that he had awakened in them. A meeting followed in the Ward

Theatre later that night. In fact, the first week of his return to Jamaica was a week of welcoming ceremonies. There was at least one negating factor to his arrival back in Jamaica. The ruling elite on the island, Black and white, were none too happy and were not a part of the thousands who came to welcome him home. The *Daily Gleaner* published the following lament upon his arrival:

> It is with profound regret that we view the arrival of Marcus Garvey back in Jamaica. And it is with more than profound regret that we picture any leader of thought and culture in this island associating himself with a welcome given to him. But Kingston has reached such a level of degeneracy that there is no knowing what she will do . . . A new spirit has passed over the lower classes which has nothing to commend it except its ignorance . . . is to receive another impetus through the dumping upon us of a man who indeed is a Jamaican but for whom the island as a whole or the more intelligent section of it has no use.

He immediately began to put his organizational house in order, and planned a trip to Central America and Europe. Mrs. Garvey gives this account of the trip:

> He had planned a trip to Central America but none of the consuls for these countries would give him a visa, so in April 1928 he left for England and Europe after setting up Headquarters. He brought down from America the Vice-President, Miss Davis, and left her in charge of the office. An American secretary also came, who traveled with him.

> During his stay in England he busied himself contacting African and West Indian seamen and students and organized and financed an underground movement. He formed a branch of the organization among the colored people and spoke in Hyde Park on Sunday afternoons. He sent circular letters to members of Parliament, leading ministers of the Gospel and liberal-minded persons, explaining his program, and pointing out to them the grave unrest in the Colonies and Protectorates because of bad living conditions, urging them to become interested before it was too late. So as to crystallize interest he planned a big meeting at the Royal Albert Hall, London. For weeks before the meeting he had a typist address envelopes from telephone subscribers' names and addresses, in which he put invitations and handbills.

To Garvey's amazement and disappointment [only] about two hundred persons attended the meeting, but he went through just the same with a concert and speaking program. Garvey did not fully realize the lack of concern on the part of the British people.

Marcus Garvey's Albert Hall speech, in addition to being one of his best thought out explanations of his program for Black people, holds its own as a piece of living literature.

In the brief few months he and Mrs. Garvey were in England, he organized a chapter of the UNIA and set up committees for the support of the organization. He and Mrs. Garvey left England at the end of September 1928. They landed in Montreal, Canada, where Marcus Garvey was arrested on a technicality—illegal entry. After some embarrassment and humiliation that seemed to have been intended, he was released. He was not allowed to land in Bermuda. The British authorities were sensitive about the conditions on the island which created a Jim-Crow paradise for white people. He was allowed to speak in Nassau, Bahamas, where a former supporter used this occasion to get a judgment against the UNIA for $30,000. These financial squabbles were now threatening to tear the organization apart while he was trying to put it back together.

In August of 1929, the sixth International UNIA Conference was held in Jamaica. This was the first conference that had been held outside the United States. It was well attended, and representatives came from most of the Black world, including a surprising representation from Africa. These representatives who came to this conference risked their lives and personal safety to defy their colonial governments in journeying across the world to a conference which was dedicated to the liberation of all colonies.

The number of legal difficulties which tied up Garvey's time that year did not deter his desire to build a political party in Jamaica that would represent working people.

In the tenth plank of his manifesto he stated that judges should be tried for dealing unjustly and as a result was sent to prison for three months and fined $200.00 (Jamaican) for contempt of court. Charged with seditious libel, arising from an editorial written by T. A. Aikman, literary editor of the *Blackman*, Garvey won the appeal. In October, he was elected Councilor of the Kingston and St. Andrew Corporation. He had to forfeit his seat since being in prison he could not attend the meetings.

During 1930–1931, Edelweiss Park became headquarters for the UNIA, and a major culture center for the Black population in Jamaica. In 1932, he started a new publication, the *New Jamaican.* The UNIA was having problems of growth and finance, and Marcus Garvey was approaching the end of his stay in Jamaica.

Mrs. Garvey gives this account of his last years in Jamaica, before going to London:

> Because of the underhand methods used to keep him out of the City Council, an article was written in the *Blackman* newspaper, which stated in part: "The Corporation is entirely opposed to the welfare of the country . . . the Government is also bereft of common decency, not to say dignity and common sense." Counsel was retained for Garvey, T. Aikman, Editor, and Coleman Beecher as Circulating Manager who were charged for seditious libel. Beecher was acquitted, Aikman (who wrote the article) was sentenced to three months in prison, and Garvey to six months. Notice of appeal was given. The Appellate Court upheld the appeal. Garvey was justified in that later on a Commission was set up to probe into the affairs of the City Council, and the body was dissolved. Garvey was opposed in the City Council in getting his resolutions passed and put into practical use. As these would have set in motion works of reproduction financed by loans from the Imperial Government at a low interest rate of three per cent, so in June 1930 he formed the Workers and Laborers Association. He headed a deputation to the Governor, asking him to investigate the appalling conditions of the masses, and to use his influence towards remedial measures. The Governor nonchalantly replied that, in his opinion, there was "no unusual suffering."
>
> Garvey's next effort was to draw up a petition to the King, through the Colonial Office, copies of which he sent to members of Parliament and liberal-minded editors in England. The result was the appointment of a Royal Commission to investigate the political and economic condition in the West Indies. At the end of September 1930 he held a mass meeting at Coke Chapel steps (the outdoor forum) to celebrate the good news.

Our first son was born September 17, 1930, and was named Marcus. Julius was born August 16, 1933. Garvey was proud of being a father, but the work of the organization and financing of it came first in his planning.

Early in 1934 he felt the full effects of the two-year depression in America, as Negroes suffered more than whites and were unable to support the work of the organization. Garvey called the seventh Convention in Jamaica, and the decision was made to remove the headquarters to England, where he would not be subjected to such colonial pressures and would have easier contacts with Africa. Before this could be done all our household furniture was sold, as he could not meet the payments on the bill of sale. I had mortgaged the home and furniture when he was in Spanish Town prison and paid the overdue installments on Edelweiss Park, the organization's property. This was also sold. After he left for England I was served with summonses for doctors' bills and overdue acceptance on printing machinery.

Letter from Mr. Armin Kohn of the firm of Kohn and Nagler, Lawyers to Mrs. Amy Jacques Garvey*

December 2, 1927

Dear Mrs. Garvey,

Now that the case of the United States against Marcus Garvey is concluded we think it would not be amiss to render to you a report concerning the various matters that have occurred, and the work done in connection therewith since Garvey's imprisonment in the Atlanta Federal Penitentiary, at least insofar as the services in connection therewith were rendered by me. Shortly after Mr. Garvey's imprisonment a warrant of deportation was lodged by the Immigration authorities with the Warden of the Prison. Prior to February 25, 1927, we understand that several applications were made in Mr. Garvey's behalf to the President of the United States for a commutation of his sentence.

In connection with these several applications you were indefatigable and conferred with many persons, both of high and low degree, in an effort to enlist their aid in securing the release of Mr. Garvey.

* Reproduced in the *Negro World*, December 10, 1927, and in the Jamaica *Daily Gleaner*, December 15, 1927.

With these prior applications we have nothing to do. Unfortunately, these several applications were denied as we were informed, upon various separate and respective grounds.

In February 1927, you enlisted our aid in connection with a further application for executive clemency, and you conferred with us many, many times; going over the grounds and even remaining in our office during the entire time that the brief upon the application was being prepared making to us, in many instances, valuable suggestions.

On February 24, 1927, the writer accompanied by you proceeded to Washington, and there met Mr. Knox, and we proceeded to the office of the Attorney General where an appointment had been made for the following morning at 9 o'clock for my appearance.

Shortly after 9 o'clock, in your presence and that of Mr. Knox, I began my argument before Attorney General John S. Sergent for a commutation of sentence. The argument continued until nearly 12 o'clock when an adjournment was taken until 2 o'clock that afternoon, and it was then continued for approximately one hour more.

Mr. James A. Finch, Pardon Attorney of the United States Government, appeared as representing the Government on this application. After the conclusion of this argument, you, Mr. Knox and I repaired to the office of Mr. Finch, where a very lengthy conference ensued. As a result of this conference I prepared a supplemental brief and through the kindness and courtesy of Mr. Finch I was permitted to submit this brief as a further argument in favour of commutation. My recollection is that I submitted a third brief that was the result of certain correspondence that passed between Mr. Finch and our office.

From February 25, 1927, down to November 18, 1927, the date when the commutation was granted, there were many conferences between you and the members of my firm, and also letters passing between the office of the Department of Justice through Mr. Finch and our office.

You were always impatient and insistent that further action be taken to bring about prompt commutation of the sentence and, if possible, the release of Mr. Garvey.

As a matter of fact, sometimes your impatience tried our

patience, but knowing your loyalty and devotion to Mr. Garvey, and the great strain and anxiety under which you were constantly laboring, we were very prone to overlook your eagerness, and to join you in exhausting every possible effort to bring about a speedy and successful determination of our application. On the afternoon of November 23, the newspapers carried a report that the application for executive clemency insofar as the commutation of sentence was concerned had been granted by the President but that Mr. Garvey would be immediately deported. That was the first information that either you or we had on the subject.

We understand that you immediately tried to reach the writer on the telephone at his office, and all of the following morning at his home, and finally we succeeded in talking on the telephone, as a result of which the writer, at your suggestion, sent a telegram to the Warden of Atlanta Penitentiary requesting information as to whether he had learned of the commutation, and also when Mr. Garvey would be removed from the penitentiary.

Shortly thereafter a reply was received to the effect that the information would have to come from the Immigration Department, and this reply was relayed to you on the telephone.

A subsequent telegram to the Immigration Department for similar information remained unanswered.

All of Thanksgiving Day you kept the wires hot in constant conference with the writer on the telephone, and bright and early the following morning you were at our office in conference with us on the subject of the next move to be made to obtain for Mr. Garvey a reasonable stay of the execution of the warrant of deportation. In the meantime, you had already sent Mr. Knox to Washington, and during the course of the day Mr. Knox reached the writer on the telephone and informed him that he had noted his appearance with the Board of Review of the Department of Labor, Immigration Division, and had arranged an appointment for the writer to appear before the Board on Saturday morning, the day following, at 9 o'clock.

That night the writer left for Washington and arrived the following morning, where he met Mr. Knox, and at 9 o'clock appeared at the office of the . . . Immigration Division. We were there informed that the Board would not convene until 10 o'clock. In the meantime, we examined the files in the department pertaining to the Garvey case. We saw some interesting correspondence. We also saw a telegram from the Commissioner of Immigration of New York advising that the port of deportation be changed from New York to New Orleans. It seems from these files that we saw, that as recently as November 25, the Immigration Department had reconsidered a previous decision and had withdrawn its authority to release Mr. Garvey on a thousand dollars bail and to detain him for immediate deportation.

Later in the morning, the writer argued his application before the Board of Review for a stay in the warrant. The chairman of the Board stated upon the argument that he did not believe it was within the power of the Board to release the defendant on bail because the commutation by the President was conditioned upon his immediate deportation. After a lengthy pro and con, in which it appeared that the chairman . . . was the attorney arguing in opposition to the application, a decision upon the application was reserved. To this reservation the writer very strenuously objected because he feared, and he so stated to the Board, that the decision would be withheld until the authorities were about ready to place the defendant on board a ship, and it would then be too late for us to take any steps to prevent his movement. However, the chairman was adamant and stated that he would telegraph the decision to our office.

The writer thereupon talked with you on the long distance telephone and made a full and detailed report as to what had occurred, and then proceeded to New Orleans on Saturday night, arriving there Monday morning.

It was our thought that we would be able to apply to the United States Court for a writ of habeas corpus and in that proceedings argue out the question of the right of the government to deport the defendant, the point involved being that he originally arrived in this country in 1917. In 1921 it became necessary for him to make a short visit to Cuba. At that time the rule was still in effect that before an alien could leave the country it was necessary for him to pay his income tax to the government and receive and exhibit to the Immigration authorities a green receipt. This green receipt issued to Garvey contained a statement by the authorities that he was about to leave the country on a trip of five weeks and would then return, hence the department considered him a resident alien.

If, therefore, he was technically and legally a resident alien, his absence from the country for five weeks and his re-entry at the end of that time, or shortly thereafter, would not constitute a re-entry within the meaning of Section 4289 J.J. of the United States Revised Statutes, which amongst other things provided that if an alien resident of this country for five years or less should commit a crime during that period, he may be deported.

In other words, Garvey having arrived in this country in 1917 and having been convicted June 18, 1923, he would not have come within the provisions of the deportation law above cited.

Upon the writer's arrival at New Orleans he immediately consulted with Mr. William J. Guste, a local attorney. We went over the facts in the matter and considered the question of applying for a writ of habeas corpus, and we both agreed that this was the proper course to pursue at the time, and after spending several hours together in conferences and study of the situation we proceeded to visit Mr. Garvey at the United States Immigration Station at Algiers.

After a conference with him, he, Garvey, decided against making the application for the writ. He took the position that in view of the fact that the Immigration Department stated that the commutation of sentence was conditional upon deportation, he was willing to accept the conditions and would not make any obtrusive move. The only thing left to be done, therefore, was to try to induce the authorities at Washington to voluntarily and without court order give Garvey a reasonable respite to enable him to return to New York and there, in the short time to be left at his disposal, put the affairs of the Universal Negro Improvement Association and its kindred interests into such shape as to permit someone else to be designated either by Garvey or the membership to take the helm and keep the ship steered in a straight course, and thus give some measure of protection to the property interests of the thousands of colored members of the organization.

With this end in view, the writer left the same afternoon for Washington, and the first thing on Wednesday morning, when he

arrived there, proceeded to the office of Secretary of Labor
Davis, where he asked for an interview. Word was sent to him
that the man in charge of this case for the department was Judge
Smeltzer, and there the writer made a very vehement plea for a
short stay of the warrant of deportation and that Garvey be
released on bail and subject to any conditions that the Department may impose. Judge Smeltzer stated that he was without
power to grant this application in view of the Presidential
commutation, subject to immediate deportation, and nothing that
the writer could say or do moved him from this position.
Thereupon the writer went to the office of the Department of
Justice and conferred with the authorities there in an effort to
persuade that department to intervene, but the commutation
matter having been concluded, that department was without
power to do anything.

*However at this office, the writer saw the copy of the
commutation of the President, and not a single word is set out in
that commutation for deportation. In other words, the commutation of sentence is a clean-cut unconditional commutation and is
not, as was stated recently by various officials in the Immigration
Department, "subject to immediate deportation."*

We, of course, do not know what these officials in the
Department of Immigration had in mind when they informed us
that the commutation was a conditional one upon deportation.
Perhaps they were under a misapprehension themselves, or
perhaps they misconstrued the warrant commutation. How they
could do this, however, in the light of the very clear and
clean-cut language used by the President in unconditionally
commuting the sentence is something beyond our comprehension.

Nothing was left to be done at Washington. The Immigration
Department was firm in its position and declined to do anything
whatsoever in the way of granting time for a stay of the warrant
and the Department of Justice was without power to do anything
as the case was concluded in that office when the commutation
was handed down by the President. We regret very much that
this closes the case, but we desire to take this opportunity of
expressing to you our high sense of appreciation for the
conscientious and intelligent aid you gave us throughout the very

many trying hours while our various applications were pending and for the unstinted time and effort you put into the work of obtaining for Mr. Garvey his freedom.

Your loyalty and devotion to the interests of Mr. Garvey never wavered for a moment, and in the face of many discouragements and obstacles you remained firm and courageous and unswervingly stuck to the task ahead of us.

We beg to thank you for this wholehearted and sincere support and cooperation, and if at any time we can be of service to you personally, please do not hesitate to call upon us.

Very truly yours,
(Sgd.) Kohn & Nagler
by Armin Kohn

Hon. E. B. Knox
Describes Leave-taking
at New Orleans*

Sunday night, December 11, Liberty Hall, New York City. If George Harris, ex-politician, ex-alderman, and several other X's, or any of the rest of the "immortal eight" who wrote friend Daugherty way back in 1923 asking him to silence and deport Marcus Garvey, had thrust their heads in at the door of Liberty Hall tonight, they would have retreated in confusion and dismay. Instead of people sorrowing over the spiriting away of their leader, they would have beheld thousands of men and women, their heads held high, in joyful mood, laughing alike at the misfire of the paid white press and the Afro-American pigmies whose masterpiece of "cheap demagogy," as the Atlanta *Independent* characterized the infamous letter to Daugherty, reacted in an entirely unexpected way.

For Liberty Hall tonight was dividing its time between rejoicing over the safe arrival of the Hon. Marcus Garvey at Kingston, Jamaica, the wonderful reception accorded him there, and listening to the Hon. E. B. Knox as he told of his parting conferences with the great leader at New Orleans, and vowing and showing—with dollars—its determination to carry the program through to complete success.

For Knox made a great hit with the membership and received full-throated endorsement as he announced that he had been appointed national representative of the President-General in America, and vowed that he would give the best that in him lay to the fulfillment of Mr. Garvey's wishes and the program. The vast audience hung on his every word as he told of Mr. Garvey's suffering in Atlanta and of the great leader's expressed belief that he had come safely out of the jaws of death by "keeping his hand in God's hand."

The meeting was enlivened by a fine musical program. The chairman said he was very pleased indeed to see such a great outpouring of members and friends on this occasion. It was a splendid tribute to Marcus Garvey, and to the conscientious men whom he had appointed in his stead to head the work in America under his assistance and guidance—the Hon. E. B. Knox. He then introduced Mr. C. Smith, a New York stalwart.

Mr. Smith delivered a very inspiring address. They were present that night he said to prove to the world that neither imprisonment, deportation, nor any other tricks can dismay the most farsighted and able leadership the Negro race has had in several generations. They wanted the world to know that Marcus Garvey was a different type of Negro—such a Negro as the world had never seen before. It was the first time in the recent history of the Negro race that efforts to mislead and fool the race have failed so utterly.

He wanted to remind the membership that it is because of their splendid loyalty to Mr. Garvey and the cause, and their admirable persistence, that Mr. Garvey "sent out of this country virtually as a prisoner, has been received like a king at his destination." It was his firm conviction that the black people of Jamaica today had more respect for Marcus Garvey than for King George of England. He wanted to commend the membership for preserving Garvey, for by preserving Garvey's leadership, they had preserved Garvey.

The Hon. Marcus Garvey on his arrival at Kingston, Jamaica, at five o'clock last Saturday afternoon received an ovation and welcome that eclipsed any that the oldest inhabitants of the island could remember. No sooner had he set foot upon the shores of Jamaica than he was acclaimed by thousands of Jamaicans, who long before the United Fruit liner *Santa Marta* had docked, had waited patiently in holiday attire to do honor to the famous leader.

The local branches of the Universal Negro Improvement Association were well represented in the welcoming throng. A great parade was staged, led by units of the divisions and their bands. A monster mass meeting was held on Sunday evening in Ward's Theatre, Kingston, from which hundreds were turned away as the spacious auditorium filled rapidly with a capacity crowd.

Word comes from Colon, Panama, where the great leader stopped en route to Jamaica, that the people there—about 50,000—had planned a monster reception, but this was prevented by the Canal Zone government. Reporting Mr. Garvey's arrival there, the New York *Herald Tribune* printed the following dispatch from its Panama correspondent:

Panama-December 8.   A committee of six fraternal brothers, with flowers and a cash purse, waited on Marcus Garvey, the "Moses of the Negro Race," on his arrival at Cristobal this afternoon on the steamship *Saramacca*, on which he was deported by the United States, en route to Jamaica.

The entire Negro population of 50,000 would have welcomed him but was not permitted to do so by the Canal Zone government, none except the committee being allowed inside the pier gates. The committee talked with Garvey for two hours. He declared that he would allow nothing to hinder him in his plan to achieve the economic independence of the Negroes throughout the world, his ultimate aim being to establish a Negro Republic in Africa.

He urged his followers to unite and foster the development of the Universal Negro Improvement Association, of which he is President-General. He has no bitter feeling regarding his conviction and imprisonment, but regretted having been "railroaded" from the United States. He said he was rushed to New Orleans, where he was given twenty-four hours in which to leave the country, while his wife and friends awaited him at New York, where he made his home.

He hopes to be allowed in a few years to re-enter the United States, from which country, he said, he was the first Negro to be deported. He plans to remain in Jamaica, return to Panama, and then tour Central and South America in furtherance of his plans for Negro improvement.

Garvey is being held aboard the *Saramacca* until the arrival of the *Santa Marta*, on which he will sail next Thursday to Jamaica. Garvey's conviction has united behind him the support of the West Indian Negroes here, where he is well known and beloved by a vast following, who believe that he meant no wrong, but was convicted on a technicality.

The Political Activities
of Marcus Garvey* in Jamaica

BY AMY JACQUES GARVEY

THE YEAR 1929 was one of the most striking and
agonizing 365 days of Garvey's stay in Jamaica. Subtle, silent,
systematic efforts were made to crush him and destroy his
movement, when he would not heed the overtures of agents sent
to plead with him (for his own good) to give up the fight to
change the condition of the black masses.

In July of that year a default judgment of G. O. Marke, a
former officer of the parent body in New York City, was taken up
by J. H. Cargill, solicitor in Jamaica. . . . Sir Fiennes Barrett
Lennard, Chief Justice . . . gave judgment and ordered the sale
of all the properties and assets of the parent body UNIA . . .
Despite the fact that an appeal was pending, everything was sold.

During the hearing the Chief Justice fined Garvey twenty-five
pounds for not producing the books of the local branch, which
Garvey did not have in his possession. The local UNIA won the
appeal, and the government had to refund the branch the price
paid for their Liberty Hall at the auction sale, which was below
market value. But Garvey got nothing for all the assets of the
various auxiliary units sold by order of the Chief Justice.

The Isaiah Morter case was going through the courts of Belize,

* *Jamaica Journal*, June 1972.

British Honduras, on to England on appeal. Mr. Morter, a black patriot, left his estate to the UNIA "for African redemption." This the Colonial Office (through the local judiciary) said was for "illegal purposes," and despite the thousands of pounds spent for barristers, and court fees, the parent body and Garvey never got the legacy. Garvey and the movement were stripped financially, but their spirit was never broken; so they held the sixth international convention in Jamaica, and delegates heralded to the world a defiance that whatever mortal men did to hamper the struggle, the spirit of Garveyism would prevail.

Feeling the mighty hand of imperialism clothed in legal authority, Garvey decided to form a political party, in order to change conditions. He and his colleagues named it "The Peoples Political Party." In 1929 they issued a Manifesto.

In the subsequent municipal elections they won three seats— they had one in the Legislative Council. They now decided to run twelve candidates, one for each parish, for the general elections to the Legislative Council. The following are the planks of their platform, which were printed on hand bills, also in *The Blackman.*

> If elected, I shall do everything in my power . . . to make effective the following:
>
> 1. Representation to the Imperial Parliament for a larger modicum of self-government.
> 2. Protection of native labor.
> 3. A minimum wage for the laboring and working classes of the island.
> 4. A law to protect the working and laboring classes of the country by insurance against accident, sickness and death, occurring during employment.
> 5. A law to compel the employment of not less than sixty per cent of native labor in all industrial, agricultural and commercial activities engaged in, in this island.
> 6. The expansion and improvement of city, town or urban areas without the encumbrance or restraint of private proprietorship.
> 7. An eight-hour working day throughout Jamaica.
> 8. A law to encourage the promotion of native industries.
> 9. Land reform.

10. A law to impeach and imprison judges who, with disregard for British justice and constitutional rights, dealt unfairly.

11. A Jamaica University and Polytechnic.

12. The establishing of a Government High School in the capital town of each parish, for the supply of free secondary education. Attached to the said High School to be a night continuation school to facilitate those desiring to study at night, in order to advance their education.

13. A public library in the capital town of each parish.

14. A National Opera House, with an Academy of Music and Art.

15. Prison reform.

16. The compulsory improvement of urban areas from which large profits are made by trusts, corporations, combines and companies.

17. The appointment of official court stenographers to take official notes of all court proceedings in the Supreme Court, Resident Magistrates Courts and Petty Session Courts of the island.

18. The creation of a Legal Aid Department to render advice and protection to such persons who may not be able to have themselves properly represented and protected in the courts of law.

19. A law for the imprisonment of any person who by duress or undue influence would force another person to vote in any public election against his will, because of obligation or employment or otherwise.

20. The granting to the townships of Montego Bay and Port Antonio the corporate rights of cities.

21. A law to empower the government to secure a loan of three million (or more) pounds from the Imperial Government, or otherwise, to be used by the government, under the management of a department of the Director of Agriculture in developing the Crown lands of the island, agriculturally, and otherwise, with the object of supplying employment for our surplus unemployed population, and to find employment for stranded Jamaicans abroad; and that the government purchase such ships as are necessary from time to time, to facilitate the marketing of the produce gathered from these Crown lands, and at the same time conveniently offering an opportunity to other producers to ship and market their produce.

22. The beautifying and creating of the Kingston Race Course into a National Park, similar to Hyde Park in London.

23. The establishment by the government of an electrical system

to supply cheap electricity to such growing and prospering centers as are necessary.

24. A law to establish clinical centers from which trained nurses are to be sent out to visit homes in rural districts, and to teach and demonstrate sanitary and better health methods in the care of home and family.

25. A law to empower the Parochial Boards of each parish to undertake, under the direction of the Central Government, the building of model sanitary homes for the peasantry by the system of easy payments, to cover a period of from ten to twenty years.

26. A law to prevent profiteering in the sale of land in urban and suburban areas to the detriment of the expansion of healthy home life for citizens of moderate means—profiteering such as is indulged in in lower St. Andrew by heartless land sharks.

As leader of the party, Garvey spoke at Cross Roads Square on September 10, 1929, presented the Manifesto, and elaborated on all proposed reforms. A few days later he was arraigned in court on a second contempt charge before the same Chief Justice, and two other judges. The basis of the charge was the tenth plank of the Manifesto. He was found guilty and sentenced to three months' imprisonment and a fine of one hundred pounds. He served the prison term at the Spanish Town prison, as a "first class misdemeanant."

On release from prison he only had a couple of weeks to campaign, and was without funds. Here are a few points he made:

Workers should be insured against sickness and accidents while employed . . . The earning capacity of the workers must be increased, which will benefit all classes of society. In this way workers will be able to spend more, by earning more . . .

No encouragement is being given to the natives to foster and promote industries. The result is that Jamaica has grown up to be a country of *consumers*. Out of our by-products of agriculture we produce nothing. We import shoes, clothes, hats etc., when most of these things could be made right here. Canning and tanning factories would be a great encouragement to the farmers in the country parishes, whose surplus fruit go to waste, and the skins of the animals bring little or nothing.

My opponents say I am against white and fair-skinned people. This
is not so. I am against the class system here, which keeps the poor
man down, and the poor are mostly black people. It is only natural,
therefore, that their interest should be nearest and dearest to my
heart. . . . Let us all work together as fellow Jamaicans, and ring in
the changes for a NEW JAMAICA.

When the election returns were announced, Garvey was a
shocked and grieved man. However, he went through the
parishes and thanked those who had voted for his party. Said he:

My speeches and utterances were recorded with the hope of
sending me back to prison . . . You were told not to vote for
Garvey as he would become too powerful; but under the party
system a man is as powerful in a Legislature as his party, which
derives its power from the voters; and intelligent voters cast their
votes not merely because they like him, but because he is bound by
the party's plans for betterment. . . .

The voters have turned back the clock of progress for another ten
years, but party system is well established in your minds, and it will
come, it is bound to come.

In a letter dated February 1, 1930, reproduced in the *Negro
World*, A. Wesley Atherton commented on the campaign thus:

Rum and human depravity blocked the path of Marcus Garvey.
The terrible reverse which he received at the polls was due in no
sense whatever to lack of organization. With the limited means at
his command, his campaign could not have been better organized.
He has lost in what was almost a rum war, a money scramble. With
the bait dangling before their gaze—the red linen of filthy
lucre—Negro sons of African slaves, in this enlightened age voted
away their birthright, and suffered themselves to be indentured for
another five years under conditions that have sucked their vitals to
the very bone. They traded on the future happiness of their
children and trampled their manhood into the dust. With the whip
of the slave master still cracking in their ears, they followed the
stream of molten gold down the hills of St. Andrew to vote against
Marcus Garvey.

They stabbed him fiercely in the back, and while now recovering from that brutal wound, he stands before the bar of public opinion, facing the charges of his traducers. Those who can, must help, and those of us who cannot, must weep.

But the mournful dirge of the Peoples Political Party, not Garveyism, will not be sung in this generation, nor in the next, It shall synchronize only with the passage of time into eternity. Both causes are immortal and must survive all human, material barriers and impositions. Marcus Garvey has secured a wider niche in the hall of fame.

In October 1929 Garvey was elected to the Kingston and St. Andrew Corporation Council, but having to serve three months in prison on the second contempt charge, he was unable to take the oath and function as a councillor. He applied for leave; it was denied by a majority of one, but the lawyer for the Corporation ruled that it was discretionary. Garvey took his seat on release from prison. Then some of the councillors maneuvered again to unseat him, but they finally lost out.

Arising out of the underhanded tactics used to keep him out of the Council, an article was written in *The Blackman* in which it was stated in part:

"The Corporation is entirely opposed to the welfare of the country . . . The government is also bereft of common decency, not to say dignity, and common sense. It is true our faith in the local administration of affairs is sorely tried; perhaps we should not be, but our confidence in British fairplay is not upheld by the manifestations we behold day by day . . ."

Garvey, T. Aikman, editor, and Coleman Beecher, circulating manager, were brought before the court for seditious libel. Although Aikman admitted writing the editorial in question, and Garvey did not see it, as he was traveling in the parishes, the same Chief Justice acquitted Beecher, and referred to Aikman as "the tool of Garvey," and sentenced him to three months' imprisonment. Garvey, he said, was criminally responsible, and sentenced him to six months' imprisonment. Garvey and Aikman appealed at great cost, and the appeal was allowed. So ended the third charge of contempt.

Later on, a special commission was appointed to probe the affairs of the City Council. On the grounds of their findings that body was dissolved.

Unable to do anything for the parishes he was not in the Legislative Council and being hampered in the Corporation Council in getting his resolutions through and put into practical use, Garvey, in June 1930 formed the Workers and Laborers Association to see what organized effort could do on their behalf.

He led a deputation to the Governor, asking him to investigate the distressing conditions of the masses of the island, and to use his influence towards remedial measures. Nonchalantly the Governor replied that in his opinion there was "no unusual suffering."

Garvey's next move was to draw up a petition to the King, through the Colonial Office. He sent copies to Labor members of Parliament, other liberal-minded men and newspaper editors in England. The result was the appointment of a Royal Commission to investigate the political and economic conditions of the West Indies. At the end of September he held a monster mass meeting in Kingston at Coke Chapel steps (the outdoor forum) to tell the people the good news.

Mr. J. Denniston, treasurer of the Workers and Laborers Association, presided and introduced Garvey. He complimented the people on their good behavior during the times of provocation, strain and misery and outlined the matters to be brought to the attention of the members of the Royal Commission.

During the time he served the municipality, the following is one of the most far-reaching resolutions he put forward. Of course he was out-voted:

> Be it resolved that the Council, for the purpose of carrying out civic improvements—particularly involving better water supply, better lighting, installing of proper sewage system, improvements to slum areas, building a Town Hall, erecting new Fire Brigade Station, laying out recreation grounds, and all such works of magnitude that may be necessary as improvements within the Corporate Area—approach government for the purpose of securing the necessary authority to float a local loan of five hundred thousand pounds, in order to undertake the carrying out of these improvements immediately.

Particularly as a means of relieving the present and continuing state of unemployment and hardships among the people. Be it further resolved that the City Engineer be requested to prepare plans and estimates involving the general costs of all these improvements, for the guidance of the Council in laying before the government the manner in which the amount asked for will be spent.

In speaking on the motion, he said that the Depression was being felt in the big cities of Europe, England and the United States of America. Their statesmen did not ignore it; in fact, they dared not. So, with initiative and planning they put into effect measures to alleviate same—the dole, relief works, feeding of schoolchildren, old age pensions, etc.

The Legislative Council instead of tackling our problems at this level ignore them and continue their individual narrow policy of getting bridges built, a stretch of road repaired or a water tank erected. Let us set them an example in sensible planning and make the people of Kingston and St. Andrew happy.

Some of us will ask where is the money to come from. It is right here in Jamaica. Just recently I read in the newspapers that a man died and left six hundred and fifty thousand pounds. There are many planters, merchants and business men who have made their money here and are wealthy; but alive or dead, they do nothing to benefit the people of their communities. They have no national spirit; but they could be asked to subscribe a loan for development, for which they would be paid interest. This act would also ease their consciences.

The opposing arguments were that such socialist planning had lost the Labor Party an election. They did not intend to assume big responsibilities as they could hardly manage what they had in hand. Put to the vote, the motion was lost. It was grievous to Garvey that legislators in both Councils refused to legislate for a better Jamaica, from the grassroots up; but he warned them that one day these docile people would rise up in the power of their wrath and tear down the barriers that keep them—the lower classes—down.

The political and economic reforms that he suggested in Jamaica set the pattern for all the other Caribbean territories. He was the pioneer, reformer and prophet.

MARCUS GARVEY IN HIS OWN WORDS

Speech at Royal Albert Hall*

The Case of the Negro for International Racial Adjustment

Mr. Chairman, Ladies and Gentlemen—fellow citizens of the British Empire—I am here this evening as the President-General of the Universal Negro Improvement Association, an organization of 11,000,000 Negroes in Africa, the United States of America, South America, Central America, Canada, and the West Indies to present to you the claim of our race upon your civilization.

For more than 500 years you assumed a leadership over us, much against our will, the result of which took us into slavery, and we labored as such slaves for 250 years in the country now known as the United States of America, and for 230 years in the countries known as the West Indies—British, Spanish, and French. I can well remember when you, the English, entered upon the slave traffic, John Hawkins, whom you afterwards elevated to knighthood, in seeking a charter to empower him to take slaves from Africa . . . said that he wanted . . . to take the slaves from Africa for the purpose of civilizing and Christianising them. Christianising and civilizing them the Queen signed the charter. That traffic removed millions of black men, women, and children from the West Coast of Africa to your dominions and colonies in the West Indies and in America.

As I have said, for 250 years we struggled in America under the

* London, June 6, 1928.

burden and the rigors of slavery. We were brutalized; we were maimed; we were killed; we were ravaged in every way. Then in America a man sprang up by the name of Abraham Lincoln, and in 1865 he liberated the American Negro slaves. A woman by the name of Victoria the Good, the Queen of England, in 1838 emancipated the West Indian Negroes. Tonight we have on the platform here native sons of Africa, descendants of the slaves in the western world, Negroes of America and Negroes from the West Indies. We have come to tell you how we feel about it and what we want done at the present time to prevent a recurrence of what happened to us hundreds of years ago.

In presenting this case I want to do so with the best of feeling towards all concerned. I came to England under instructions from those millions of people to approach you, through your government, through public opinion, through your King and through the crowned heads and the governments of Europe, especially those that have dominions at the present time in Africa. England, France, Italy, Spain, Belgium, Portugal, have assumed within the last fifty years the right politically to parcel out the land of our fathers without anybody saying a word to us. At the Versailles Conference, at the League of Nations, the representatives of those governments created certain mandates without asking us—nearly 300,000,000 people—one word about it. We are here in Europe to say something about it. We are here to let not only Europe but the world know that the new Negro is not going to be railroaded into slavery, into becoming a peon, into becoming a serf, as was so easily done in the centuries gone by.

We are men; we have souls, we have passions, we have feelings, we have hopes, we have desires like any other race in the world. The cry is raised all over the world today of Canada for the Canadians, of America for the Americans, of England for the English, of France for the French, of Germany for the Germans. Do you think it unreasonable that we, the blacks of the world, should raise the cry of Africa for the Africans?

Somebody with an evil mind has placed a wrong interpretation upon our motives and upon my expressions. They have tried to make me all kinds of things. They tried to make me a Socialist and a Bolshevist, and when they found out that I was neither they said I was a crook and they sent me to prison as a favor (they said) to the colored people; and after they kept me in prison for two years and ten months and found it was not a pleasure but a grave displeasure they found an excuse to commute my sentence, and then they deported me from America. I thought of coming from America at the request of my organization to speak to the English people about whom I read so much and about whom I heard so much for their liberal attitude towards all men; I thought I would have had a fair hearing in England to present a clear case not only for the organization I represent but for the Negroes of the world and to clear my character. The first thing they said about me when I arrived here was that I was a desperate crook, and the person who wrote that about me never saw me, knew nothing about me, had had no dealings with me, but he and others were willing to state a case against me so as to prejudice the success of this meeting, without investigating.

Do you know what I went to prison for? They said that some unknown employee of mine, because I was President of the Black Star Line, a steamship corporation, and an auxiliary of the organization that I represent now, posted a letter to somebody. In the evidence an envelope was presented to the witness which he identified as addressed to him; but he could not identify any letter contained in the envelope, and the prosecuting attorney presented it in evidence as a fair assumption that the envelope bore mailed matter from the Black Star Line . . . And because of that—an empty envelope—I was sent to prison in America for five years; and you call me a criminal for that; and the newspapers in England have published only that evil side of it without seeing the good that the organization which I represent has done in its fourteen years of existence. What have we done in fourteen years? In fourteen years we have organized 11,000,000 black men. We have made an effort to prove to you who have helped us—some of you with very good intentions—to help ourselves that we were capable of doing something for ourselves. We started a steamship line called the Black Star Line, the object of which was to offer an opportunity to the Negroes in the western world who were desirous of going back to Africa as missionaries and as settlers to help develop their country. Preparing the way for that, we started a commercial relationship with the nearby Negroes of the West Indies and America—a big fruit company in America that has exploited the Negroes of the West Indies for fifty years and piled up a reserve of nearly $1,000,000,000—started with one little three-masted schooner and today [has] a steamship line of 150 ships. When they saw that we were in earnest and we were making a serious effort to help the Negro from a commerical point of view, they influenced the politicians and influenced servants of the American government, bribed our employees, so as to make it impossible for this little venture of ours to succeed.

After they had done everything in conjunction with others who were desirous of preventing us from entering into any serious business proposition, after they had destroyed the possibility of success, they found some person to complain and after some pretense, they indicted me for the failure of the company; they found somebody who would vouchsafe to say that he bought stock in the Black Star Line on my urge, on my request. After indicting me they seized the books of our corporation with 35,000 names and sent out a questionnaire to the 35,000 stockholders of the corporation asking them if they were satisfied with the investments they had in the undertakings of Marcus Garvey, did Marcus Garvey influence them to buy stock, and so on—there were over one hundred other questions—and out of the 35,000 they got eighteen people to say that they were dissatisfied. Those eighteen people were all employees of the American [U.S.] government. Those are the people they used to convict me in America.

In addition to the fact that for six years twenty-five per cent of our employees were secret service agents of the United States government, it is peculiar also for you to realize that the Counsel-General to me and to my organization, on whose advice I acted, I not being an American citizen but a British subject and not knowing [was] paid, like myself, from the common funds of the organization. An American citizen who was responsible for the legal phase of our business, [the Counsel-General] while in our employ was also in the employ of the government. When I was indicted they called him out from serving us as Counsel-General, and, after convicting me, they made him Assistant Attorney General of the United States. If anybody should have been indicted the Counsel-General of the organization who gave the advice to the organization, should have been indicted. . . . Those are the morals of politics in America.

And I am surprised that the English press should influence the English public to condemn me without a hearing, trying to state that I am a criminal and an ex-convict under those circumstances.

Now, I am not here to present my story, but I am forced to make a statement so as to clear your minds, and I regard you as good friends who have come here in spite of all the vicious and wicked things that have been said. You have come to hear what I have to say on behalf of my race and on behalf of my organization, though secret propaganda has been engineered to prevent the success of this meeting simply because those who were chiefly instrumental in my imprisonment in America and those who profit most by interrupting the success of this organization, desired to do that. It is such a grave question that I will endeavor to present it briefly in parts. But erase from your minds that I am here as an ordinary criminal trying to influence you to do something that is not right. I am here because I am in earnest, because of my love not only for my own race but because of my love for humanity.

Since I arrived in London the many interviewers of your race who came to see me only wanted to know if we intended to use force in getting possession of Africa, and they wanted to know what part of Africa and all the rest of it. We are not evil-minded. As the Chairman said, we believe in righteousness. We have a righteous cause, and we are going to present it from that angle. But you Britishers, you Englishmen, have suffered as much as we have suffered, because you, although far removed from the period today, were as much slaves hundreds of years ago as we were slaves sixty, seventy, or eighty years ago in the western world. You grew out of slavery, the slavery imposed upon you by the Romans; you have developed wonderfully to the point where you are in a position today to treat with others.

We want to place you mentally back into the position that you were in 55 B.C. when you were slaves to the Romans. Surely you do not feel well about it. It is because of that that you have become such a sturdy race, determined that you shall never be slaves again—that Britain shall ever rule the waves and that Britons never never shall be slaves. As you feel about it, so do we feel about it. You are human beings; we are human beings; we are not asking for anything that is unfair and unreasonable; we are only asking for the right to repossess ourselves of our country. Would you like anybody to go into your country and dispossess you of it? Surely not. You love the old homeland too well, too much, for that.

So tonight we come to you Englishmen and Englishwomen, you who form public opinion, before going to the government; because we interpret government as only an executive for the people. Before we go to the government we go to the people to test the sentiments of the people so that you can, by that sentiment, direct the attitude of those who represent you. . . . We do not contemplate rushing on the government without proper preparation, for the government to excuse itself by saying, "Well, we are not instructed to do this and we cannot assume the responsibility of doing this." That is why we have come to you in your public forum to get your opinion about the matter. We want to find out if you Englishmen, if you Englishwomen, who make up the bone and sinew of your nation, intend that Africa must be exploited, must be taken away from its native peoples, that black men from Africa must be kicked about all over the world without a home, without a vine and fig tree of their own. If you say you empower your government to carry that out, then we will know exactly the attitude of the English people and how to deal with the matter. But we do not believe that the hearts of Englishmen and Englishwomen are so depraved, so unreasonable, so unfair, so unjust, as to instruct their government to go into the black man's country and dispossess him of every bit of his native rights in his own home, and, if he goes abroad will tell him—as a lady told me in Hyde Park last Sunday—"Go back to your country," when I asked a question of a speaker speaking on the anti-Socialist platform.

Now, this is something about which you ought to be serious. If you want me to go home, should not you make it so [that] that home is really home to me and not [one] in other lands where I am not wanted? The joke of deporting a Negro from America! Have you looked upon it from the humorous point of view? It was all a joke to me. I never took myself to the Western World. They, of their own free will, went 300 years ago to my native land, where I was happy and at peace with myself and with my God, and took me into the bosom of their own country, and then after 300 years deported me. Now, is it not a joke?

They claim that I am an undesirable alien. Just imagine, after 300 years, a Negro becoming undesirable in America. It is such a huge joke that we have not finished laughing at it yet. But those are the little things that weaken you, that weaken white civilization, in the eyes of the thinking darker peoples of the world. Those are the little incidents that cause us to think that you are not serious.

We are not here to do anything that is unreasonable. We are here to present a just claim. You who know your relationship with the Negro know that we have done everything possible to assist and to help you. The history of the centuries tells it. In nearly all your wars we assumed a common responsibility with you so as to preserve the Empire. Why, we ourselves are responsible for adding so much domain to your Empire. Nearly all your possessions in Africa were made possible by the blood of our men under your direction. The West India Regiment, which you have just disbanded, the West African Regiment, that you have just disbanded, tell a tale in history. You used the British West India Regiment to add nearly all West Africa to your Dominions; you used the West Indian and African Negro soldiers in the last war to take over the territories that you have taken over from Germany.

Not only have we fought to add new territory to the British Empire, but we have fought to save the American Union; we have fought to make American independence possible. The first man who shed his blood in America for the independence of the American Colonies was a black man on Boston Common by the name of Crispus Attucks. In the Civil War, the black soldiers saved the day many a time. The great Theodore Roosevelt that you have heard of—Theodore Roosevelt the Blessed—was saved to serve his country and humanity not by his own Rough Riders but by black men.

Do you know that we have gladly borne your burdens for hundreds of years? The cotton mills of Lancashire, the great shipping port of Liverpool, tell the tale of what we have done as black men for the British Empire. The cotton that you consume and use in keeping your mills going has for centuries come from the Southern states of the United States; it is the product of Negro labor. Upon that cotton your industry has prospered and you have been able to build the great British Empire of today. Have you no gratitude for a people who have helped with all that God gives them to give in fellowship and in good grace to others? We are not before you tonight asking you to pay us for 300 years of labor in slavery. No! We are only asking you now for common justice. With the terrible system of dishonor that existed in Europe you were forced into a great war—the war of 1914 to 1918; a war that never concerned me; a war that never concerned any black man in the world, because for the last 3,000 years the black man has been a man of peace. It was your war; but when it was too much for you you called for help, and two millions of us black men went from Senegal, from the Sudan, from West Africa, from East Africa, from the West Indies, from the United States of America; and tonight the blood of our boys has soaked the soil and their bones are buried in Flanders where the poppies grow. Not for any political reason on behalf of the Negro but in answer to the call to save the world for democracy and to protect the rights of weaker peoples. That was the urge that called us into war. Two millions of us answered, and hundreds of thousands of us paid the price.

At Versailles when the Peace Treaty was to be signed, you called everybody in and you distributed the spoils of war to everybody. You gave to the Jew Palestine; you gave the Egyptians a larger modicum of self-government; you gave the Irish home-rule government and Dominion status; you gave the Poles a new government of their own. But what did you give to the Negro? What did you do to the Negro? You threw his dead body on the streets of Cardiff, smashed the coffin and kicked the corpse about and made a football of it after he came back from the war. In America, 200,000 boys had hardly taken off their uniforms when, on parading in the streets, one of them was lynched in the very uniform of the United States. Is that a just reward for service so generously given?

Yet we are not sore about it; we are not vexed about it; we

only want you people to know the truth, because we do not believe that the hearts of all Englishmen are bad; we do not believe that the hearts of all the American people are bad. When I spoke of the lack of morality in politics in America I did not mean . . . among the people, but I mean . . . without any reserve among the politicians now in power.

Now, I consider myself honored to have been indicted and to have been sent to prison at the time the Administration of such a rogue and vagabond as the ex-Attorney General of the United States of America, Harry Dougharty, the very man who engineered my indictment, plotted my indictment with others, was such a rascal that they had to kick him out of office and indict him for fraud in connection with $7,000,000 alien enemy funds, and whose only plea to the jury was that he had an old mother. But because he belonged to the party in power they convicted the other fellow, who acted under his urge, and let him go. As I have said, I feel honored to have been indicted under the administration of such a rogue.

When I was in the federal prison in America I was associated with whom? I was associated not with the ordinary criminal of the streets, I was an associate of and a fellow convict in company with men like ex-Governor McCray of the State of Indiana, and of senators and congressmen of the United States; so you will understand that being imprisoned in the United States is not like being imprisoned in England. Therefore, you should not condemn me without trying me on the principles of English justice. I do not believe there is any law on your statute books that would convict a man because some unknown agent of his posted an empty envelope. Yet you say I am a criminal because I was convicted on such a flimsy charge in the United States of America.

But, men, let me show some of the things that are being done against us. My imprisonment in America was only the means to an end in the commercial and industrial schemes of men who are creating so much trouble in the world today. Take the great rubber shortage.

There was a great rubber shortage from 1922 up till 1925 on the part of the Americans. You English had cornered the rubber market; you had all the rubber plantations under your control in the Malay Peninsula. The Americans had no rubber reserve. Mr. Hoover acted as foster father of all American rubber interests. He set out to get control of rubber lands in any part of the world where he possibly could get control of them. Just about that time my organization, in carrying out its serious program of rebuilding Africa through the help and influence of the educated Negroes of the West going home, had completed an agreement with the Liberian government for that government to place at our disposal four sections of the little country so that we could start our experiment in helping to build Liberia and make her a worthy worthwhile Negro state in West Africa. We sent four delegations out to Liberia who were received by the President of Liberia and by the Liberian government. An agreement was entered into. They advised us at what time we should start sending out our colonists to Liberia. Acting on their instructions and on their urging we spent fully half a million dollars in buying machinery and materials and in securing one of the best steamships afloat, known as the S.S. *General Goethals*, a German liner taken during the War. She was a well constructed boat of 5,500 tons; we bought her from the Panama Railroad Company and paid nearly $260,000 for her and in purchasing equipment. After we had spent nearly half a million dollars, after we had entered into agreements with expert civil engineers and mechanical engineers and mining engineers and had taken from a company in America one of their best expert civil engineers to be the director-general of our work in Liberia, after we had everything ready, Firestone's agent found out that it was possible to grow rubber in Liberia. He, therefore, influenced the President of Liberia—Charles King, the man who had entered into a sacred agreement with us—to abrogate the contract between his government and my organization and to place at his (Firestone's) disposal the land that was to be given to our organization. Without any advice, without any instructions, when our advance agents landed in Liberia, instead of receiving them, as they promised they would, [the government] deported them.

When the ships of the Bull Line arrived with our material aboard, nearly $200,000 worth of materials, they landed the materials and have kept them up to now. They also gave Firestone 1,000,000 acres of land which they had placed at our disposal for colonization purposes. Firestone was backed by Mr.

Hoover, the Secretary of Commerce in America. Therefore you will understand that it was convenient at that time, in 1924, to rush me to prison, because just at that time I was able to make not only trouble for Charles King, but for Firestone for double-crossing us in Liberia. I had enough influence to have unseated Charles King as President in the next election. Firestone and the then American government knew that: Mr. Hoover knew that I had enough influence in Liberia to prevent Charles King being returned for a third time as President of the country, and so as to weaken my influence and make it impossible for me to prevent King being returned, so that he and his senate could ratify the agreement, they thereupon railroaded me for five years and kept me there for six months after Charles King was reelected. That is the kind of thing they do. The President of the United States of America said to the ex-Counsel-General of my organization, "I know Garvey has not done any wrong, but he was a bad business man." That President had it in his power not only to commute my sentence the very day I was sentenced but to pardon me, yet he never did anything until two years afterwards when it was convenient from a political point of view and from a commerical point of view to let me go; and then they deported me without giving me a chance of going back to my office in New York, where I represented the interests of 4,000,000 American citizens, involving millions of dollars. They called me a rogue and vagabond and did not give me a chance to go back to New York and straighten out the affairs of these people, although I asked to be allowed to do so, and the Secretary of Labor said "No." They commuted my sentence on November 24. The executive authority said that my commutation release should be immediate, but they kept me until nearly the first day of the following month, without notifying me that I was commuted, although I should have gone away from prison at that time. The reason was that they were devising schemes during those few days as to how they could get me out of the country without my returning to New York. Therefore, I never knew the condition of my commutation until I was on the ship.

So you will realize that being imprisoned in the United States of America is not like being imprisoned in England, where you have morality and principle and justice and law before you can take away the name of a man and deprive him of his character.

Consequently I appeal to you Englishmen and Englishwomen who are here tonight not to come to any hasty conclusion touching my character; because I feel it coming before you that, before my God, I can match my character against the character of any man in the world. I dare any man in all the world to say that I have ever defrauded him of one penny—any man in the world . . . So that I trust you will not make it a point of prejudice against me and against the organization I represent that I was sent to prison, because that is a minor and an insignificant matter in considering the grave question that we have before us for settlement.

As I have said, I am here as the representative of 11,000,000 people. They naturally will look towards any treatment meted out to me as a similar treatment meted out to them. I trust you will not make the mistake of thinking that the Negro is so simple at this time as to accept any insult without returning it. So that any rebuff you give as touching the representation I make on behalf of the people will not be an insult to Marcus Garvey but an insult to 280,000,000 Negroes whom I represent through the Universal Negro Improvement Association.

We look upon your representatives as the ambassadors of your race. We want to treat with them as honorable men. All this vile propaganda that you have read of within the last week is purely a misrepresentation of the statements I have made as touching the aims and object of this organization. I gave clean and intelligent and aboveboard statements to the press; they have not published those statements, but they have published things to make me a buffoon, to make me look ridiculous before you, and to defeat the object of this meeting here tonight. I want you, therefore, to know that the Negro is no longer asleep. The intelligent representatives of the race are thinking; but we are intelligent enough to know that you should not be judged and held accountable for the conduct of men who do not truly and throughly represent you.

We want to be the friends of the English people; we want to be the friends of the white races the world over; because neither the black race nor the white race nor the brown race nor the yellow race can achieve anything in the world lastingly except through peaceful methods. We want peace. The Negro has always been on the side of peace. We are not a vile people. You

know our history throughout the last 3,000 years. We have
committed no outrages upon humanity; we have committed no
outrages upon civilization. We have at our disposal today no
great armaments; we have no battleships, we have no navies, we
have no standing armies; therefore, you must conclude that we
are a people who love peace. Our attitude and our acts prove
conclusively that we are not inclined to disturb the peace of the
world. All we want is justice; and we are appealing to the hearts
of you Englishmen at home and abroad to listen to the plea of
bleeding Africa.

I have recounted to you the history of slavery; I have
recounted to you our present economic and social difficulties. In
your respective countries you do not want us. We cannot go to
Australia and get a living; we cannot go to Canada and get a
living; we cannot come to England and get a living; you will not
employ us. Nearly ninety per cent of the blacks in England are
unemployed because you are prejudiced against employing us.
That is not fair. In our countries we treat you with consideration.
In the colonies where you send out your men both as emigrants
and as colonial administrators, we treat them with the greatest
courtesy. I have but to recall the treatment of Negroes in Africa
towards Stanley and towards Livingstone to show our disposition
towards strangers. You sent consumptive Livingstone to us; he
lived in our midst; we fed him; when he was sick we gave him
medicine; when he died and we could do nothing more for him
we took his dead body upon our shoulders and walked hundreds
of miles through the forests of Africa and brought his remains to
you, to the sea, whence you could remove them at your pleasure.

The consumptive Cecil Rhodes went to Africa; we treated him
with kindness and consideration. What is the result? They have
made Rhodesia so that a black man cannot walk on the sidewalks
of that country. That is not a fair return for all that we have done.
We have laid our hearts and our souls bare before you. We have
always been willing to suffer and to help you in all circumstances,
in season and out of season; and therefore we are only asking you
now for a reasonable consideration of our case.

We are 280 millions of homeless people, with no country and
no flag. In America they make a joke of it that every nation has a
flag but the coon. You will find that in mimicry and in song.

Tonight I am appealing to the hearts of you Anglo-Saxons, or you Anglo-Americans, to listen to the plaintive cry of the black man who has been abused for nearly 300 years in the Western World. I understand that a great scare was laid around me as a deterrent to holding this meeting here tonight. I want to say to you that up to now you do not understand the Negro. You cannot scare the Negro any more. The Negro is a man. We represent the new Negro. His back is not yet to the wall; we do not want his back to the wall because that would be a peculiar position and a desperate position. We do not want him there. It is because of that we are asking you for a fair compromise.

Now, you have sent your agents to me asking what part of Africa we want. It is for you to decide; it is for the British government to decide; it is for the French government to decide, it is for the governments of Belgium also and of Portugal and of Spain, all in conference with us, to decide what part of Africa they will place at the disposal of the natives so that they can live in peace in their own native land.

The Belgians have control of the Belgian Congo which they cannot use—they have not the resources to develop nor the intelligence. The French have more territory than they can develop; the Italians have more territory than they can develop. You English also have more territory than you can develop. There are certain parts of Africa in which you cannot live at all; now it is for you to come together and give us a United States of Black Africa. If you want South Africa, you can keep South Africa. If you want East Africa, we are reasonable enough even to say, "Have it." But we are going to have our part of Africa whether you will it or not. We are going to have it. Because we are not going to be a race without a country. God never intended it; and we are not going to abuse God's confidence in us as men. We are men, human beings, capable of the same acts as any other race; possessing, under fair circumstances, the same intelligence as any other race. You do not know Africa. Africa has been sleeping for centuries—not dead, only sleeping. You have all read the story of Rip Van Winkle who got up and walked around. Today Africa is walking around, not only on its feet but on its brains. You can enslave, as you did for 300 years, the bodies of men, you can shackle the hands of men, you can shackle the feet of men, you can imprison the bodies of men, but you cannot shackle or imprison the minds of men.

No race has the last word on culture and on civilization. You
do not know what the black man is capable of; you do not know
what he is thinking. You are thinking in terms of battleships, of
dreadnoughts, of submarines, of aeroplanes. Do you know what
we are thinking about? That is our private business.

So give us credit for being able to use our minds; and with
people becoming conscious of themselves, determined to use
their minds, you do not know to what extent they can go.
Liberate the minds of men and ultimately you will liberate the
bodies of men. And I am here tonight as a representative of the
new Negro in finance, the new Negro in art, the new Negro in
literature, the new Negro in music, the new Negro in economics,
the new Negro in science.

Gentlemen, do not you know that one of the ablest scientists of
the world today is a black man in the Tuskegee Institute of
Alabama in the United States? Do you know what a scientist can
do for the world? You had a little fellow over here the other
day—I believe his name was Matthews—who had an idea that he
had discovered the death ray, and everybody's eyes were set on
him. France wanted the secret; England wanted the secret;
America wanted the secret; but when they got hold of him they
found he had not discovered anything yet.

But the new Negro is also thinking in terms of perpetual
motion; the Negro is also thinking in terms of the hidden
mysteries of the world; and you do not know what the oppressed
and suppressed Negro, by virtue of his condition and circumstance, may give to the world as a surprise.

Do you know that when men are forced to do things they do
them with greater effect than when they are not forced to do
them? Are you going to force us into a corner where we have to
think, and think evil? I trust you will not do that. For God's sake
do not force 280 million black men to think evil; because
probably a unit of that great number may think so dangerously as
to be a menace to the world. By the time it gets up with him he
will have gone away with the world. Do not force us to think that
way. Give us a chance to live in ease as you are living, so that we
may have a chance to bring out those latent, hidden powers
which made a Newton, which gave us a Darwin and a Huxley.
We are capable of giving such men to the world if we are forced
into a corner to think. But, as I have said before, we are a

peace-loving people. We love humanity; we love your race not for social fellowship but in the common brotherhood that God intended we should live. We love the white race because we believe the white race has a right to peace and happiness and all those things conducive to a happy life. We believe the yellow man has such claims, and we are not going to deny ourselves the privilege.

I thank you for coming out here tonight, and I compliment you upon the independence of spirit which has forced you to come to this meeting; because you could have adopted the attitude of other Englishmen who are not here tonight, under the persuasion of the propaganda to destroy me, holding me up in the way that you have read of. The fact that you have come here shows that you are in search of information. I would not for one minute accuse all Englishmen of dishonor; I would not for one minute accuse all the white American people of dishonor; I have good friends in America, and I think I recognize one of them in the audience here, a man who has stuck by me all through because he believed that we were right. He represents one wing of his race, the purity side of his race, and he has been struggling for that and we have upheld that; we honor him and his organization for that; we want to see a pure white race, and we are going to work so that we are going to have a pure black race.

Circumstances sometimes create conditions over which we have no control. Men who are thrown into foreign places where their own people do not domicile naturally do not do things because they are right but because they are convenient. Those are the side shows and incidents we will not discuss, but the bigger issue reveals the fact that we respect the white race remaining as it is, and we also demand that you allow the black race to remain as it is. In the Colonies you have treated us unfairly; you went to Africa and you have given us there a mongrel population; in America also you have given us a mongrel population—nearly 4,000,000 people—and so we are aggrieved socially. But we are not going to press this grievance; we are only going to ask you to give us a fair chance, a fair opportunity to express ourselves in terms of reason.

Negro Progress Postulates
Negro Government*

W HETHER IT BE viewed from the moral, legal, industrial and economic, social or political standpoint, there is no reasonable ground of objection to the establishment of a system of government by Negroes for Negroes. And such a system will not be characterized, as some persons fear, by the primitivism of intertribal strife and savage, perpetual warfare for temporary supremacy of this or that tribal leader. For the race is endowed with the instincts of government that bore the marks of a high standard of civilization, to which, in certain features, our boasted Western Culture has not made a worthy approach.

The Race has fallen but her instincts are not dead. The silence of centuries has been broken. Her winter has passed and her springtime is here with the promise of a bountiful harvest, for Negro genius has again been fanned into activity, and is ready to infuse into Negro life the qualities and characteristics that made Negroes great in their institutions of the past.

The Seat of Empire Northward Moves was true to history and poetry during the period of Negro decline. But its Northern limit has been reached, and with the revival of Negro activity its path has again turned South. For Empire has not only a Seat but a Home and that Home is Africa.

It is well for black men to think on these things and to notice the movements that are contributory to this end. Jamaica is to be favored in August with the General Convention of the UNIA movement. And while we can make only the briefest reference to that subject today we would ask Negroes to say what is their mind upon the matter. What do they expect to see and hear? They possibly have read concerning former conventions held in New York. These have been wonderful happenings in a wonderful country. What is their conjecture concerning that to be held in Jamaica? Hundreds and hundreds of Negro delegates from all parts of the world will meet from day to day for a whole month in discussion on Negro problems, and world issues as they affect the Negro. What is the aim? What will be the effect? Can Jamaica Negroes and the Jamaica community be the same after the convention?

And will not this convention in its implications and bearings be significant in regard to the growing consciousness of kinship of Negroes in whatever part of the world they are found? Can it leave us without a strong, irresistible urge to realize the meaning of a common, permanent government, with a fixed habitation and a name? The convention will be a demonstration of the possibilities of Negro Government that no one can deny.

The World as It Is*

One Mr. Sparks and His Anthropology
South Africa and the Natives
Politicians and General Elections

One Mr. Sparks of 60 Slipe Road, Kingston, has written us a letter, dealing on the question of, as he terms it, "anthropology." The letter really is a castigation of us for referring to an esteemed fellow citizen a couple days ago as being of colored blood. For what we know of anthropology we find ourselves very unlearned, when we have to admit Mr. Sparks' new definition of the subject. This is what Mr. Sparks says in his "anthropology" which is very amusing to us: "For your information white men having children with Negro women do not make those children Negroes as the man reproduces his race, no matter who the woman may be." Now isn't this a foolish statement for Mr. Sparks to make, and call it anthropology?

Now answer us this—if a white man has a child by a black woman and the child is to be called a white man because of the father's reproduction, when this child marries another black woman and has a child, according to you, this child would also be a white man and this child in turn will marry another woman and have a child; now how ignorant a proposition is it to suggest that this child would be a white man?

* The Blackman, May 8, 1929, Pages 1 and 8.

Your anthropology hasn't any legs to stand on, it is blatant ignorance, but we must admit that you have suggested it as an excuse for colored people not calling themselves Negroes. The laugh is with us Negroes and the white people over those who do not want to admit themselves Negroes as members of a race.

South Africa is a hot bed of trouble between the natives who are black and the colonists who are European. There are two million Europeans in and around the Union of South Africa with more than six million natives. These two million have been trying to rob the entire South Africa from the natives who originally owned the country. This leaves no room for any good will between the two peoples. What the outcome will be, only God can tell. There is one thing however, that we know, and that is, the natives are not going to die without striking back and so we may look forward to a terrible time of unrest from that section of the world. It is a pity because the great question in dispute could be settled amicably by being just fair to the natives. . . .

The World as It Is*

A Brutal Man

A poor black boy, trying to earn a living by running tasks in carrying bananas for the Jamaica Fruit and Shipping Company, at the No. 3 Pier, was beaten up a couple days ago by the Assistant Wharfinger. He was boxed out of line by this man and kicked severely on his jaw. The poor boy was brought to our office and showed plainly the effects of his maltreatment. A reputable doctor has given a certificate touching on the boy's condition and there are many witnesses to prove the gross advantage taken of him by this brutal Wharfinger.

An occurrence of this kind could not have taken place anywhere in the civilized world without calling forth the gross indignation of the community. In Jamaica where the poor black people are not counted, such an occurrence goes unnoticed until this time. We have here a society for the protection of cruelty to animals, which very often prosecutes cruel persons for ill-treating animals. None of the people interested in such a society have said anything about the brutal treatment of this black boy, but we are determined to see that justice is done him—we feel somewhat sure that the managers of the Jamaica Fruit and Shipping Company, whose bananas he was handling, have not sanctioned such brutal treatment by their employees to laborers; we are now bringing the matter prominently before the Jamaica public and the government. Jamaica is being scandalized by the barbarous handling of the black people on the waterfront. Some of these men who are in charge take it as a delight to hit the poor laborers with sticks, abuse them and treat them most wickedly especially on the approach of tourist ships, so as to show off to the tourists the social relationship between the people here so that they go away with the impression that the black people are dogs. All self-respecting Negroes must be incensed at such an action. Any man occupying the position of Assistant Wharfinger who did anything of the kind ought to be regarded as an unsafe person to invest with any authority. The Jamaica Fruit Company, like other fruit companies, is making its fortune out of these poor black laborers; common decency ought to teach them that they should treat the people with courtesy and consideration. If this thing had happened in America, the Assistant Wharfinger would have been immediately arrested, but nothing has been done to him up to the present, although complaint has been made.

He calculates that because the boy only earns an average of 3/6d per week it would be impossible for him to spend that to find a lawyer in prosecuting him and so he took the advantage of beating the poor boy. He is just a ragged boy, but that makes the case even more important in that the Wharfinger is so low down as to have taken advantage of the boy because of his helpless condition. He knew well that because the other poor Negroes were anxious to get a day's work they would not retaliate in protection of the boy. He even inspired them to help beat the boy—that is another awful state of affairs; it borders on slavery.

Uncle Tom's Cabin as brought to us by Harriet Beecher Stowe is strikingly similar. Still, we are nearly 100 years removed from slavery. Are we going to stand for this in civilized Jamaica? Surely not. What the men on the waterfront should have done when the Assistant Wharfinger attempted to beat up one of their kind was to get hold of him and chuck him into the sea; but I suppose that the men were too cowardly to do that, calculating that they would have lost their employment, or that they would have been brutally treated by the forces the Jamaica Fruit Company would have called in to handle them.

Not very long ago the same advantage was taken of a large number of Jamaica laborers in Santa Maria and when they attempted to retaliate, the Colombian soldiery was called in to shoot them down like dogs. That could not have happened in Jamaica today, because those of us who are on guard in protecting the rights of the black people would have immediately got in touch with His Excellency the Governor or the Secretary of State to see that the power of the law be not used by any class to take advantage of another.

If the associates of this boy had held on to the Assistant Wharfinger and given him a good whipping or thrown him into the sea they would have been justified. We hope this is the last we will hear of this brutality on the waterfront because we are going to encourage our men to hit back and hit hard and to hold on to anyone attempting to take advantage of them. In this case we are going to take the matter to the court to see that the boy is protected. We hope the Jamaica Fruit Company will do the right thing by dismissing this brutal Assistant Wharfinger.

The World as It Is*

Insulting Negro Womanhood

It is an unfortunate thing that the Negro womanhood of Jamaica in particular and of the West Indies in general can be so abused without any protection given them or interest taken in the matter. We have before us the case of a prominent man, who is only one of many, who has taken gross advantage of a Negro girl, yet he continues to enjoy public respect. Unfortunately, the man himself is a Negro; his action toward a member of his own race is worse than if it were committed by a man of any other race. This man is wealthy, he was not always so, he was once a poor man. When he was poor, he got engaged to a colored girl, probably with the best intention; when he started to get rich, he started to ignore this colored fiancée, to "put her off" and tell her all kinds of false tales with the object of breaking his pledge. According to the man's way of thinking he had become sufficiently prominent and rich to enter "into society" and so he wanted a white wife, apparently, as most successful Negro men of a certain turn of mind do after amassing fortunes. The colored girl refused to release him from his obligation and so because he feared a suit for breach of promise he has not yet married a white woman but he doesn't want to marry a colored girl any more, yet during the time he has been taking advantage of colored girls and in one instance has made one a mother.

* *The Blackman*, May 17, 1929, Pages 1 and 8.

This treatment to colored girls is common among us and it is time a halt be called—if by no one else, by the *Blackman* in exposing such cases to the public. It is a dirty trick on the part of successful Negroes to spend two-thirds of their lives amassing wealth from among the Negro people, [that] then when they become rich they marry people outside of their own race to die shortly after, leaving their fortunes, made from the Negro people, to go into the coffers of other people who are sufficiently independent and provided for, while the Negro race still remains in poverty. It is a shame, and so we shall make it a point of our duty to at all times bring any abuse of our womanhood to the attention of the public.

Not long ago a prominent doctor died and left a fortune. The fortune went to the white lady he married and, naturally, to her relatives. The doctor, like most of our successful men, came up through difficulties; his poor Negro parents labored hard to give him an education. Nearly everything he got by way of education and start in life came through Negroes. The success of his profession was insured through Negroes because all his patients were Negroes, yet when he became rich instead of marrying a Negro woman like his mother, he married a white woman, and now that he is dead all of his wealth is gone out of the race.

There is one thing that we have to admire the white man for and that is he is never found disloyal to his race. We find isolated cases where individuals of the white race marry Negro women, but not where they have to give their fortunes to these women or their relatives; it is always the case [that] the Negro women are rich when marriages take place between them and white men. We hope that public sentiment will be stirred as to make it impossible for successful Negro men to so insult our womanhood, and we hope the gentleman we have in mind will marry the poor nurse he has dishonored.

The World as It Is*

The Internal Prejudices of Negroes

According to the arrangement of the "colored" leaders, the following plan is decided and acted upon; it is made very successful in the West Indies and is now being successfully fostered in America and elsewhere. In countries where the blacks outnumber the whites, the "colored" build up a buffer society through the financial assistance and patronage of the minority whites. They convince the minority whites that the blacks are dangerous and vicious, and that their only chance of successfully living among them is to elevate to positions of trust, superiority and overseership of the "colored" element who will directly deal with the blacks and exploit them for the general benefit of the whites. The whites being not strong enough to stand alone accept our acquiescence and thus the "colored" element is elevated to a superior position and naturally becomes attached to the whites. The skillful group, however, by its ability to acquire wealth through the privileged position allowed, immediately starts out to socially equip itself educationally and culturally to meet the whites on equal terms. They also skillfully strengthen their positions by stirring up the blacks against the whites explaining to the former that all their ills are caused by the whites, then they go back to the whites and intimidate them by drawing their attention to the great danger of the dissatisfied blacks, and offer as a solution the uniting of the whites and "colored" in a social and economic union to offset the supposed common danger from the blacks. By this artful method the "colored" elements of the colonies have socially subdued the white man, who now looks on and sees the prosperous "colored" gentleman leading away his sister or daughter in the bonds of marriage without the ability to raise the voice of protest.

The "colored" elements have arranged it so that the blacks are always kept down, so that they can use their dissatisfaction and disaffection as an argument to strengthen and further perpetuate their positions of social equality and economic privilege and preferment with the whites.

Such is the game that is being played over in America by the Du Bois–Weldon Johnson group of "colored" persons of the National Association for the Advancement of Colored People. The Universal Negro Improvement Association stands in opposition to this association on the miscegenation question, because we believe in the racial purity of both the Negro and white races. We feel that the moral disadvantage of slavery should not be perpetuated. That where our slave masters were able to abuse our slave mothers and thereby create a hybrid bastardy, we ourselves, at this time of freedom and culture, should not perpetuate the crime of nature.

We desire to standardize our race morally, hence our advocacy of all elements and shades within the race coming together and by well understood and defined codes build up a strong and healthy Negro race with pride and respect in itself, rather than seeking, as the Du Bois group does, to practice an unrestricted intercourse of miscegenation.

All the hate that the leaders of the small "colored" group can find has been levied at me for my interference with and interruption of their plans. My indictment, conviction and imprisonment are but a small effort of theirs to help destroy and ruin me because of my effort to save the Negro race from extinction through miscegenation.

That "colored" group has scientifically arranged their method of propaganda. In America and the colonies, they hold out certain baits and hopes to the educated and financially prosperous men of the darker groups, such as encouraging them to marry the very lightest element of their women and adopting them into their society. These darker men, for the special privilege and "honor" are used as active propagandists to deceive the great mass of dark people so that they would not suspect the motive or the design of the "colored" element. Generally the darker men who marry the very lightest "colored" women who sometimes pass off as white, become more hostile to their kind in the mass as well as by individual contact than the very leaders as the leaders are generally careful not to attract or arouse suspicion of their motive. The majority of the "colored" leaders who seek after white women and the darker men who marry very light "colored" women are seldom on social terms with their own mothers if they are dark. If they have their mothers in their homes, which is generally never so, they hide them away either in the kitchen or a back room where they do not come in contact with either their light "colored" or white guests. Such is the great problem that I have sought to solve, and no one will wonder why I have been made a criminal in the struggle to rescue and save the Negro race from itself and from continuous suffering and ultimate extermination.

The Negro's Place
in World Reorganization*

GRADUALLY WE ARE approaching the time when the Negro peoples of the world will have either to consciously, through their own organization go forward to the point of destiny as laid out by themselves, or must sit quiescently and see themselves pushed back into the mire of economic serfdom, to be ultimately crushed by the grinding mill of exploitation and be exterminated ultimately by the strong hand of prejudice.

There is no doubt about it that we are living in the age of world reorganization out of which will come a set program for the organized races of mankind that will admit of no sympathy in human affairs, in that we are planning for the great gigantic struggle of the survival of the fittest group. It becomes each and every one engaged in this great race for place and position to use whatsoever influence possible to divert the other fellow's attention from the real object. In our own sphere in America and the western world we find that we are being camouflaged, not so much by those with whom we are competing for our economic, political existence, but by men from within our own race, either as agents of the opposition or as unconscious fools, who are endeavoring to flatter us into believing that our future should rest with chance and with Providence, believing that through these agencies will come the solution of the restless problem. Such

* The Blackman, Saturday, February 1, 1930.

leadership is but preparing us for the time that is bound to befall us if we do not exert ourselves now toward our own creative purpose. The mission of the Universal Negro Improvement Association is to arouse the sleeping consciousness of Negroes everywhere to the point where we will, as one concerted body, act for our own preservation. By laying the foundation for such we will be able to work toward the glorious realization of an emancipated race and a constructed nation. Nationhood is the strongest security of any people and it is for that the Universal Negro Improvement Association strives at this time. With the clamor of other peoples for a similar purpose, we raise a noise even to high heaven for the admission of the Negro into the plan of autonomy.

On every side we hear the cry of white supremacy—in America, Canada, Australia, Europe, and even South America. There is no white supremacy beyond the power and strength of the white man to hold himself against others. The supremacy of any race is not permanent; it is a thing only of the time in which the race finds itself powerful. The whole world of white men is becoming nervous of touching its own future and that of other races. With the desire of self-preservation, which naturally is the first law of nature, they raise the hue and cry that the white race must be first in government and in control. What must the Negro do in the face of such a universal attitude but to align all his forces in the direction of protecting himself from the threatened disaster of race domination and ultimate extermination?

Without a desire to harm anyone, the Universal Negro Improvement Association feels that the Negro should without compromise or any apology appeal to the same spirit of racial pride and love as the great white race is doing for its own preservation, so that while others are raising the cry of a white America, a white Canada, a white Australia, we also without reservation raise the cry of a "Black Africa." The critic asks, "Is this possible?" and the four hundred million courageous Negroes of the world answer: "Yes."

An Apostrophe to Miss Nancy Cunard*

NATURE, FOR HER own purpose, made us racially separate, and almost distinct; if from no other point of view, from the physiological; in so much so that we are Chinese, Japanese, English, French, Dutch, African, Indian and the rest of it. In the course of our human growth we recognize, and strongly so, this great difference, but what may be missing in this particular seems to be made up for, and is common to all of us, and that is, in the *ability to think;* but even in the realms of thought men differ, hence our manifold systems of politics, philosophy, and religion. We do not think all alike on any of these subjects or questions; but in the great world of things, whether we are Chinese, Japanese, Anglo-Saxon, Teuton, Latin, or African, there is always a circle of mental companionship wherein we see and admire things from the same viewpoint. We not only think them, but we feel them, so that the student can well appreciate a member of one race in comradeship with the member of another, whether the racial difference be white, or black, or yellow or brown. The world wonders why Miss Nancy Cunard thinks sympathetically black. It is with the same reason that the black man thinks sympathetically white whenever any outrage is attempted or perpetrated upon the white race anywhere.

Black men have shouldered arms in wars to protect the lives of

* *The New Jamaican,* July 28, 1932.

white men, not because they, the black men, were particularly affected, but because of that deep human sympathy and mental viewpoint of right as against wrong. It was the same among white men during the time of the American Civil War, when Garrison, Lovejoy and Lincoln thought that it was cruel to hold black men in bondage. If we were to resurrect the world and should awaken thought with it, we would find strange company in the realms of thought, because Socrates may forsake the companionship of the Greeks to find more pleasant mental atmosphere with the Romans; Cicero may forsake the Romans to find better companionship with the Africans; Theodore Roosevelt may forsake the American white race to find mental comradeship with Booker T. Washington, the sage and seer of Tuskegee, and in the same realm, now resurrected, Miss Nancy Cunard and myself may stand in the same company, forsaking all relations that would otherwise separate us in race.

Companionship of minds is a grand and noble thing; it destroys the peculiarity of selfishness of race. It holds out a reward far above the common level of human things. To the philosopher the physical man is nothing, it is the mental man that counts. The mental man is the soul possessor, is the soul owner, the soul captain and master of himself. This soul he expresses in poetry and in prose. It confines him to no particular race or any particular country. The mind of Shakespeare was not purely English, nor was the mind of Cicero purely Roman, neither were the minds of Socrates and Plato purely Greek. The Empire of those minds extended around the world; it is a company to which only noble characters particularly are admitted. It is the company in which Miss Nancy Cunard finds herself at this particular time which the narrow selfishness of her own race does not understand. Those who live for the companionship of the mind live in an atmosphere higher and loftier than anything temporarily physical. We must remember that when all that is physical decays, all that is higher and nobler mentally, lives on. The good deeds of men never die, whether we record them on parchment, bronze or marble. The ages keep company with them, and so, whilst the ashes of Socrates moulder with Greek dust; whilst the ashes of Cicero moulder with Roman dust; whilst the ashes of Hegel and Spinoza, Darwin and Huxley, Ladd and James and

Marx moulder with their national earth, the mental spirit of the
men goes on and on to inspire and to ennoble others as they
succeed to the careers of previous generations. When Miss
Cunard is gone (as she must go) the way of physical beings, her
kindly thoughts, her gentle mental sympathies for a race
downtrodden and oppressed shall live forever; when the millions
(sterling) of her fathers shall corrode and rust and probably be
lost to the Cunard generations, for her deeds, she shall be
remembered. We are, therefore, encouraging her in this companionship of minds. Forsake not the great task that lies before you,
but pursue it because it leads to immortality and the continuous
worship at a shrine that shall ever blossom with the fragrance of
the sweet rose. How can man live or die better than by tracing
the footsteps of immortality.

It is not the common mind that establishes immortality, it is
the high mind, the lofty mind, the conscious, self-possessed,
mental sparkle of divinity. We are divine in our thoughts,
because thoughts are the creators of all things visible and
invisible. The Divine mind is master of the universe; the human
mind is master of its particular world. So that we should always
dignify and ennoble that divine attribute, that links us to
Supreme Divinity.

The source of all good thought is love—Divine Love—and how
could we rise to loftier and nobler heights without emulating that
love even to the human limit. It is the possession and the
execution of this love that link Miss Nancy Cunard with the
Negro race. It is the same love that makes the black man think
kindly even of an offending world towards him. These are the
thoughts that will save us. These are the thoughts that inspire
Divine goodness with patience, notwithstanding the vicious and
wicked sins of men. I must conclude in saying that Miss Nancy
Cunard is in the highest company that man can select, and that is
the noble company of minds that think alike for the good and
salvation of the world.

The Communists
and the Negro*

A CABLE DESPATCH from London stated that a Communist body, at a gathering of its members, decided to suspend propaganda work among colored Americans because of the "inherent ignorance" of the colored races, which makes their unity impossible.

The Body also declared that it was a futile endeavor to enlighten "born fools."

We are peculiar in our opinions—peculiar only because these opinions are arrived at through mature consideration and ripe experience, which is not consistent with local opinions, because we are accustomed to express ourselves locally, more through sentiment than facts.

While we have a good deal of sentiment in us, we also have a superabundance of seriousness, calculated to be interested only in those things that are right and stating only those things that are true. To be responsible for such opinions in Jamaica is sometimes to be very unpopular among sentimental people, who never like the truth but who prefer to hide it.

That the colored man is sentimental goes without saying. It is this very flimsy sentimentality that is going to destroy him as a race group. He is now being destroyed in America, at a rapid rate, because he will not become serious enough to think on the problems that confront him and work seriously to solve them.

* The New Jamaican, September 5, 1932.

The colored or Negro race seem to think that the world owes an obligation to them, to cuddle, pamper, tickle and tolerate them as children are generally treated in the nursery. They have not yet grown to realize that they are living in a serious world, and to hold their place in it they must be serious and assertive on their own account.

We feel confident in saying that no one in our present time has had more experience with the colored or Negro race than we have had. We, therefore, feel ourselves competent to pass judgment or an opinion on the colored people.

The term colored is confused with the term Negro. In America when both terms are used they mean the same thing. We are using them from the American understanding. We state this because we do not want any local confusion.

The Communists have declared that the colored people are "born fools." There is something significant in this. We agree, not only in the sense that all men are born fools, until they are able to absorb and understand, but the colored people are peculiarly ignorant of their rights and privileges. They take more talking to and more persuasive influencing than any other group of people in the world, and even when you think you have achieved something, in pointing them to that which should be theirs, when you least expect it, you find them just where they were before. That must have been the experience of the Communists with the Negroes in the United States and in other parts of the world where they have been trying, at least for six years, to radically influence them toward Communism.

Again the Communists say that the colored people are cursed with "inherent ignorance." We suppose they mean ignorance toward their political rights. Again we agree.

In agreeing with the statements of the Communists, we must state clearly that we are not supporters of Communism. Communists have been our bitter foes for the last ten years. They have done us a great deal of harm in the United States. They made attempts several times to operate an organization of four million colored people, of which we were head, and when we stopped them and stubbornly resisted them all around, they initiated a vile and wicked propaganda against us, calling us capitalists, bourgeoise, opportunists and Uncle Toms.

We declared then, as we declare now, that the Negro should not allow himself to be absorbed by Communism, because, ultimately Communism in its treatment of Negroes will be no better than the other "isms" we have had since the Negro came in contact with European civilization. We declared then and still declare that Communism among Negroes was only an effort to line up another powerful minority group with other discontented minority groups of the world, to strengthen the hands of Communism to smash [the present order] out of which would rise a universal Communism that would be as dangerous to the peace of the world and as oppressive to control as any other system that went before.

We claimed then and we claim now that a European Communist will be no different, when he gets into power, to the Southern Cracker of the United States. The Cracker has in his blood the desire (wish) to kill and brutalize the Negro because of his vaunted image of superiority based upon the difference of color.

When you scratch the Communist beneath the surface, you will find him the same vicious Southerner whose political belief will not surmount his racial prejudices and for this, we have always kept Communism at bay; hence no one will mistake us for having any sympathy for the Communists as far as bringing the Negro into Communism is concerned. We are interested only to watch the results of their mighty effort and to seize our chance to be what we ought to be, by not being "born fools."

Can we blame the Communists for calling us "born fools" in America, when the opportunity was ripe, pointed the Negro toward the building up of great industrial enterprises, the establishment of steamship lines to link up the commerce of the race throughout the world, and particularly between Africa, the West Indies and North America. The intellectual "fools" of the Negro race laughed when I told them it was time to get hold of Liberia and make it the center of world Negro activities, thereby demonstrating to the other nations that the colored man was able to build and control a nation of his own. The Negro intellectuals laughed again.

We organized a plan for building four modern cities in the Republic of Liberia as the first concentration centers for the

Negroes of the West Indies and America to link up their intelligence with the native African in the scheme of nation building.

When we were able to influence the Liberian government to give a concession of lands, and a budget of two million dollars was prepared to start the work, and engineers and experts landed on the spot in Liberia, a black president of Liberia, by the name of Charles Dunbar King, who had acquiesced to the proposition, saw the possibility of getting graft from Harvey Firestone, the American millionaire of the Firestone Rubber Company. He gave to the Firestone interests the landed concessions in Liberia that were intended to be the concentration centers of Negro colonists, who were to go there to build up the Republic and prove to the world that the Negro was capable in government.

Just at this minute, we have on our desk a confidential report we have received from Geneva—a plea from an ambassador from Liberia, asking us to help now to do the thing that we attempted to do eight years ago, because the Firestone interests have ravished the country and have reduced the people almost to a state of serfdom, to be mildly relieved only by the timely effort of the League of Nations. Do you wonder that the Communists call a race so childish and simple "born fools?"

The Communists must have had their experience to have come to the conclusions that we, by experience, felt long ago, and which made us aggravated because so much could have been done otherwise.

We know that most of the Negroes who have led Communism in America and in other parts of the world have done so only because of the easy money they could collect from the Soviet Union or from the Communist Party.

The Negro has not yet learned to project honorable and honest leadership. The Communists are therefore tired of paying out to the Negroes to help themselves. We feel sure that the Negroes are paying very little into Communism, because, outside of the great effort we headed in America and outside of the churches and a few organizations that keep the Negro sentimental all the time, he is not willing to foot his own bills. Politically he is not willing to pay his price. Anything political must be contributed to and paid for by somebody else for him, otherwise he is not interested.

These are only fringes of the truth that could be told, but why tell them except to help? We have hinted enough to help us to realize the sad position we are in, and we do hope that some good will come out of the charge that the Communists have made against the colored people.

Part Six

The Last Years, 1934-1940

Commentary

BY JOHN HENRIK CLARKE

HE WOULD NOW go to the seat of the British Empire
and petition directly for the redemption of Africa. He did not
succeed. In fact, his presence in London caused the British no
fear. The Empire was spread around the world and the sun was
not setting on the British flag. It was the last of England's age of
splendor, domination and arrogance. They were not inclined to
listen to this subject of the Crown who was acting like a citizen
and demanding the basic rights that go with being a citizen.
During the early part of Marcus Garvey's London years the
Italian-Ethiopian War had broken out and had destroyed his
dream of a place in Africa where Africans could go and start
nation-building. He cautioned Haile Selassie, but to no avail,
against leaving Ethiopia during its hour of trial.

The last five years of Garvey's life were years in which he
struggled to hold on to a semblance of the once-great mass
organization. Funds and supporters of the organization had
dwindled almost to nothing and while the Great Depression was
over for a lot of white people due to the beginning of the war in
Europe accentuating employment, this was not true in the Black
community, where depressions come early and stay late; and so
the last years of Marcus Garvey were years in which he lived in
poverty without losing one iota of the Jamaican-Maroon pride
that had projected him out into the world thirty years before. His
death came at a time when a lot of his predictions were coming

to pass. European powers were engaged again in a massive world struggle, and the colonized people were once more beginning to defy European rule. The legacy that he left behind would be part of the stimulus for the African freedom explosion that would come 20 years later.

In a long article in the Magazine *RACE*, published in London in 1967, the writer Richard Hart has said that "The last five years of Marcus Garvey's life marked the decline in influence and popularity, almost to the point of oblivion, of a man who had once inspired millions." [1] The statement is only partly true. The Italian-Ethiopian War started soon after Marcus Garvey re-established residence in London. This attack on Ethiopia, the last remaining independent African nation, awakened Black people around the world. It also gave a rebirth to Garveyism. In the midst of this war and in the Depression years many conservative Blacks became radical and nationalists and a new political consciousness was born. A young Ghana student, Kwame Nkrumah, came to the United States and began his studies in this atmosphere. During those years he came under the influence of Garveyism.

Black Americans were becoming more Africa-conscious. The Italian-Ethiopian War was responsible for this new interest and anger about Africa. A number of study groups showed interest in African history. The best known of these groups was the Blyden Society, named after the great nationalist and benefactor of West Africa, Edward Wilmot Blyden.[2] I personally remember Kwame Nkrumah attending several meetings of this society.

The American Black press improved its coverage of news about Africa. In the reporting on the Italian-Ethiopian War this press was fortunate in having in its service at least two reporters who had been well schooled in African history in general, J. A. Rogers, an historian and journalist, and Dr. Willis N. Huggins, historian, teacher and community activist. In his dispatches from Ethiopia, J. A. Rogers gave an astute analysis of the war to the Pittsburgh *Courier*. He was the only reporter on the scene who was looking at the Italian-Ethiopian conflict from a Black point of view. Rogers also commented on the political intrigues in Europe that led to this conflict. Later, in a small book, *The Real Facts About Ethiopia*,[3] he digested his reports and produced the most revealing document about the Italian-Ethiopian War that has so far appeared in print.

Dr. Willis N. Huggins, a high school history teacher and founder of the Blyden Society for the Study of African History, went to Geneva and reported on the League of Nations meetings concerning the Italian-Ethiopian War for the Chicago *Defender*. Dr. Huggins had already written two books on Africa: *A Guide to Studies in African History*,[4] and *Introduction to African Civilizations*.[5]

The "Back to Africa" teaching of Marcus Garvey was now being reconsidered. The Harlem literary renaissance had died. The Black urban communities, especially in the North, were entering a renaissance of African consciousness and nationalism. The first nation-wide Black student unions, which included African students from all over the continent, were formed. The attack on Ethiopians and the re-emergence of Garveyism and the hardships of the Depression years had created a semblance of unity among Black Americans.

Kwame Nkrumah's plans for the eventual independence of his country were formulated during his student years in the United States. In the book *Kwame Nkrumah*,[6] by Bankole Timothy, we are told that Nkrumah dreamed of organizing all Africans in the United States so that they might return and perform useful services for Africa. He was the moving force behind the organizing of the first General Conference of Africans in America, in September 1942. At the same time, he dreamed of a West African Federation and together with Nuamdi Arikiwe of Nigeria and Durosimi Johnson of Sierra Leone, planned on returning to their respective countries to start political agitation toward this objective.

While Nkrumah was finishing college in America and writing his important booklet, *Toward Colonial Freedom*,[7] Marcus Garvey was in London trying to hold together the structure of the UNIA while war clouds were gathering in Europe.

Mrs. Amy Jacques Garvey has written this account of her husband's last London years:

> While in England he published *The Blackman* as a monthly magazine. He had pneumonia in the winter of 1936. As all of the

finances had to be used for the work of the organization, he did not send for his family until June 1937.

Every summer he was allowed to go to Canada and conduct meetings and conferences, which American Garveyites attended. In 1937 he left from Halifax and visited and spoke at all port cities of the Leeward and Windward Islands down to Guyana. He had enthusiastic crowds and appreciative listeners.

In June 1938 Junior contracted rheumatic fever because the bedroom was not adequately carpeted. He was in hospital with a drawn knee after the fever subsided. At the end of the summer the specialist and the school doctor decided that as the knee could not keep straight without a plaster cast, he would have to be sent to an orthopedic home in the south of England, or I could take him back to the West Indies, as he needed sunshine on his limbs. This I did, and we stayed at my mother's home. Julius, who had bronchitis in the winter, was glad to be able to play outdoors all year round. Garvey was in Canada convening the eighth International Convention. He sent us $20.00 some months, but not regularly as money was coming in slowly, agents did not pay promptly for the magazine, and rent and staff had to be paid.

In January 1940 he had the first paralytic stroke; his condition improved, but in May a black reporter in England maliciously gave out the news that Garvey had died in poverty in England. Cables and letters poured into the office, and although his secretary did not let him see them, he suspected that something was wrong, by the constant ringing of the door bell. He demanded that he see the correspondence. When he saw the black streamer headlines of the Negro newspapers, he motioned to her that he wanted to dictate a statement; but he cried out aloud in anguish, and fell back on his pillow. He was unable to speak again, and the brave soul returned to his Creator on the tenth of June 1940. But his message to the world had been delivered.

> O Africa awaken
> The morning is at hand
> No more art thou forsaken,
> O bounteous Motherland.
>
> From far thy sons and daughters
> Are hast'ning back to thee
> Their cries ring o'er the waters
> That Africa shall be free.

In his lifetime Marcus Garvey managed to convey to African people that Africa was their homeland, and it had to be reclaimed.

The Black nationalists and freedom fighters before and after Marcus Garvey were saying no more or less than what Garvey had said in word and in deed: "Up, up you mighty race. You can accomplish what you will."

The Last London Years, 1935-1940

BY RUPERT LEWIS

MARCUS GARVEY LEFT Jamaica in April 1935 for England, where he re-established the headquarters of the UNIA. Before leaving he undertook a lecture tour of the island where he addressed audiences on "The Vision of a New Jamaica" and on his own platform at Edelweiss Park in Kingston he spoke on the "Economic Future of Jamaica." His activity was now being guided by the perspectives of the 1934 International Convention of the UNIA.

Having been deported from the United States as an undesirable alien, Garvey was kept under strict surveillance in Jamaica and his British passport was restricted so he was barred from entering the Central and South American republics where the UNIA was very well organized among West Indian laborers. The American Government kept Garvey away from his American supporters and the British Government from the Garveyites in the Central and South American republics.

Garvey's last eight months in Jamaica had been hectic. He had presided over the seventh International Convention of Negro Peoples of the World in August 1934 which coincided with the centenary of the emancipation of Black slaves in the West Indies, then gone on to chair several private and public sessions of the Permanent Jamaica Development Convention which had been formed by the Jamaican representatives attending the International Convention. The task of the Jamaica Convention was to consider proposals for the social, economic and cultural reconstruction of Jamaica. After outlining the plans, representations were made to the British government for the raising of a twenty-million-dollar (Jamaican) loan. Garvey had also started work on the Five Year Plan which had been decided on at the International Convention. After the International Convention and the Jamaica Convention Garvey figured prominently in the very controversial 1935 election to the legislature.

The only just way to write about Garvey's last London years is to reconstruct the vision that was not started in one man's head but rooted in the historical movement of the colonized against the colonizer. After looking at the network of imperialist diplomacy then we can deal with the fact of secret-service agents in the organization. The most glaring case of this was the fact that the UNIA's legal advisor was in the pay of the American government and after Garvey was indicted he was appointed an Assistant Attorney-General.

Much of Garvey's activity in Jamaica can be understood as a contribution to the democratic movement in the West Indies, whose political testament was C. L. R. James' *A Case for West Indian Self-Government* (1928). The principles on which the Peoples Political Party founded by Marcus Garvey were based are inherent in a memorandum Garvey addressed as a young man to Major Moton of Tuskegee Institute when he came on a visit to Jamaica in 1916. Garvey wrote:

> If you desire to do Jamaica a turn, you might ask those around you on public platforms to explain to what proportion the different people here enjoy the wealth and resources of the country. Impress this, and let them answer it for publication, and then you will have *the whole farce in a nutshell.*

In Jamaica Garvey brought the racial question to the forefront. He did so by distinguishing between racism in the United States and that in the West Indies. Here Garvey is not concerned primarily with discrimination by itself, but sees that correctly in sequential terms. . . . We have to grasp the significance of the

principles which guided Garvey's activities. If we don't, then we
see him undertaking a multiplicity of tasks, forming a political
party, publishing newspapers, pamphlets, writing poetry and
holding an international organization together and then we fall
back onto a redemptive understanding based on Black Moses.
These principles bear out the essential unity of his activities.
They were developed and agreed on by members of an international organization. In the United States Garvey had said:

> To fight for African redemption does not mean that we must give
> up our domestic fights for political justice and industrial rights.

That is the first principle. The second, which is found in a
confidential "Booklet of Information and Instructions to Presidents of UNIA Divisions" (1929) reads:

> The culmination of all the efforts of the UNIA must end in a Negro
> independent nation on the continent of Africa. This is to say,
> everything must be contributed toward the final objective of
> having a powerful nation for the Negro race. Negro nationalism is
> necessary. *It is a political power and control.*

Garvey's activity in Jamaica was not based on a decision to do his
next best where he was, for he had worked out the basis for his
activity in the colonial outpost which was also his home and this
excluded subjective meanderings. In Jamaica an international
movement took on its national form whose particular expression
was developed within boundaries marked off by British colonial
rule in plantation society.

In Jamaica the UNIA fought against great odds, not least
among them being the colonial bureaucracy whose post-office
"security" did what the restricted passport was incapable of. The
lesson was clear. No international organization could function
effectively in a colonial outpost.

Apart from the Black Moses understanding of Marcus Garvey,
we need also to combat the very subjectivist view of a dejected
Garvey which has been swept into the last London years. No
movement which is historically based can be understood in these
terms. Garvey had no illusions as to where his vision came from.

As he wrote in reply to a Costa Rican evangelist who was his supporter and saw him as a prophet, he said his vision was based on the practical side of life. Garvey himself was then combating the Black Moses understanding. The last London Years stand in clear perspective only in relation to this whole.

Nineteen thirty-five was an important year for the struggle of colonial peoples against imperialism, a struggle accelerated by the Italian invasion of Ethiopia. Not only did Marcus Garvey arrive in London that year, but also George Padmore. C. L. R. James discusses these years in a series of articles, "Notes on the Life of George Padmore," written for the *Nation* newspaper (of which he was the editor) in Trinidad. Padmore was first active in the International African Friends of Ethiopia organized by James. Among its members were Jomo Kenyatta and Durosimi Johnson (Sierra Leone). The International African Friends of Ethiopia became the International African Bureau which Padmore was in charge of.

James expresses the theoretical basis of their political activity this way:

> Between 1930 and 1939 all of us saw African emancipation as dependent upon the breakdown of imperialist power in Europe. Armed rebellion was sure to be crushed unless the imperialist powers were impotent, and this could only be the result of revolutions within the metropolitan powers themselves. The theory is very clearly stated in *The Black Jacobins*.[8]

There are two other quotations from James' articles without which the last London Years cannot be understood. The first one is related to the revolutionary significance of the International African Bureau, specifically, but is a general commentary on the importance of anticolonial struggle outside of Africa itself:

> The Africans have told us that the movement was kept alive and its continuity was maintained by the work that we did in London and distributed to the African territories.

The second deals with the relationship between Africans and West Indians in London:

The Africans were not politically active, but it was clear that they were rebellious in spirit and resented not only West Indians but the whole British regime which they identified with the maintenance of colonialism.

Most West Indians in London at that time embodied British colonial rationalizations of themselves and other people. Garvey had written about this and tried to show the educated West Indian what had been made of him. James points out that he was an exception and completely accepted by the Africans precisely because these rationalizations had been negated.

In London Garvey sets up the headquarters of the UNIA. In Hyde Park he has his own platform. There are reports in the Jamaican press of Garvey attracting thousands and also of him taking the reactionary side in relation to colonialism at a Hyde Park debate between him and an English Socialist. At this time Garvey was arguing the need for Black colonial representation in the imperial legislature as the outpost legislature was ineffective. He was basing this claim partly on the representation French colonials had in their imperial legislature. Moreover, he had been delegated by the Jamaica Convention of September 1934 to make representations to the British Secretary of State for the colonies for raising the twenty-million-dollar loan. The continuity of his work is evident in that he not only solicited a reply of non-commitment from the secretary of State, but was working with the Jamaica Convention which exists not in name but in action. Again, the platform-understanding of Marcus Garvey is incomplete without bearing in mind the actual relations of the organization pitted in an objective war with imperialism and the tactics he had to employ. The actual relations forestalled opportunism, though they couldn't stop it, as several leading Garveyites clung to their [greedy] tactics and were lost to the whole unity of the struggle for African redemption.

To grasp the actual relations we have to move outside the UNIA itself to consider the West African Students Union, the Colonial Seamen's Union (African and West Indian Seamen) and West Indian labor in revolt in the late 1930's. Garvey's contact with the West African Students Union was Ladipo Solanke. Mrs. Amy Jacques Garvey relates that at times her husband financed their publication called *WASU* and that this contact was an underground one. Ladipo Solanke contributed an article to the July–August 1936 issue of *The Blackman* magazine in which he discussed "Life and Conditions in West Africa." African seamen were of great importance as they were purveyors of UNIA literature, confidential correspondence and firsthand information on developments in Africa. This made them invaluable propagandists. Several of these seamen had married Englishwomen who themselves were involved in UNIA work, for example, distributing handbills during Garvey's Hyde Park meetings and performing other tasks. They could not become members of the UNIA but an auxiliary of the organization was formed for them.

Garvey left Jamaica in 1935 with colonial state officials in panic at the number of disturbances occurring in the country. During the election campaign the Riot Act had to be read in one country parish and labor organizations had sprung up among the workers and the unemployed. A weekly newspaper known as *Plaintalk* had started publication at the printery which had earlier published Garvey's newspapers and pamphlets. *Plaintalk* had started out gingerly by supporting progressive politicians in the Jamaica legislature and reporting on the activities of the UNIA in Jamaica. However, it got caught up in the forward movement of agricultural and industrial labor in the Caribbean and had to develop, though it did not do so in a revolutionary way. The paper's development also owed much to the Ethiopian cause in which *Plaintalk* played the leading journalistic role in the British Caribbean.

One of the important political documents published in *Plaintalk* came from the International African Bureau and was signed by George Padmore and Wallace Johnson, a memorandum to the West Indies Commission investigating the strike among the oilfield workers in Trinidad. It started out by stating the political position of the African Bureau:

> The strikes in Trinidad have been basically for economic demands, but they have taken a form which prove conclusively that the population of the island has reached a stage far beyond the constitution under which it is governed. The International African Service Bureau claims that the future of Trinidad and other West Indian islands should be decided by the people themselves.[9]

Garvey at this time was returning from Canada after attending the 1937 Regional Conference of the UNIA. His boat had stopped at several Eastern Caribbean ports and also in Guyana. He was allowed entry into Trinidad but not permitted to speak because of the unrest caused by the oilfield workers strike and colonial officials evidently saw his speeches as adding more oil to the fire of labor.

Before he left for the Summer Conference in Canada, Garvey had written a memorandum on behalf of about 70,000 West Indian laborers in Cuba as the Cuban government was repatriating them by the hundreds. This was published not only in *Plaintalk* but in a number of other newspapers including the *Panama Tribune* (whose editor was a Garveyite). On the basis of this memorandum Garvey made representations to the British Secretary of State for the colonies once more. Garvey wrote:

> Several years ago, owing to the very bad economic conditions then prevailing in certain of the British West Indian islands, namely Jamaica, Barbados, Trinidad, the Windward Islands, Leeward Islands, large numbers of British West Indian Negroes were forced to leave their respective countries for the Republic of Cuba where there was a boom in the sugar and banana industries.

He discusses the travails of the West Indian laborer working in these countries and goes on to state near the end of the memorandum:

> The different West Indian Islands from which these immigrants hail *have resources sufficient within them to guarantee proper employment to these people* if they should be returned, but the governance of these resources must be undertaken not by private ownership which is always selfish but under government direction without prejudice to the class of people who need consideration and assistance.

When he wrote of the West Indies labor riots in the *Blackman* magazine, Garvey made his position clear:

> We are glad the Jamaica laborer has struck. He has struck at a time when those at the helm in England were making much of imperial unity . . .

Britain was a declining imperial power, so she had to make much of the myth of imperial unity in order to hold her shaky empire together. Labor in the British Caribbean at this time was fulfilling its historical task; no one else, especially those who were at the pinnacle of the oppression could stop that. That historical role was grasped by Garvey when in the article he pointed out:

> Money and color count in Jamaica more than anything else and it would take more than a colonial governor or an ordinary imperial colonial secretary to *change the class distinctions and improve the economic conditions to the benefit of the poorer people in Jamaica.*

The *Blackman* magazine published not only articles discussing the Italian invasion, seeing it as the start of the Second World War, but also poetry, and biographies of Ethiopian warriors, so fulfilling a vital journalistic role. E. U. Essien-Udom[10] in his study of Black nationalism has dealt with the support Garvey organizations in America gave to the Ethiopian cause. The attitude that Garvey took toward Haile Selassie after he arrived in England from Abyssinia was bitterly criticized. But this is how he viewed the situation:

> Haile Selassie ruled over a state with more than twelve million people and one of the richest in the world in natural resources; his best friends surely cannot compliment him for leaving that country in the hands of a foreign foe, and by *the methods he adopted.* He kept his country unprepared for modern civilization, whose policy was strictly aggressive. He resorted sentimentally to prayer and to feasting and fasting, not consistent with the policy that secures the existence of present-day freedom for peoples whilst other nations and rulers are building up armaments of the most destructive kinds as the only means of securing peace and protection . . .

> The results show that *God* had nothing to do with the campaign of Italy in Abyssinia, for on the one side we had the Pope of the Catholic Church blessing the Crusade, and the other the Coptic Church fasting and praying with confidence of victory . . . The Italians triumphed by the use of mustard gas. It is logical therefore that God did not take sides, but left the matter to be settled by the strongest human battalion.[11]

In leaving his London headquarters on his regular summer trips to Canada for the Regional Conferences of the UNIA, Garvey usually left detailed instructions on the running of the office. In 1938 in "Instructions for Mrs. Garvey," he writes:

> All employees are supposed to report for work at 9 a.m., leave at 1 p.m.; return at 2 and work each and every day up to 5 p.m. Any employee who is absent half an hour in any day will not be paid for the amount of time and if more than two hours in a week, the same to be deducted at the end of the week. There shall be no leave of absence during my absence and any absence from work shall not be paid for that particular time.

These instructions were in fact written for the five employees of the organization—his wife, two contributing editors to the *Blackman* magazine, one of whom was the chief clerk of the office, an English stenographer, and Garvey's private secretary. Finances were very low and he had budgeted down to the last cent. One understands the need for such careful budgeting when one reads the financial statement presented in Toronto at the UNIA Convention: "Salary and miscellaneous to Mr. Garvey from June 1935 to June 1938 amounted to 1000 dollars (US)." The weekly pay roll for the headquarters amounted to $22 (Jamaican).

The English stenographer was given the special task of mailing out lessons for the School of African Philosophy. The School of African Philosophy, Garvey said, was the result of five years of planning. It was based on the recognition that in the twenty-three years of the UNIA's existence, it had not paid attention to training new leadership. The School of African Philosophy was based on a study of the organization's work over the past two decades and related to concrete tasks that division presidents had to do. It covered forty-two subjects based on the UNIA and ACL's work.

Garvey maintained regular correspondence with his family after they returned to Jamaica in September 1938 due to the illness of Marcus, Jr., and expressed concern for their security in writing:

> . . . I shall not be returning to Jamaica and . . . in case anything happens to me I want you to know that I have opened [a] Post

Office account at the West Kensington, North End Road, W. 14, Post Office in your name.

In another letter he assured his sons that the organization would take care of them after he died. It was of course unable to. His final handwritten letter to his sons was dated January 6, 1940. Very soon after that he suffered a second serious stroke and all his letters had to be dictated to his secretary or written by one of his assistants with the usual five Jamaican dollars enclosed for pocket money. At times he attempted to scrawl "Dad" at the end of the letter. However, by now Garvey was gravely handicapped and unable to resume a normal life. His private secretary confided in a letter to his wife, "If anything happened to him he wanted his body sent to his UNIA people in Jamaica." Garvey died June 10, 1940, during the Blitz in London.

The UNIA was the first major vehicle to carry the principles of Garveyism, and its worldwide activities accelerated the African revolution. Because of this Garveyism moved into the mainstream of the African struggle on the homefront. Since the UNIA's work had to be underground and anonymous, it was known only to a few patriots. That is why Garvey said in his 1937 Toronto address to the Detroit delegation:

> Those of you who thought the UNIA was dead or is dead have made a terrible mistake. It hasn't started to live in its reality.

During these last years Garvey made some very fundamental observations about the organization. Garvey saw himself like this:

> If I were of another age I probably would not see the need of the UNIA. It happens to be true that I am a child of the twentieth century and I do things that are right, that are done within the period of which I was born . . . If I were of another age I probably would not see the need of the UNIA.

Another type of person would have bureaucratized the UNIA in terms of a sterile Black Nationalism, but this time Garvey was lopping off sections of the UNIA which had become redundant. At the 1938 Convention he took the position in a debate about the Legions, the military section of the UNIA, that it ought to be disbanded.

Garvey made a number of errors, but on fundamental issues he was hardly ever wrong. The Garvey movement was an historical praxis of antiimperialist struggle. It is with this fact in mind that we understand Marcus Garvey and his creativity. Everything he did developed concretely out of the struggle he was involved in and had committed his life to.

In a speech to a London audience in 1928 Garvey said:

> But the new Negro is also thinking in terms of perpetual motion; the Negro is also thinking in terms of the hidden mysteries of the world; and you do not know what the oppressed and suppressed Negro, by virtue *of his condition and circumstances*, may give to the world as a surprise . . .

It is with a conception like this one in mind that one can understand Garvey's impatience with Black intellectuals and also with the cultural criticism of creative artists like Claude McKay and Paul Robeson.

Garvey was spiritually religious; he believed that his Creator had endowed him with an unquenchable spirit as man—to struggle to survive, to fail and go right on trying to attain the goal; seeing the masses of his people at the base in poverty and frustration, he said, "My place is with them, not looking down at them, but helping them to reach the top en masse . . ."

In order to fully rehabilitate the race, he had to reorientate their religious concepts; so he established the African Orthodox Church with Archbishop George Alexander McGuire as titular head. These church groups in Africa played a great part in spreading Garveyism. Through the International Convention he proclaimed a bold concept visualizing the Creator-God as Black (in our own image and likeness), the Mother of the Redeemer as a saintly Black woman like the Madonna of Guadalupe, and Simon the Cyrenian—the Bearer of the Cross—as a Black man. Psychologically this heightened the religious fervor of the masses giving them new courage to strive for creative perfection as children of a dusky Deity. During those last London years, Garvey never departed from the principles which guided his historical task. Neither imprisonment, betrayal nor financial deprivation could deter his activities or lead him to despondency as he saw the forward movement of colonial peoples gaining momentum against imperialism.

The Death of Marcus Garvey*

BY DAISY WHYTE

TWICE DURING HIS last stay in England he had
pneumonia and was advised by his doctor (who by the way was
an eminent Indian specialist) that the climate was damp and very
bad for him as he was subject to asthma. But the government
would not permit him to return to the United States or to go to
Africa, and he felt that he could not lead a world movement
hemmed in in this small island, so he disregarded medical advice
and remained in England where he could make better world
contacts and not be hampered by petty official red tape.

In January of 1940 he became ill. His English housemaid came
over to the office one day and asked me to rush home as she did
not know what to do for him. A male clerk and I went
immediately and saw him trembling as if he had taken a chill, and
unable to speak. I sent for the nearest doctor. He examined him
and said he did not know what was the cause of his illness but
prescribed medicine for him. I gave him one dose, but saw no
change in him and got his Indian specialist. He said it was a
stroke, which caused paralysis of the right side. He also said that
his heart was weakened as he had had pneumonia twice before
and if it could bear the strain, with good nursing he could live,
but a weak heart was a very uncertain organ, and that I should

* Daisy Whyte was Marcus Garvey's private secretary at the time of his death. This
account was published in the magazine *Voice of Freedom*, London, August 1945.

notify his family immediately to expect the worst. I cabled the American Secretary-General, and also Mrs. A. J. Garvey, who had returned to Jamaica previously with the two children on account of the older boy being crippled with arthritis.

Mr. Garvey improved under the care of his Indian specialist and my nursing. He was soon able to speak again and conduct the business of the UNIA from his home in Talgarth Road, West Kensington. He insisted on reading all his letters and newspapers too, although the doctor advised against this. He also dictated letters and had interviews at his bedside. He worked himself to death. He never wanted people to know how ill he was, although the doctor told him his condition was dangerous and he needed absolute rest.

In May, a London reporter wickedly sent out a news release that he had died. Newspapers all over the world carried the news and each one enlarged on it; some even described his supposed death from their imagination. As he opened all his letters and cables, he was faced with clippings of his obituary and pictures of himself with deep black borders. After the second day of this pile of shocking correspondence, he collapsed in his chair and could hardly be understood after that.

His Indian specialist by this time had returned to India on account of his strong nationalist feelings, and I had to call in an English doctor. Mr. Garvey steadily grew worse and passed away on June 10, 1940.

I am not surprised on my return here [Jamaica] to hear that some people did not believe that he was sick for so many months as he was seen driving in Hyde Park. Well, we did take him driving in Hyde Park during his illness, when he felt brighter, and many of his former audiences in the Park greeted him not knowing that he was unable to walk. He was very sensitive about this, as he never wanted people to know that he was crippled in one side.

During many of the long winter and spring days, when Hitler was stalking through Europe and drawing nearer and nearer to England, Mr. Garvey would talk, as his strength permitted, on the war and its effect on peoples of Africa and of African descent. Sometimes he would recall with anguish his years of warning to them to prepare for just such an opportunity. Sometimes he would speak of the future as it affected our race.

He believed that before many years have passed people will be glad to lay claim to the African blood in their veins, for the future of nearly twelve million square miles of Mother Africa, with its untold wealth, is a heritage of which any people should be proud. The Caribbean peoples also have a great future as members of our noble race if they can unite and build a sound economy and continue to press for political recognition. The surplus population of the small islands should find outlet for industrial activity in the broad areas of British Honduras and British Guiana, and thereby balance the economy of the islands. Unity alone can achieve this. Because of the scientific and educational environment of our people in America, they have the opportunity of being real leaders in these fields and to be an incentive to others. He had faith in the American people that they would care for and educate his two boys; he little knew that war and distance would deny them these necessary aids. He said, "I have nothing to leave for them, but the service I have cheerfully given to my race is guarantee for their future."

He believed that in his grandchildren's day a United States of Africa will be a possibility, and this will be hastened through the exigencies of war and the patriotic devotion of our people everywhere to the cause of African redemption.

His last request was to have his body brought back to Jamaica and not left in the "land of Strangers." As soon as shipping permits, Mrs. A. Jacques Garvey, with the help of his followers, is making arrangements to have him laid to rest in this sunny isle.

Let the Negro
Accumulate Wealth*

It Will Bring Him Power

Our economic condition seems, to a great extent, to affect our general status. When it is considered that twentieth century civilization pays homage to and worships peoples and nations only on the basis of wealth, it should not be surprising to understand why the Negro is universally ignored. Economic independence or wealth is the recommendation of a people to the full consideration of others. With all that may be said of the morals and ethics of our time, carrying with it the suggestion of rights, liberty and justice, the whole fabric is based upon economic wealth. Either the wealth of the individual, the race or the nation. So it behooves the Negro to think in terms of economic expansion through which he may enforce the consideration that is necessary for his political, social and other betterment.

The Universal Negro Improvement Association, as everyone will admit—the most thoughtful Negro movement in the world— is now, according to the need of time, emphasizing economic expansion and solidarity among Negroes. We have to make new conquests in the economic field. We have to bring under control every available resource to which the Negro is allied on his native

* The *Blackman* magazine, July 1935.

ground or wheresoever he happens to find himself in its midst. Be assured of this, that in the Negro's rise to wealth will come the adjustment of most of the wrongs inflicted upon him. We must have wealth in culture, wealth in education and solidly wealth of real economic values.

The program laid down by the last Convention of the Universal Negro Improvement Association in Jamaica, 1934, covers a wide range of economic expansion. This is a program that every sensible Negro, in affiliation with the Universal Negro Improvement Association, must work for, and so the urge is for greater loyalty to the work, because it is only through proper organization that the real work can be done. Be not deceived, wealth is strength, wealth is power, wealth is influence, wealth is justice, is liberty, is real human rights. The system of our world politics suggests such and as a fact it is. Show wealth to your statesmen and they will couch their language in terms satisfactory, show wealth to the soldiers and they will enlist in your army, show wealth to the neutral populations and they will turn on your side. It is by the accumulated wealth of the Jew that he is winning support from a hostile world, it is the accumulated wealth of the Negro that will force him to the front and compel men and nations to think of him in terms of human justice. All this is achievable through a greater economic expansion. That must be our purpose and to this the Universal Negro Improvement Association dedicates itself.

P.S. No message of mine would be complete to the Negro peoples of the world without again reminding them of their obligations to the parent body of the Universal Negro Improvement Association. Divisions, branches, chapters and members must do their duty. The greatest duty now is to report regularly each month and for each member to pay in his Assessment Tax; if not convenient to pay it to the divisions pay it direct to the parent body, Universal Negro Improvement Association, 2, Beaumont Crescent, West Kensington, London, W. 14, England.

M.G.

The World as It Is*

A REPORT FROM New York reveals the terrible truth about a form of barbarism in America known as lynching, which is a greater blot on civilization than anything we know of by way of human conduct. It is said that lynching is being carried on at the rate of one every six days. At least this has been so for a couple of months. As far as we know, the record at certain times has reached a higher mark, so that there isn't much exaggeration in stating that at least once a week there is a lynching in the United States.

The Emperor of Abyssinia was right when by his retort he told Mussolini that there was more savagery outside of his country than inside, as practiced by the so-called civilized peoples. If lynching is not barbarism, we have yet to understand what it means. Yet no one can deny that America is a highly civilized country. It shows that even though a country may be civilized, things happen within its borders not consistent with its civilization and which it may find itself unable to immediately restrain or prevent.

The slavery that is supposed to exist in Abyssinia is not as bad as the lynching that goes on in the United States. If the world can give the government of the United States time to abolish lynching, surely the same time ought to be given to Haile Selassie to abolish any form of slavery that he may have in his country. Since no one has attempted to conquer America and to dominate

* The *Blackman* Magazine, October 1935.

the country because lynching goes on, we can see no reason why Italy should want to invade and control Abyssinia so as to put down what is called slavery.

The Haitian government is really one of enlightenment. They are now attempting to place the educational system of the country on a high standard. A commission is to investigate the entire school system, the ultimate object being the establishment of a Haitian University based upon the best and highest standard. Bravo for Haiti!

Haiti is the lone black Republic in the West Indian Archipelago. It won its freedom from France through the military prowess of the black slave soldier Toussaint L'Ouverture. On the fields of Santo Domingo he defeated the best soldiers of Europe—those of France, England and Spain, and made it possible for his fellow black slaves to become a free and independent people, culminating in what is known today as the free Republic of Haiti.

The present President of Haiti must be a patriot and a far-seeing man in having the desire to better educate his country. A Haitian University will mean a great deal to Negroes. It will enable them to do a lot of things experimentally and otherwise which they may not be able to do today elsewhere. The University is generally the home of creative genius. The Negro wants that opportunity. It is hoped that out of the University of Haiti will come the philosophy, the science, the creative art, that will place the Negro in line with the other leaders of our civilization.

Messrs. Generals Smuts and Hertzog of South Africa are wonderful men. They like to glory in their African patriotism. Of late, whatever they say is regarded in certain British circles as being of great significance, but when they do speak of South Africa as far as we know, they generally have in mind only that limited white section of South Africa that makes up the population of the self-governing Dominions. They never include the millions of natives who are really the heirs to all things South African. There is a studied scheme among them to discard the existence of the native from the political, social and economic points of view.

Legislations under their respective governments have always been of the nature suppressive of the Negro's rights and discouraging to his ambition. The condition of the natives is known to be that bordering on the worst within the British Empire. These natives have everlasting cause to be dissatisfied, yet Messrs. Smuts and Hertzog go on making fine speeches about humanity, civilization, justice, morality, etc., forgetting that when brought to book they cannot well justify their high-sounding ideals because they are not consistent with the attitude adopted toward the natives of South Africa.

We are interested in Generals Smuts and Hertzog only because they are a part of the British Empire. Because of that we would suggest to them to think a little more deeply than they have been doing heretofore. We may give then this free advice. No country ever perpetuates its happiness or its prosperity when it has in its midst a larger number of discontents than satisfied people. Wherever such a condition exists it is always easy on the approach of an enemy to destroy the prosperity and happiness of the few in that it is never difficult for the enemy from without to succeed against the particular country considering that there is always a local majority population ready to go over to the enemy so as to invite a change in their condition.

If Messrs. Smuts and Hertzog will think this over they will find how necessary it is to immediately treat the natives very decently and give them the same opportunities as the white people of South Africa, so that in the future any enemy attempting to invade South Africa would find a united South African people, willing—each and every one—to lay down his life for something that he loves and something that has been of benefit to him and his children. We do not charge you for the suggestion, gentlemen!

Jamaica, the little island in the British West Indies, has had three devastating storms within the last three weeks. The staple crops of the country have been ruined. We can imagine a lot of destitution following the havoc of these storms. In fact, Jamaica has always been a country of sorrow for the poorer classes of people in that nobody has ever made any effort to improve their bad conditions. Whether there is a storm or not, or earthquake or

not, the people suffer. It probably may sound strange to those
outside Jamaica, but the common people in Jamaica look upon
these catastrophes as their best opportunity for getting work and
a chance to live. It is only when these calamities come that they
are considered at all as being necessary in the economic life of
the country. Probably these visitations come upon that island
because they are the only opportunities that the people have for a
larger life. . . .

There are a few good men in Jamaica, and they do not include
many of the ministers, but they are too few to really influence the
country for good. The national disposition seems to be that of
enthroned selfishness. There is no patriotism, no love of country
for its sake. Further, there is no love of countrymen, and so
anyone going to Jamaica will see that the most prosperous people
on the island are aliens, particularly Asiatics. Their control of the
island is made easy because the people who are natives hate
themselves to such a terrible extent that they easily open up the
way for the outsider to get the advantage. The Jamaicans hate
themselves because they constitute a mixed population and their
color is the standard for everything. The people in Jamaica
worship color, that is the color of the skin. They think it is the
greatest and best thing in life, hence people who are even related
by blood, if they are not of the same complexion, hate and
despise each other. A British governor in an island like Jamaica is
supposed to be a master diplomat to be able to get anywhere in
his administration, because he finds when he goes to Jamaica a
country not united, but a country divided on the shades of color.
The few real white people who are in the country being more
sensible than the rest, allow the native population the freedom of
their own thoughts, and so the colored and black peoples carry
on among themselves a peculiar prejudice that affects the natural
life of the country. Not even hurricanes and earthquakes do
much in getting them to realize their oneness. Probably Nature
will have to invent some other method of making the Jamaicans
realize that as a people they ought to pull together and be
sensible.

Paul Robeson, the Negro actor, has left London for Hollywood.
He has gone there to make another slanderous picture against the

Negro. He is to be one of the stars in the new picture, *Stevedore*. This is a propaganda play engineered for the purpose of emphasizing Negro inferiority and white superiority . . .

We admire Paul Robeson as an artist, but as a representative of the race he is a poor specimen, in that he always allows himself to be featured in those plays that do more harm than good to his race . . .

For quite a while some Negroes used to look upon any Negro adopted by white people and placed in any remunerative position as a great man of the race. Today, that kind of a sentiment is changed. The people are becoming more critical, and he is not regarded in the same light by thoughtful Negroes . . . It is hoped that he is making enough money for himself so that when he retires from the stage he may be able to square his conscience with his race by doing something good for it.

The War*

MUSSOLINI'S WAR in Abyssinia is progressing. He has succeeded in landing scores of thousands of Fascists and other Italian soldiers made up of Europeans and black natives of Africa, along with his so-called modern mechanical and gaseous implements of destruction. So far, he has taken Adowa and a couple of other towns over which enthusiastic celebrations were conducted in Rome and in other parts of Italy. High Masses were even said . . . All this goes to the glory of Benito Mussolini, the arch-barbarian of our present age.

Mussolini's hope for glory is based on Roman traditions. Probably if he is not made "a saint" immediately or some time after his death, he will be referred to as one of the "gods" of modern Italy. The only thing is that he will not be a myth, like the old Roman gods, but will be remembered as a real "brute-god" who plagued the twentieth century with his inhumanity. He has bombed and gassed innocent women and children of the civil population of Ethiopia. He has used poison gas against the native soldiers of Abyssinia and has carried out such outrages as to make him typically Roman in his character; but whilst we give him the honour of having taken Adowa and a few other towns, the world must know that all this was done not by his Fascist soldiers of Italy, nor the European soldiers of Italy, but by the black native soldiers whom Mussolini has been using as the advance guards and shock troops of his so-called army of conquest.

* The *Blackman* Magazine, October 1935.

The European soldiers have been marching behind the native soldiers, so all the victories that have been won already by Italy are victories due to the native African soldiers who are being used by Italy. The Abyssinians have not started to fight. In fact, they have only retreated from these different towns. Their retreat is their strategy of inveigling the invader into farther parts of the country through which he will be unable to retreat with possible hope of success when attacked by the . . . troops who are preparing for him. Up to now the Italians have not shown their ability to fight Abyssinia. Outside of bombing from the air and using their big tanks, they have done no actual fighting, because what has been done up to now, as stated, was done by native troops. Mussolini's glory up to the present, therefore, is not his. It is still the glory of Africa. We hope he will realize this and be satisfied that up to now the Italian has not been able to whip the African.

Lest We Forget*

THE ITALO-ABYSSINIAN war affords only another example of what unpreparedness means to a people. The entry of Italy into Abyssinian territory is positively due to the fact that the Abyssinians were not sufficiently equipped from a military point of view to oppose the invaders. That will mean experiencing greater difficulties than would have been necessary in dislodging them. This unpreparedness is characteristic of the Negro, contrary to the doctrines of the Universal Negro Improvement Association preached even from the housetops for the last twenty years.

All of us are hoping that Abyssinia will win in her fight with Italy, even if it be miraculous. Our hearts, our souls, everything we possess by way of thought goes out to Abyssinia because it is the land of our fathers. But as anxious as we are, scattered all over the world, to help Abyssinia, we are as helpless in our habitats as if we were newborn children.

In America there are millions ready to help Abyssinia who cannot move. In the West Indies there are other millions, and so in other parts of Africa. Why is it they cannot move? Because prior to the crisis they had no organized sentiment . . . which would give them the immediate advantage of acting in an organized manner. The crisis was brought upon us suddenly, and in the very suddenness we became passionate, enthusiastic, and emotional, which is really characteristic. Without preparation for

* The *Blackman* Magazine, October 1935.

handling the situation, our enthusiasm, our passion count for nought. Immediately after the crisis passes over we shall forget that there was ever such a moment in our lives. It is hoped nevertheless that we shall not forget our difficulties in the present crisis, but that we will use them as a guide to our conduct in the future.

If the Negroes of the world were prepared Italy would not have struck at Abyssinia; but Mussolini and his agents all over the world knew the slackness, the indifference, the unpreparedness of the Negro, and so he felt sure of his grounds when he stood up in one of the provinces of Italy and told Italians that they have always whipped the Negro. Yes, the Negro will be whipped every time he enters the fight unprepared. He will come out victorious, all things being equal, fighting against any man when he is well prepared.

We must, therefore, suggest action, and emphasize the suggestion that we keep ourselves prepared and ready for every human contingency. The Negro cannot afford to ignore the essentials of life. The things that count in the daily life of the other fellow must also count in his life. The tomfoolery about eschewing politics, government, industry, science and all other practical phases of human life must be done away with. It is all bunkum to talk about not paying attention to the things that attract the attention of other men. The Negro should copy the worthy deeds of every other race in the world leading up to anything useful. In addition to his copying, he should create and if possible lead in all human events.

It is only when the entire race is bent upon such a purpose to maintain it by proper preparation [that] fellows like Mussolini [will] find it difficult to challenge units of the race anywhere. In feelings, in passions, we may be at this moment equal to Mussolini if we were to meet him man to man; but that is not the way the fight is being conducted in Abyssinia today. It is being conducted with machine guns, tanks, aeroplanes and other instruments of destruction. What can the Negro do fighting against such odds? It is evident that he must fail when not prepared, and who wants to be identified with a race that is always failing?

The present generation of Negroes is an ambitious one. It seeks within the human range all that is possible to other human beings, therefore, if this ambition is to be maintained, we must not only think, but we must act. The urge is that we act manly, courageously, thoughtfully, and prepare ourselves so that when the particular event takes place we will be ready to hold our own. Let the Abyssinian fight keep our memories fresh, lest we forget.

The American Mind
and the War*

The politics of America is dominantly the ruling force in the life of the American people. Big business in America does rule to a certain extent, like everywhere else, but it is limited there in its obedience to politics. The politician is really the national god, because ultimately he uses the political machine to discipline all elements in the economic and social life of the country. The game, therefore, is to play politics and play it well. Mr. Roosevelt, who is now on the last lap of his first term, is looking forward to repeating himself as President of the United States. To successfully achieve this, he must play good politics. The Italo-Abyssinian war is an important political issue, and so Mr. Roosevelt has to handle the situation with the sensible view of securing himself from any reaction that will endanger his re-election. This being so, we can well understand why America is adopting such a peculiar attitude. The country is neutral, yet not neutral. It is neutral for those who will be fooled by her neutrality, and not neutral for those who will take advantage of the loopholes.

The Negro, naturally, will be fooled, because he is not sufficiently artful in diplomacy and political trickery to know the underlying causes of certain actions. The Italian-American cannot be fooled, and so by his usual systematic organization he is using the peculiar neutrality to help Mussolini and Italy. That is

* The *Blackman* Magazine, December 1935.

why the President found it difficult to stop the American oil supply to Italy, a stoppage which would have immediately handicapped the Italians in Abyssinia. Italian finance in America and Italian political power have combined to influence American businessmen to break through the neutrality to assist Italy, whilst Abyssinia goes floundering because the Negroes in America cannot bring a similar pressure to prevent the Italians getting the advantage. Mr. Roosevelt is steering his ship clear of the trouble. That is to say, he cannot afford to displease the Italian-American who is able to mobilize his friend to make it difficult for the President to have himself re-elected if he doesn't show some hidden sign of being on the side of Italy, even though he doesn't want to.

If the American Negro could bring such a pressure upon things politically in America, then the President would be in a quandary and ultimately he would have had to show his hand. We regard Mr. Roosevelt as a friend, and would not like to embarrass him, but it is our duty to bring to the attention of our race situations as they do arise and the difficulties that they have to overcome.

Unpreparedness a Crime*

The Negro Is Guilty

Positively no useful purpose is served in continuously deceiving others or oneself. This is more so evident when the deception applies to an entire race or set of people. Among the peoples of the world the most susceptible to deception is the Negro. As a fact, he likes deception. He thrives on it. He doesn't appreciate being told the cold, blunt truth. He likes to be complimented and flattered, even to his own destruction, and so, those who desire to profit out of his peculiar mentality and spirituality indulge wholesalely in the scheme of deception. This is practiced on him by individuals, by societies or organizations, by some of his churches and by government itself, and so the poor Negro stands before the world, in an enlightened onward moving civilization as the object of pity as observed by the thoughtful and sensible while the rest of the world goes on doing and achieving and adding new laurels to the honor of man.

Those who know me as a Negro leader cannot say that I have ever flattered the race or tried to deceive it against its own interest. I have always been frank and brutally so, even to my own disadvantage. I intend to be frank in this article and to be brutally so for the purpose of again drawing to the attention of the sleeping Negro the seriousness of his position in a material civilization. . . .

Because of the lack of vision of bygone years, Ethiopia stands

* The *Blackman* Magazine, March 1936.

today at the crossroads left alone to fight a mightily equipped European nation having at her disposal the most modern scientific implements of war and tacitly assisted by other European governments equally prepared, and which have used their diplomacy to deceive the Negro, pretending friendship for Abyssinia, when as a fact assisting Italy to devastate the one remaining black kingdom on the continent of Africa.

There is much suspicion that Abyssinia has invited her own trouble by not adhering to a positive racial nationality. To what extent this is true will go without discussion for the present; but in showing up the Negro's unpreparedness we cannot eliminate Abyssinia from the fold of Negrodom. Just as the individual Negro kept himself unprepared for cooperative action in the preservation of his race, so Abyssinia unfortunately kept herself unprepared to meet an ancient foe. Unfortunately, the great diplomatic machinery that should have been at the disposal of Abyssinia for the last fifty years to supply her with all the information necessary for her preservation was never contemplated. At the outbreak of war we found no Abyssinian embassies in the different countries of Africa as there should have been, nor of Europe, Asia and the Americas, and particularly among Negroes. There was no Ambassador in Haiti, in Liberia, in the United States, nor in countries of the West Indies where millions of Negroes live. If these embassies had existed with their consulates, similar to the embassies and consulates of Italy and other big countries, at the outbreak of war Abyssinia would have been able to lay claim of fellowship among nations and peoples that would have been consistent with her position as an African imperial power.

The scattered Negroes of themselves in all parts of the world had no imperial or racial cooperative spirit. Nothing was ever undertaken except the effort of the Universal Negro Improvement Association to organize the Negro as a solid commercial, industrial, educational, political and scientific phalanx to meet any attack from without. When I endeavored to place on the ocean steamships, with the idea of building up a great merchant marine, the ignorant of the race laughed at me as well as the intellectuals. When I undertook the responsibility of projecting big commercial corporations the same Negroes used the force of government to smash me. They could not understand that the future, which is part of today, calls for the preparation of the race to meet scientific competition whether on the battlefield, in the laboratory or other active walks of life. All of a sudden, therefore, when the Italo-Abyssinian war broke out, the Negro thought he could, by some miracle, match the forces of a prepared country like Italy. Outside of the ancient preparation of Italy for nationalistic expansion, Mussolini engaged himself for the last fifteen years in preparing his attack on Abyssinia. Every field of industry and science was organized for that specific purpose; during which time, the Negro, as usual, dreamt his dream and went about laughing and skylarking as if the world owed him nothing. This is a crime, a crime that penalizes the Negro today. It is hoped that this will open his eyes for tomorrow.

It is surprising that a large number of Negroes, and a goodly number of them members of the Universal Negro Improvement Association, expected me to have done wonders when the Italo-Abyssinian war broke out. Ignorant as they are, they thought that I could alone, singlehanded, stop Italy from invading Abyssinia after these very people for twenty years ignored my warning and destroyed my purpose. It is amusing, it is laughable. Negroes, why are you such fools? Are you going to continue playing the fool, expecting to find yourselves among the living in another century? This is a warning. If you Negroes do not readjust and steady yourselves and think intelligently as the age demands, your next fifty years will not see you defeated, but will see you wiped out entirely from civilization. I have no wonders to perform, but I have, by my sober judgment, advice to give, and I am advising you to prepare yourselves as individuals, as a group, as a race, and fight your battles, and fight them well. Nothing will be achieved by any man, by any group, by any race, by any nation except that which is undertaken by self and carried through with reliance on self and the help of the gods that be. The God of Africa, the God of the black man is the eternal God, but that God moves only in a mysterious way, and that way is first initiated when the subject has given good reason or cause to deserve a blessing. The man, the race, the nation, that helps itself is helped by God. The individual, the race or nation that leaves its destiny to forces completely exterior is doomed, and in the destruction there is no remorse, there is no shedding of tears by anyone but the sufferer himself.

Let the Negro cut loose from the fantasy of exterior help and fall back on his own initiative. Let us, therefore, prepare with the vision of a people capable of seeing down the ages. Let us with one determination create in our minds today the conditions of another fifty years, as Mussolini created twenty years ago the conditions that exist today. If I were Italian I would be with Mussolini. I am Negro, I am against Mussolini; but that Mussolini has whipped the Negro or is whipping him is no fault of Mussolini. It is the fault of the Negro himself. Let the Negro realize that. Throw off the mask of ignorance. Throw off the cloak of superstition and be yourselves.

The Negro fights himself too much. His internal racial conflicts constitute the puzzle of our age. No one knows better than I. As head of the largest Negro organization ever organized, my experience has been one where the Negro keeps up a continuous fight against himself. He never agrees with himself for long. Every other day he is smashing up what he has made, and so the process goes on. He never permanently constructs. We now realize that the system takes us nowhere.

I have done my duty. I will still continue to do that duty, not by deceiving the Negro but by telling him the truth—the cold, blunt, truth. "So help me God." I am vexed in soul, through the fools you have made of yourselves. My destiny is linked with you and you keep me down when I should be rising up and be up. If you can understand this, you know how I feel toward every Negro who hinders the progress of his race. I shudder, I weep, I hang my head in shame. How long must this continue? How long must the Negro walk the world the outcast of the races, the laughingstock of civilization? How long must he be internationally kicked and abused and fooled by everybody? The answer is left to you members of the race. I hope you will now prepare.

Italy's Conquest?*

MUSSOLINI OF ITALY has conquered Haile Selassie of Abyssinia, but he has not conquered the Abyssinians nor Abyssinia. The Emperor of Abyssinia allowed himself to be conquered, by playing white, by trusting to white advisers and by relying on white governments, including the white League of Nations.

We can remember in 1920 inviting the government of Abyssinia to send representatives to the International Convention of the Negro Peoples of the world in common with other Negro governments, institutions and organizations. Whilst others replied, and most of them sent representatives to that greatest of all Negro conventions, the Abyssinian government returned the communication unopened. Its policy then, as during the Italo-Abyssinian war, was no doubt to rely completely on the advice and friendship of white people. They ignored Negro relationships from without and throttled Negro aspirations from within. The result was that they dragged along without any racial policy, except that of the ruling classes, believing themselves white and better than the rest, with a right to suppress the darker elements which make up the tremendous population.

When Haile Salassie departed from the policy of the great Menelik and surrounded himself with European advisers, he had taken the first step to the destruction of the country. It is true that he became heir to the very bad conditions prevailing in Abyssinia, but he had an advantage over previous emperors. He traveled to Europe and America, he saw what European civilization was like. He saw the freedom of the peoples of the different countries and must have been impressed with their high social, educational and cultural developments. A wise monarch, like Peter the Great, would have gone back to his country, if he were patriotic and humane, with a program to lift the standard of his people and push forward the status of his country. This Haile Selassie did in a small way, but too small to be effective, to the extent of saving himself and his country from the designs of the very European sharks whose representatives were advising him. He inherited a vendetta from Italy. He knew that Italy one day would strike. Why he kept the majority of his countrymen in serfdom and almost slavery is difficult to tell. Why he refused to educate on a large scale thousands of the youths of his country, so that they would be able to help him to carry on the government and lead the masses in a defensive war against Italy, cannot be understood.

When all this is considered it is not difficult to understand why Mussolini defeated Haile Selassie. We gave all the support that we possibly could during the Italo-Abyssinian war to Abyssinia. We tried our best to influence the British government at home by our speeches and writing so as to secure support for Abyssinia, not only at the League of Nations but independently. This support, at the very start, was given by Great Britain, but the conditions prevailing in Abyssinia, created by the Emperor himself, defeated the possibility of immediate success. Italy was attacking Abyssinia from the presumptive high morality of freeing the slaves and developing the country for the good of the people. Everybody knows that this was a lie, that the real motive was to create Abyssinia as a part of the new Italian Empire and to exploit it for the good of Italians. Nevertheless the appeal of Italy for the cause of humanity arrested the attention of humanitarians the world over and gave Mussolini allies that he never would have had if there were no such conditions in Abyssinia to cause him to pretend as he did.

Abyssinia has been reputed to be one of the richest sections of Africa. In fact, it is so. With such a rich country at its disposal a patriotic and sensible government would have sought its development. It is true that the prejudice against the Negro is great, and that foreign states would not readily give a loan to an Abyssinian government for its development, but the proper manipulation of the financial affairs of the Abyssinian government could have brought it to a state of independence whereby it could have developed the country without humiliating itself, without having to beg for foreign loans. With twelve million people in Abyssinia, the Abyssinian government could have issued a domestic paper currency backed up by the wealth of the country for local use, and with such a currency labor could have been paid for the exploitation of the country's resources. With the production of that wealth, markets could have been found all over the world ready to accept the products which not only stabilize its own domestic currency but give it a proper credit with other nations. But the Abyssinian government never even sought a substantial loan. The first time an effort on a loan was made was during the war, when it was too late to raise money.

That the country could stand a tremendous loan is well demonstrated by Mussolini now seeking to raise a loan of more than eighty million pounds for the development of the country. If Mussolini can borrow eighty million on the resources of Abyssinia, the Abyssinian government could have in thirteen years borrowed twenty or thirty million pounds for civilizing purposes.

The Emperor's reliance on the League [of Nations] was unfortunate, but more so was his reliance on his white advisers. Would one imagine the cats advising the rats? Would one imagine the lions advising the sheep? Can you imagine the English advising the Japanese, or can you imagine the German advising the French? Yet Haile Selassie having his hand in the lion's mouth allowed the lion to advise him. What else, but be swallowed by the lions as he has been swallowed by the League of Nations? It is too sad, brutally sad, to see the hopes of a people dashed to pieces by bad diplomacy, by bad leadership; but Abyssinia is not yet conquered. She will not be conquered. She shall be free. It will take time, for Italy is only stirring up trouble for herself in the future. The spirit of the Negro will never go to sleep. In fact, the Negro will never die . . . He has learnt too much. He knows too much. The day will shortly come with the blessing of God, when he will stretch forth his hands. Probably it is through Italy in Abyssinia that "Ethiopia shall stretch forth her hands unto God and Princes shall come out of Egypt."

The Rise of
African Sentiment*

AFRICA TO THE white man is just a vast area for his exploitation. At the present moment he has absolutely no other idea than to by force or otherwise establish himself as lord and master of a continent. Whether it is Italy, France, England or any of the other colonial powers, the supreme urge is for the possession of the economic wealth of Africa and to use that wealth in the development of their respective countries.

As far as Africa itself is concerned, there is absolutely no thought of the natives securing for themselves any form of government other than that imposed upon them by the invader, but the thinking and thoughtful Negro looks at Africa as the new hope of the race, for which he is constantly fighting. To him Africa looms as a tremendous possibility for racial energy. Whether it be South Africa or Tripoli or any section of the continent, everything to the student looks hopeful in the trend of the commanding thought that is gradually penetrating the minds of its students.

Although we have lived for a long time in the world, whether we are white or black we do not seem to learn certain lessons in history. If we were to recast our minds over the political development of Europe and consider that everything that happens there was the result of the human urge toward a larger

* The *Blackman* Magazine, July 1938.

civilization, then we will readily admit that what has been true of Europe because of its humanity can be true of any other part of the world.

The African himself need not be downhearted. He must learn his lesson well, and if he does he can see for himself the coming of a day when he will be master again in his own country. It is true that the powerful military pranks of the white race seem to threaten a long reign of sovereignty over other peoples, but this position of military superiority is due only to the development of science in a certain direction. As civilization grows and the Negro becomes more keen in his observation of it, he will find his scientific methods of coping with or outdoing anything that would possibly hinder his advancement. It is in this direction that the thoughtful Negro should be concerned if he ever hopes to override the apparent powerful rule of the white man.

The thoughtful Negro, therefore, looks to the cultural and intellectual development of the race as the only hope through which a new civilization can be projected and a new conquest become evident. To live without a hope of being free would be almost a waste of time. The proud and self-respecting Negro never feels obedient absolutely to imposed authority, except that authority comes from within his own ranks. Gradually the whole race will take on this attitude and as it becomes more formidable so will Africa rise not only as one nation but as many nations such as we have in Europe today among the different groups of the same race.

The African at home must gather a new thought. He must not only be satisfied to be a worker but he must primarily be a figure. It is the thoughts of men that make the nation. As a fact where there is no vision the people perish.

The African Negro has a straight case. It admits of no compromise. It is very good for the Africans, those at home and those abroad. In working for [such an] achievement it isn't necessary for us to imagine that this can happen in a day. Such effort will take decades, and in some cases hundreds of years, but there must be the constant and steady effort toward the end. When Africa at home thinks in these terms and Africa abroad works toward the accomplishment, the united energies of the people of the Negro race is bound to bring beneficial results . . .

there should be no admission of anything that would tend to interfere with the solidity of that achievement. In our modern economic situation many things are brought to bear as the reason for the Negro's particular position, but whatever is said and done, the Negro should have one determined effort, and that is to believe in no one but himself as far as his national outlook is concerned.

Any race that is continuously subjected to another admits its inferiority. The Negro will never be able to hold up his head as a man and speak as a man until he is able to do the things that other races have done and are doing. This is the urge that forces men on to the accomplishment of those things that are worthwhile, and it is hoped that the African at home as well as the African abroad will work toward that end.

Part Seven

The Marcus Garvey Revival, 1940 to the Present

Commentary

BY JOHN HENRIK CLARKE

A REVIVAL IN thinking about Marcus Garvey and his movement started about five years before his death, with the Italian invasion of Ethiopia and the destruction of the last sovereign nation in Africa. I am mindful of the existence of Liberia in West Africa and its pseudo-independence since 1847. But most Black Americans think of Liberia as an American colony, and this thinking is not too far wrong. Garvey's attempt to establish settlements in Liberia failed, and it failed precisely because American influence in Liberia prevented it.

With the loss of Ethiopia, Black people began to revive their relation to Marcus Garvey's dream of nationhood. This revival in thinking was to continue through the Second World War and in part to stimulate the convening of the Fifth Pan-African Congress in Manchester, England, in 1945. This Congress was the political incubator for a large number of African future heads of state, especially, Kwame Nkrumah.

With the publication of the books *Black Moses: The Story of the Universal Negro Improvement Association*[1] in 1962, by Edmund D. Cronon, and *Garvey and Garveyism*,[2] by Amy Jacques Garvey, in 1963 (reprinted 1970), the new interest in Marcus Garvey went beyond the papers written by students, many of whom considered Marcus Garvey an academic curio piece.[3] He has now become part of a new literature. Both Professor Cronon and Mrs. Garvey have called attention to a lot

of material on the rise and fall of the Garvey Movement and the
Garvey revival is now something of an epidemic. (Mrs. Garvey
maintains that her husband was the forerunner of the "Black
Power" and "Black is Beautiful" concept in this century.[4])

Certainly Garveyism was one of the main ingredients that
helped to set the African independence explosion in motion. Mrs.
Garvey says:

> Let us trace the source and course of Black Power to determine its
> effectiveness as a weapon of defense of a black minority. I propose
> to do so by submitting questions sent me by a student of research
> on the work of Marcus Garvey. I added other questions, and the
> answers, so as to round out my subject. Here they are.

> Is there any connection between Marcus Garvey's teachings and
> the philosophy of Elijah Muhammad and Malcolm X? Have
> Garvey's teachings been corrupted?

> This question can partially be answered by my quoting from a
> letter written by Mr. Thomas Harvey, President-General of the
> Universal Negro Improvement Association to the Jamaica *Gleaner*,
> November 17, 1964, in which he states: "Please allow me space to
> express my thanks to your government for inviting us down from
> America to attend the ceremonies in connection with the reinter-
> ment of Marcus Garvey in George VI Park. I think I am in a
> position to speak on behalf of Negroes in America and Canada, and
> to affirm our belief in the sincerity and courage of Marcus Garvey
> as the only international Negro leader at the close of this century.
> He paved the way for all local leaders who have emerged since his
> death. Most of them were his understudies or followers who were
> inspired by his dynamic leadership and the universality of his
> appeal for justice, equality and independence for the Negro
> peoples throughout the world. For instance Elijah Muhammad was
> formerly a corporal in the uniformed ranks of the Chicago division.
> Malcolm X's father was a vice-president of the Detroit division, so
> Malcolm X grew up under the influence of Garveyism. Mrs. M. L.
> Gordon of the Peace Movement of Ethiopia was formerly an active
> member of the organization in Chicago. The Ethiopian Federation
> is also an offshoot of Garveyism."

Here are some of the events that tend to support Mrs. Garvey's
assumption:

1957: Dr. Nkrumah as Prime Minister of Ghana in their independence year launched the Black Star Line Steamship service in memory of Marcus Garvey.

1963: Mrs. Garvey wrote and published *Garvey and Garveyism*, the world distribution of which brought about the renaissance of Garveyism.

1964: Garvey's remains returned to Jamaica and reburied at George VI Park. Proclaimed Jamaica's First National Hero.

1965: Marcus Garvey Scholarship for Boys established by the government of Jamaica.

1968: Mrs. Garvey wrote and published a collection of essays updating Garveyism.

1969: Human Rights Year. The government offered a prize of $10,000 in the name of Marcus Garvey to a person who contributed most to world peace. The award was made posthumously to Dr. Martin Luther King. His widow, Mrs. Corretta King, received the award at a public ceremony at the National Stadium.

The Federal Republic of Cameroon, West Africa, issued a fifty-franc commemorative stamp bearing the likeness of Marcus Garvey.

1971: The government of Jamaica issued a ten-cent-stamp and fifty-cent note in honor of Marcus Garvey.

1972: A plaque unveiled in London to mark the office where Garvey worked. Ground-breaking ceremony for Marcus Garvey East Village in Brooklyn, New York. (This is part of a state urban renewal project which is being built at a cost of $11,950,000.)

In Jamaica, Marcus Garvey's home, the subject of repatriation is once more being discussed.[5] In February 1972 a number of African organizations in Jamaica, West Indies, came together and formed the Joint Committee on Repatriation. The Joint Committee has since that time been working steadily to effect the return of Africans in Jamaica to their motherland, Africa.

In pursuit of this aim, the Committee has started a drive to collect 100,000 signatures to support a petition to the United Nations to take up the matter of the repatriation of the descendants of the Africans formerly held as slaves. The campaign has been well received initially. There have been good attendances at outdoor meetings and the majority of the people giving their names for repatriation have been under thirty years of age. This shows the awakened interest of Black youth in Jamaica in their ancestral motherland of Africa.

Garveyism:
Some Reflections on Its
Significance for Today

BY MARCUS GARVEY, JR.

SO MANY COMMENTATORS writing about the late
Marcus Mosiah Garvey have used the term "Back-to-Africa
leader" and have concentrated exclusively on this aspect of
Marcus Garvey's thought and work that the general reading
public must be excused for thinking there was nothing more to
Garvey philosophy than packing all the Blacks on boats and
dumping them in the African bush. This, of course, is not an
accident. The white liberals and the pseudo-intellectual Blacks
who have been most vocal in interpreting and denouncing
Garvey adopted the same line for different reasons. The liberals
have never wanted the Black race to develop strength and power
in their motherland of Africa. In that case they would be out of
business. The pseudo-intellectuals on the other hand have always
been wary of any scheme which would take them too far away
from their favorite avocation—pursuit of the white female. For
these reasons principally, commentary on Marcus Garvey has
usually taken the form of a Black and white minstrel show built
around the general theme [of a] crazy, egotistic and noisy Black
who thought up a scatterbrained scheme to remove the Black
people from their American paradise to the African jungle.

Nevertheless, there exists a sufficient body of the speeches, sayings and writings of the late Marcus Garvey to lead us to an understanding of the concrete, rational and orderly ideas which constitute the philosophy of Garvey—Garveyism. In his ideology Garvey proved himself an African Nationalist par excellence, and Garveyism remains today the highest form of African Nationalism. Let us proceed to a sectional evaluation of the concepts.

The first concept that Marcus Garvey laid down was what may be termed Black Awareness, the belief that we as a race and a people must be aware of ourselves as Black men, that we must be familiar with our culture, our heritage and our history. "Black man, know thyself," was his familiar and powerful injunction. He never wearied of pointing out that when our forefathers were cultured and civilized the whites of Western Europe were howling barbarians who committed human sacrifice and worshiped the mistletoe:

> But, when we come to consider the history of man, was not the Negro a power, was he not great once? Yes, honest students of history can recall the day when Egypt, Ethiopia and Timbuctoo towered in their civilizations, towered above Europe, towered above Asia. When Europe was inhabited by a race of cannibals, a race of savages, naked men, heathens and pagans, Africa was peopled with a race of cultured black men, who were masters in art, science and literature; men who were cultured and refined; men who, it was said, were like the gods. Even the great poets of old sang in beautiful sonnets of the delight it afforded the gods to be in companionship with the Ethiopians. Why, then, should we lose hope? [6]

The reason for the great teacher's insistence on knowledge of Black history was to confute the lies of the white propagandists who pretended that the African was a man without history and had never advanced beyond the stage of primitive savagery except under the tutelage of other races. His views are clearly stated:

> To read the histories of the world, peoples, and races written by white men would make the Negro feel and believe that he never amounted to anything in the creation.

History is written with prejudices, likes, and dislikes; and there has never been a white historian who . . . wrote with any true love or feeling for the Negro. The Negro should expect but very little by way of compliment from the pen of other races.[7]

It is essential for the African Nationalist to be familiar with the history of the continent in order to ground his legitimate claim to the mother continent of our race. Both the Arabs and Berbers in the North and the Western Europeans in the South are invaders and usurpers. The fact that the theft and spoliation have been hallowed by time has no relevance to the man with Black skin and woolly hair who because of his familiarity with his history knows that he, and he alone, has the right to the title African. Marcus Garvey realized that the judgment of history awarded Africa to our race and that it was our God-given right to occupy the land and reconstruct the glories of our ancestors in this time and age. It is difficult for a man to know where he is going to if he does not know where he is coming from.

An important concept of Garveyism was pride in the Black race. Marcus Garvey never permitted advertisements for bleaching creams and hair straightening in his paper, the *Negro World*. He called on the people of his race to respect their own kind of beauty, to accept the shape of their lips and noses, and to appreciate the woolly hair of the African:

Take down the pictures of white women from your walls. Elevate your own women to that place of honor. They are for the most part the burden-bearers of the race. Mothers! give your children dolls that look like them to play with and cuddle. They will learn as they grow older to love and care for their own children and not neglect them. Men and women, God made us as his perfect creation. He made no mistake when he made us black with kinky hair. It was Divine Purpose for us to live in our natural habitat—the tropical zones of the earth. Forget the white man's banter that he made us in the night and forgot to paint us white. That we were brought here against our will is just a natural process of the strong enslaving the weak. We have outgrown slavery, but our minds are still enslaved to the thinking of the Master Race. Now take these kinks out of your mind instead of out of your hair.[8]

In furtherance of his belief in Black pride, Garvey was instrumental in producing Black dolls for African children in the United States. He more than any other mass leader understood the need for early indoctrination of the youth.

In his campaign for Black pride, Marcus Garvey always inveighed against miscegenation, which he considered a sure way to race suicide. The statement "What We Believe" which appeared over his signature in January 1924, is revealing.

> The Universal Negro Improvement Association advocates the uniting and blending of all Negroes into one strong, healthy race. It is against miscegenation and race suicide.
>
> It believes that the Negro race is as good as any other, and therefore should be as proud of itself as others are.
>
> It believes in the purity of the Negro race and the purity of the white race.
>
> It is against rich blacks marrying poor whites.
>
> It is against rich or poor whites taking advantage of Negro women.

It was this insistence on race pride and race purity, as far as that was possible, which earned him many enemies among the Black upper class. However, these very views, which he expounded so forcefully, have been the reason why he is today considered by many people of African origin as the father of Black pride.

In the world of Garvey's time, contempt for Black skin and African hair was the norm. His pioneering work in assailing the belief in European standards of beauty and the acceptance of African features has borne a rich harvest in today's world.

The constitution of the Universal Negro Improvement Association was a lucid and comprehensive document. One of the doctrines which its provisions clearly expressed was that the Black organization should be racially exclusive. No Black organization was valid in the race struggle if it included non-Africans in its membership. In fact, the constitution expressly stated that no high office in the organization could be held by a Negro who was married to a person of alien race. There was no doubt of the

separatist nature of the Garvey movement. In every strong
nationalism which the world has witnessed there has been an
element of racial exclusiveness and a desire for national privacy.
Garveyism clearly laid down the basic principle of Black Power,
that the Black man must create himself his own Black institutions
under Black leadership. Marcus Garvey poured contempt on
those Black organizations which existed on the philanthropy of
the white liberal and which were always proud to state the white
gentlemen and ladies who were associated with them in their
good work. He realized that these bigger organizations had not
been created by the sacrifice and dedication of their own people
and, as they were manipulated by the whites who financed them,
were practically useless in the cause of African redemption and
race uplift. The correctness of his analysis and outlook cannot
now be doubted. Any race unable to build and create by its own
genius, perseverance and ability, is unfit to claim equality with
other peoples and races that have so built and so created.

The white man has always reviled the Black man because in
recent times the Black man has not been able to create a modern,
efficient nation of his own. Yet, many so-called intellectuals of the
African race state unequivocally that we can do nothing without
the help and assistance of the European. Marcus Garvey always
derided such self-defeating philosophy and maintained until his
death that the Black man's only salvation was to create his own
Great Nation by dint of his own efforts in his motherland of
Africa.

"I know no national boundary where the Negro is concerned,"
he said. Garvey was stating his firm belief that the problem of the
Black man was universal in that all peoples of African stock
suffered to greater or lesser degree at the hands of alien races.
Hence, their salvation could not depend on national boundaries.
In addition, the Black man had not delineated these national
boundaries nor had he placed himself within them. He was
therefore under no duty to respect them. Marcus Garvey's
philosophy and thinking was for the entire Black race. He was
the first truly international African. He saw that the condition of
the race was unaffected by national situations—all stronger racial
groups were prepared to give the Negro a kick in the pants. To
correct this universal racial imbalance the Black man needed

Black unity in the national and international sense. Black movements had to be created which transcended national boundaries and which set the entire race about the task of racial reconstruction.

Toward that end the *Negro World*, the chief propaganda instrument of the Garvey movement, was published in English, Spanish and French. It reached out to Black communities all over the world and was smuggled into the interior of Africa where it was forbidden reading. The imperialists of Britain, France and Portugal were afraid of the effect of the inflammatory doctrines of the Garvey movement on the populations of their African colonies. It was the unscrupulous machinations of these European bandits which aborted the colonization scheme of Marcus Garvey in Liberia. Land which had been designated for settlement by Garveyites was afterwards handed over to the white American rubber king Firestone. The Garvey movement was, and remains, the greatest international movement of the African race in modern times. From the beginning to the end it was international in conception and scope. Marcus Garvey preached unity of the national communities of those of African stock; this was concomitant with racial solidarity on the global scale.

The kernel of Garveyism consisted of his unyielding belief that the salvation of the race demanded the creation of a great nation in Africa capable of spreading its protective umbrella over all the African peoples scattered across the world in the great Black diaspora. This was the fifth basic concept of Garvey philosophy: To put it in modern language—the Black man must do his own big thing in his home base, Africa. This fundamental of Garveyism may be best expressed in his own words.

> For five years the Universal Negro Improvement Association has been advocating the cause of Africa for the Africans, that is, that the Negro peoples of the world should concentrate upon the object of building up for themselves a great nation in Africa . . .[9]

> Races and people are only safeguarded when they are strong enough to protect themselves, and that is why we appeal to the four hundred million Negroes of the world to come together for self-protection and self-preservation. We do not want what belongs to the great white race, or the yellow race. We want only those

things that belong to the black race. Africa is ours. To win Africa we will give up America, we will give up our claim in all other parts of the world; but we must have Africa. We will give up the vain desire of having a seat in the White House in America, of having a seat in the House of Lords in England, of being President of France for the chance and opportunity of filling these positions in a country of our own.[10]

In his poem "Hail United States of Africa!" written in 1926 in Atlanta prison Garvey expressed the ideals of all African unity and foresaw the need for an African superstate when most Black leaders at that time were wallowing in the morass of tribalism and communal isolationism. His vision of Africa was prophetic to an uncanny degree. In his home country of Jamaica, he is considered by many for these and other reasons to have been a combination of prophet and seer. His great battle cry—Africa for the Africans, those at home and those abroad—resounded around the African world and remained to stimulate and dynamize such African nationalists as Kwame Nkrumah and Nuamdi Arikiwe. Although a United States of Africa has not yet materialized, the Organization of African Unity is a small step in the right direction which gives great hope to the oppressed people of African race everywhere.

We now turn to Garvey's concept of God. What is or what can be our concept of God? Every race and every people who have emerged since the beginning of time have had some concept of a God or gods. In every case a people has sought a religion which gives them strength and points them in a direction of positive achievement. No race or people have made any impact on the world who have allowed themselves to become enslaved to a religion which made them nothing. Those people who have conquered, those people who have built civilizations, are people who have had a religion which made them strong, which made them positive, which enabled them to assert themselves. We cannot have a religion which tells us that we are inferior, which tells us that we must remain in the place which the Lord has allotted us. Such a religion, such a God, ensures that we will be slaves and inferior to another race and another people. Our God must make us strong; our God must heed our every need and every purpose, otherwise he is not our God. Marcus Garvey understood this and when he spoke, his words led us directly to the concept of the Black God:

> If the white man has the idea of a white God, let him worship his God as he desires. If the yellow man's God is of his race let him worship his God as he sees fit. We, as Negroes, have found a new ideal. Whilst our God has no color, yet it is human to see everything through one's own spectacles, and since the white people have seen their God through white spectacles, we have only now started out (late though it be) to see our God through our own spectacles. The God of Isaac and the God of Jacob, let him exist for the race that believes in the God of Isaac and the God of Jacob. We Negroes believe in the God of Ethiopia, the everlasting God, God the Father, God the Son and God the Holy Ghost, the One God of all ages. That is the God in whom we believe, but we shall worship Him through the spectacles of Ethiopia.[11]

The belief in the God of Africa and the Black race, who has created his Black sons and daughters in his own image and likeness, was an essential part of the total philosophy of Garveyism. Just as the white man uses all the external paraphernalia of his religion so must we Africans do likewise. Each race or people since prehistoric times has visualized its God as having a physical form corresponding to their own. It is only the inferior race which worships an alien God. Marcus Garvey taught us to see our God through the spectacles of Ethiopia, and it was for this reason that he together with Archbishop McGuire raised the Black Christ and the Black Madonna of the African Orthodox Church. If we follow the great teacher, then we accept that the African must have a theology rooted in his own ancestry and heritage and illustrated in conformity with his own physical appearance.

In the second half of the decade beginning in 1960 a powerful cry arose from the oppressed Africans of the United States of America, a cry that reverberated around the world and set in motion changes in speech, dress and thought that are even now continuing. This cry was for Black Power. It answered the needs of Black people in the '60's just as the thunder of Garveyism had answered the needs of the Blacks in the '20's. What is the real difference between the two philosophies? The answer is that both doctrines coincide to an amazing extent but Garveyism emphasizes far more than Black Power; [Garveyism stresses] the need for a great nation in Africa as a part of the final solution. Marcus Garvey realized that minority groups existed in countries at the whim and fancy of the majority, and, that irrespective of the temporary achievement of the group, they could be dispossessed and despoiled if they did not have a powerful home nation to protect them when the majority coveted or envied their supposed advances. The fate of the Jews at different times in their long history of vagrancy is eloquent and sad testimony of this fact. Black Power has now spread from the United States to the islands of the Caribbean and will eventually make its presence felt in the mother continent, Africa. Each community has tended to give its own interpretation to Black Power ideas. The result is that the original ideas propounded by Carmichael, Hamilton and others, have been transformed to concepts which after appear stupid, ineffective and negativistic. This is, of course, because so many opportunists have tried to mount the Black Power band wagon. Black Power, with its strident demand for local power in the Black community, has seemed to many a panacea for the ills of the Black man, but it must be realized that any solution which is not based on the creation of an African superstate equipped with modern weaponry and disposing massive military force is no solution at all.

Marcus Garvey preached Black pride; he called to Black people to acquaint themselves with their glorious history and to take pride in their culture; he at all times propounded Black institutions financed by Black people. He was an unrepentant separatist. He said, "A race without authority and power is a race without respect," and "Power is the only argument that satisfies man Except the individual, the race or the nation has POWER that is exclusive, it means that that individual, race or nation will be bound by the will of the other who possesses this great qualification. . . . Hence it is advisable for the Negro to get power of every kind." It is not too much, then, to say that he was the first and original exponent of Black Power.

The high noon of Garveyism was 1919 to 1925; Marcus Garvey died in 1940. [Let us] consider the relevance of Garveyism at the present time.

The integrationists and the self-seekers are always quick to point out the gains of the Black man in the United States and the rash of small independent countries in Africa and the Caribbean as major advances since Garvey's day. They then proceed to say that much of what Garvey worked for has already been obtained so [that] his philosophies are irrelevant in the present improved situation and [that] we shall overcome the remaining obstacles to racial progress in due course. This is to my mind a load of rubbish.

Marcus Garvey would not be impressed by the Black man's situation in the world today. He would still ask where are the Black man's armies? Where are his navies? Where are his men of great affairs? The answers must be that the Black man has no armies or navies which are worthy of note and his men of great affairs are usually to be found in the antechamber of powerful white men begging for loans, alms and grants-in-aid.

Despite the fact of independence, the African in today's world finds himself under the control of men of alien race. In all the so-called independent countries of Africa and the Caribbean, searching questions reveal the powerlessness of the African in his own countries where he is an undisputed majority. Who owns the new skyscrapers that are being built? Who owns the banks? Who owns the industries? Who owns and dominates the commerce? The white man, the yellow man, or the East Indian brown man. The identity of the dominant minority groups may vary from country to country, but the basic situation is the same whether in Kenya, Ghana, Jamaica or Trinidad. The Black man, the African, works for other racial groups who own and dominate the economy and [skim the] cream of the major share of wealth for their own kind. The African everywhere suffers from what Kwame Nkrumah called neo-colonialism.

In the United States and South and Central America, the African remains at the bottom of the social scale. He is crammed into crumbling ghettoes and is the victim of mortality rates which are always much higher than in the surrounding white communities with their superior living standards. Drug addiction, unhealthy living conditions, communal crime and inferior education keep the Blacks of the Americas in general situations of degradation and inferiority.

Garveyism was relevant to the oppressed Blacks of the '20's. I submit that it is equally relevant to the oppressed Blacks of the '70's. In addition, the emergence of two super powers, the U.S.A.

and the U.S.S.R., and the coming emergence of another, the People's Republic of China, witness the foresight of the great teacher of African Nationalism. If it was necessary for the Black man to create a great nation in Africa in 1920, then it is even more necessary for him to do so in 1970. The white man has the U.S.A. and the U.S.S.R.; the yellow man has China; the brown man has India. Where is the Black man's massive and monolithic political entity? Garveyism demands that we set about creating one now. At the time that Garvey formulated his ideas, capitalism appeared to be the norm and communism the aberration therefrom. Fifty years later we have witnessed the tremendous changes wrought in the Soviet Union and China by communist methods of social and economic organization. However, communism has not proved to be an undiluted blessing. Production has lagged in agriculture and in the Soviet Union capitalist incentives have had to be adopted where communist idealism has failed. Regimentation and the curtailment of individual freedoms have been part of the price for rapid industrialization and military power. The African has noted the failures of capitalism and communism. He must, I feel, seek his own middle road which can help him to build the powerful superstate that is our only salvation.

The solution, as I see it, lies in linking the African Nationalism of my father to an African Socialism based on principles rooted in our African culture and heritage. This compound doctrine may properly be called African National Socialism. It constitutes a total philosophy for the African race and is applicable to Black communities throughout the world. The newly independent nations of Africa and the Caribbean have in the years since independence failed to satisfy the high expectations of their peoples. A few who have worked with the neo-colonialists have prospered off the perquisites of office or have managed to amass wealth by dubious means. The remainder have been at the mercy of steeply rising prices in the midst of chronic unemployment. Wealth and ownership have been concentrated in too few hands.

A race or people cannot expect salvation from doctrines formulated by alien races for their own peculiar environment and circumstances. Neither atheistic communism nor monopoly capitalism will provide the Black man with an African paradise. What is the nature then of the African Socialism which I predicate?

The first basic idea is that the wealth of the Black community should be in the hands of the Black people. Too many Black doctrinaire thinkers have sent themselves into tenuous tantrums worrying about the division of an economic cake which the Black man does not possess anywhere in the world. Our first job is to seize the cake from the alien races who have so far been happy to leave us with the crumbs. This can be accomplished in independent African countries (whether in the Caribbean or in Africa) by economic boycott of business interests owned by minority non-African groups. Another effective method is to restrict activity in certain lucrative fields by trade licensing and the grant of these licenses only to Africans. Government contracts would also be limited in certain cases to African firms. Finally, nationalization should be used to deal with large undertakings. In the countries of the Caribbean it would be legitimate to expropriate English, Canadian and American holdings as compensation for the slave labor of our African ancestors. The Jews received reparations from Germany, it is time that we Africans got our reparations from the Western white man.

If the Black man controls the economy, it is then appropriate to think of models for the distribution of wealth and the ownership of property. It was natural for our African ancestors to consider that grazing and hunting land should be held for the tribe and should not be arrogated to the individual or family. But at the same time they appreciated private ownership of certain items of wealth. Thus state ownership on behalf of the people of the nation is a legitimate concept of African Socialism. Equally people's cooperatives covering a wide range of industry, commerce and agriculture are an inherent part of the system. The aims must be to reduce exploitation of man by man, to enforce a leveling of individual incomes and reduce wide disparities, and to place the major means of production in the control of the workers and peasants through their government agencies and cooperatives. At the same time, the total abolition of individual ownership would have a stifling effect on personal initiative and effort and would retard the development of small enterprises which depend on individual expertise and personal service. This would be a ridiculous example of doctrinaire thinking at a time when the Black people need to mobilize their total resources, by all means possible, for rapid development.

It is convenient, therefore, to consider all activity divided into large, intermediate and small-scale enterprises. There would then be state ownership of all large-scale enterprises and those other enterprises vital to national security. Individual ownership of small-scale enterprises would be permitted; and there would be an overlap between state and cooperative ownership in the intermediate range. In all cases worker participation in ownership should be accepted. African Socialism should be flexible and pragmatic; it should be based on the essential unity of the African family, our common history of suffering and degradation, and our need to complete the work of racial reconstruction.

No philosophy can be all-embracing and at the same time immutable. We live in an age when the rapid ebb and flow of climacteric events shape and reshape our contemporary world with bewildering rapidity. Garveyism will adapt to this time by becoming part of the wider philosophy of African National Socialism. [The] Black man cannot sacrifice life and limb in a struggle against one form of oppression in order to fall into a Black system of inequality and minority privilege. The greatest good for the greatest number will temper all revolutionary activity among Africans in the foreseeable future. That Garveyism can be absorbed almost intact into the wider philosophy speaks volumes for the genius of its creator. If there is one point at which we must diverge from the great teacher, it is in the use of the appellation "Negro." As African Nationalists only one word can be applied to the people of the dark skin and woolly hair—African. Let us speak in future of American Africans, Trinidadian Africans and Brazilian Africans. It is time for the word Negro to die a natural death.

African National Socialism postulates that the children of the Black God of Africa have a date with destiny. We shall recreate the glories of ancient Egypt, Ethiopia and Nubia. It is natural that the children of Mother Africa scattered in the great diaspora will cleave together once more. It seems certain that the world will one day be faced with the Black cry for an African "Anschluss" and the resolute demand for African "Lebensraum." One God, One Aim, One Destiny for our glorious African race.

The Flowering of Black Nationalism: Henry McNeal Turner and Marcus Garvey*

BY EDWIN S. REDKEY

AFRO-AMERICANS HAVE reacted in different ways to the problems they have faced in the United States. Quite understandably, many have tried to get along as best they can, eking out a living, trying to avoid trouble, never losing hope for a better day. Others have protested to whites, asking for fair treatment, civil rights, and integration into American life. And others have militantly called for separation from whites, unity and pride in the Black community, and a new political arrangement in which they control their own destinies. This last approach, generally labeled "Black Nationalism," has taken a number of different forms through the years, but the basic elements of Black separatism and solidarity, race pride and political independence, have always been recognizable.

Some Black Nationalists have called for all-Black states, cities, or towns within the United States; others have wanted to carve a separate country out of American territory. Often Black Nation-

* From *Key Issues in the Afro-American Experience*, edited by Nathan I. Huggins, Martin Kilson and Daniel M. Fox, Vol. 2, copyright © 1971, Harcourt Brace Jovanovich, Inc., New York.

alists have proposed establishing ties with Blacks in other parts of the New World and in Africa. Recently this has taken the form of a sophisticated cultural identification with Black Africa, whose peoples have inspired Afro-Americans by gaining political independence after a century of European domination. In earlier years, Black Nationalists urged that a significant number of Afro-Americans emigrate to their fatherland and establish there a powerful new nation. Twice between 1890 and 1925 this "Back to Africa" form of Black Nationalism generated widespread enthusiasm among Black Americans. Although few Blacks actually emigrated to Africa, the movement's stress on race pride and the rejection of white America was indelibly impressed in many minds and inspired a new generation of militant Black Nationalists.

Conditions in the South in 1890

Although the concept of emigration to Africa to establish a powerful new Black nation had been formulated before the Civil War, most notably by Martin R. Delany, the idea was then limited to a few Black intellectuals, mostly free Blacks in the North. As a mass enthusiasm, Black Nationalism first flowered during the 1890's among the Black peasants who farmed the cotton plantations of the South. It was clear to them that, even though it was twenty-five years after the end of the Civil War, most white Southerners intended to keep Blacks as near slavery as possible. Having built up elaborate intellectual defenses for slavery during the early nineteenth century, the whites were not willing or able to change their concept of Blacks as inferior, almost subhuman beings. Nor could they imagine for them any role in society other than that of the lowest class, possessing a minimum of rights, power, and status. When ex-slaves tried to assert their rights and privileges as citizens, whites used every possible means to keep them "in their place."

Violence had been a frequent tool of repression in the days of slavery, and it continued to be used during and after Reconstruction. Lynching was a particularly terrifying means of social control, for it deprived its victims of any chance to prove themselves innocent of whatever charges were made against them; frequently they were brutally tortured and humiliated before being hanged, shot, or burned to death. The rate of lynchings increased rapidly during the 1880's and reached a peak in 1892.

Whatever political power Blacks had gained during Reconstruction, Southern whites now whittled away through violence, fraud, and deceit. By 1890 it had become evident that Northern whites, who had supported the Blacks for political reasons, had grown tired of their efforts and were no longer going to interfere in Southern racial politics. White Southerners quickly took advantage of this development and began formally and legally to strip away what little political power remained to the Blacks. Mississippi led the way in 1890 with the passage of a new state constitution that effectively stopped Blacks from voting. During the next eighteen years most Southern states followed Mississippi's example. Though legally free, Blacks could not use politics to protect their freedom.

The economic life of Blacks was also restricted by whites, who, as they had before the Civil War, still owned the land and controlled the economy. Blacks worked the farms and paid a large share of their crop to the white landowners as rent. And the portion of the crop retained by the sharecropper was probably already mortgaged to the white storekeepers for food and supplies. Therefore, after the merchants and landowners were paid off, the farmer was left with little or no profit from the harvest and usually remained in debt. When cotton prices declined, as they did in the late 1880's, or when a general depression gripped the nation, as it did during most of the 1890's, the Black farmer could see little improvement in his situation since slavery.

Reactions to this social, political, and economic oppression took several forms. Undoubtedly, most Blacks, unsophisticated in business and politics and dominated by the landowner, the merchant, and the sheriff, simply endured the hardships and made the best of a bad deal, no matter what dreams of escape they may have had. The spokesman for this group was Booker T. Washington, who made "accommodation" an ideology. He urged his people to work hard, live clean, quiet lives, save money, and demonstrate their worthiness so that whites would someday recognize and honor their virtue and thrift. Others, mainly intellectuals and middle-class Northern Blacks, protested and appealed to the conscience of the nation to grant them equality and integrate them into white American life. Frederick Douglass was the early spokesman for this viewpoint; others, including W. E. B. Du Bois, followed. But as conditions in the rural South worsened during the 1890's, a significant number of Blacks began to despair of ever attaining the good life in the United States. Neither accommodation nor protest seemed to make life any better for the vast majority of Black farmers and workers, who had little chance of earning enough or learning enough to reach the middle-class standard of living. For a time, in the late 1880's, some Black farmers joined with their white counterparts in the Populist movement, which sought better economic conditions for all farmers. But racial prejudice soon split the Populists, and the Blacks realized that the main reason for their hardships was their color, not their occupation. Many began to dream of establishing a nation of their own where they could be free of white oppression, own their own land, and control their political destiny. The Black nation of their dreams would be a credit to the entire race and gain respect for Blacks wherever they lived. The chief advocate of this brand of Black Nationalism during the years between the Civil War and World War I was Bishop Henry McNeal Turner. . . .

Urban Blacks and Marcus Garvey

During the war years 1914–1918, the general situation of hundreds of thousands of Blacks changed radically. Ever since the days of slavery Blacks had looked upon the North as a kind of promised land of political and social freedom. But after Emancipation the economics of cotton farming had kept ninety percent of them in the South. Bishop Turner, among others, realized and publicized the fact that there was much prejudice and racism in the North, especially among recent immigrants from Europe who were competing with Blacks for jobs. Nevertheless, a small but steady stream of Blacks, mostly from Virginia and Kentucky, migrated to the industrial cities of the North and founded communities there.

With the coming of World War I, however, the labor situation in the North changed dramatically. Immigration from Europe was drastically reduced, while the demand for manufactured goods expanded. Industrialists in Chicago, Detroit, Cleveland, New York, Philadelphia, and other cities were crying for unskilled labor and began sending agents into the South to recruit Blacks. Afro-American newspapers also summoned Southern Blacks to the new bonanza, while letters home from early arrivals lured still others away from their cotton farms. In 1915 and 1916 those cotton farms were having hard times anyway, as the boll weevil marched across the South, destroying crops and making life even more difficult than usual for Blacks.

The result of these forces was a sudden, dramatic spurt in the migration from the Deep South to the cities of the North. Almost overnight major cities gained large Black populations. Attracted by jobs that paid in dollars instead of credit at the local store, by the growing all-Black communities inside the cities, and by the relative political and social freedom in the North, nearly half a million Black migrants had moved into the Northern cities by 1920, and the tide was to continue for several decades to come.

But the North was hardly a paradise for Blacks. Friction over jobs, housing, and life styles quickly arose. And when the war ended, returning soldiers and new European immigrants displaced many of the Black workers. Furthermore, the infamous Ku Klux Klan, with all its virulent racism, was revived and began to reach into the North as well as the South. The expanding Black settlements spread from block to block in the major cities, displacing whites, changing neighborhoods, and altering political patterns. To these friction-generating changes were further added 400,000 Black soldiers who had been away helping to "make the world safe for democracy," but who came home from Europe to find the same old racial oppression in the United States.

The result was a long series of race riots, many in Northern cities, in which Blacks invariably suffered the most. During the economic recession that followed the war, urban Blacks, who had been "last hired," found themselves "first fired" and frequently out of work. Although the North still offered more opportunities than the South, and despite the fact that Blacks continued to pour into the cities, it became clear that even in the "promised land" Black people were oppressed. Uprooted from familiar surroundings, crowded into small quarters in expanding ghettos, shunned by whites and restricted to the lowest levels of society, some Blacks began to recall Bishop Turner's African dream of a free and powerful Black nation outside the United States. Into this urban scene of Black newcomers with new homes, new jobs, and new problems stepped Marcus Mosiah Garvey, the man who was to mobilize them in the second mass flowering of Black Nationalism. . . .

Garvey also read Booker T. Washington's autobiography, *Up From Slavery*, and suddenly perceived that his own life work was to be a leader of the Black race. Returning to Jamaica in 1914, he set about building an organization that would "unite the 400,000,000 Negroes of the world for the purpose of building a civilization of their own." [12] He called the organization the Universal Negro Improvement Association and African Communities League (UNIA) and began work among the Black peasants of his home island. Among his goals was the creation of industrial schools to teach trades and skills—schools patterned after Booker T. Washington's Tuskegee Institute. . . .

Central to Garvey's philosophy was the need to unite all Black people and to give them a racial self-confidence that would enable them to throw off white oppression. Like Bishop Turner a generation earlier, Garvey hoped to stimulate race pride both by direct propaganda and by the establishment of a powerful Black nation in Africa. Whenever he spoke, he urged Afro-Americans to shed the old thinking that "white was right" and that Blacks were powerless. "Up you mighty Race! You can accomplish what you will!" was one of his mottoes. To the thousands of Blacks who were caught in the anonymity of the big cities and who felt as helpless under the grinding wheels of Northern society as they had under the oppression of white Southerners, those words held out new hope.

To help stimulate pride and independence, Garvey demanded

racial purity. He was himself of unmixed African descent, and, reflecting the three-way split in West Indian society, he despised mulattoes. Such distinctions between brown and black, however, were not as important in the United States. But Garvey's stress on the glories of the African heritage helped many Afro-Americans, both brown and black, to find new confidence in themselves and in one another. Garvey advised them not to be too concerned with political rights and social equality in the United States, but rather to become as independent as possible in the white man's country. He organized his followers into marching units of uniformed African Legions and Black Cross Nurses whose colorful parades inspired thousands of Harlem residents.

Economic independence was another factor in the UNIA plan. Garvey urged his followers to "buy Black"—to patronize their own businessmen. Following Booker T. Washington's stress on self-sufficiency, the UNIA opened several business projects, including the Negro Factories Corporation, to assist Black businesses. More important, Garvey founded the Black Star Steamship Line to serve as a commercial and spiritual tie among Blacks wherever its ships traveled. Like Bishop Turner's shipping attempts, the Black Star Line was intended to carry freight as well as passengers. But contrary to popular belief, carrying emigrants to Africa was not one of the original motives of Garvey's enterprise. Black Star Line stocks were sold to Blacks only, and Garvey promised stock buyers that they would not only be helping their race but might also make a handsome profit. To the surprise of his critics, Garvey collected enough money between 1919 and 1925 to buy four secondhand ships and to begin trade with the Caribbean.

For Garvey, the major path to Black pride and economic independence was the redemption of "Africa for the Africans." "The only wise thing for us ambitious Negroes to do," he wrote, "is to organize the world over and build up for the race a mighty nation of our own in Africa." [13] It would be "strong enough to lend protection to the members of the race scattered all over the world, and to compel the respect of the nations and races of the earth." [14] He believed that "power is the only argument that satisfies man," and that "it is advisable for the Negro to get power of every kind . . . that will stand out signally, so that other races and nations can see, and if they will not see, then FEEL." [15]

The Garvey movement reached a peak in August 1920 at a month-long convention held in New York City. At least 25,000 people attended the many meetings, at which Garvey used all of his oratorical power to proclaim Black Nationalism. The emphasis was on the redemption of Africa. "The other races have countries of their own and it is time for the 400,000,000 Negroes to claim Africa for themselves," he announced, "and we mean to retake every square inch of the 12,000,000 square miles of African territory belonging to us by right divine." [16] Garvey was designated "Provisional President of the African Republic"; other officials of the UNIA were given similar titles. The convention adopted a long "Declaration of the Rights of the Negro Peoples of the World," which embodied most of Garvey's philosophy. A truly impressive affair in its magnitude and splendor, the convention brought Garvey to the attention of the world. He had managed to do what Bishop Turner and many other Black leaders had failed to do: he had mobilized the Black masses. Thousands of urban Blacks were drawn to the red, black, and green flag of Black nationalism. Many more read the *Negro World* and responded eagerly to the agents of the Black Star Line who circulated among them selling stock.

Garvey was aware that many difficulties stood in the way of the redemption of Africa. European imperialists controlled most of Africa by military force. Furthermore, the Africans themselves would need help in learning to cope with the powers and problems of the twentieth century. Garvey therefore proposed sending a limited number of Afro-Americans with skills, professions, and capital (twenty or thirty thousand families to begin with) to settle in Liberia. Liberia was at that time the only independent West African nation, and it was governed by an elite group of descendants of earlier Afro-American settlers who ruled the indigenous Africans. After 1920 several teams of Garvey's representatives visited Liberia to lay the groundwork for the newcomers. But the UNIA seemed a threat to these Americo-Liberian rulers, especially after they discovered Garvey's secret plan to take over the country. With the approval of the European colonial powers, which also felt threatened by Garvey's "Africa for the Africans" policy, Liberia broke off negotiations and refused to allow any UNIA members to settle there.

Thus ended Garvey's only real attempt to repatriate the descendants of Africa. The enormous appeal he had for Afro-Americans, however, was not based solely on the Back to Africa idea. Although he maintained that "the future of the Negro . . . outside of Africa, spells ruin and disaster," he did not actually call for mass emigration of American Blacks. But mass emigration to escape oppression in the United States was an appealing concept to many of Garvey's working-class followers, and he did little to discourage that popular misinterpretation of his plans.

It was not only the Liberian government and the European colonial powers that were alarmed at Garvey's promises to redeem Africa through his African Legion and Black Flying Eagles; many Afro-Americans also opposed the UNIA leader. The Black elite of businessmen and intellectuals resented Garvey just as they had resented Bishop Turner. Labor leader A. Philip Randolph, of the socialist journal *Messenger*, thought Garvey's Africa would be a reactionary dictatorship, not a democracy. Robert Abbott, of the influential *Chicago Defender*, arranged to have Garvey harassed for selling stock in Illinois without a license. Black churchmen resented Garvey's establishment of an African Orthodox Church, which threatened to win the allegiance of Black Christians to a Black God. W. E. B. Du Bois, editor of the NAACP magazine *The Crisis*, accused Garvey of being the worst enemy of the Black race. Du Bois was then involved in a series of pan-African conferences which tried to bring together intellectual and upper-class Blacks in an organization aimed at pressing for independence for colonial Africa. Although the Pan-African movement shared some basic goals with the UNIA, its style was quite different and its membership much smaller than that of the UNIA; Garvey despised Du Bois. The Black elite, or "talented tenth," as Du Bois called them, not only opposed Garvey's Black nationalism but also criticized the man himself for being uneducated, a foreigner, and a "demagogue." Many whites, including federal government officials, also viewed the UNIA as a dangerous "anti-American" movement.

At first, such opposition did little to dim Garvey's popularity with the Black masses, but the Jamaican also had to take his "friends" into account. Although the UNIA was far-flung, its organization rested chiefly on Garvey himself rather than on strong local leaders. Nevertheless, the UNIA attracted a number of men who saw in it an opportunity to gain personal power or profit. At first Garvey was too trusting of his associates and allowed them to make decisions that later hurt the movement, especially their financial decisions for the Black Star Line. Despite the fact that millions of dollars had apparently been collected from UNIA members, most of it was never accounted for. And, although the organization eventually bought four ships, they either turned out to be unseaworthy or were lost because of debt. The other financial affairs of the movement were also apparently mismanaged, so much so that Garvey's opponents, including some defectors from the UNIA and some disgruntled stock owners, alerted the United States government and charged that the Black Star Line was making false claims about its finances. . . .

Garvey's opponents were delighted, of course, and they published the details of how the UNIA members and Black Star Line investors had lost their money. They expected the movement to quickly collapse. During Garvey's two years in prison there was indeed a decline in the activities of the UNIA, for it had been held together primarily by the personality of Garvey himself. Nevertheless, some local chapters continued to function, waiting for the day when their leader would again rally them to the cause of Black Nationalism. But when Garvey was released from prison and tried to rekindle the old enthusiasm from a distance in Jamaica, he had little success. Even though there was a temporary rally, particularly in the West Indies, the damage had been done. Vestiges of the UNIA lingered on in the United States, but it was torn by factionalism, dissension, and bankruptcy. By 1930 it had ceased to be a major organization in Afro-American life. Garvey died in London in 1940, still clinging to the dream of a powerful African nation that would unite the descendants of Africa scattered around the world. But this second flowering of mass Black Nationalism in the United States had withered. Yet another generation would pass before such ideas again stirred American Blacks.

Turner and Garvey in Perspective

Garvey's UNIA, of course, received much more public recognition than had Bishop Turner's movement. The reasons lie in the differences between their followers. Turner lived and worked in the South, where most Blacks were farmers and where white oppression was much more personal and pervasive. Garvey, on the other hand, worked primarily in the large cities, where communications were better, leisure time more plentiful, white oppression less personal, and mass meetings more feasible. Furthermore, Turner's followers rarely saw much cash, whereas the urban Blacks, though underpaid and underemployed, were paid cash wages. This made it easier for Garvey to raise money for his operations. In addition, many UNIA members, having recently moved to the North, found it easy to think of moving to get another "promised land." These factors partially explain why Garvey, rather than Turner, succeeded in creating a large, visible nationalist organization.

However, Garvey and Turner shared not only a dream of African redemption and Black pride but also certain personal qualities that influenced their activities. Although neither was superhuman and each had his glaring weaknesses, both possessed an overwhelming desire to see the Black race achieve honor and equality with whites. They shared a vision of African power. Both were impressive speakers with a flair for the dramatic and a willingness to speak bluntly about white racism, and to speak it in the language of the masses. But, although Garvey and Turner were competent organizers on a surface level, neither possessed the shrewdness or ability to mobilize his followers efficiently and fend off attacks both by whites and by other Blacks.

In contrast, Booker T. Washington, the dominant Black leader in the years between Turner's and Garvey's heydays, was able to use people, publicity, politics, and personality to maintain his own power for almost twenty years. Of course, Washington paid a price for that power—namely, the humiliation of Southern Blacks in their own eyes and in the eyes of whites in return for telling white businessmen what they wanted to hear about "happy, docile Blacks." And although Washington's power gained him the respect of many Blacks, he commanded little enthusiasm among the Black lower class because he had no great, militant vision of the future of Afro-Americans. But he was a shrewd and capable organizer and manipulator of ideas and men. In the final analysis he was the most powerful Black man in American history.

Had either Bishop Turner or Marcus Garvey combined Washington's organizational ability with their Black Nationalist understanding of what had to be done, the outcome might have been different. Although Turner fought for African redemption and Afro-American emigration throughout most of his long life, he had other interests, particularly church affairs, and so did not give his wholehearted attention to Black Nationalist agitation. Garvey had only one consuming passion, but his fatal weakness was his failure to select competent and loyal assistants.

There were other reasons why neither Turner nor Garvey was able to achieve ultimate success. Each had active opponents and, in the end, was overwhelmed by them. For, just as Turner's propaganda was taking effect in the mid-1890's, Booker T. Washington gained national attention and soon dominated Black leadership. Garvey was overwhelmed, not by a new leader with new ideas, but by a concerted attack from his opponents, who succeeded in physically removing him from the scene. Both Turner and Garvey failed to get substantial support from the Black upper class—the small but influential elite who had skilled jobs, professions, or college educations and who yearned for stability and integration more than race pride. Although Garvey was much more successful in getting money and ships, in the end neither he nor Turner was able to arrange a strong settlement of Afro-Americans in Africa or otherwise create a powerful Black nation. Each man was so aware of the pervasive reality of white oppression and the powerlessness of Blacks around the world that he ignored the necessary details of organization and nation building.

It was the concept of Black Nationalism rather than its organization that fired the imaginations of Turner's oppressed Southern followers and Garvey's Northern urban admirers. To be sure, there was a major element of escapism in the popular interpretation of Black Nationalism. That escapism forced both leaders to include mass emigration in their thinking, even though both maintained that a full exodus was both impractical and unnecessary for the establishment of a free Black nation in Africa. But Blacks seemed to want a nation of their own that would command the respect of the world, an idea they clearly adopted from whites; both the 1890's and 1920's were times of intense nationalism in both Europe and the United States. Southern and Northern whites proclaimed that this was a "white man's country." The ideas and arguments employed by Turner and Garvey were learned from these whites.

Central to the concept of Black Nationalism was the unity of all Blacks in all parts of the world. Unity meant more than strength in numbers; the international approach reinforced the nationalists' awareness that the root of their problems lay not in racial inferiority, personal traits, or bad luck, but in white oppression. This was true not only in the United States and the Caribbean but in Africa as well. Bishop Turner watched in alarm as the European powers established their imperial control over the homeland during his lifetime. Both he and Garvey were early contributors to the small but growing movement for African nationalism among the Africans themselves, a movement that eventually led to their independence.

For Turner, Garvey, and their followers, Africa became a symbol more powerful than reality. As the home of their ancestors, it had a strong appeal to Afro-Americans, whose knowledge of Africa was clouded by generations of separation and years of brainwashing. New World Blacks easily romanticized Africa and ignored its difficult problems—first of European control, second of economic growth in societies that had not yet begun to industrialize, and third of nation building on a continent containing hundreds of different ethnic groups. Both Turner and Garvey tried to learn about Africa, however, and their visions of an independent, powerful African nation were more than empty dreams.

The primary impact of both Turner and Garvey, of course, was on American Blacks. Black Nationalism gave Afro-Americans a feeling of independence and power in the face of suffocating, ever present white oppression. It also gave them a sense of working toward the day when Black men would indeed have their own nations and be respected in the councils of the world. This sense of purpose drew together a people who had been lost in an American society supposedly very individualistic but actually very group-oriented, especially where race was involved. It got some of them—for a time, at least—to work together, to dream, to build, and brought a self-pride that mere rhetoric could never have produced.

The flowerings of Black Nationalism under Bishop Turner and Marcus Garvey left seeds that are still growing. First, the promise of African freedom inspired Africans to work for independence from Europe. Second, the stress on Black accomplishments built a new pride in the Afro-American lower class that would one day blossom into a new Black power and independence.

Marcus Garvey
and African Nationalism*

BY JABEZ AYODELE LANGLEY

I

Nearly every work on African nationalism has asserted the influence of Garveyism on the growth of race consciousness in Africa. The nature of this influence is more often asserted than analyzed. The testimonies of the King of Swaziland (who is reported to have told Mrs. Garvey that the only two Black men he knew in the Western world were Jack Johnson, the boxing champion, and Marcus Garvey) and ex-President Nkrumah (who recollects that Garvey's *Philosophy and Opinions* had a profound influence on him during his student days in America) are usually cited as examples of Garvey's influence on African nationalist thought and politics. As Professor Essien-Udom has pointed out in his introduction to the second edition of Garvey's *Philosophy and Opinions*, "Garvey's influence on the Negro freedom movements in the United States and Africa, will never be fully known." [17] Sufficient material exists in African and American sources for a preliminary assessment of the extent and significance of this influence.

* *RACE*, Vol. X, No. 2, October 1969. Copyright by Institute of Race Relations, London.

Concerning the Pan-African movement of W. E. B. Du Bois, opinion in nationalist circles in English-speaking West Africa was generally a mixture of enthusiasm, mild criticism, and an attitude which implied that there was no direct rapport between Du Bois' Pan-Africanism and the new pan-West African nationalism of the 1920's. It was a grand movement, to be admired and held up as an indication of a new and vigorous race-consciousness determined to assert itself in the postwar world, but was at the same time not directly related to peculiar economic and political problems of British West Africa. As far as Garvey's Pan-Negro movement was concerned, however, the position, contrary to the opinion of certain European contemporary writers, was different. As Thomas Hodgkin has suggested, the Garvey movement may have had a more significant and widespread effect on African nationalist thought than is commonly supposed.[18] Professor Shepperson has already argued the thesis of Negro American influences on African nationalism, particularly East and Central African nationalism, although the extent and significance of this influence varied somewhat, as we shall show in the West African case. Some of the radical Negro newspapers found their way into Africa; for example, the *Crusader*, frequently quoted by West African papers, wrote:

> The *Crusader* serves . . . the colored people of the world. It circulates in nearly every big town in the U.S. . . . It has circulation in the West Indies and Panama, in South America, and in the coastal districts of West, East and South Africa, penetrating as far as Kano on the Nigerian railway, as far as Coquilhatville on the Congo River, and in South Africa as far as Pretoria.[19]

And an American writer, describing the network of influence linking Negroes throughout the world, wrote as follows: "Indeed, a reader in Sierra Leone writes to the *Negro World* (March 26, 1921): 'We have been reading the *Negro World* for about two years. We have been reading other Negro papers, such as the *New York Age*, the *Washington Bee*, *The Crisis*, the *Colored American*, the *Liberian West Africa*, the *Liberian Register*. . . .' "[20]

Even as late as 1933 there were African nationalists in South

Africa who, in spite of police surveillance, were receiving copies
of Garvey's *Negro World*. One James Stehazu, for example
(signing himself 'Yours Africanly'), wrote to the *Negro World*
editor "to express the feeling of our African brothers towards the
American or West Indian brothers." His observations were frank
and sharp:

> The Africans are now wide awake in affairs affecting the Black
> races of the world, and yet the so-called civilized Negroes of the
> Western Hemisphere are still permitting the white men to deceive
> them as the Negroes of the old regime, Uncle Tom stool pigeons. If
> the "motherland" Africa is to be redeemed, the Africans are to
> play an important part in the ranks and file of the UNIA and ACL.
> I have studied comments and opinions of twenty-nine leading
> American newspapers (all colored) and to my horror it is only one
> problem that is still harassing. The 250-year-old policy, 'Please and
> Thank You' (Sir, Kick Me and Thank You). But the lion-hearted M.
> Garvey has cut it adrift from the new Negro. He is now admitted as
> a great African leader. . . . The intellectuals like Dr. Du Bois,
> Pickens, Hancock and others are obviously put to shame, hope-
> lessly moving like handicapped professors who are drunk with
> knowledge, who cannot help themselves. . . . The red, the black
> and the green are the colors talked about by the young men and
> women of Africa. It shall bury many and redeem millions. Today in
> Africa, the only hope of our race is gospel of UNIA—is sung and
> said as during the period of the French Revolution.[21]

Yet another South African (E. T. Mofutsanyana) wrote criticizing the anticommunist craze in South Africa:

> These pretenders, these destroyers of happiness, these exploiters,
> profiteers and parasites . . . under cover of justice and religion are
> busy formulating a law that they believe will lock up Communism
> in an iron box never to peep out again . . . Communism is like
> grass. They cannot cut it; they can burn it to ashes, but when the
> time comes for revolution, it will positively get up like fire. . . .[22]

While Garveyism did not have any permanent influence, the
available evidence suggests that it excited more interest and
controversy and was a more powerful utopia among African

nationalist groups than the Du Bois movement. In both French and British West Africa between 1920 and 1923, there were a few individuals and organizations associated with Garveyism. It was in Lagos, however, that the movement was strongest where a small but vigorous branch of UNIA was actually established in mid-1920, almost at the same time as the National Congress of British West Africa came into being. In March 1920, the Rev. Patriarch Campbell, one of the Congress leaders in Nigeria, was approached by some Lagosians on the subject of the Garvey movement and with a proposal for forming a committee of the UNIA in Lagos. Campbell advised them to postpone discussion until the meeting of the National Congress of British West Africa (hereafter referred to as NCBWA) where he would take the matter up. He thought there was something to be said for the commercial aspects of Garvey's Pan-Negroism, especially the project of the Black Star Line, but advised loyal British subjects against participation in UNIA politics "as conditions in both hemispheres differ altogether from each other." [23] Campbell then discussed the idea with delegates at the Accra meeting of the NCBWA and the conclusion reached was that Garvey's politics should be ignored and the Black Star Line patronized, "it being a Negro undertaking and its object being solely for the purpose of facilitating and giving us more and brighter prospects as Africans in our commercial transactions." [24] The *Times of Nigeria* editorial endorsed the view of the NCBWA dwelling almost exclusively on the economic aspects of Garveyism.

> The idea of establishing a line of steamers owned and controlled by Africans is a great and even sublime conception for which everybody of African origin will bless the name of Marcus Garvey. . . . The inclusion, however, of such a tremendous political plan, as the founding of a pan-African Empire, is too obviously ridiculous to do aught else than alienate sympathy from the whole movement. We do not suggest that our brethren in America ought not to aim at political autonomy. Liberty is man's highest right . . . particularly in the case of our American brethren, for whom the hardships and disadvantages under which they exist in the land of their exile make it desirable to have some portion of their ancestral land, where they could unmolested shape their own destiny and spread

culture among their less enlightened brethren—"De ole folks at home." [25]

The *Times* went on to argue, in a manner reminiscent of present pan-African disagreements, that the NCBWA concept of independence was incompatible with the UNIA concept of a pan-Negro Republic: "If at all the day should come—and come it must in the process of evolution—when Africa shall be controlled by Africans, each distinct nation, while having the most cordial relations with every other sister nation, will infinitely prefer remaining as a separate political entity to being drawn into one huge melting pot of a Universal Negro Empire." The NCBWA was cited as an example of a movement working towards the gradual independence of British West Africa within the British Empire, and Garvey was told that what Africa needed was banks, schools, industries, modern universities, and the Black Star Line, not "wild-cat schemes" like a pan-African Republic. [26]

Towards the end of 1920, with the government taking a serious view of the unrest the Garvey movement could cause in the colonies, the majority of the Lagos elite dissociated themselves from the UNIA branch which was being run by Ernest S. Ikoli. The conservative *Nigerian Pioneer* wrote on November 26: "We advise the police to keep an eye on the Garveyites in Nigeria." Some of the leading members of the UNIA Lagos branch included the Rev. W. B. Euba and the Rev. S. M. Abiodun. At the unveiling of the UNIA branch charter on November 26 at Lagos, the Rev. Euba, whilst insisting on their loyalty to Britain, made it clear that "cooperation among Negroes is the first necessity without which it will be futile to try to co-operate with other peoples." The *Lagos Weekly Record* condemned Garveyism because of "it's aggressive and militaristic tendencies" but said of the Lagos branch: "To us they are neither traitorous nor revolutionary, neither fantastic nor visionary." [27] . . .

If the middle-class nationalists were opposed to UNIA politics, there were a few Lagos radicals like J. Babington Adebayo who mercilessly criticized the Lagos branch of the NCBWA and the conservative Lagos press. He criticized the Rev. J. G. Campbell for accusing Garveyites of sedition and disloyalty and for concerning himself with conservative bodies like the Peoples

Union, the Lagos Anti-Slavery Society, and with such institutions
as the intercolonial cricket match. Adebayo went on to attack the
criticisms the *Nigerian Pioneer* made of the Garvey movement—
criticisms like: "The thousands of tribes in any section of Africa
never at any time regarded themselves as one people or one
nation"—the standard argument of the conservatives who were
also opposed to the NCBWA. According to Adebayo, his fear was
that the trouble with most Africans, especially those with the
mentality of the *Nigerian Pioneer*, was that they clung too closely
to "the best traditions of British rule," forgetting that sometimes
these "best traditions" were not always in their own interests: "It
is this we consider and believe the greatest obstacle and one that
can scarcely be annihilated. We need not be reminded that the
best traditions had not always been upheld among us without a
break," and drove home his point by quoting Paul Lawrence
Dunbar's poem about the oppressed yet eternally forgiving
African. It was this attitude, he said, that constituted "the
greatest obstacle to the materialization of this glowing Utopia"
(i.e. Garvey's Utopia).[28] As for the Lagos branch of the NCBWA,
Adebayo thought that though its leaders were sincere, their
methods were dictatorial, publicity poor, and internal struggles
disastrous; office-holders were far too numerous, "chairman came
over chairman, officers galore as lieutenants in the Haitian
Army." [29]

Whereas the *Times of Nigeria* took a sympathetic view of the
Garvey movement, the *Nigerian Pioneer*, representing conservative opinion in Lagos, was openly hostile to any such Pan-African
movement. . . . The *Sierra Leone Weekly News*, perhaps representing the majority view on Garveyism, took a very constitutional view, confusing Garveyism with revolution and socialism:

> We, as British subjects, may be opposed to any novel line of policy
> which administrators of his Majesty's Government may elect to
> pursue and recommend, and which we judge may hamper our
> racial progress and deprive us of our civil liberty, but in seeking
> redress we are not prepared to confound maintenance of rights
> with disloyalty to rulers . . . with a declaration of racial independ-
> ence which may sound well in words, but has no meaning in
> reality. . . . We want no gospelers to lead us into the whirlpool of
> revolutionary Socialism. . . .[30]

The Colonial Office, aware of the unrest Negro American activity had created in other parts of the continent, took the Garvey movement seriously, for in 1922 it sent a secret dispatch to Sir Hugh Clifford, inquiring about UNIA activities in Nigeria, especially the operations of the Black Star Line. Sir Hugh in turn furnished the reports of two lieutenant-governors on the subject, indicating that the Lagos Garveyites were harmless. According to him, the movement appeared to be "inspired mainly by a not unnatural desire on the part of Marcus Garvey and his associates to obtain money from natives of Africa for which it is not proposed to make any very adequate return." [31] According to his source of information, financial contributions and subscriptions had in fact been made in some cases and sent to America by "malcontent Africans living in Nigeria and in the employment of the Government." Sir Hugh, however, had little to fear from Garveyism because, he said, from what he knew of the West African, he felt certain that his "notorious ability to take care of himself where money is concerned" would provide a powerful check on any commercial exploitation by Garvey or others. H. C. Moorhouse, Lieutenant-Governor of the Southern Provinces, added that a Negro American called Cockburn, formerly employed by the Nigerian Marine, was rumored to have been given command of one of the Black Star ships, and that Garveyism "has made very little headway here and if as appears probable the association becomes discredited in America, it will . . . gradually die out here." [32] According to W. F. Gowers, Lieutenant-Governor of the Northern Provinces, investigations in early 1921 in the north had shown that copies of the *Negro World* were being circulated among Africans and West Indians "to a very small extent in some Provinces, among them Kano, Munshi, and Illorin," but that there was no evidence of UNIA propaganda. He added: "There is no likelihood at all of the principles of the Marcus Garvey movement finding any encouragement outside a very limited class of native, not indigenous to the Northern Provinces . . . there is even less interest taken in Marcus Garvey and his movement than there was last year." So far as he knew, there could be no question of pan-Africanist activity in the north.[33]

The Nigerian Deputy Inspector-General of Police then outlined the aims of UNIA and dwelt a little on the Black Star Line, stating that a number of West Africans had bought shares. Branches of the UNIA had been formed in Africa, America, and the West Indies, and in Nigeria its headquarters was at 72 Tinubu Square, Lagos, the president of which was Winter Sohakleford, a clerk to S. Thomas & Co. The secretary was Ernest S. Ikoli, editor and manager of the "African Messenger," but he had been succeeded by the Rev. Ajayi of the CMS in 1922. Membership was around the 300 mark, but paying members amounted to a mere twenty-eight—heavy subscriptions and levies ensured a rather lukewarm support. There was also a brass band which the movement owned; official instructions from headquarters in New York stated that the African National Anthem ("Ethiopia, Land of My Fathers") was to be played on all public occasions. It was also stated that the Nigerian agent for the industrial wing of the UNIA was a Mr. Agbebi, but no shares had been sold in Lagos though there was some interest in the matter. According to the police, Mr. Ikoli had resigned as secretary of the local branch "on the grounds he was opposed to its political aims, though he approved of the industrial scheme." [34] He (the Deputy Inspector-General) had also seen a private letter from Herbert Macaulay when the latter was in England, to a friend of his in Lagos, "warning him to be very careful in having anything to do with this Association as it is perilously near the border line of treason and sedition." [35] In conclusion, the report noted: "The movement is not meeting with much local success and with the exception of the leaders, the members are lukewarm and the public generally are not in favor of it. They recognize they are much better off under British rule and have no desire to change . . . for American Negro rule. . . ."

Apart from Lagos, Garveyism attracted considerable attention in Liberia, where its activities inevitably involved Liberian-American and British relations, and the interests of the Firestone Rubber Company.[36] Apart from Liberia and Lagos, the UNIA does not seem to have had much impact on other parts of West Africa. . . .

II

The admirers of Garvey, however, were not all "semi-educated," "ignorant and gullible." As M. Labouret argued in the 1930's, there were a few of the nationalist intelligentsia in British Africa who had studied Garveyism closely and had related it to nationalist politics.[37] And it certainly comes as a surprise that the most outspoken and eloquent commentator on the Garvey movement among this intelligentsia was "that remarkable Cape Coast lawyer" (as Thomas Hodgkin rightly describes him), William Essuman Gwira Sekyi (or Kobina Sekyi), Gold Coast philosopher, nationalist, lawyer and traditionalist. A controversialist and prolific writer, Sekyi was one of the most interesting personalities in Gold Coast public affairs and an example *par excellence* of the African intellectual in nationalist politics.[38] Sekyi devoted two interesting chapters to the Negro question in America in his violently anticolonial book which recommended as little contact as possible between Africans and European colonials.[39] Writing in defense of the Garvey movement he argued that any manifestation of solidarity between Africans and other Negroes was generally regarded with great suspicion by the white man who had "got so hopelessly alarmed by the *necessary spadework* that Marcus Garvey is doing towards the erection, in the not very remote future, of [an] abiding edifice of racial collaboration, that he has further overlooked the truth of the well-known remark: Abuse is no argument." . . . Unlike the majority of the pan-African utopians, however Sekyi was able to perceive that the African diaspora, for various historical and sociological reasons, had ceased to have any of the attributes of a nation and that West Indians and Black Americans, in spite of the new race consciousness and pan-Melanism, had inherited Anglo-Saxon prejudices against the African and were *ipso facto* disqualified from assuming any political leadership in the African continent:

From Marcus Garvey's announcements regarding Africa, it is clear that he does not know even the level of acquaintance with Western ideals and of capacity to assimilate and adapt whatever comes from or is traceable to the modern world. What is much more important is that he does not understand how we Africans in Africa feel about such matters as the Colonial Government; neither can he and his set . . . realize that republican ideals in the crude form in which they are maintained, in theory, at least, in America go directly against the spirit of Africa, which is the only continent in the whole world peopled by human beings who have in their souls the secret of constitutional monarchy. . . . What Marcus Garvey and any other leader of Afro-American thought has first to appreciate before he can present a case sufficiently sound for Africa to support in the matter of combination or cooperation among all Africans at home and abroad, is the peculiar nature of the African standpoint in social and political institutions. *The salvation of the Africans in the world cannot but be most materially assisted by the Africans in America but must be controlled and directed from African Africa and thoroughly African Africans.*[40]

Sekyi's other strictures against the pan-Africanism of Black Americans and West Indians . . . indicate a different concept of pan-Africanism on the part of the West African nationalist intellectuals [and] because they illustrate the dilemma posed by the Black American "double consciousness." To the Black American, Africa in the abstract was both a romantic illusion and a sharp reminder that he was an American first, and this dichotomy, in Sekyi's view, meant that political leadership of Africa must come from within Africa. . . .

On the basis of the evidence, it is reasonable to conclude that, in spite of their objections to Garvey's concept of a pan-African state, the majority of the petty-bourgeois nationalist leaders of the National Congress of British West Africa, on the whole, tended to be more sympathetic to Garvey's pan-Negro nationalism and its economic goals than to the more majestic, more intellectual, but ineffective movement of Du Bois. As I have shown elsewhere,[41] the leadership of the NCBWA attempted between 1920 and 1930 to blend pan-African idealism with a realistic consideration of their socio-economic interests.

III

Garvey's ideas not only reached nationalist circles in West Africa and South Africa; they also reached French-speaking Africans and West Indians in Paris in the 1920's though the Dahomean Marc Kojo Tovalou Houenou who sent copies of the *Negro World* to Dahomey and founded the pan-Negro *Ligue universelle pour la defense de la race noire* in 1924. Houenou was definitely a supporter of Marcus Garvey, and visited the United States in 1924 as guest of Garvey's Universal Negro Improvement Association. His sister (Mme Rose Elisha of Cotonou) informed the author that Houenou was a "friend of Marcus Garvey" and that Garvey's activities were well known in Cotonou and Porto Novo in the 1920's. In fact, *Les Continents* (the journal of Houenou's *Ligue*) carried several articles on Negro American literature and politics, with reprints of Garvey's speeches and accounts of UNIA meetings in America. Houenou was himself nominated UNIA representative in France, and was so involved in UNIA affairs that he rashly attempted to "liberate" Dahomey with some Negroes in 1925, and was promptly arrested.[42] In fact Garvey visited France in July 1928 and met French Negro groups in Paris, claiming that UNIA had "already cemented a working plan with the French Negro by which we hope to carry out the great ideals of the UNIA. My visit to France is, indeed, profitable, and I do hope for great results." [43]

Although Garvey's movement had no direct contact with Equatorial Africa, French and Belgian officials were prone to attribute any local disturbances in their colonies to Garveyism and to the pan-African movement in general. Between 1920 and 1923 syncretistic and prophet movements sprang up in West, Central and Equatorial Africa, the most serious being the prophet movement in the Belgian Congo led by Simon Kimbangu and Andre Yengo. Belgian officials saw these as nationalist movements inspired by Garveyism and its Negro American missionaries . . . [who] were alleged to have distributed copies of Garvey's *Negro World* with seditious literature and hymns in the Congo, especially around Kinshasha and Stanley Pool.[44] A few

other European journalists regarded Garveyism as a bad influence on the Congo, and as a clever plot by the American
government to rid itself of turbulent Negroes by encouraging
their anticolonial activities in Europe and Africa.[45]

Garvey did not achieve the "great results" he hoped for, but to
argue, as James Weldon Johnson did in *Black Manhattan*,[46] that
he was neither moderately successful nor successfully moderate,
is to miss the point by judging him solely on the basis of
immediate practical success. The political thought of great men
does not have to be evaluated on the basis of the historian's
success story for its significance to be appreciated.[47] As Samuel
Butler has reminded us, "It is not he who first conceives an idea,
nor he who sets it on its legs and makes it go on all fours, but he
who makes other people accept the main conclusion, whether on
right grounds or on wrong ones, who has done the greatest work
as regards the promulgation of opinion."[48] And this is what, in
my view, Marcus Garvey did for Pan-Negro nationalism. . . .

The Garvey Movement:
A Marxist View*

BY WILLIAM Z. FOSTER

THE UNIA TOOK root immediately on American soil and flourished like a green bay tree. . . .

Whatever the actual paid-up membership of his UNIA may have been, the incontestable fact is that Garvey had a tremendous following among the Negro people. His movement was based on the migrants from the South; it was led by the petty bourgeoisie, and it consisted mainly of workers. Garvey moved the Negro millions as never since Reconstruction days and the Populist period. Garvey's militant program and spectacular organizing methods had a tremendous attracting power for the harassed Negro people in this country, both North and South. The movement also exerted a considerable influence throughout the world. Everywhere that masses of Negroes lived Garvey's name was familiar; and to the UNIA conventions came delegates from Africa, the West Indies, and Central America.[49]

The growth of the UNIA was without parallel in Negro history. The basis for its great expansion in the United States was to be found in the severe conditions of exploitation and oppression under which the Negro masses suffered. This was a time of hard economic conditions in the South, of mass migration, of brutal

* *Political Affairs*, February 1954.

lynchings and race riots, and of KKK terrorism. Behind the ensuing Negro discontent were also the tremendous employers' offensive and the workers' defensive struggle of the period. Especially pronounced were the influence of the great Russian Revolution, with its stirring slogans of national and social equality, and also the international revolutionary spirit of the working class in Europe. Negative causes for the success of the movement were the failure of the conservatively-led NAACP and Urban League to give militant leadership to the embattled Negro people, and the widespread white chauvinism in the AFL, Socialist Party, farmers' organizations, etc. Garveyism came as a flash of hope to the doubly exploited and oppressed Negro masses. Its militancy fitted in with the indomitable fighting spirit expressed by the Negro people during the bitter years following World War I.

A Negro commentator thus describes the enthusiasm behind Garvey's leadership: "The bands of black peasant folk flock to Garvey. They worship him. They feel he is saying the things which they would utter were they articulate. They swarm to hear his fiery rhetoric. They pour their money into his coffers. They stand by him through thick and thin. They idolize him as if he were a black Demosthenes." [50] Negro women took an active part in the whole movement. . . .

Back to Africa

The central political slogan of the Garvey movement was "Back to Africa." Garvey held that it was impossible for Negroes to get justice in countries where they formed a minority, and that they must migrate to Africa, their traditional homeland. He cultivated this plan with all the skill of a great master of mass agitation. In this respect he has hardly been excelled by any agitator in American history. In the early, militant stages of his movement, he understood profoundly how to appeal to the oppressed and insulted Negro people and give them a new sense of national pride, dignity, hope, and power. He went beyond mere verbal propaganda, actually setting up in the United States a miniature replica of the governmental regime that he hoped to create in Africa. In 1921, he organized the Empire of Africa with himself as head and also set up "armed forces," with which eventually to clear Africa of white invaders. . . .

The Back-to-Africa movement undoubtedly exerted a strong pull upon the Negro people. It expressed their traditional longing for land and freedom, and it dovetailed with historic tendencies among the Negro people to migrate out of the South—to Africa, to the West Indies, to Canada, to the West, to the North—anywhere to escape from the purgatory of the Southern planters. But the Negro people were realistic enough, even during the high thrills and excitement of the Garvey movement, to realize that, at most, comparatively few of them could ever reach Africa, at least within a measurable time.

A most important factor that accounted for the great upswing of the Garvey movement during its early stages was its aggressive protest against the wrongs inflicted upon the Negro people and its ringing demand for their redress. This fitted right in with the rising militancy of the Negro people during these crucial postwar years of offensives by the employers and struggle by the masses. This was the time of the "New Negro," as expressed in the *Messenger, The Crusader, The Challenge, The New Emancipator,* and other fighting journals and books of the period. The "New Negro," as conceived by the *Messenger,* was one who was quite willing to die, if need be, in defense of himself, his family, and his political rights. He stood for "absolute social equality, education, physical action in self-defense, freedom of speech, press and assembly, and the right of Russia to self-determination." [51] Garveyism flourished in its initial militancy and expanded in the midst of this growing spirit of struggle.

Disastrous Business Ventures

Translating his burning nationalist evangelism into deeds, Garvey proceeded to prepare for the actual transportation of his people to Africa. . . . These business ventures were most unfortunate for Garvey and the UNIA. How much Garvey was responsible for the welter of corruption that developed in the organization is problematical. The probability is that he, personally, was financially honest, but he was surrounded by a number of crooks and incompetents who flocked into the company when the money began to pour in. . . . Garvey was a very great political agitator; but he obviously knew little of the complexities of business and less of the wiles of business thieves. . . .

The Political Decay of Garveyism

While the financial debacle of the Black Star Line was in the making, the UNIA itself was going through a process of political decay. Garvey was gradually shedding his early radicalism, and taking on a conservatism which amounted to a surrender of the Negro people into the hands of their worst enemies on a national and international scale. Garvey tended more and more toward the supplicating line of his friend, Booker T. Washington. The political degeneration of the Garvey movement was directly related to the subsiding of the great postwar struggle of the workers in this country and also to the temporary lull in the profound revolutionary movement which shook Europe in the early years after World War I. Garvey took the line of surrender characteristic of Social-Democratic and national reformists. This collided with the basic interests of the harassed Negro masses, and his movement proceeded to fade away. Its decline set in early in 1921.

Garvey dropped his demands for Negro rights and concentrated everything upon his utopian plan of a mass return to Africa. Benjamin J. Davis, Jr., later stated that "Garvey would surrender the fight for the complete freedom of the Negro in America, and in other lands which they helped to build, for the fantastic dream of a trek to Africa." [52] Indeed, although denying it, Garvey actually became an enemy of all struggle for Negro rights in the United States. He sharply opposed trade unions (which had long Jim Crowed Negroes), and warned the Negro "to be careful of the traps and pitfalls of white trade unionism. . . . It seems strange and a paradox, but the only convenient friend the Negro worker or laborer has, in America, at the present time, is the white capitalist. . . . If the Negro takes my advice he will organize by himself and always keep his scale of

wages a little lower than the whites until he is able to become
. . . his own employer." Garvey also stated that "Capitalism is
necessary to the progress of the world, and those who unreasona-
bly and wantonly oppose or fight against it are enemies to human
advancement." [53]

Garvey deprecated all struggles for social equality for Negroes.
He said, "Let foolish Negro agitators and so-called reformers,
encouraged by deceptive and unthinking white associates, stop
preaching and advocating the doctrine of social equality." [54] As
Robert Minor put it, "By a process of elimination, all demands
which were offensive to the ruling class were dropped one by one
and the organization settled down to a policy of disclaiming any
rights for the Negro people in the United States." [55] Instead of his
early threats to refuse to obey segregation laws and to oust the
imperialists from Africa, Garvey later put out the slogan, "The
Negro must be loyal to all the flags under which he lives." [56]
From holding a friendly attitude toward the USSR, Garvey
became a militant Soviet hater.

The UNIA degenerated into a mass deportation movement,
hardly to be distinguished from the old reactionary American
Colonization Society, launched in 1817. Garvey appealed to the
white chauvinism of the ruling class with his offer to settle the
Negro question by getting rid of the Negroes altogether, by
shipping them off to Africa. He visited Colonel Simmons,
Imperial Grand Wizard of the Ku Klux Klan,[57] invited him to
speak at the UNIA convention and praised the KKK publicly. He
also negotiated with various anti-Negro Southern senators and
congressmen for cooperation. Du Bois charged that Garvey had
plans afoot to get the Klan to finance the Black Star Line and
that "the Klan sent out circulars defending Garvey and declaring
that the opposition to him was from the Catholic Church." [58]
Characteristically, in April 1938, when Senator Bilbo of Mississippi introduced a bill to deport 13,000,000 Negroes to Africa,
Garvey's wife supported it.[59]

After Garvey's imprisonment, the UNIA, a prey to internal
disruption and outside pressure, rapidly declined. Factionally
split, remnants of it still exist, however.[60] The movement gave
birth to a series of minor groupings, such as the 49th State
Movement, the Peace Movement for Ethiopia, and others.

Garvey and his UNIA constituted a definite threat to the established leadership of the Negro people, as represented by the NAACP, the Urban League, and the leading Negro journals. Garvey's movement not only menaced their policies, it also strove to destroy the whole groundwork of these organizations by turning the Negro people's attention to Africa and, if possible, by transporting masses of them there. Consequently, the leaders of the established Negro bodies generally met Garvey's offensive with a strong counterattack. Garvey made few attempts to conciliate these enemies; instead he called them "opportunists, liars, thieves, traitors, and bastards." [61]

W. E. B. Du Bois, the influential editor of *The Crisis*, chief organ of the NAACP, characterized Garvey as "a sincere, hard-working idealist," but also, "a stubborn, domineering leader of the mass." [62] But this attack was mild compared with the blasts coming from other Negro leaders. The A. Philip Randolph group, who initially were members of the UNIA, were especially violent, denouncing Garvey in every key. Eight of them went so shamefully far as to write a letter to U.S. Attorney General Dougherty, on January 19, 1922, demanding that Garvey be deported and that his "vicious movement be extirpated." They assailed Garvey with every insult, even regarding his physical appearance.[63]

The Communist Party, then newly established, took a critical, although friendly attitude toward the Garvey movement. Robert Minor called the UNIA "the most important mass phenomenon to be found in the sphere of Negro activities since Reconstruction days. In a thousand sleepy villages today, tens of thousands of suffering and oppressed Negro laborers are meeting together and talking about their wrongs." [64] The Communist Party, which opposed the Back-to-Africa slogan, sent a letter to the 1924 convention of the UNIA, criticizing mistakes of the organization and pledging support to the general liberation fight of the Negro people. The letter, signed by Charles E. Ruthenberg and William Z. Foster, thus stated the Party line: "We stand for driving the imperialist powers out of Africa and for the right of self-determination of the peoples of Africa. In taking this stand, we point out that it need not and must not involve a surrender of the Negroes' rights and equality in America or any other land." [65]

Garveyism: Negro Nationalism

Garvey's was the voice of the Negro petty bourgeoisie, seeking to secure the leadership of the Negro people by subordinating their national feelings and needs to class interests. It was trying to develop commercially, industrially, and politically. This was the significance of the whole string of cooperative enterprises—grocery stores, laundries, restaurants, hotels, printing plants, and, above all, the Black Star Line—which his movement built up. Planning to create a great Negro state in an industrialized Africa, Garvey was obviously speaking not merely in the vague, indefinable terms of "race," but in concrete and definite concepts of bourgeois nationalism. What he had in mind for Africa was some kind of replica of capitalist society in the United States. . . .

Marcus Garvey, Pan-Negroist: The View from Whitehall*

BY ROBERT G. WEISBORD

FUTURE HISTORIANS MAY well view Marcus Mosiah Garvey as the central figure in twentieth-century Negro history. Some students of America's seamy record of race relations, not to mention countless ghetto militants, already regard Garvey as the patron saint of Black Nationalism and the progenitor of Black Power. . . . More than any other Black leader, the charismatic Garvey in his worldwide activities underlined the international character of the color problem. He was a pan-Negroist without equal.

During his era Great Britain could still boast of an empire containing a sizable number of the four hundred million colored people for whom Garvey was the self-proclaimed leader. Therefore, Whitehall's concern with Garvey, especially in his heyday, is not at all surprising. The depth and scope of that concern have not been fully understood. Fortunately, pertinent Foreign Office and Colonial Office documents, until recently inaccessible to scholars, are now open for examination at the Public Record Office in London. Dispatches from embassies, legations, and consulates on at least three continents repeatedly touched on the threat posed by Garvey and his local followers during the years of his American period (1916–1927).

* *RACE*, 1968, Institute of Race Relations, London.

A document recently discovered in America's National Archives reveals that in 1919 unrest among Negroes in the United States and elsewhere was being closely watched by the British Government.[66] In that year a strictly confidential report was sent to the Department of State listing groups important to radical Negro movements and providing notes on individual Black agitators and propagandists. . . .

To be sure, Garvey's influence was greater in West Africa than in East Africa, and in 1923 there were rumors that the Black Moses was planning a sojourn to the land of his fathers. The Acting Governor of Nigeria was of the opinion that Garvey should be refused a passport to visit that colony, and the majority of the Executive Council in Sierra Leone strongly believed that he should not be permitted to land at Freetown. In a letter, dated May 28, 1923, to the Colonial Secretary, the Duke of Devonshire, the Acting Governor of Sierra Leone stated that Garvey appeared to "advocate an open repudiation of obedience to the established European governments in Africa accompanied with violent abuse of them." He described Garvey's views as mischievous and seditious. The *Negro World*, though not absolutely prohibited in Sierra Leone, had been carefully regulated. To support his description the Acting Governor cited an ominous article in that newspaper:

> When it comes to Africa we feel that the Negro has no obligation to anyone but himself. Whatsoever kind of Government we have in Africa . . . has been imposed on us by stealth and deception; therefore we are not compelled to recognize them. . . . If it takes a thousand years we shall work for, and probably fight for, the freedom of our Fatherland.[67]

It is interesting to note that UNIA adherents from Sierra Leone had been active not only in their native land, but also in neighboring Senegal. They were instrumental in setting up branches in Dakar, Rufisque, and Thies, in widely disseminating information about Garvey's program, and in collecting subscriptions for his schemes. After nervously scrutinizing the UNIA's activities for some months, the French authorities had in 1922 deported some of the Sierra Leoneans in question. To the British

Consul-General in Dakar the French move presented a curious spectacle of the UNIA, presumably an anti-European movement originating in the United States, indulgently tolerated in four British colonies, and sternly repressed in eleven French dependencies.[68] . . .

In 1920 Garvey dispatched Elie Garcia to consult the Liberian Government about colonization possibilities for New World Negroes. . . . [The UNIA] promised to do everything possible to help Liberia liquidate its debt to foreign governments. On June 14 Edwin Barclay, Secretary of State, writing to Garcia at the behest of President Charles D. B. King, stated that his government "appreciating as they do the aims of your organization as outlined by you, have no hesitancy in assuring you that they will afford the Association every facility legally possible in effectuating in Liberia its industrial, agricultural and business projects." [69] In March of the same year he had been even more specific when he told UNIA officials that his government would "be glad to have your Association occupy . . . certain settlements already laid out." [70]

On the strength of these commitments and others made by Mayor Johnson, early in 1924 three reportedly well-financed representatives of the UNIA arrived in Liberia to propose a settlement scheme involving three thousand Blacks. The plan was allegedly to establish six communities, two on the British border and four on the French frontier. According to the British Chargé d'Affaires, Francis O'Meara, President King did actually offer a trial concession of five hundred acres, but not in the areas desired by the UNIA.

According to Garvey the delegation had been successful in having a committee formed to receive the repatriated Negroes due to arrive later in 1924. That committee consisted of influential Liberians. The initial settlement was to be established near Cape Palmas on the Cavalla River in Maryland County. While not satisfied on a number of points, the UNIA instituted a campaign to raise two million dollars to construct the first colony.

But in midyear when a rumor was bruited about in Liberia to the effect that three thousand disciples of Garvey would be departing for Monrovia in November, the government abruptly reversed its decision. Barclay, in a letter to Messrs. Elder

Dempster and Co. Ltd., shipping agents, stated categorically that no member of the Garvey movement would be allowed to enter the country.[71] Steamship companies received the same notification. British officials were delighted, to say the least.

When three followers of Garvey did actually disembark on July 25 they were immediately placed under police guard and deported in short order. Later in the year, after the deportation of Reginald C. Hurley, a Barbadian with Garveyite leanings, the Chargé became alarmed over the possibility that other British subjects would enter Sierra Leone as a result of expulsion from Liberia.[72] In October, O'Meara was instructed by cipher telegram to forewarn the governor of any British colony to which deportation of UNIA personnel might be contemplated.

President King in his message to the legislature of Liberia delivered on December 9, 1924 dealt with the Garveyite problem in extremely strong terms. He stated that the apparent intention of the UNIA was "to use Liberia as its base for the dissemination of its propaganda of racial hatred and ill will." The President was particularly disturbed by the "loud and continued boasts of members of that association, in America, to the effect that they had obtained a firm foothold in Liberia, and that the Republic would be used as a *point d'appui* whence the grandiose schemes of their leader . . . would be launched." Therefore it was necessary for the government to take such steps as "would show to our friendly territorial neighbors and the world at large, that Liberia was not in any way associated or in sympathy with any movement . . . which tends to intensify racial feelings of hatred and ill will." President King proceeded to denounce political incendiarism, whether Negro or not, and asserted that the objective of his country was not racialism, but nationalism. Negroes in the United States who desired to settle in the Republic and were willing to take an oath of exclusive allegiance to Liberia would be heartily welcomed. However, and there can be no doubt that King was talking about Garvey here, Liberia's doors would be securely closed to a movement which planned to launch "a race war against friendly states in Africa." [73]

Early in January 1925 when the Liberian president visited Sierra Leone, the governor of that colony applauded his "statesmanship":

Your Excellency by slamming the door on spurious patriots from across the Atlantic, men who sought to make Liberia a focus for racial animosity on this Continent, deservedly earned the gratitude not only of every West African government but of all who have the true welfare of the African at heart.[74]

Edmund Cronon in his classic, *Black Moses*, explained Liberia's volte-face by alluding to the *Liberian News* which averred that both Britain and France coveted the country and Garveyism would provide a convenient excuse for partition.[75] Cronon also commented that the contents of the Garcia report, so disparaging about the Americo-Liberians, "the most despicable element in Liberia," had become known to the government.[76] It is also noteworthy that shortly after Liberia unequivocally disavowed the Garveyite program, an agreement was concluded with the Firestone Rubber Company. Some of the same territory earmarked for development by the UNIA was leased to Firestone for rubber exploitation.[77]

At the time he carried out his research (1950–1951) Cronon could not determine the extent to which England had instigated the Liberian rejection of Garvey. Relevant British official records were closed to him under the old fifty-year rule. Now open for inspection, they do *not* indicate that Britain played any active role. . . .

To offset UNIA propaganda, representatives of the British government in the United States did help to finance a new magazine called *The British West Indian Review*. It was hoped that the publication would affect the interests of West Indians residing in New York, a group which was drawn to the Garvey crusade. The Consul-General even assisted in the preparation of the first number of the magazine which appeared in April 1923.[78]

Generally, it may be said that as apprehensive as the British were about the destructive impact that Garvey might have on the Empire, they felt that the United States government was chiefly responsible for him within its borders. UNIA activities in British colonies or in countries where British interests were vitally involved were another matter. Garvey's *Negro World* was banned in many dependencies; and members of the UNIA were denied entry to others. Just days after Garvey was convicted in June

1923 for using the mails to defraud investors in the Black Star Line, the Foreign Office began to predict his moves after imprisonment. If, after the expiration of his term, Garvey applied for a passport to travel to any British West African colonies, facilities were not to be granted. Ironically, Garvey, the passionate apostle of "back-to-Africanism," never did set foot on African soil.

Garvey would doubtlessly have been amused by the way in which British officials impugned his motives. One minuted in 1923 that "it is more than suspected that Garvey's efforts . . . are not without considerable financial profit to himself and his immediate associates." [79] As previously mentioned, the governor of British Honduras saw Germany as the evil force behind Garveyism. Others claimed that the UNIA was linked with the "Wobblies," the International Workers of the World.[80] In the judgment of one observer, Garvey's paper attacked Britain "with a malignity reminiscent of the *Irish World*." [81] Clearly, *Negro World* malignity was no greater than that of an official who lamented in 1924 about Garvey: "It's a pity the cannibals do not get hold of this man." [82]

Diehard champions of the erstwhile British Empire might well share those intemperate sentiments for the reverberations of Garveyism are still being felt. *Mzee* Jomo Kenyatta, putative leader of the Mau Mau and today President of an independent Kenya, once related to C. L. R. James "how in 1921 Kenya nationalists, unable to read, would gather round a reader of Garvey's newspaper, the *Negro World*, and listen to an article two or three times. Then they would run various ways through the forest, carefully to repeat the whole, which they had memorised, to Africans hungry for some doctrine which lifted them from the servile consciousness in which Africans lived." [83]

On the eve of independence Kwame Nkrumah acknowledged Ghana's debt to Marcus Garvey.[84] And in his autobiography Nkrumah stated that Garvey's *Philosophy and Opinions* did more to fire his enthusiasm than any other book.[85] James Coleman in his book *Nigeria: Background to Nationalism* has written that: "Many themes in latter-day Nigerian nationalism have been cast in the spirit if not in the exact words of Garvey." [86] Garveyite ideas deeply impressed Nigerians who were involved in proto-nationalistic organizations such as the Nigerian Youth Movement and the National Congress of British West Africa.

Ten years after his death, the Kingston *Gleaner* stated:

> . . . it would be true to say of Jamaica, and to a lesser extent of the other British West Indies, that national consciousness received its main impetus, if it was not actually born, from the racial movement associated with the still revered Marcus Garvey.[87]

Fittingly, a bust of Garvey now graces King George VI Memorial Park in Kingston and a thoroughfare is named in his honor. His remains were disinterred and taken to Jamaica in 1964.[88]

Today in England itself Garvey is lauded, even deified, by Black Power advocates from the West Indies and Africa. In a very real sense, as far as the British Empire is concerned Garveyism has triumphed. Whitehall had had good reason to be worried.

Some Aspects of
the Political Ideas
of Marcus Garvey

BY TONY MARTIN

I

The political ideas of Marcus Garvey contained all the classic elements of success. They were sophisticated and complex and based on wide practical experience and deep study. Yet in their main essentials they could be expounded simply enough to be easily grasped by the mass of oppressed Black people. Upon these ideas were built the most successful Pan-African organization in the history of the race, and as we of the present generation continue the historic quest for the liberation of our people a close examination of the ideas of Garvey must of necessity repay the effort.

Central to Garvey's ideas was the concept of God. This is an aspect of Garveyism which sits uneasily on the consciousness of the present generation. Thus Garvey's motto "One God! One Aim! One Destiny!" is nowadays rendered "One People! One Aim! One Destiny!" There is nothing necessarily wrong with this change, and it probably faithfully represents a well-founded disenchantment with Christian religion based on the experience of centuries.

This apparent departure from an important tenet of Garveyism is, however, less of a departure from the original use of the concept of God in Garveyism than would appear at first sight. For Garvey was also an avowed enemy of the institutional church, but faced with the overwhelming importance of God and religion in the lives of Black people, and mindful of his own familiarity with the Christian religion, he seems to have preferred to use the idea of religion while skillfully reinterpreting it for use as an agent of liberation. In other words, faced with the choice of launching a frontal assault against religion on the one hand, and co-opting it for the struggle for nationhood on the other, he preferred the latter. By this stratagem he was presented with a ready-made vehicle which was already familiar to potential Garveyites.

The God of Garveyism did not have too much in common with the God of the rest of Christendom. The God of Isaac and Jacob was cool for those who believed in Isaac and Jacob, he expounded, but God for Garveyites was "the God of Africa, Great and Almighty." Furthermore, as Garvey explained, "whilst our God has no color, yet it is human to see everything through one's own spectacles . . ." He was therefore a Black God.

Furthermore, the God of Garvey was a God of self-reliance. Instead of telling Black people to be meek and mild he told them that they would have to sacrifice and struggle for their freedom, or perish. Garvey was fond of quoting Napoleon to the effect that God is on the side of the stronger battalion. The God of Garvey preoccupied himself with the spiritual side of man's dual nature. He would not presume to interfere in the affairs of men's bodies. As Garvey summed it up in 1937 (at the same time taking a sly dig at Father Divine),

> We are not going to get it [freedom] by worrying God about it, because HE is not a political agent of anybody. He is not a surveyor. God has given you the character to get anything you want without playing God, and there is only one man playing God, and that is Father Divine. We are not going to play God, we are just going to play man. What man has done we are going to do.

Later that same year at a UNIA convention in Toronto, Garvey explained that while he was a believer in religion "when it is

delivered in the proper way," he was nevertheless not an
advocate of that religion. "I," he said, "have selected the job to
save the bodies of men because I believe it is as necessary to save
the body as the soul, and if God didn't intend that he never
would have made man with a body."

Garvey's theory of the separation of functions between God
and man led logically to a ruthless advocacy of Social Darwinism.
His whole attitude to liberation could be summed up in a
sentence from an issue of the *Blackman* of 1938: "It is a crime to
be a fool." And since it was a crime to be a fool, then Black
people who preferred to live in ignorance rather than bestir
themselves could not justifiably blame the white man for their
woes. Garvey may appear to some to have overstated this point,
but it is a point which has always had to be overstated to shake
oppressed people out of the lethargy of subjugation.

The doctrine of self-reliance inevitably emerged as the criterion by which Garvey judged other leaders of the race. Thus,
although he certainly did not agree with every aspect of Booker
T. Washington's program, he did consider the UNIA as the
continuation, on a higher level, of some positive aspects of
Washington's program. Indeed he went further and asserted that
no one since Washington (except, of course, for the UNIA) had
come up with "a positive and practical uplift programme for the
masses—North or South."

His admiration for the self-help aspects of Washington's
philosophy were matched by a deprecation of the dependence on
white liberal sustenance as characterized at that time by W. E. B.
Du Bois. In Du Bois he saw a Black man who had been educated
and sustained by white philanthropy. He went so far as to suggest
that if Du Bois and Garvey could both start from scratch again
Garvey would inevitably outdistance Du Bois, for Garvey was a
self-made man. And when Du Bois most unfortunately ridiculed
Garvey's Liberty Hall while praising other Black-occupied (but,
unlike Liberty Hall, white-owned) buildings, Garvey was quick to
emphasize the flaw in his adversary's argument:

> This shows the character of the man—he has absolutely no respect
> and regard for independent Negro effort but that which is
> supported by white charity and philanthropy, and why so? Because
> he himself was educated by charity and kept by philanthropy.

Father Divine, too, was judged by the yardstick of self-reliance. While refraining on one occasion from an outright attack (he was careful to emphasize that his information was secondhand and that he had reason to know the inaccuracies of the lying propaganda against race leaders), he expressed concern over the white support which was reputed to be propping up this new Harlem phenomenon.

But the leader who, together with Du Bois, was the recipient of the severest attacks on this score was Haile Selassie, emperor of Ethiopia. Much of Garvey's political efforts in England during the last years of his life were taken up with the question of the invasion of that country in 1935 by the Italian Fascists under Mussolini, whom Garvey poetically characterized as "the Italian dog," which line was duly made to rhyme with another calling him a "violent hog." Garvey frequently bemoaned the circumstance that Haile Selassie had prayed and trusted to God while Mussolini, even though his Fascist hordes had been blessed by the Pope for good measure, preferred to place his emphasis on modern technology and thorough training.

There can be no doubt that Garvey's criticisms of the race were harsh and uncompromising. But this was a harshness born of love. For Garvey the genocide practiced against the Indians in North America and elsewhere in the hemisphere, as well as the disappearance of African populations in South American countries where the race had formerly been numerous, were indications of what could happen to African populations in the United States and elsewhere, should they be lulled for too long into complacency. There was only one method of self-preservation:

> The Negro must make his own material life. The weeping, sobbing, pining, cringing Negro must ultimately die. If he doesn't kill himself his environment will kill him. Following the Darwinian theory of the "survival of the fittest," every creature that is too puny, too weak, too imbecilic, must ultimately go down before the superior species, even though the creature be man.

This is why, too, he sometimes preferred the cold reality of the Ku Klux Klan (though it would be wrong to call him a Klansman, as his enemies did, or to suggest that he condoned any atrocities perpetrated by this group) to the smooth flattery of would-be liberals. For the Klan at least might force Black people into a realization of the real dangers which faced them. In any case, if white people felt like asserting their authority over their environment they could hardly be blamed for this: "I am not criticizing the white people. In fact, I am criticizing the Black man. I am a queer critic, but I am a logical one."

Garvey, obviously, was about the business of building a Black nation. And as such he was a firm believer in the primacy of race over other considerations making for cohesiveness. "The Ethiopian," he reasoned, "cannot change his skin; and we shall not." His thesis was that the universally oppressed African people of the world would have, as their primary objective, to emancipate themselves as a race. And this would only be feasible in terms of a program built upon racial solidarity. And while Garvey did not completely dismiss the progressive elements of other races he had little patience with arrogant racists of alien races who pretended to have the interests of African people at heart while persecuting their leaders. In his last Liberty Hall speech before his incarceration in the Tombs prison he expressed amusement at the fact that his persecutor, the district attorney, "said that he was more interested in Negroes than Marcus Garvey." Garvey was incredulous. "It is a lie for any Jew to say he is more interested in Negroes than Negroes are in themselves. It is an unnatural lie to talk about one race being more interested in another race than that race is interested in itself."

For Garvey a race (and particularly an oppressed race) was more than just a race. It was a *political unit*. (These were his words). It was largely for this reason, and not for any of the ridiculous reasons advanced by some commentators, that Garvey hated the divisiveness introduced into the race by some elements among those of lighter hue. It was no case, as has been alleged, of a simplistic transference of attitudes developed in the West Indies to an alien context where the objective situation was different. Instead, Garvey saw, in color-caste manifestations such as the "Blue Vein Society," a trend which, if left unchecked, would culminate in the pronounced aristocracy of light skin which existed in the islands, and which was undeniably present in the United States, though, in his opinion, to a lesser degree.

Garvey justifiably claimed a portion of the credit for the

appearance, in the 1920's, of the so-called New Negro, new, that is, in his resolve to retaliate massively against the lynchers and oppressors of the race. In the field of artistic endeavor the New Negro is remembered for what has been dubbed the "Harlem Renaissance." This so-called renaissance witnessed an efflorescence of literary and other artistic work with no real parallel before the late 1960's. But Garvey, possibly alone among important leaders of the race in that period, was able, because of his deep racial pride, to identify a nagging contradiction in the literary outpourings of the renaissance. He expressed his concern in a *Negro World* editorial of 1928:

> Our race, within recent years, has developed a new group of writers who have been prostituting their intelligence, under the direction of the white man, to bring out and show up the worst traits of our people.

The immediate cause of this editorial was Claude McKay's *Home to Harlem*, which Garvey described as "a damnable libel against the Negro." The 1930's found Garvey once more in a dissenting minority on a similar subject. This time it was Paul Robeson who incurred his displeasure for acting in productions such as *Emperor Jones*, *Sanders of the River*, *Stevedore*, and others which showed the Black man as a savage or a laughable idiot. For Garvey it was not sufficient for the Black artist to succeed in the white man's world. He had to go beyond that and place his artistic ability at the disposal of his struggling race, a struggling race which could not afford the luxury of its most acclaimed representatives being used to reinforce negative stereotypes inflicted upon the race.

Garvey, therefore, believed in the primacy of race as a focal point in the liberation of Black people. But to say this is to leave much unsaid. For Garvey, despite his firm commitment to a struggle in racial terms, seems to have largely avoided the reactionary pitfalls of cultural nationalism and Negritude. We can hardly imagine Garvey saying, like the poet of Negritude, "Hurrah for those who have never invented anything." And we could scarcely conceive of Garvey reveling, like the latter-day high priests of Negritude, in the supposed superiority of the emotionalism of the so-called Negro over the precise technology of the Anglo-Saxons. Fanon called this "banal exoticism" and Garvey would have agreed. For Garvey the Black man "must cast off his superstition, sentimentality and emotionalism, and . . . become a realist in a world where men depend upon organized force and strength . . ."

Though Garvey kept up a running battle with the class doctrines of the Communists (about which more anon) he, unlike some of the exoticists of Negritude, had no illusions about the realities of class distinctions among Black people. Replying to an article written by Du Bois in the *Century* magazine, Garvey said,

> Admitting that Marcus Garvey was born poor, he never encouraged a hatred for the people of his kind or class, but to the contrary devoted his life to the improvement and higher development *of that class within the race* which has been struggling under the disadvantage that Du Bois himself portrays in his article [emphasis mine].

Garvey's writings and speeches are full of similar sentiments. In the wider context of Black versus white America, his was a race struggle, but within the confines of the race he was simultaneously engaged in a bitter class struggle. It must not be forgotten that his first recorded militant struggle was as the leader of a strike against the boss class of Jamaica, and far from inducing in him a distrust of working-class organizations, as his American biographer asserts, this incident set the tone for his entire career. As late as 1930, after his deportation from the United States, we find him forming a "Workers and Laborers Association" in Jamaica and he was robbed of victory at the polls (for the Jamaica Legislative Council) only by the fact that the British imperialists still deprived the Black masses of the vote under the guise of "property qualifications" legislation.

Garvey's enemies were well aware of his threat to entrenched privilege, even within the race. Amy Jacques Garvey quoted his Black opponent in the 1930 elections to the Jamaica Legislative Council as saying, apropos of Garvey's demand for minimum-wage legislation and the eight-hour day, "Could the smaller people who had to employ labor send such an impossible man to the Council?" The same fear of Garvey's arousal of the Black masses can be seen through the warped reasonings of the eight traitors to the race who organized the "Garvey Must Go" campaign that resulted in his deportation. In their letter to the Attorney General of the United States they claimed that the UNIA was extremely dangerous since "it naturally attracts an even lower type of cranks, crooks and racial bigots, among whom suggestibility to violent crime is much greater." The letter also characterized Garvey's followers as "the most primitive and ignorant element of West Indian and American Negroes." Charles S. Johnson in an editorial in *Opportunity* magazine expressed a similar uneasiness at the phenomenon of the Black workers, peasants and lumpenproletarians on the move. He spoke inanely of "Those dark, dumb masses to whom he has offered an opiate for their hopeless helplessness . . . a fantastic world beyond the cold grasp of logic and reason. . . ."

And for his complete dedication to the Black masses Garvey was repaid by a loyalty which astounded friend and foe alike. The very shareholders he was supposed to have defrauded in an indictment of the United States government in their alleged solicitousness after the welfare of Black people, were the ones who in 1923 raised $15,000 bail money in cash; who subscribed enough money to launch a new steamship company while the case involving the Black Star Line was pending on appeal; and who finally paid the costs of that appeal. And in 1926, with Garvey in jail, 150,000 of his followers turned out in Harlem to parade behind his portrait and ceremonial robes. The Black man was as ready in those days as he will ever be. Queen Mother Moore even recalls an occasion in Louisiana when Garvey's followers forced the local police to let Garvey speak by dint of a massive display of armaments.

Despite the class basis of Garvey's movement his relations with Communists, Black and white, were frequently stormy. His ideas on the subject of Communism were complex and undoubtedly influenced by the particular Communists with whom he came into contact. In the first place, he seems to have had a deep admiration for Lenin and Trotsky. This obviously did not necessarily mean an endorsement of all the principles of Marxism-Leninism. There is no evidence that he made any deep study of these doctrines anyhow. His wife Amy Jacques Garvey, in her biography, suggested that his admiration for Lenin was based on the fact that "Nicolai Lenin, as a leader of the masses of Russia deserved respect for what, in all sincerity, he tried to do for them. Said he, 'the masses need peace, bread, liberty and land!' " These were clearly the same things which Garvey was fighting for. Garvey was also on record as suggesting that Communism was all right for Russia, though not necessarily for other areas. Yet he was not unmindful of the similarity in aims between the revolutionary movements among oppressed white people and his own movement. In a front page editorial in the *Negro World* he even suggested that the Black masses could learn from white revolutionary movements:

> The royal and privileged classes of idlers who used to tyrannize and oppress the humble hordes of mankind are now experiencing difficulty in holding their control over the sentiment of the people . . . the Negro has been a slave to the white man's ideas for three hundred years, and the hour has now struck for him to imitate the masses of white society and cut away from royalty and privilege.

His admiration for Lenin and Trotsky was matched by the fact that his denunciations of Communism frequently included some such qualification as "as taught in America." And certainly his experiences with Communists in America were not calculated to encourage his confidence in the movement. Some, such as the prominent Harlem radical W. A. Domingo, had been former members of the UNIA who were expelled on doctrinal grounds. Many other less well-known Black Communists were infiltrated into the organization, and Communist organs such as the *Daily Worker* made no secret of their ambition to convert the Garvey movement to the path of joint action between Black and white toilers under the leadership of a Communist organization.

Another element in Garvey's attitude to American Communism was a very real fear of repression. This fear was sometimes repeated by leader-writers and columnists in the *Negro World*. A fact which seems to have been forgotten by analysts of Garvey's movement is that the years between Garvey's arrival in the United States (1916) and his incarceration in 1925 witnessed a savage repression of white Communists and other radicals which has no parallel outside of the McCarthy era. It was in this period that the revolutionary Industrial Workers of the World were bludgeoned into ineffectiveness by a combination of wholesale

arrests, deportations, pitched battles sometimes resembling civil
war and other means. This was also the period of the notorious
Palmer Raids, when Communists were rounded up by the
thousands. The question which therefore recurred in Garveyite
circles was this: If to be Black meant to be lynched and
exploited, and to be a Communist meant to be ruthlessly
suppressed and deported, then what would be the fate of a large
movement that was both Black and avowedly Communist? And
would the white radicals remain steadfast when, as would
inevitably happen, Black revolutionaries were called upon to
bear the brunt of official repression?

Garvey also seriously doubted whether white workers in
America and Europe were ready to forgo their racial privilege for
class interests on any large scale. He argued, like Lenin, that
white workers enjoyed a relatively favorable condition at the
expense of oppressed Black toilers all over the world. These same
workers, he pointed out, comprised the lynching parties and
armies of oppression which spread devastation in African communities, at home and abroad. Stalin's rapprochement with
imperialism in the 1930's encouraged him in his view that
Communism might be perverted by white opportunism. (Many
Black Communists, notably George Padmore, broke with Moscow, though not always with Marxism, in this period.)

Nevertheless, Communist attempts to infiltrate and capture
Garvey's movement must be seen as a tacit acknowledgment of
the success of Garveyism, and the meteoric rise of Garveyism did
not fail to teach a few lessons to these rival claimants for the
allegiance of Black workers and peasants. So that by 1928, at the
urging of Stalin, Lenin's thesis on the right of self-determination
for national minorities was officially accepted as applicable to the
Afro-American, and thereafter the demand for a separate Black
state became official Communist Party policy. Shortly afterwards
the demand for a redeemed Africa was seen to make its way into
the demands of the American Negro Labor Congress, a violently
anti-Garvey organization closely aligned to the Moscow line
(despite occasional disclaimers to the contrary in their organizational press).

And one of the most eloquent tributes to Garvey and his
movement came in an official statement of the Workers (Communist) Party of America shortly after his imprisonment in 1925.

This statement demanded his unconditional release without
deportation, as well as the unhampered furthering of links
between Afro-America and Africa. It read, in part,

> The Workers [Communist] Party, composed of Negro workers as
> well as white workers, and standing for the solidarity and
> emancipation of the working class on terms of equality of all races,
> cannot stand idly by while the capitalist dictatorship attempts to
> destroy a mass organization of the exploited Negro people.

And Communist Robert Minor had noted a year earlier that "The
lickspittles of capitalism in Washington do not love Marcus
Garvey. This alone ought to make anyone of the working class
think twice before condemning the man."

The central idea in Garvey's philosophy was the idea of
nationhood—the building of a strong independent Black nation
which would take its rightful place in the comity of nations.
Nationhood entailed first of all changing the self-image of the
Black man. All the activities of the Universal Negro Improvement Association were designed ultimately to serve this purpose.
And this was expensive business. In the words of Amy Jacques
Garvey in the *Negro World*, "Nation building is our program, not
building apartment houses or churches, that's too small a job for
us."

Nationhood inevitably involved the Garvey slogan of "Africa
for the Africans—those at home and those abroad." But the exact
significance which Africa occupied in the thought of Garvey is
the subject of controversy. Garvey's utterances on the subject
were ambiguous enough to lead many to conclude that he
advocated a wholesale return of New World Africans, and
particularly Afro-Americans, to the Motherland. But two people
who were in a better position to know than most—Amy Jacques
Garvey and Bishop George Alexander McGuire, head of the
African Orthodox Church, both explained that Garvey never
intended anything more than "select colonization by pioneering
people."

Whatever the scale of migration, Garvey's idea was never to
neglect the New World for the continent. For an important
element in his desire to make Africa strong was the fact that "A
strong man is strong everywhere." So a strong Africa would of

necessity redound to the good of New World Africans. This argument was resuscitated by Malcolm X and given practical expression in the linkages he established with the Organization of African Unity. It is still enjoying currency among our own generation of Pan-Africanists.

Garvey's belief in the necessity to fight for political gains in America and elsewhere was given expression in the Universal Political Union, which sought to use UNIA votes to the greatest advantage. He even commended the example of Afro-Americans to Africans elsewhere:

> The American white man has established his system of politics around self . . . The sensible Negroes, therefore, have realized that it is only by playing the white man's politics in America as he plays it, can they get anything out of it, and so they are playing it with a vengeance and we compliment them.

Marcus Garvey loved Black people. He sacrificed his health, his money, his family life and his liberty for the cause of Black people. He is said to have wept after witnessing the sadly depleted ranks of Black veterans marching down Lenox Avenue after World War I. The thought of these men without a land to call their own, called upon to make the supreme sacrifice in a cause which was not theirs, and the reward for which would often be a lynching while still in uniform, was too much for him. So Garvey wept.

But like all Black leaders of any importance in the struggle for human dignity, Marcus Garvey could not bring himself to emulate the blind hatred of the oppressors of his race. Said he:

> The Negro isn't going to revenge anybody. He has never murdered anybody in bed, although the white man has taught him all these vicious and wicked things . . . it is the white man who is going to injure himself. He is about destroying himself by his system of injustice, not only to others but to the different groups of his own race.

The Declaration of Rights of the Negro Peoples of the World*

* Issued at the first International Convention of the Universal Negro Improvement Association, New York City, 1920.

THE FOLLOWING DECLARATION was signed by 122 convention delegates. Some fifty signers went on to take leading roles in the affairs of the Association.

Among the signers were Garvey's secretaries, Janie Jenkins and Mary E. Johnson; J. J. Cranston, head of the Baltimore division; Reynold F. Austin, head of the Brooklyn division; the Jamaican delegates Frederick Samuel Ricketts, Carrie M. Ashford and James Young; heads of Canadian divisions, Richard Edward Riley, T. H. Golden and I. Braithwaite; Edward Alfred Taylor of Pittsburgh; Frank O. Raines of New York; Shedrick Williams of Cleveland; Emily Christmas Kinch of Liberia; Prince Alfred McConney; and UNIA field representative Sara Branch.

PREAMBLE

Be it Resolved, That the Negro people of the world, through their chosen representatives in convention assembled in Liberty Hall, in the City of New York and United States of America, from August 1 to August 31, in the year of our Lord, one thousand nine hundred and twenty, protest against the wrongs and injustices they are suffering at the hands of their white brethren, and state what they deem their fair and just rights, as well as the treatment they propose to demand of all men in the future.

We complain:

1. That nowhere in the world, with few exceptions, are black men accorded equal treatment with white men, although in the same situation and circumstances, but on the contrary, are discriminated against and denied the common rights due to human beings for no other reason than their race and color.

We are not willingly accepted as guests in the public hotels and inns of the world for no other reason than our race and color.

II. In certain parts of the United States of America our race is denied the right of public trial accorded to other races when accused of crime, but are lynched and burned by mobs, and such brutal and inhuman treatment is even practised upon our women.

III. That European nations have parcelled out among them and taken possession of nearly all of the continent of Africa, and the natives are compelled to surrender their lands to aliens and are treated in most instances like slaves.

IV. In the southern portion of the United States of America, although citizens under the Federal Constitution, and in some states almost equal to the whites in population and are qualified land owners and taxpayers, we are, nevertheless, denied all voice in the making and administration of the laws and are taxed without representation by the state governments, and at the same time compelled to do military service in defense of the country.

V. On the public conveyances and common carriers in the Southern portion of the United States we are jim-crowed and compelled to accept separate and inferior accommodations, and made to pay the same fare charged for first-class accommodations, and our families are often humiliated and insulted by drunken white men who habitually pass through the jim-crow cars going to the smoking car.

VI. The physicians of our race are denied the right to attend their patients while in the public hospitals of the cities and states where they reside in certain parts of the United States.

Our children are forced to attend inferior separate schools for shorter terms than white children and the public school funds are unequally divided between the white and colored schools.

VII. We are discriminated against and denied an equal chance to earn wages for the support of our families, and in many instances are refused admission into labor unions, and nearly everywhere are paid smaller wages than white men.

VIII. In Civil Service and departmental offices we are everywhere discriminated against and made to feel that to be a black man in Europe, America and the West Indies is equivalent to begin an outcast and a leper among the races of men, no matter what the character and attainments of the black man may be.

IX. In the British and other West Indian Islands and colonies,

Negroes are secretly and cunningly discriminated against, and denied those fuller rights of government to which white citizens are appointed, nominated and elected.

X. That our people in those parts are forced to work for lower wages than the average standard of white men and are kept in conditions repugnant to good civilized tastes and customs.

XI. That the many acts of injustice against members of our race before the courts of law in the respective islands and colonies are of such nature as to create disgust and disrespect for the white man's sense of justice.

XII. Against all such inhuman, unchristian and uncivilized treatment we here and now emphatically protest, and invoke the condemnation of all mankind.

In order to encourage our race all over the world and to stimulate it to a higher and grander destiny, we demand and insist on the following Declaration of Rights:

1. Be it known to all men that whereas, all men are created equal and entitled to the rights of life, liberty and the pursuit of happiness, and because of this we, the duly elected representatives of the Negro peoples of the world, invoking the aid of the just and Almighty God do declare all men, women and children of our blood throughout the world free citizens, and do claim them as free citizens of Africa, the Motherland of all Negroes.

2. That we believe in the supreme authority of our race in all things racial; that all things are created and given to man as a common possession; that there should be an equitable distribution and apportionment of all such things, and in consideration of the fact that as a race we are now deprived of those things that are morally and legally ours, we believe it right that all such things should be acquired and held by whatsoever means possible.

3. That we believe the Negro, like any other race, should be governed by the ethics of civilization, and, therefore, should not be deprived of any of those rights or privileges common to other human beings.

4. We declare that Negroes, wheresoever they form a community among themselves, should be given the right to elect their

own representatives to represent them in legislatures, courts of law, or such institutions as may exercise control over that particular community.

5. We assert that the Negro is entitled to even-handed justice before all courts of law and equity in whatever country he may be found, and when this is denied him on account of his race or color such denial is an insult to the race as a whole and should be resented by the entire body of Negroes.

6. We declare it unfair and prejudicial to the rights of Negroes in communities where they exist in considerable numbers to be tried by a judge and jury composed entirely of an alien race, but in all such cases members of our race are entitled to representation on the jury.

7. We believe that any law or practice that tends to deprive any African of his land or the privileges of free citizenship within his country is unjust and immoral, and no native should respect any such law or practice.

8. We declare taxation without representation unjust and tyrannous, and there should be no obligation on the part of the Negro to obey the levy of a tax by any law-making body from which he is excluded and denied representation on account of his race and color.

9. We believe that any law especially directed against the Negro to his detriment and singling him out because of his race or color is unfair and immoral, and should not be respected.

10. We believe all men entitled to common human respect, and that our race should in no way tolerate any insults that may be interpreted to mean disrespect to our color.

11. We deprecate the use of the term "nigger" as applied to Negroes, and demand that the word "Negro" be written with a capital "N."

12. We believe that the Negro should adopt every means to protect himself against barbarous practices inflicted upon him because of color.

13. We believe in the freedom of Africa for the Negro people of the world, and by the principle of Europe for the Europeans and Asia for the Asiatics, we also demand Africa for the Africans at home and abroad.

14. We believe in the inherent right of the Negro to possess himself of Africa, and that his possession of same shall not be regarded as an infringement on any claim or purchase made by any race or nation.

15. We strongly condemn the cupidity of those nations of the world who, by open aggression or secret schemes, have seized the territories and inexhaustible natural wealth of Africa, and we place on record our most solemn determination to reclaim the treasures and possession of the vast continent of our forefathers.

16. We believe all men should live in peace one with the other, but when races and nations provoke the ire of other races and nations by attempting to infringe upon their rights, war becomes inevitable, and the attempt in any way to free one's self or protect one's rights or heritage becomes justifiable.

17. Whereas, the lynching, by burning, hanging or any other means, of human beings is a barbarous practice, and a shame and disgrace to civilization, and we therefore declare any country guilty of such atrocities outside the pale of civilization.

18. We protest against the atrocious crime of whipping, flogging and overworking the native tribes of Africa and Negroes everywhere. These are methods that should be abolished, and all means should be taken to prevent a continuance of such brutal practices.

19. We protest against the atrocious practice of shaving the heads of Africans, especially of African women or individuals of Negro blood, when placed in prison as a punishment for crime by an alien race.

20. We protest against segregated districts, separate public conveyances, industrial discrimination, lynchings and limitations of political privileges of any Negro citizen in any part of the world on account of race, color or creed, and will exert our full influence and power against all such.

21. We protest against any punishment, inflicted upon a Negro with severity, as against lighter punishment inflicted upon another of an alien race for like offense, as an act of prejudice and injustice, and should be resented by the entire race.

22. We protest against the system of education in any country

where Negroes are denied the same privileges and advantages as other races.

23. We declare it inhuman and unfair to boycott Negroes from industries and labor in any part of the world.

24. We believe in the doctrine of the freedom of the press, and we therefore emphatically protest against the suppression of Negro newspapers and periodicals in various parts of the world, and call upon Negroes everywhere to employ all available means to prevent such suppression.

25. We further demand free speech universally for all men.

26. We hereby protest against the publication of scandalous and inflammatory articles by an alien press tending to create racial strife and the exhibition of picture films showing the Negro as a cannibal.

27. We believe in the self-determination of all peoples.

28. We declare for the freedom of religious worship.

29. With the help of Almighty God, we declare ourselves the sworn protectors of the honor and virtue of our women and children, and pledge our lives for their protection and defense everywhere, and under all circumstances from wrongs and outrages.

30. We demand the right of unlimited and unprejudiced education for ourselves and our posterity forever.

31. We declare that the teaching in any school by alien teachers to our boys and girls, that the alien race is superior to the Negro race, is an insult to the Negro people of the world.

32. Where Negroes form a part of the citizenry of any country, and pass the civil service examination of such country, we declare them entitled to the same consideration as other citizens as to appointments in such civil service.

33. We vigorously protest against the increasingly unfair and unjust treatment accorded Negro travellers on land and sea by the agents and employees of railroad and steamship companies and insist that for equal fare we receive equal privileges with travellers of other races.

34. We declare it unjust for any country, state or nation to enact laws tending to hinder and obstruct the free immigration of Negroes on account of their race and color.

35. That the right of the Negro to travel unmolested throughout the world be not abridged by any person or persons, and all Negroes are called upon to give aid to a fellow Negro when thus molested.

36. We declare that all Negroes are entitled to the same right to travel over the world as other men.

37. We hereby demand that the governments of the world recognize our leader and his representatives chosen by the race to look after the welfare of our people under such governments.

38. We demand complete control of our social institutions without interference by any alien race or races.

39. That the colors, Red, Black and Green, be the colors of the Negro race.

40. Resolved, that the anthem "Ethiopia, Thou Land of Our Fathers," etc., shall be the anthem of the Negro race.

THE UNIVERSAL ETHIOPIAN ANTHEM
(poem by Burrell and Ford)

Ethiopia, thou land of our fathers,
Thou land where the gods loved to be,
As storm cloud at night suddenly gathers
Our armies come rushing to thee.
We must in the fight be victorious
When swords are thrust outward to gleam;
For us will the vict'ry be glorious
When led by the red, black and green.

Chorus:
Advance, advance to victory,
Let Africa be free;
Advance to meet the foe
With the might
Of the red, the black and the green.

II

Ethiopia, the tyrant's falling,
Who smote thee upon thy knees,
And thy children are lustily calling

From over the distant seas.
Jehovah, the Great One has heard us,
Has noted our sighs and our tears,
With His spirit of Love He has stirred us
To be One through the coming years.

CHORUS: Advance, advance, etc.

III

O Jehovah, thou God of the Ages
Grant unto our sons that lead
The wisdom Thou gave to Thy sages
When Israel was sore in need.
Thy voice thro' the dim past has spoken,
Ethiopia shall stretch forth her hand,
By Thee shall all fetters be broken,
And Heav'n bless our dear fatherland.

CHORUS: Advance, advance, etc.

41. We believe that any limited liberty which deprives one of the complete rights and prerogatives of full citizenship is but a modified form of slavery.

42. We declare it an injustice to our people and a serious impediment to the health of the race to deny to competent licensed Negro physicians the right to practice in the public hospitals of the communities in which they reside, for no other reason than their race and color.

43. We call upon the various governments of the world to accept and acknowledge Negro representatives who shall be sent to the said governments to represent the general welfare of the Negro peoples of the world.

44. We deplore and protest against the practice of confining juvenile prisoners in prisons with adults, and we recommend that such youthful prisoners be taught gainful trades under humane supervision.

45. Be it further resolved, that we as a race of people declare the League of Nations null and void as far as the Negro is concerned, in that it seeks to deprive Negroes of their liberty.

46. We demand of all men to do unto us as we would do unto

them, in the name of justice; and we cheerfully accord to all men all the rights we claim herein for ourselves.

47. We declare that no Negro shall engage himself in battle for an alien race without first obtaining the consent of the leader of the Negro people of the world, except in a matter of national self-defense.

48. We protest against the practice of drafting Negroes and sending them to war with alien forces without proper training, and demand in all cases that Negro soldiers be given the same training as the aliens.

49. We demand that instructions given Negro children in schools include the subject of "Negro History," to their benefit.

50. We demand a free and unfettered commercial intercourse with all the Negro people of the world.

51. We declare for the absolute freedom of the seas for all peoples.

52. We demand that our duly accredited representatives be given proper recognition in all leagues, conferences, conventions or courts of international arbitration wherever human rights are discussed.

53. We proclaim the 31st day of August of each year to be an international holiday to be observed by all Negroes.

54. We want all men to know we shall maintain and contend for the freedom and equality of every man, woman and child of our race, with our lives, our fortunes and our sacred honor.

These rights we believe to be justly ours and proper for the protection of the Negro race at large, and because of this belief, we, on behalf of the four hundred million Negroes of the world, do pledge herein the sacred blood of the race in defense, and we hereby subscribe our names as a guarantee of the truthfulness and faithfulness hereof in the presence of Almighty God, on the 13th day of August, in the year of our Lord one thousand nine hundred and twenty.

Notes

INTRODUCTION

1. Roi Ottley, *New World A-Coming*, World Publishing Co., Cleveland and New York, 1971.

2. W. E. B. Du Bois, *Dusk of Dawn: An Essay Toward an Autobiography of Race Concept*, Harcourt, Brace and Company, New York, 1940; Schocken Books, Inc., New York, 1968 (paperback reprint).

3. W. E. B. Du Bois, *Souls of Black Folk*, New American Library, New York, 1969 (paperback reprint).

4. Robert Campbell, *A Pilgrimage to My Motherland: An Account of a Journey Among the Egbas and Yarubas of Central Africa in 1859–60*, republished in *Search for a Place: Black Separation and Africa, 1860*, University of Michigan Press, Ann Arbor (Ann Arbor Paperback), 1971.

5. Dorothy Sterling, *The Making of an Afro-American: Martin Delany*, 1812–1885, Doubleday, New York, 1971.

6. Edwin S. Redkey, *Black Exodus: Black Nationalists and Back-to-Africa Movements, 1890–1910*, Yale University Press, New Haven, Conn., 1969, pages 47–72.

7. W. E. B. Du Bois, *History of the Pan-African Congress*, George Padmore, ed., Hammersmith Bookshop, Ltd., London, 1962, pages 13–15.

8. Vincent Bakpetu Thompson, *Africa and Unity: The Evolution of Pan-Africanism*, Longmans, London and New York, 1969, pages 24–41.

I. THE FORMATIVE YEARS, 1912–1920

1. C. L. R. James, *The Black Jacobins*, Vintage Books Edition, Random House, New York, 1963, pages 396–404.

2. W. E. B. Du Bois, *Dusk of Dawn: An Essay Toward an*

Autobiography of Race Concept, Harcourt, Brace and Company, New York, 1940; Schocken Books, Inc., New York, 1968 (paperback reprint), pages 229–277.

3. *Ibid.*, pages 230–231.

4. Booker T. Washington, *Up from Slavery*, Doubleday, New York, 1933.

5. Edwin S. Redkey, *Black Exodus*, Yale University Press, New Haven, Conn., 1969, pages 24–25.

6. Anne Kelley, *Bishop Henry McNeal Turner, A Political Biography*, graduate paper, Cornell University.

7. Amy Jacques Garvey, *Garvey and Garveyism*, Collier Books, New York, 1970, pages 12–13.

8. Roi Ottley, *New World A-Coming*, World Publishing Co., Cleveland and New York, 1971.

9. Adam Clayton Powell, Jr., *Marching Blacks*, Dial Press, revised version, 1973.

10. Marcus Garvey, *The Philosophy and Opinions of Marcus Garvey*, Amy Jacques Garvey, ed; Atheneum, New York, 1969.

11. W. E. B. Du Bois, *History of the Pan-African Congress*, George Padmore, ed., Hammersmith Bookshop, Ltd., London, 1962, pages 14–15.

12. Garvey, *op. cit.*

13. Sidney King, "A Birth of Freedom," *New World Magazine*, Special Independence Issue, May 5, 1966.

14. P. H. Daly, "Revolution to Republic," *Daily Chronicle, Ltd.*, Georgetown, Guyana, pages 14–22.

15. *Ibid.*

16. *Ibid.*

17. *Ibid.*

18. James Rodway, *History of British Guiana from the Year 1668 to the Present Time*, 3 volumes, reproduction of 1894 edition, Negro University Press.

19. Daly, *op. cit.*, page 13.

20. Gleaner Co., Ltd., *The Gleaner Geography and History of Jamaica* (revised 1967), Jamaica, 1968, pages 40–43.

21. Beatrice Jackson Fleming and Marion Jackson Pryde, *Distinguished Negroes Abroad*, Associated Publishers, Washington, D.C., 1946, pages 181–185.

22. Gleaner Co., *op. cit.*, page 47.

23. C. Roy Reynolds, "Tacky and the Great Slave Rebellion of 1760," *Jamaica Journal*, Quarterly of the Institute of Jamaica, Vol. 6, No. 2, June 1972, pages 5–8.

24. Gleaner Co., *op. cit.*, pages 51–54.

25. Russell L. Adams, *Great Negroes Past and Present*, Afro-American Publishing Co., Inc., Chicago, 1969, pages 16–19.

26. Robert G. Weisbord, "J. Albert Thorne, Back-to-Africanist," *Negro History Bulletin*, Washington, D.C., March 1969.

27. *Daily Gleaner*, January 23, 1935. The report of Garvey's speech stated: "Mr. Garvey cited historical facts to prove how people sought to secure useless revenge . . . and went on to deal with the Car Riot in which innocent persons were shot. He was an eyewitness and was one of two men—Mr. Elliot the photographer being the other—who shielded the Governor of the day from attack." The latter reference was to Governor Sydney Olivier.

28. *New Jamaican*, August 1932.

29. *New Jamaican*, October 26, 1932.

30. Richard Hart, "The Life and Resurrection of Marcus Garvey," *Race*, Vol. IX, No. 2, 1967, page 220.

31. Quoted in Len Nembhard, *Trials and Triumphs of Marcus Garvey*, Kingston, 1940, page 111.

32. "Some Worthy Efforts," *Jamaica Times*, October 17, 1914.

33. The University of Edinburgh. Scotland occupies an especially significant place for other Pan-African figures from the West Indies, most notably Dr. J. Albert Thorne of Barbados and Dr. Theophilus E. S. Scholes of Jamaica. See also, Edward Dixon, "The American Negro in Scotland in the Nineteenth Century," University of Edinburgh, M. Litt. thesis, 1970.

34. Marcus Garvey, "The Negro's Greatest Enemy," *Current History*, September 1923, page 14.

35. The source of greatest information on Duse Mohammed Ali is the recently completed Ph.D. thesis by Ian Duffield of the University of Edinburgh. See also his two articles, "The Business Activities of Duse Mohammed Ali: An Example of the Economic Dimension of Pan-Africanism, 1912–1945," *Journal of the Historical Society of Nigeria*, Vol. IV, No. 4, June 1969, pages 571–600; and "John Eldred Taylor and West African Opposition to Indirect Rule in Nigeria," *African Affairs*, Vol. 70, No. 280, July 1971, pages 252–268.

36. Ian Duffield, in a communication with the author dated October 27, 1971, comments: "I have radically changed my analysis of his book *In the Land of the Pharaohs* since [1968]. I have found that, paradoxically, although it was certainly well received and influential, it was substantially plagiarized from Cromer's *Modern Egypt*, W. S. Blunt's *Secret History of the English Occupation of Egypt*, and Theodore Rothstein's *Egypt's Ruin*. This does not, needless to say,

prevent it from being a work of considerable historical importance, and indeed the best things in it are quite original."

37. For information on the Congress see Michael D. Biddiss, "The Universal Races Congress of 1911," *Race*, Vol. XIII, No. 1, 1971. Its significance for the emergence of early twentieth-century Pan-African consciousness is described in Imanuel Geiss, "Notes on the Development of Pan-Africanism," *Journal of the Historical Society of Nigeria*, Vol. III, No. 4, June 1967, pages 729–730.

38. *African Times and Orient Review* (A weekly Review of African and Oriental Politics, Literature, Finance, and Commerce), London. July 1912–December 1913, as a monthly; March 24, 1914–August 19, 1914, as a weekly; January 1917–October 1918, as a monthly.

39. "*African Times and Orient Review*, and Duse Mohammed Ali," Minutes, November 1917, Colonial Office 554/35, Public Record Office, London.

40. Duffield, "John Eldred Taylor and West African Opposition to Indirect Rule in Nigeria," *op. cit.*, pages 261–262.

41. National Archives, Record Group 165, Records of the War Department, General and Special Staffs, Military Intelligence Division, 10218-261/36, November 22, 1918.

42. National Archives, Record Group 59, Department of State, 811.108G191/3, London, April 6, 1921. The reference to intended libel action against the magazine *World's Work* would have applied most certainly to the article written by Truman Hughes Talley, "Marcus Garvey—The Negro Moses?" Vol. XLI, No. 2, December 1920.

43. Tuskegee Archives, Box 73, Folder 561, letters dated April 4, 1922 and June 20, 1922. The letters never received a reply.

44. Garvey, it would appear, had a special fondness for the "mirror" image contained in the title of the article. He employed the same metaphor in a later article which he wrote shortly after arriving in the United States, "West Indies in the Mirror of Truth," *Champion* Magazine, Chicago, January 1917.

45. From the end of the nineteenth century, sparked by the emergence in Jamaica of Dr. J. Robert Love's "People's Convention" movement, all the early Jamaican protest movements centered their energies on trying to make the "unjust bureaucracy" of colonial rule accountable and responsive to the needs of the people. The West Indies was in reality an administrative dictatorship under Crown Colony rule. Probably the most serious challenge to the domination of the colonial bureaucracy, and one with which Garvey had been involved as a young man, came in the period 1909–1911 with the formation of the National Club under the leadership of S. A. G. Cox, "The People's Sandy," as he

was called. In April 1910 Garvey was elected one of three secretaries of the National Club.

46. Colonial Office 351/IND 18937, Jamaica Register of Correspondence, Public Record Office, London. Unfortunately, the actual letters have been destroyed, leaving only the entries in the Register of Correspondence. One further item listed in the Register may be of some interest. It was dated June 24, 1914, and stated: "Patronage. Garvey, Miss L., Passage to Colony, states her circumstances and asks for assistance to obtain." It is possible that this referred to Garvey's sister, Indiana, who had been working in London in the service of a family around the same time Garvey had gone there.

47. Garvey, "The Negro's Greatest Enemy," *op. cit.*, pages 14–15.

48. Foreign Office 371/9580, Public Record Office, London. Ian Duffield will shortly publish a research paper entitled "The 'Darker Races' in London, 1911–1921," which will undoubtedly shed a great deal of light on the social and political composition of the African and Afro-West Indian community in England during this formative stage in the growth of early Pan-African consciousness. Letter to the author, October 27, 1971.

49. Duffield, "John Eldred Taylor and West African Opposition to Indirect Rule in Nigeria," *op. cit.*, pages 259–260.

50. Magnus J. Sampson, *Gold Coast Men of Affairs*, London, 1937, page 163. See also his *West African Leadership: Public Speeches Delivered by J. E. Casely Hayford*, London, 1951.

51. A useful compendium of Blyden's work has recently been published: Hollis Lynch, ed., *Black Spokesman*, New York, 1971. See also the biography by the same author, *Edward Wilmot Blyden, Pan-Negro Patriot, 1832–1912*, London, 1967. A point of historical interest is the fact that Blyden's most renowned work, *Christianity, Islam, and The Negro Race*, was published in 1887, the year of Garvey's birth.

52. Hayford's proposal for the formation of "Ethiopian Leagues" was based upon his admiration for the precedent of the Irish League, whose principal aim was the preservation of the national language as "the safest and most natural way of national *conservancy* and evolution." [*Ethiopia Unbound*, page 195.]

53. For the impact of Garveyism on the emergence of Gold Coast nationalism, see David Kimble, *A Political History of Ghana: The Rise of Gold Coast Nationalism, 1850–1928*, Oxford, 1963, pages 543–550. For Hayford's speech to the founding conference of the NCBWA see Magnus J. Sampson, *op. cit. The Times of Nigeria*, March 22, 1920, ascribed to the Congress movement the "glorious goal of race free-

dom and race redemption." For a recent historical assessment see G. I. C. Eluwa, "The National Congress of British West Africa: A Study in African Nationalism," *Presence Africaine*, No. 77, 1971, pages 131–149.

54. Kimble, *op. cit.*, page 550.

55. For the first full-length biography, see Christopher Fyfe, *Africanus Horton: West African Scientist and Patriot 1835–1883*, Oxford, 1972.

56. James Africanus Horton, *West African Countries and Peoples 1868*, with an introduction by George Shepperson, Edinburgh, 1969, page xiv.

57. Shepperson provides the following biographical information which strengthens this symbolic aspect: "It appears that, during his stay in Great Britain, he [Horton] began to call himself 'Africanus,' not only adding this to his two other first names, but also, on occasion, using it in place of them. It is clear from the meager records that survive of his Scottish student days that Horton had begun to call himself 'Africanus' by the time he reached Edinburgh . . . This Africanist spirit was revealed further in the preface to his published thesis in which he wrote 'that this Publication may be the means of exciting some interest . . . on behalf of Africa is the sincere wish of AFRICANUS HORTON!' And it will be noted that, while the title page of *West African Countries and Peoples* bears his full name, Horton signed the preface, as he had done in his *Political Economy* pamphlet and as he was to do in subsequent writings, simply as 'Africanus Horton.' " Introduction pages xvi–xvii.

58. James Hunt, "On the Negro's Place in Nature," *Memoirs of the Anthropological Society of London*, 1863–1864, pages 26–27.

59. *Ibid.*, pages 51–52. That it was Hunt whom Africanus Horton had principally in mind in writing his "vindication" cannot be in doubt. The title of Part I of *West African Countries and Peoples* was "The Negro's Place in Nature." Moreover, the pamphlet published three years earlier by Horton, and on which he substantially based the later book, was also directed at the same target, as can be seen in the full title, *Political Economy of British Western Africa; with the requirements of the several colonies and settlements* (THE AFRICAN VIEW OF THE NEGRO'S PLACE IN NATURE), London, 1865. For the proceeding discussions surrounding Hunt's paper, see *The Anthropological Review*, Vol. I, 1863, pages 386–391, and Vol. II, 1864, pages xv–lvi. Along the same line, see also Henry F. J. Guppy, "Notes on the Capabilities of the Negro for Civilisation," *The Anthropological Review*, Vol. II, 1864, pages ccix–ccxvi.

60. W. E. B. Du Bois, in his 1897 address to The American Negro

Academy entitled "The Conservation of Races," stated the problem thus: "The American Negro has always felt an intense personal interest in discussions as to the origins and destinies of races: primarily because back of most discussions of race with which he is familiar, have lurked certain assumptions as to his natural abilities, as to his political, intellectual and moral status, which he felt were wrong. He has, consequently, been led to deprecate and minimize race distinctions, to believe intensively that *out of one blood God created all nations,* and to speak of human brotherhood as though it were the possibility of an already dawning tomorrow."

61. "Universal Negro Improvement Association: Address Delivered by the President at the Annual Meeting," *Daily Gleaner,* August 26, 1915.

62. The original UNIA statement of objects has happily been preserved in the Booker T. Washington Papers, Library of Congress. The statement, along with other correspondence between Garvey and Tuskegee Institute, has in addition been published by Daniel T. Williams in his very useful bibliography, *The Perilous Road of Marcus M. Garvey,* Tuskegee Institute, Alabama, 1969.

63. "Jamaica, Her Needs and the Negro Problem," *Daily Gleaner,* March 29, 1921.

64. Daniel T. Williams, *The Perilous Road of Marcus M. Garvey,* Tuskegee Institute, Alabama, 1969, Garvey to Major R. Moton, "On Visit to Jamaica," February 29, 1916.

65. Colonial Office 137/705, Marcus Garvey to Lewis Harcourt, Secretary of State for the Colonies, September 16, 1914, Public Record Office, London. The following minute, signed by a Colonial Office official, Mr. Grindle, was appended to the dispatch containing Garvey's letter: "I blush to think that I once suggested to Mr. Marcus Garvey that he should go to the workhouse. Acknowledge with expression and appreciation of H. M. of the loyal sentiments expressed by the Assn." A later dispatch, dated June 2, 1915, contained a "Birthday Message to the King from the UNIA," but this dispatch has not been kept. (Dispatch No. 212, June 2, 1915, C.S.O. Governor to the Secretary of State for the Colonies, answered by the Secretary of State No. 178/15.)

66. *Current History,* September 1923, pages 15–16.

67. *Williams,* Garvey to Moton, February 29, 1916.

68. *Ibid.*

69. *Ibid.*

70. So far as the present writer has been able to discover, the only extant copy of this important pamphlet is in the West India Reference Library in Jamaica. The acquisition stamp is dated June 22, 1918, but the pamphlet itself is undated.

II. THE YEARS OF TRIUMPH AND TRAGEDY, 1920–1925

1. Elliot M. Rudnick, "Du Bois versus Garvey: Race Propagandists at War," *Journal of Negro Education*, Vol. 28, No. 4, Fall 1969, pages 422–423.

2. *Ibid.*, pages 425–426.

3. W. E. B. Du Bois, *History of the Pan-African Congress*, George Padmore, ed., Hammersmith Bookshop, Ltd., London, 1962.

4. W. E. B. Du Bois, *Dusk of Dawn: An Essay Toward an Autobiography of Race Concept*, Harcourt, Brace and Company, New York, 1940; Schocken Books, Inc., New York, 1968 (paperback reprint) pages 276–277.

5. W. F. Elkins, "The Influence of Marcus Garvey on Africa: A British Report of 1922," *Science and Society*, Summer 1968, pages 321–323.

III. THE MOVEMENT IN TRANSITION, 1925–1927

1. In an article in the *Crusader* magazine, entitled "Figures Never Lie But Liars Do Figure."

2. The Negro radicals referred to are Richard B. Moore, Otto Huiswoud, W. A. Domingo, Cyril Briggs, and Hubert Harrison before his degeneration. Domingo was never a member of the Party. Huiswoud, Briggs and Moore were members of the Communist faction in the African Blood Brotherhood.

3. Alain Locke, *The New Negro*, Atheneum, New York, 1968.

IV. MARCUS GARVEY AND HIS CRITICS

1. "Marcus Garvey and the NAACP," *The Crisis*, February 1928.

2. Emma Lou Thornbrough, *T. Thomas Fortune, Militant Journalist*, University of Chicago Press, 1972, pages 356–363.

3. J. A. Rogers, *World's Great Men of Color*, Collier Books, New York, 1972, pages 415–430.

4. Charles Willis Simmons, "The Negro Intellectuals' Criticism of Garveyism," *Negro History Bulletin*, November 1961, pages 33–35.

5. James Weldon Johnson, *Black Manhattan*, Alfred A. Knopf, New York, 1930, page 256.

6. Of the fifteen names of his fellow officers in 1914 not a single one appears in 1918: of the eighteen names of officers published in 1918 only six survive in 1919; among the small list of principal officers published in 1920 I do not find a single name mentioned in 1919.

7. Mrs. Garvey boasts February 14, 1920: "This week I present you with the Black Star Line Steamship Corporation recapitalized at $10,000,000. They told us when we incorporated this corporation that we could not make it, but we are now gone from a $5,000,000 corporation to one of $10,000,000."

This sounds impressive, but means almost nothing. The fee for incorporating a $5,000,000 concern in Delaware is $350. By *paying $250 more the corporation may incorporate with $10,000,000 authorized capital without having a cent of capital actually paid in!* Cf. "General Corporation Laws of the State of Delaware," edition of 1917.

8. He said in his "inaugural" address: "The signal honor of being Provisional President of Africa is mine. It is a political job; it is a political calling for me to redeem Africa. It is like asking Napoleon to take the world. He took a certain portion of the world in his time. He failed and died at St. Helena. But may I not say that the lessons of Napoleon are but stepping stones by which we shall guide ourselves to African liberation?"

9. Marcus Garvey, *The Philosophy and Opinions of Marcus Garvey*, Amy Jacques Garvey, ed., Atheneum, New York, 1969.

10. Marcus Garvey, "The Negro's Greatest Enemy," *Current History*, Vol. XVIII, September 1923, pages 951–957.

11. Robert Campbell, *A Pilgrimage to My Motherland: An Account of a Journey Among the Egbas and Yarubas of Central Africa in 1859–60*, republished in *Search for a Place: Black Separation and Africa, 1860*, University of Michigan Press, Ann Arbor (Ann Arbor Paperback), 1971.

12. Amy Jacques Garvey, *Garvey and Garveyism*, Collier Books, New York (paperback reprint), 1970.

13. Theodore G. Vincent, *Black Power and the Garvey Movement*, Ramparts Press, New York, 1971.

14. *Ibid.*

15. Anatoli Vinogradov, *The Black Consul*, Viking Press, New York, 1955.

16. Rogers, *op. cit.*

17. H. P. Davis, *Black Democracy, The Story of Haiti*, revised edition, Biblo and Tannen, New York, n.d.

18. Rogers, *op. cit.*

19. Robert A. Bone, *The Negro Novel in America*, Yale University Press, New Haven, Connecticut, 1958, page 6.

20. Marcus Garvey, *op. cit.* note 18.

VI. THE LAST YEARS, 1934–1940

1. Richard Hart, "The Life and Resurrection of Marcus Garvey," *RACE*, Vol. IX, No. 2, London, 1967, pages 234–235.

2. Kwame Nkrumah, *Ghana: The Autobiography of Kwame Nkrumah*, New World Paperbacks, International Publishers, New York, 1971, pages 14–54.

3. J. A. Rogers, *The Real Facts about Ethiopia*, J. A. Rogers Publications, New York, 1936.

4. Willis N. Huggins, *A Guide to Studies in African History*, New York Federation of History Clubs, New York, 1934.

5. ———, *Introduction to African Civilization, with Main Currents in Ethiopian History*, Avon House, New York, 1937.

6. Bankole Timothy, *Kwame Nkrumah; His Rise to Power*, Allen & Unwin, London, 1955.

7. Kwame Nkrumah, *Toward Colonial Freedom*, Heinemann, London, 1962.

8. C. L. R. James, *The Black Jacobins*, Vintage Books Edition, Random House, New York, 1963.

9. *Plaintalk*, September 11 and 18, 1937.

10. E. U. Essien-Udom, *Black Nationalism: A Search for Identity in America*, University of Chicago Press, 1962.

11. *Blackman* Magazine, January 1937.

VII. THE MARCUS GARVEY REVIVAL, 1940–PRESENT

1. Edmund D. Cronon, *Black Moses: The Story of the Universal Negro Improvement Association*, University of Wisconsin Press, Madison, 1962.

2. Amy Jacques Garvey, *Garvey and Garveyism*, Collier Books, New York, 1970.

3. Richard Hart, "The Life and Resurrection of Marcus Garvey," *RACE*, Vol. IX, No. 2, 1967.

4. Amy Jacques Garvey, *Black Power in America: Marcus Garvey's Impact on Jamaica and Africa*. Privately published pamphlet, Kingston, Jamaica, 1968.

5. "Repatriation Battle Resumes in Jamaica," *African Opinion*, November–December 1972, pages 8–9.

6. Marcus Garvey, *The Philosophy and Opinions of Marcus Garvey*, Amy Jacques Garvey, ed., Atheneum, New York, 1969, page 77.

7. *Ibid.*, page 82.

8. *Ibid.*, page 27.

9. *Ibid.*, page 68.

10. *Ibid.*, page 107.

11. *Ibid.*, page 44.

12. Marcus Garvey, *The Philosophy and Opinions of Marcus Garvey*, Amy Jacques Garvey, ed., page 95.

13. *Ibid.*, page 58.

14. *Ibid.*, page 52.

15. *Ibid.*, pages 21, 22.

16. *Ibid.*

17. See E. U. Essien-Udom's introduction to the second edition of *The Philosophy and Opinions of Marcus Garvey*, Frank Cass and Company, 1967, London, pages xxv and xxiv. See also Edmund D. Cronon, *op. cit.*

18. T. Hodgkin, *Nationalism in Colonial Africa*, Muller, London, 1956, pages 101–102. See also G. Shepperson, "Pan-Africanism and 'Pan-Africanism': Some Historical Notes," *Phylon*, Vol. XXIII, No. 4, 1962, page 356.

19. Frederick German Detweiler, *The Negro Press in the United States*, University of Chicago Press, 1922, page 16.

20. *Ibid.*

21. *Negro World*, July 16, 1932, page 6.

22. *Negro World*, June 3, 1933, page 2. See also "An Appreciation of Garvey's 'Africa for the Africans,'" *Abantu-Bantho*, August 7, 1926, page 10, Johannesburg; Joseph Masogha, Kimberley, South Africa, to the editor of *Negro World*, August 14, 1926, page 10; *ibid.*, April 30, 1872, page 2; Benjamin Majafi, Liddesdaale, Evaton, South Africa, to S. A. Hayes, president of the Pittsburgh division of UNIA, in *Negro World*, April 30, 1927, page 5; "What They Think of Garvey," *Negro World*, August 18, 1928; "Organization Work in Africa Growing," *Negro World*, May 21, 1927: "The Universal Negro Improvement Association and African Communities League Making Progress in Lagos," *West Africa*, November 27, 1920, pages 1,513, 1,496, and West Africa, December 11, 1920, page 1,533.

23. J. G. Campbell to the Editor, *Times of Nigeria*, May 24, 1920, pages 4–5.

24. *Ibid.* See also resolution 5, *Conference of Africans of British West Africa, Held in Accra, 1920*, page 3.

25. *Times of Nigeria*, May 24, 1920.

26. *Ibid.*

27. *Lagos Weekly Record*, November 27, 1920, page 5.

28. J. Babington Adebayo, "The British West African Congress: Marcus Garvey's Pan-Negroism and the Universal Negro Improvement Association," *Lagos Weekly Record*, November 27, 1920, page 7.

29. *Ibid.* See also Ralph Korngold, *Citizen Toussaint*, Left Book Club, London, 1945, page 67.

30. *Sierra Leone Weekly News*, quoted in *West Africa*, December 11, 1920, page 1,553.

31. Sir Hugh Clifford, *Report on UNIA Activities in Nigeria*, C.O. 583/109/28194, February 27, 1922, paragraph 2.

32. *Ibid.*

33. *Ibid.*

34. *Ibid.*

35. *Ibid.*

36. George Padmore, *Pan-Africanism or Communism?* Dobson, London, 1956, pages 97–101.

37. H. Labouret, "Le Mouvement Pan-Negre aux Etats-Unis et Ses Repercussions en Afrique," *Politique Etrangere*, 1937, page 320; Hans Kohn and W. Sokolsky, *African Nationalism in the Twentieth Century*, Van Nostrand, Princeton, New Jersey, 1965, page 34.

38. Magnus J. Sampson, "Kobina Sekyi as I Knew Him," Sekyi Papers, Cape Coast Regional Archives, 716/64.

39. Kobina Sekyi, *The Parting of the Ways* (1922?).

40. *Ibid.*, pages 23–24.

41. Jabez Ayodele Langley, "West African Aspects of the Pan-African Movement, 1900–1945," Ph.D. thesis, University of Edinburgh, 1968, chapters 3 and 5.

42. ———, "Pan-Africanism in Paris, 1924–1936," *Journal of Modern African Studies*, Vol. VII, No. 1, April 1969.

43. Marcus Garvey, *Negro World*, August 4 and 11, 1928.

44. Ch. Du Bus de Warnaffe, "Le Mouvement Pan-Negre aux Etats-Unis et Ailleurs," *Congo*, May 1922; "Le Garveyism en Action dans Notre Colonie," *Congo*, June–December 1921, pages 575–576; and Pierre Daye, "Le Mouvement Pan-Negre," *Le Flambeau*, Brussels, No. 7, July–August 1921, pages 359–375.

45. R. Eaton, "Le Bolshevisme au Congo," *Congo*, June–December 1924, pages 752–757.

46. James Weldon Johnson, *Black Manhattan*, Alfred A. Knopf, New York, 1930, page 256.

47. *Ibid.*

48. E. H. Carr, *What Is History?* London, 1961, pages 48–49.

49. *Journal of Negro History*, October 1940.

50. Eric D. Walron, *The Independent*, January 3, 1925.

51. *Messenger*, August 1920.

52. *The Daily Worker*, June 14, 1930.

53. Marcus Garvey, *op. cit.*, note 21, pages 69, 70, 72.

54. ———, *An Appeal to the Soul of White America*, New York, 1924.

55. *The Workers Monthly*, April 1926, New York.

56. *The Communist*, June 1930, New York, page 549.

57. *The Liberator*, October 1924, New York.

58. *The Century*, February 1923, New York.

59. *Congressional Record*, May 24, 1938.

60. Amy Jacques Garvey, *Memorandum to the United Nations*, Kingston, Jamaica (1944?).

61. Gunnar Myrdal, *An American Dilemma, the Negro Problem and Modern Democracy*, Harper & Row, Evanston and New York, 1944, page 746.

62. *The Crisis*, February 1928.

63. *Messenger*, March 1923.

64. *The Liberator*, October 1924.

65. *The Daily Worker*, August 5, 1924.

66. The entire report can be found in W. F. Elkins " 'Unrest Among the Negroes': A British Document of 1919," *Science and Society*, Vol. XXXII, No. 1, Winter 1968, pages 66–79.

67. C.O. 267/600, Acting Governor of Sierra Leone to Duke of Devonshire, May 28, 1923.

68. F.O. 371/7286, Consul-General, Dakar, to Foreign Secretary, August 17, 1922.

69. Barclay to Garcia, June 14, 1920, in Amy Jacques Garvey, ed., *Philosophy and Opinions of Marcus Garvey*, 2nd rev. ed., Frank Cass & Co. Ltd., London, 1967, page 365.

70. Cronon, *op. cit.*, page 125.

71. F.O. 371/9553, Barclay to Messrs. Elder Dempster and Co., June 30, 1924.

72. O'Meara to Foreign Secretary, August 23, 1924.

73. C.O. 267/607: Message of President King to the Liberian legislature, December 9, 1924.

74. Speech by Governor of Sierra Leone, January 22, 1925.

75. Cronon, *op. cit.*, page 130.

76. *Ibid.*, pages 124, 130.

77. A. J. Garvey, ed., page 384. Speaking in June 1928 at the Royal Albert Hall in London, Garvey stated that Firestone's agent had influenced President King to reverse himself. He also blamed his imprisonment on the fact that Firestone, backed by Herbert Hoover, then Secretary of Commerce, knew that he could prevent President King's re-election.

78. F.O. 371/8513; Armstrong, Consul-General to His Majesty's Ambassador in Washington, D.C., April 18, 1923.

79. Maurice Peterson minute on Garvey Press Release, February 9, 1923.

80. F.O. 371/5684, R. H. Hadow minute, February 21 and 22, 1921,

on Governor Willcocks of Bermuda to Churchill, January 16, 1921. The same claim was made by the secret report of 1919, "Unrest Among the Negroes."

81. F.O. 395/389, Angus Fletcher report, June 12, 1923.

82. F.O. 371/9633, minute of June 20, 1924 (author not identified) on British Embassy, Washington, D.C., to MacDonald, June 6, 1924.

83. C. L. R. James, *The Black Jacobins*, Vintage Books Edition, Random House, New York, 1963, page 397.

84. Kwame Nkrumah, *I Speak of Freedom*, Frederick A. Praeger, New York, 1962, page 107.

85. Kwame Nkrumah, *Ghana: An Autobiography*, Nelson's, London and New York, 1957, page 45.

86. James Coleman, *Nigeria: Background to Nationalism*, University of California Press, Berkeley and Los Angeles, 1965, page 190.

87. Quoted in Cronon, *op. cit.*, page 217.

88. Adolph Edwards, *Marcus Garvey 1887–1940*, New Beacon Publications, London and Port of Spain, 1967, pages 33, 35.

Bibliography

Adams, Russel L. *Great Negroes: Past and Present*, p. 91, 1963, 1964, Chicago, Afro-American Publishing Co.

Baker, Ross K. (ed.) *The Afro-Americans*, pp. 279–282, 1970, N.Y. London, Van Nostrand, Reinhold Co.

Bennett, Lerone *The Challenge of Blackness*, p. 196, 1972, Chicago, Johnson Pub. Co. Inc.

——— *Pioneers in Protest*, pp. 231–238, 1968, Chicago, Johnson Publishing Co., Inc.

Bracey, John H., and August Meier *Black Nationalism in America*, pp. 158–160, 1970, Indianapolis, Bobbs-Merrill Co., Inc.

Brisbane, Robert H. *The Black Vanguard*, p. 43, 1970, Valley Forge, Pa., Judson Press.

Broderick, Francis L., and August Meier *Negro Protest Thought in the Twentieth Century*, p. 82, 1965, Indianapolis, Bobbs-Merrill Co., Inc.

Brotz, Howard *Negro Social and Political Thought 1850–1920*, pp. 24–27, 1969, N.Y., Basic Books.

Brown, Ina C. *Story of the American Negro*, p. 114, 1936, N.Y., Friendship Press.

Cronon, Edmund Davis *Black Moses, the Story of the Universal Negro Improvement Association*, 1955, 1962, Madison, University of Wisconsin Press.

Daley, P. H. *Revolution to Republic*, p. 67, Georgetown, Guyana, Daily Chronicle, Ltd.

Davis, Daniels *Marcus Garvey*, 1972, N.Y., Franklin Watts, Inc.

Delany, M. R., and Robert Campbell *Search for a Place*, p. 47, 1971, Ann Arbor, University of Michigan Press.

Delboca, Angelo *Ethiopian War 1935–1941*, p. 38, 1965, Chicago, University of Chicago Press.

Dowd, Jerome   *The Negro in American Life*, p. 465, 1926, 1927, N.Y., London, New Century Co.

Draper, Theodore   *The Rediscovery of Black Nationalism*, pp. 50–56, 1970, N.Y., Viking Press.

Drimmer, Melvin   *Black History*, pp. 324–510, 1967, Garden City, New York, Doubleday & Co.

Dubusdewarnaffe, Vicomte Charles   *Le Mouvement Pan-Negre aux Etats-Unis et Ailleurs*, 1922, Bruxelles, Goemaere.

Edwards, Adolph   *Marcus Garvey 1887–1940*, 1967, London, New Beacon Pub.

Essien-Udom, E. U.   *Black Nationalism: A Search for Identity in America*, pp. 36–39, 1962, Chicago, University of Chicago Press.

Fax, Elton C.   *Garvey*, 1972, N.Y., Dodd, Mead & Co.

Franklin, John Hope   *From Slavery to Freedom: A History of American Negroes*, pp. 489–492, 1967, N.Y., Alfred A. Knopf.

Frazier, E. Franklin   *The Negro in the United States*, p. 225, 1948, 1949, N.Y., Dryden Press.

Garvey, Amy Jacques   *Garvey and Garveyism*, 1963, Kingston, Jamaica; 1970, N.Y., Collier Books.

———   *Tragedy of White Justice*, 1927.

———   *United States of America vs. Marcus Garvey: Was Justice Defeated?*, 1925, N.Y.

Garvey, Marcus   *The Philosophy and Opinions of Marcus Garvey*, 1969, N.Y., Atheneum.

Gilbert, Peter (ed.)   *Selected Writings of John E. Bruce*, p. 101, 1971, N.Y., Arno Press.

Gosnell, Harold F.   *Negro Politicians*, pp. 338–339, 1935, Chicago, University of Chicago Press.

Guerin, Daniel   *The West Indies and Their Future*, p. 92, 1961, London, Dennis Dobson.

Harris, Robert   *Black Glory in the Life and Times of Marcus Garvey*, 1961, N.Y., African Nationalist Pioneer Movement.

Harris, Sheldon H.   *Paul Cuffe*, pp. 11, 42, 1972, N.Y., Simon and Schuster.

Haywood, Harry   *Negro Liberation*, pp. 197–198, 1948, N.Y., International Publishers.

Henry, Edward Barnes   *The Predictions of A Great Race in Fullfillment*, 1953, N.Y.

Huggins, Nathan I., Martin Kilson, and Daniel M. Fox   *Key Issues in the Afro-American Experience*, 2 vols, p. 18, vol. I, p. 105, vol. 2, 1971, N.Y., Harcourt Brace Jovanovich, Inc.

Hurwitz, Samuel J. and Edith F. Hurwitz   *Jamaica*, pp. 190–192, 1971, N.Y., Frederick A. Praeger.

James, Cyril *A History of the Negro Revolt*, pp. 72–82, 1969, Washington, D.C., Drum and Spear Press.

McKay, Claude *Harlem: Negro Metropolis*, pp. 143–180, 1940, 1968, N.Y., E. P. Dutton & Co. Inc.

Maglangbayan, Shawna *Garvey, Lumumba, Malcolm*, 1972, Chicago, Third World Press.

Manoedi, M. Kokete *Garvey and Africa*, n.d., N.Y., New York Age.

Mezu, S. Okecukwu, and Ram Desai *Black Leaders of the Centuries*, p. 185, 1970, Buffalo, Black Academy Press, Inc.

Murray, R. N., and E. H. Carter *18th Century to Modern Times*, p. 173, 1967, London, Thomas Nelson Ltd.

Myrdal, Gunnar *An American Dilemma*, pp. 746–749, 1944, 1962, N.Y. & Evanston, Harper & Row.

Nettleford, Rex M. *Identity, Race and Protest in Jamaica*, pp. 31–33, 1972, N.Y., William Morrow & Co., Inc.

Ottley, Roi *New World A-Coming*, pp. 67–81, 1943, Cleveland, World Publishing Company.

——— and William J. Weatherby *The Negro in New York*, pp. 209–222, 1967, N.Y., Oceana Publications, Inc.

Ovington, Mary White *Portraits in Color*, pp. 18–30, 1927, N.Y., Viking Press.

Padmore, George *Pan-Africanism or Communism*, pp. 116–117, 1971, N.Y., Doubleday & Co.

Paschal, Andrew G. *A W. E. B. Du Bois Reader*, 1971, N.Y., MacMillan Co.

Peeks, Edward (ed.) *The Long Struggle for Black Power*, pp. 180–200, 1971, N.Y., Charles Scribner's Sons.

Powell, Adam C., Jr. *Against the Tide*, pp. 70–71, 1938, N.Y., Richard R. Smith.

——— *Marching Blacks*, pp. 49–50, 1945, N.Y. Dial Press.

Redkey, Edwin S. *Black Exodus*, pp. 193–196, 1969, New Haven, Yale University Press.

Record, Wilson *The Negro and the Communist Party*, pp. 39–43, 1971, New York, Atheneum.

Reid, C. H. *Marcus Garvey: A Social Phenomenon*, unpublished Master of Arts thesis, Evanston, Ill., Northwestern University, 1928.

Report of the Joint Legislative Committee of New York Investigation Seditious Activities, Vol. II, 1920.

Rogers, J. A. *The World's Great Men of Color*, pp. 415–431, Vol. II, 1972, N.Y., Collier Books.

Sochen, June *The Black Man and the American Dream*, p. 313, 1971, Chicago, Quadrangle Books.

Standing, Theodore G.   *A Study of Negro Nationalism*, unpublished Master of Arts thesis, 1929, University of Iowa.

Sterne, Emma Gelders   *This Was the Voice*, 1971, N.Y., Collier Books.

Stuckey, Sterling   *Ideological Origins of Black Nationalism*, p. 28, 1972, Boston, Beacon Press.

Thompson, Bakpetu Vincent   *Africa and Unity*, p. 36, 1969, London, Longmans, Green & Co. Ltd.

Thornbrough, Emma Lou   *T. Thomas Fortune*, pp. 356–363, 1972, Chicago, University of Chicago Press.

Toppin, Edgar A.   *Blacks in America: Then and Now*, p. 49, 1969, Boston, Christian Science Pub. Society.

Tuttle, William M., Jr.   *Race Riot*, p. 256, 1970, N.Y. Atheneum.

Uya, Edet   *Okon, Black Brotherhood*, p. 172, 1971, Lexington, Mass., Hetch & Co.

Vincent, Theodore G.   *Black Power and the Garvey Movement*, 1971, N.Y., Ramparts Press.

Walden, Daniel (ed.)   *W. E. B. Du Bois: The Crisis Writings*, pp. 303–329, 1972, Greenwich, Conn., Fawcett Publications.

Weatherford, W. D.   *The Negro from Africa to America*, 1924.

Weinberg, Arthur Myron   *Passport to Utopia*, pp. 214–222, 1968, Chicago, Quadrangle Books.

Williams, Eric   *The Negro in the Caribbean*, 1945.

Williams, Lee E., and Lee E. Williams II   *Anatomy of Four Race Riots*, p. 13, 1972, University and College of Mississippi.

Zickefoose, Harold E.   *The Garvey Movement*, unpublished Master of Arts thesis, 1931, Iowa City, State University of Iowa.

Index

A

Abbott, Robert S., 228, 396
Abiodun, Reverend S. M., 406
abolition movement, xiii, xiv, 25
Abyssinian Church (New York City), 118
Accabreh, 18
accommodation, ideology of, 390–91
Adams, John Quincy, xix
Adams, Russell L., 25–27
Adebayo, J. Babington, 406, 407
Adler, Felix, 5
Adoe (slave leader), 18, 24
Africa: European exploration of, 15–16; gold trade, 15; honor system in, 16–17; idea of uniting, xxiv; *See also* names of countries
Africa for the Africans, 220, 394, 395, 438
Africa as Seen by American Negroes (Diop), xxv–xxvi
Africa and Unity: The Evolution of Pan-Africanism (Thompson), xxiv–xxv
African Abroad, The (Farris), 197
African Blood Brotherhood (ABB), 213, 223, 224
African Bureau, 333, 335–36
African Civilization Society, 215
African Colonial Enterprise, 27
African Colonization Movement, xxi, 197

B

M

N

Q

R

V

Contributors

CYRIL BRIGGS, one of the editors of the *Amsterdam News* in his early years, later joined the American Communist Party, and was one of the most active opponents of Marcus Garvey.

W. E. B. DU BOIS, considered to be one of the greatest American intellectuals, author of more than twenty books, one of Marcus Garvey's best known, though not the fiercest, adversaries.

A. F. ELMES was a New York journalist and free-lance writer.

WILLIAM Z. FOSTER was formerly General Secretary of the American Communist Party. He was the author of *A History of the Communist Party in the United States*.

E. FRANKLIN FRAZIER was head of the Department of Sociology at Howard University. He was noted for his writings on the Black family in the United States. His best-known book is *Black Bourgeoisie*.

AMY JACQUES GARVEY, widow of Marcus Garvey, was the literary executor of the works of Marcus Garvey and the author of the first important book on his life and movement, *The Philosophy and Opinions of Marcus Garvey*. She was also the author of *Garvey and Garveyism*, and *Black Power in America*. She died in Jamaica in 1973.

MARCUS GARVEY, JR. is Garvey's oldest son. He is a science teacher in the Jamaican school system.

ROBERT A. HILL is a Research Fellow at the Institute of the Black

World, Atlanta, Georgia, and associate professor in the Department of Afro-American Studies at Northwestern University, Evanston, Illinois.

JABEZ AYODELE LANGLEY studied at the University of Edinburgh in Scotland, where he did extensive research on the impact of Garveyism on the French speaking African community. He has since returned to his country Gambia, in West Africa.

RUPERT LEWIS is a member of the African Studies Association of the West Indies, and is an instructor in political science at the University of the West Indies in Kingston, Jamaica.

KELLY MILLER is a writer, civil rights activist, former professor at Howard University, and author of *Race Adjustment* and *Out of the House of Bondage*.

ROBERT MINOR is a former head of the American Communist Party and a journalist.

RICHARD B. MOORE was proprietor of the Frederick Douglass Bookstore in Harlem for over twenty-five years. He later became an active member of the American Communist Party, and after leaving the party, participated in several organizations working for the betterment of the Harlem community in particular, and the American Black community in general. He is President of the Afro-American Institute and author of the book, *The Word Negro: Its Origin and Evil Use*.

CAPTAIN HUGH MULZAC was Captain of one of Marcus Garvey's ships, and also lived to be one of the few Black captains of a liberty ship during the Second World War. His involvement in the Garvey Movement and the Black Star Line is told in his autobiography *A Star to Steer By*.

EDWIN S. REDKEY was formerly associate professor of history at the University of Tennessee, and is presently a professor at Yale University. He is the author of *Black Exodus*.

ROBERT G. WEISBORD is a professor at the University of Rhode Island, and author of several conference papers and articles on Afro-American life.

DAISY WHYTE was Marcus Garvey's secretary during his last London years.

ABOUT THE EDITOR

JOHN HENRIK CLARKE was born in Union Springs, Alabama, and grew up in Columbus, Georgia. He went to New York City in 1933 to pursue a career as a writer. After four years in the U.S. Air Force, where he was a sergeant major, he attended New York University and majored in history and world literature. Beginning with his early years, Mr. Clarke studied the world history of African people.

He has published over fifty short stories in magazines in this country and abroad. His best-known short story, "The Boy Who Painted Christ Black," has been translated into more than a dozen languages. His articles and conference papers on African and Afro-American history and culture have been published in leading journals throughout the world. He has served as a staff member of five different publications and was co-founder and associate editor of the *Harlem Quarterly* (1949–1950).

Professor Clarke has been a feature writer for the *Pittsburgh Courier* (1957–1958), Research Director of the first African Heritage Exposition (August 1959), Associate Editor, *Freedomways* magazine (1962–Present), Director, Heritage Teaching Program, HARYOU-ACT (1964–1969), and Special Consultant and Coordinator of the C.B.S. TV Series, "Black Heritage: The History of Afro-Americans" (1968). He is an Associate Professor in the Department of Black and Puerto Rican Studies at Hunter College, New York City, and a Distinguished Visiting Professor of African History at the Africana Studies and Research Center at Cornell University. Among the books he has written or edited are *American Negro Short Stories* (1966), William Styron's *Nat Turner: Ten Black Writers Respond* (1968), *Malcolm X: The Man and His Time* (1969), and *Harlem U.S.A.* (1971).